HURRAH FOR THE
LIFE OF A SAILOR!

John Winton

HURRAH FOR THE LIFE OF A SAILOR!

Life on the lower-deck of the Victorian Navy

MICHAEL JOSEPH · LONDON

First published in Great Britain by
Michael Joseph Limited
52 Bedford Square
London WC1B 3EF
1977

ISBN 0 7181 1580 5

Filmset and printed in Great Britain by
BAS Printers Limited, Wallop, Hampshire
and bound by J. M. Dent & Sons (Letchworth) Limited

I've braved the stormy ocean,
In foreign lands I've been,
To misfortune I've not been a stranger,
I've had my share of troubles,
Many curious sights I've seen,
But I've managed all right through the danger.
The clouds they may gather,
The sky it may look black
There's a sweet little cherub
Keeps watch for poor Jack!
So away with melancholy,
We'll all be gay and jolly;
Hurrah for the life of a sailor!

Nineteenth-century sailor's song

CONTENTS

Acknowledgements

The illustrations in this book are reproduced by kind permission of the following (numbers refer to page numbers):

Boy's Own Paper: 212, 289;
The Graphic: 157, 263;
Illustrated London News: 113, 128–9, 135, 153, 154–5, 240, 242–3, 249, 251, 269, 286;
National Maritime Museum, London: 8, 10, 19, 29, 32, 33, 40–1, 57, 83, 100, 111, 146, 147, 154–5, 159, 194, 203, 208;
The Navy & Army Illustrated: 228, 298, 300;
Punch: 199, 200;
Radio Times Hulton Picture Library: 6, 94, 178, 199, 219.

The Publishers also wish to acknowledge The History of the Victoria Cross by Philip Wilkins for the illustrations on pages 125, 146, 147, 163, 275 and 278; and to acknowledge Oliver-Sutton Antiques, Kensington Church Street, London W8 for kindly supplying the Staffordshire pottery figures for reproduction on page 120.

ILLUSTRATIONS

The British Tar:
the early nineteenth-century Navy

On 4 July 1816, Lieutenant W. Edward Parry RN wrote home to his parents from Canada. He was serving in the 38-gun, 1000-ton frigate *Niger*, then lying in the St Lawrence river. Parry, later Sir Edward Parry, the Arctic explorer, was a very able young officer, conscientious, and with the interests of his sailors at heart; years later, he was responsible for improving the sailors' lot in a number of ways. Conditions in *Niger* simply disgusted him.

> I should not have believed her to belong to the same service as *La Hogue, Maidstone, Carron*, &c., &c., if I had not before my eyes my own commission for her as one of His Britannick Majesty's ships, & if I did not constantly see about me a Captain & Officers who, thank Heaven, *still* are what British seamen *ought* to be. The men (for I will not disgrace the name of 'seamen' by applying it to them) are anything but what they used to be, ragged dirty thieves and quite ignorant of the duty of seamen.

Parry makes his points with sarcastic emphasis, underlining words with a stab of his pen:

> Their raggedness is the natural & unavoidable effect of the liberal policy of Government in giving <u>no bounty to seamen</u>. They are given two months' advance of wages, <u>including</u> a bed & blanket (25/-) which a man cannot do without. They have <u>no</u> <u>pay</u> <u>abroad</u>, so that our prime seamen are <u>tempted</u> to enter the service of their country by a <u>liberal</u> promise of receiving two months' advance, which is to last them for <u>three years</u> on a foreign station! Do they think our men such idiots as to enter under such circumstances? No: the consequence naturally must be that none but such as are starving from want of employment will come near the rendezvous appointed for manning the navy. Of this truth the *Niger* is a melancholy instance. They have lost no less than 27 men since she came to America, & it is actually more necessary to make the ship a <u>prison</u> than ever it was during the war. Captain Jackson on one occasion spoke to the principal men among the ship's company, & asked them if the desertion was to be attributed to any ill-treatment or other cause of complaint. They replied No, but that they believed one half of the ship's company only came <u>out</u> <u>for</u> <u>a</u> <u>passage</u> to America!!

Parry was writing about one ship, but the conditions he described were general throughout the Navy at that time. The great French wars were just over and the country was about to enjoy a very long period of peace, but the sailor of 1816 was still the sailor of Trafalgar, of Copenhagen and the Nile and a hundred lesser fights. He went into action barefooted and bare to the waist, with a scarf twisted round his forehead to keep the sweat from his eyes. He often wore a pigtail, and he chewed tobacco which he prepared in long rolls, the same colour, appearance and almost the same consistency as hemp rope. He was paid 25s. 6d a month, with 8s. a month more as an able seaman, and his pay was always months and sometimes years in arrears. He lived on hard ship's biscuits, salt beef or pork which was often many years old, and sometimes a mixture of oatmeal and molasses called 'burgoo' for breakfast. His drinking water was stored in wooden casks and went foetid after a very few days at sea. But he was entitled to half a pint of spirits, or a pint of wine, or a gallon of beer every day. Not surprisingly, he was drunk at every possible opportunity, ashore and on board. Drunkenness and the consequent leave-breaking and insubordination were by far the most frequent punishable offences.

The sailor of 1816 was still subject to the lash. He could still be flogged round the fleet, so many lashes inflicted at the gangway of each ship. For very serious offences, such as mutiny, he could be sentenced to death and hanged on board. Awaiting court-martial, he could be gagged, and bound hand and foot, in irons, for indefinite periods. Grim punishments such as keelhauling and spreadeagling belonged to the very recent past. Lesser punishments were 'toeing the line', that is, standing on the same spot on the quarter-deck for hours on end, or banishment to the rigging for half a day.

The sailor of the post-Napoleonic War period had very little formal training, but picked up his craft from his fellows or from his own experience. He was seldom or never allowed ashore during a commission, for fear he would desert. On discharge from a ship he was free to go where he wished, and to join another ship or not, just as he pleased. There were no arrangements, except by a few far-sighted captains, to improve the sailor's professional competence, or his health, or his living conditions, or his morals. He had no uniform, but wore what was convenient or what he could afford. A ship's commission might last five, six or seven years, but the sailor had no formal terms of service or sickness benefits. If he were discharged to shore with wounds, not he nor his wife nor any of his dependants were any official concern of service or state. There was little prospect of his becoming an officer, except by some act of extreme gallantry in the presence of the enemy. His occupational diseases were many and severe: tuberculosis, from the damp, generally insanitary living conditions, and overcrowding on the mess-decks; typhoid, cholera, dysentery and tropical diseases from service abroad; ruptures from the heavy, manual labour; scurvy from the lack of antiscorbutic acid in his diet over long periods; syphilis from his contacts ashore. Every ship's commission in sail suffered a steady wastage of men lost overboard and drowned, or killed or maimed after falling from aloft. Throughout the nineteenth century, these 'operational' casualties far outnumbered losses due to enemy action.

The ships of 1816 were wooden-hulled and powered entirely by sail. Their main weapon was still the broadside, in which muzzle-loaded guns of various calibres fired solid iron roundshot simultaneously—or as near simultaneously as the state of gunnery would allow—through apertures cut in the ship's side.

The gun-barrels were made of iron. Other weapons were the Congreve rocket, fired from the deck or, more usually, from a ship's boat; or simply boarding with cutlass and pistol. Nearly a thousand men were needed to man a line-of-battle-ship, the great majority of them for working aloft. Except possibly for some refinements in navigational instruments, HMS *Victory*, Nelson's flagship at Trafalgar, had no major technological improvements over the *Sovereign of the Seas* built two centuries earlier.

In many ways, the social status of the sailor and the way he saw himself hardly changed throughout the nineteenth century. The bluejacket considered himself—just as society did—as someone apart, from another sphere, exotic. The sailor on a run ashore was a creature from another existence. 'Jack Tar' remained synonymous with bravery, honesty, devotion to duty and good humour, to be celebrated in song and on the stage. He thought himself invincible: he could not be beaten by anybody, ashore or afloat. He was almost always right. And even if he were, temporarily, bested, he believed that he and his fellows would come back and win in the end. In this he was proved always right. He was superstitious, about cats and women and parsons and meteorological phenomena and corpses and whistling. He was always fond of animals and children, and as generous with his money as his oaths. He always reacted to officers in the same ways, ready to work and fight his heart out for a good officer, sullen, unwilling and very occasionally murderous with bad. He hated ship's thieves and ship's police equally. He was always suspicious of those who issued his pay, his rum and his food. Slumps, depressions and declines in local industries affected recruiting, but it was still astonishing how many boys joined the navy because they came from seafaring families and had been brought up to the sea, or simply had a sudden, young man's urge to run away and see something of the world for themselves.

He was also, like the Navy itself, very conservative. Although the radical spirit grew and flourished in the nineteenth century, none of the Navy's necessary reforms were brought about by the sailors themselves. Very few were even pioneered by the Admiralty; indeed, almost all reforms were bitterly opposed by the majority of naval officers. The Navy was forced to change its ways almost entirely because of outside pressure, from Parliament and public opinion. Towards the end of the century a few sailors were expressing criticism openly (though pseudonymously) in print. But most sailors' grievances were restricted to guarded entries, in diaries and logs, or were kept bottled up until they could be safely recounted in retirement, Otherwise they could only be expressed in awkward doggerel verse, with bathetic and limping scansion, or in muttered conversations in the watches or mess-decks which were perilously close to the official definition of mutinous assembly.

As always in times of peace, the Navy entered a period of decline after the end of the French wars. The number of ships in commission was rapidly run down from 713 in 1815 to 134 in 1820, having been as low as 121 in 1818. Manpower was cut just as dramatically, from 140,000 in 1815 to 23,000 in 1820, having been as low as 19,000 in 1817. The sailors had no formal engagements; they were simply landed on shore to make their way as best they could, as was recounted in a ballad of the time, 'The British Tars':

Come all you thoughtless young men, a warning take by me,
And never leave your happy homes to sail the raging sea,
For I have ploughed the raging main this twenty years or more
But now I'm turned adrift to starve upon my native shore.

When war at first assail'd us I quickly left my trade,
Our country was in danger, I flew to lend my aid.
And in my country's service, long, long fatigues I bore,
But now I'm turned adrift to starve upon my native shore.

By storms and raging tempest shipwreck'd three times I've been,
And many a bloody battle upon the seas I've seen;
I've seen the cannon's glaring flash, I've heard its murderous roar,
Tho' now I'm turned adrift to starve upon my native shore.

The British seaman's valour to all the world is known,
We conquer still where'er we go, the action is our own.
The meteor flag of England triumphantly we bore;
But now we're turned adrift to starve upon our native shore.

Should hostile fleets e'er venture upon the raging main,
True hearts of oak we British Tars we'll push to sea again;
And bravely bring their ships to port as we have done before.
So help us now while we're in want upon our native shore.

Come pity, ye gentle strangers, a luckless British Tar,
In your defence he yet may hurl the thunderbolts of war.
Come lend some kind assistance, and heaven will bless your store,
For now I'm turned adrift to starve upon my native shore.

While the men were discharged, the officers continued to serve; indeed, their numbers actually increased from 5,017 to 5,664 between 1815 and 1820, some having been promoted to increase their half-pay. But only a few officers were serving at sea, and there were fifty competing for each appointment. Captains without political or family connections, 'interest' as it was called, could wait thirty years between appointments. For most it was a case of literally waiting for dead men's shoes. The result was that the Navy entered its next major conflict, the Russian War of the 1850s, with an aging officer corps, abnormally resistant to change and innovation even for the Navy, with flag officers in their sixties and seventies, and octogenarian admirals by no means unknown.

At a time of few sea-going appointments and little chance of promotion for gallantry, those captains who succeeded in getting a ship were determined not to jeopardise their careers by allowing any indiscipline or even idiosyncrasy in their ships. When initiative or undue kindliness could lead to unwelcome publicity, captains lashed their crews into submission. Discipline was fiercely enforced. The successful ship was not necessarily a fighting ship but a smart ship: the sailors drilled for drilling's sake, cleaned for cleaning's sake. Any bosun's mate or midshipman could 'start' a man by beating him over the head and shoulders with a rope's end in which a large, fist-sized Matthew Walker knot had been tied. A man could be flogged for spitting over the side.

In the scarcity of first-hand accounts of life below decks, the ballads, to a certain extent, fill a gap. 'The Saucy *Scylla*' was a frigate on the 'Bahama station' and she 'bore a great name'. Her crew had to be able to pass their hammocks through a ring, 'all made up so neat', or 'to carry them all day on our shoulders was our fate'. *Scylla*'s day began at 4.00 a.m. and continued with cleaning and drills. In the space of a few lines, the balladeer gives a great deal of information about the ship's routine, the normal time taken for evolutions, the kinds of punishment on board, and the feelings of the sailors when exercised beyond what they thought reasonable limits:

> Two bells in the evening—'twas the drummer once more—
> Beat all hands to quarters with your bayonet and swords.
> 'Cast loose, clear for action,' our lieutenant cries,
> With the rest of good drilling and much exercise.
>
> After quarters was over, there was one thing more,
> All hands to reef topsails, which grieved us full sore;
> 'Men, man the rigging,' our lieutenant would cry,
> Rise up, and lay out your reef points to tie.
>
> In less than two minutes our topsails must be reef'd,
> All sail set above them so snug and complete;
> For black-listing and drilling grieved us to the heart,
> For our six-watered grog it measured just one quart.

To be 'on the black-list' (later modified and called '10A') was a form of punishment which made an already hard existence almost intolerable. The offender was shaken awake earlier than the rest of the ship's company, had to eat his meals on the upper-deck under the eye of a sentry, was set to work while the rest were having their meals, and had to face paintwork for hours on end after 'pipe down'. But the most disliked punishments were stoppage of grog and 'six-water grog', in which six parts of water were added to a man's rum instead of the usual one.

Unexpectedly, the ballads reflect the sailor's awareness of his position. Although officially helpless and entirely submissive to naval discipline, the sailor knew that he was being abused, knew that he deserved better. The fact that he could compose such ballads was in a sense a victory for the lower-deck. A ballad about life on a particularly hard ship sums up the ironic contrast between the Navy's glorious traditions and the treatment meted out to sailors. The ship was the *Vanguard*, and the chorus is:

> Then let us sing the *Vanguard*'s praise, proclaim her valiant name,
> Cruel usage I have met with since I sail'd in the same.

The singer, who calls himself 'a saucy mizen-top man', is not afraid to name names. At four o'clock, when the ship's company are holystoning the decks, 'Then Mr Croycraft comes on deck, and he'll begin to curse and swear'. He has no love for the ship's police, nicknamed the 'Jonty' or 'Jondy' (an abbreviation of the French *gendarme*):

> There's a man on our lower-deck, he is called Jondy Cross,
> If I had my will of him, I'd overboard him toss.

But the ballad's final shaft is directed at the captain, the most hated and feared man on board:

> But if to sea I go again, I'd sooner swing in a halter.
> Before I'd sail in any ship commanded by Mickey Walker.

On some foreign stations, though not normally the West Indies, the men readily deserted at the first chance they had. Boat's crews were best placed for deserting, and many times the midshipman of a boat returned to find it empty. The United States had a powerful attraction. Service in the United States Navy was much to be preferred to the Royal Navy. As Parry explained, *Niger* had lost twenty-seven men in the first four months of her commission. They were all, as he remarks, 'useful seamen, whose loss I have too much reason to regret almost every hour of my life'. Many of them must have joined the American Navy. Parry thought that the American 74-gun ship *Washington* would 'drub our whole squadron on this station'. The American sailors were better paid, better found and better treated. It was a bitter thought for Parry and the rest of *Niger's* officers that 'perhaps at this moment some of *Niger's* deserters are enjoying their £4 a month on board the *Washington*, & laughing, as well they may, at their old shipmates here, labouring twice as hard for one shilling or one & twopence per day!'

Parry commented upon the most absurd anomalies in the Admiralty's administration of sailor's pensions. It was not just an anomaly but a gross injustice that a pension granted to a seaman for former service was taken away from him if he entered again, 'that is,' Parry explained,

> they cease to receive it, tho' their time goes on, while serving in our ships. On the other hand, if they serve in merchant ships, their pensions *do* go on. What, in the name of common sense, is the meaning of this? These pensions after 20 years' servitude amount in some cases to 1s. to 1s. 6d pr. day. Well, then, our best seamen, who are entitled to this, find on enquiry that, if they re-enter the navy on a fresh term, their pension ceases!!!

Parry conceded the strict bureaucratic view that sailors in the Merchant Navy were, 'I *suppose*', unemployed by His Majesty. But, he concluded, and here he summed up the whole system, 'if it *be* of importance to the national interest that our small peace-time navy should be good & effective as far as they go, the sooner the whole system is changed, the better.' Here, Parry had put his finger on a problem which was to trouble the Admiralty for much of the nineteenth century: how, without using compulsion, to maintain a peacetime navy which could be rapidly augmented in time of emergency.

'The Bombardment of Algiers, 1816', as depicted by
G. Chambers.

As a result of a shortage of men, *Niger* herself had, since Parry began his letter, 'been on shore in the St Lawrence, literally for want of a seaman to heave the lead. Luckily it was a flowing tide, & smooth water, so that she only hung on the ground a few minutes, and then went off. On mustering the leadsmen we find *four* who understand this branch of a seaman's duty!!! four out of 255!!!' Even so, the master told Parry that he had to stand beside the leadsman the whole time to see that he did not report the wrong soundings. *Niger* was in fact luckier than *Chesapeake*, where the officers had to heave the lead.

While Parry was serving in Canada, events in the Mediterranean were moving towards one of the last 'wooden-wall' actions of the old Navy. The defeat of the French had left the British undisputed masters of the Mediterranean, though the Turks in Algiers, Tunis and Tripoli still made a profitable business from piracy and from ransoming their captives. Press and public opinion at home forced the Admiralty to take action. Lord Exmouth, the Commander-in-Chief, was ordered to 'show the flag' by taking the fleet to all three pirate ports. Tunis and Tripoli agreed to Exmouth's demands readily enough, but the Dey of Algiers, at first friendly to the British, became intransigent, although finally agreeing to a compromise. After the murder of some fishermen who were under British protection at Bona, which was some 250 miles south of Algiers, public opinion became really inflamed. Exmouth was charged with no less a task than to abolish slavery. To attempt to do this, he would first have to destroy the Turkish gun emplacements ashore in Algiers and sink or capture the Turkish fleet of frigates inside the harbour.

Exmouth promised the Admiralty that he would complete the operation with only five ships of the line. The officers competed for the appointments which Lord Exmouth left to the Admiralty to arrange, not extending any patronage, even to his own relatives. Recruiting the seamen was another matter. In spite of the promise of the bounty of two months' wages, most ships had difficulty in completing their complements for sea, and some sailed short-handed.

Lord Exmouth was then sixty-five years old and this was the first time he had commanded a major fleet in action. But he was an excellent seaman, with a fine record in action, one of the ablest and most dashing commanders of his day. He was also a methodical and careful man. He worked out his own plan of battle, without the aid of a staff, and he placed his ships at ranges from the shore forts most suitable for them and most disadvantageous to their opponents. The ships damaged worst in the action were those that did not position themselves as Exmouth had ordered.

His handling and training of seamen were exemplary. He had frequently held gunnery practices against towed targets. On passage out to Algiers in his flagship *Queen Charlotte* (100 guns) he had a 12-pounder gun mounted on the quarter-deck, angled to fire upwards and outwards at 10-inch long by 5-inch high bulls-eyes targets secured to the foretopmast studding-sail boom. With constant practice the standard of gunnery became so good that the gun crews were able to hit the targets repeatedly. The whole squadron carried out firing practice twice a week, each ship firing six full broadsides. *Queen Charlotte*'s guns were fitted with a special gunsight and the first and second captains of every gun were given daily exercises in using it.

Exmouth's squadron arrived off Algiers on the evening of 26 August 1816. It consisted of five line-of-battle-ships, two heavy and two light frigates, five gun brigs, four bomb vessels and a sloop fitted out as an 'explosion vessel'. Besides the gun crews, the sailors who were to man the howitzers and Congreve rockets in the ships' launches and specially designed flat-bottomed boats had all been rehearsed in their duties. The whole force of small ships, including the gun brigs and the bombs, had had a full-scale rehearsal at Gibraltar. Similarly the cable parties and upper-deck hands had been specially rehearsed in laying anchors and working the ships into position. The officers were briefed on the strength, numbers and positions of the enemy. Every captain was briefed as to what position his ship should occupy and what her role should be. Below decks, the ships were stripped for action, all bulkheads, furniture and unnecessary 'tween-decks fittings being landed before the action. Even the duties of the Arabic interpreter were rehearsed. The sailors under Exmouth could be certain that every tactical and logistical precaution had been taken to ensure success.

The squadron closed the Algerian forts at midday on 27 August. After some preliminary negotiations and deliberations amongst the Algerians, *Queen Charlotte* anchored only seventy yards off the Mole, unchallenged, and opened fire shortly before 3.00 p.m.

The firing went on, with breaks, for several hours. Exmouth did not call a halt until nearly midnight, by which time many of the fortifications ashore had been destroyed and many casualties inflicted. The rocket boats and launches had gone into the harbour and destroyed much of the Algerian fleet. But the explosion sloop *Vesuvius* missed her intended target, a battery near a lighthouse, because of a mistaken helm order, and she exploded further north. Exmouth's gun crews had performed extremely well, helped by some of their wives, who, for almost the last time in the Navy's history, served the guns by bringing up powder and shot in the frigate *Severn*. The fleet lost 173 killed, and 744 were wounded. Many of the casualties were in *Impregnable* (98), whose captain had anchored in a much more vulnerable position than Exmouth had intended him to take.

The Dey surrendered, prisoners were given up, slaves freed and tribute money paid. But, needless to say, piracy and slavery were not abolished. In a few years' time, pirates were operating along the North African coast much as before.

The bombardment of Algiers was also commemorated in a ballad:

> On the twenty-seventh of August, just by the break of day,
> We espied the city of Algiers to windward of us lay;
> 'All hands, all hands to quarters,' it was the general cry,
> 'Come load your guns with round and grape before we draw too nigh.'

There is a note of pride in the ballad; the narrator, a sailor in *Superb*, clearly feels himself not only technologically but morally superior to the enemy. He and his mates 'fought like any lions bold to set the Christians free'. It is a victory of right over wrong, civilisation over barbarism, Christian over heathen. Even the Dutch are represented as admiring the British tar's bravery. 'Take pattern by those English lads,' the Dutch admiral is made to say, 'they show you gallant play.' But it was not just gallantry. It was a conviction that naval force was necessary and justified to keep the King's peace at sea. Possibly no other navy in history has ever expended as much of its own blood, labour and skill to keep the sea open and free for all on their lawful occasions as did the Royal Navy in the nineteenth century. This mighty effort began with the ordinary bluejacket, who was supremely confident that God was on the side of himself and the Navy.

One of the rare books of memoirs by a bluejacket of this period was written by John Bechervaise, who was born in about 1790 at St Aubin in Jersey. He came of seafaring stock, his father being a master mariner. He was educated at boarding schools in the Isle of Wight and Southampton, and after trying a few jobs ashore he was apprenticed to a relative of his father's to learn 'the art, trade and mystery of a seaman'. He ate his meals with the captain and had other small privileges, which made the other lads on board jealous so that they 'exerted all their little powers' to make Bechervaise uncomfortable. But he was not a regular apprentice and he did not obtain the necessary practical experience, as he admitted himself, so that he was not qualified to command a vessel when placed in charge of one.

One of the most familiar images of the nineteenth-century sailor: Robert Cruikshank's drawing, first published in 1827, was still appearing seventy years later in advertisements of the nineties.

Bechervaise was philosophical about his difficulties, and he certainly had his ups and downs. He sailed in a brig to Newfoundland, was captured by a French privateer, recaptured the vessel himself, was legally deprived of his salvage money by the Navy, awarded eighty guineas by Lloyds, went to sea again, and was captured and recaptured by an English revenue cruiser. After his father died and left him some money, he got married and went to sea as a chief mate; when his captain died at sea he brought the ship back. He bought a share in a sloop but his partner went bankrupt and he spent some time in a debtors' prison. With his clear, forceful prose, the picture Bechervaise builds of himself is of a mature man and a competent seaman, who has knocked about the world a bit. In 1820, when he was about thirty years old, he joined the Royal Navy because it seemed the only course open to him.

For Bechervaise, as for any merchant seaman, this was a great psychological gulf to cross. 'The dread of a ship of war was next to a French prison,' he wrote. But that was the 'Old Navy'. In the 'New' Bechervaise soon settled down and eventually he wrote approvingly of it: 'It is possible the pay may be a little less, that I allow, but taking into consideration the regularity of diet, routine of duty, and comfort of the whole system, it makes up for everything, and pensions for old age.'

Bechervaise joined the frigate *Rochfort*, serving in the Mediterranean, and because of his experience he was quickly rated up to petty officer first class. He was contented, he accepted naval discipline, he knew his duties, his wife approved and his small son had entered the naval school at Greenwich. Unfortunately, Bechervaise's happiness had a setback. *Rochfort* paid off in 1824 and he could not get another ship. He joined *Bulwark* but she was delayed with a defective bowsprit, and, more out of desperation than anything else, he joined *Blossom* for Captain Beechey's expedition to the Arctic, one of the many the Royal Navy were to mount in the nineteenth century.

Blossom sailed from Spithead on 17 May 1825. Before sailing, Bechervaise had what he called the 'melancholy pleasure' of seeing his family. He thought of the coming voyage with gloom and foreboding. 'There seemed little prospect of again meeting,' he said. He had the true sailor's fatalism. Perhaps it was a good thing, he thought, that one could not see into the future, 'for if one half of the suffering I had to go through then had been exposed to my view I should have declined; but the ways of providence are inscrutable.'

The voyage was full of incident. Fourteen men deserted at Rio de Janeiro, most of them boat's crews. Beechey got them back by a trick, sailing one afternoon and slipping back after dusk, by which time the men had emerged from hiding, thinking themselves safe. They were all arrested and brought back except two boys who, according to Bechervaise, 'were of little use'. At Pitcairn Island, Bechervaise saw the last of the *Bounty* mutineers, Adams. He was then an old man, and *Blossom* was the first man-of-war he had set foot in since *Bounty*; even thirty-five years later, he was chary of coming on board and had to be reassured by Beechey. They cruised for some months in the Pacific, visiting various islands, surveying and collecting hydrographic information. One of their tasks was to rendezvous in the Arctic with Franklin;

Blossom spent some three and a half years away but never actually met him.

Blossom's officers, led by Beechey himself, seem to have been considerate and popular. On one occasion Beechey presented Bechervaise with a note containing the welcome information that he had been confirmed in his rate, meaning a small increment in pay. As Bechervaise said, 'To a man who has a family however trifling the addition of pay may be, it is welcome; but the addition was given me in a manner so kind, so gentlemanly, that it was doubly pleasing.' In the nineteenth century, as throughout the Navy's history, the sailors appreciated style and manners in an officer.

Bechervaise himself was wise in his generation and knew when to keep silent. He was sent ashore alone one day to walk round a beach and stick a pole up at a point with a flag on the top. He had just finished when he saw a large she-bear with cubs. Bechervaise, armed only with a small hatchet, took to his heels and ran for his life. Happily the bear did not follow but ambled away into the wood with her offspring. One of the ship's officers 'who had been spying at me nearly all the time made a laugh of it, asking me what the bear had said to me; it struck me to say that the bear had told me never to obey foolish orders again; I, however, kept in, sensible I was addressing my superiors.'

Bechervaise served in the Navy until the 1840s, a period in which the Admiralty slowly, reluctantly, but nevertheless steadily, introduced a number of reforms. In 1823 an unprecedented experiment was carried out in *Thetis*: the rum ration was halved, tea and cocoa was issued every day instead, and two shillings a month was added to each man's pay. For months men from *Thetis* (inevitably known as 'Tea Chest') were beaten up by others ashore who thought they would be responsible for a cut in the rum ration. The experiment was judged a success; in 1825 the rum ration was halved throughout the Navy. But at the same time the custom of having 'banyan' or meatless days was abolished and meat was issued every day of the week. In 1831 the beer ration was abolished; in 1850 the rum ration was halved again, and the evening grog issue was abolished. Wondering officers noted that the first evening of this new regime was the quietest on board that they could remember (although William Ashcroft, serving in *Caledonia* in the Mediterranean, thought that it led to more drunkenness because sailors redoubled their efforts to smuggle spirits on board).

The Admiralty made an attempt to standardise uniforms. *Instructions to Pursers* issued in 1824 gave a list of clothing to be carried on board every ship: it included blue cloth jackets and trousers, knitted worsted waistcoats, white duck trousers and frocks, shirts, stockings, hats, mitts, blankets and black silk handkerchiefs.

Every reform moved the Navy a little further towards a permanent state of manning. In June 1827 an Admiralty Circular announced that henceforth petty officers of first or second class could not be punished by flogging, except by sentence of a court-martial. Captains could, however, still disrate petty officers by summary punishment on board, as in the past. When a ship paid off, the petty officers were to be discharged to the flagship as supernumaries and, after reasonable leave, they were to be given another sea-going

'A Scene between Decks', by W. J. Huggins, published in 1833.

appointment, at the same pay and rate as before. Also, to improve the status of the petty officers, they were permitted to wear the badge of their rate, the second class petty officer a white cloth anchor on his sleeve, the first class the anchor surmounted by a crown.

In July 1838 the Admiralty sanctioned the supply of libraries to sea-going ships. Large ships were issued with 276 books, small ships with 156. The books were mostly religious or of an 'improving' nature. Various societies and private individuals also contributed. As early as 1816 a Lieutenant Baker and a Dr Quarrier supplied the *Leander* frigate, fitting out at Woolwich, with a library of several hundred books. Mrs Elizabeth Fry later persuaded the Admiralty to issue libraries to naval hospitals and to the coastguard.

As a senior rating, John Bechervaise was in a position to see how these reforms were received on the lower-deck. Of the cut in the rum ration he heartily approved. He himself was a teetotaller and although he did not advocate total abstinence throughout the Navy there was no doubt in his mind that the less spirits issued the better. From his own experience, Bechervaise knew of the punishments inflicted, the accidents caused, the opportunities lost, the careers spoiled, on account of drink.

The libraries, too, were welcome. Bechervaise served for many years as a petty officer before the libraries were issued. Then, a book was a great rarity on the mess-deck. If any mess had one, it was read and re-read and lent from man to man 'until it became difficult to tell the original colour'. Such books as there were, were 'of a kind that frequently injured rather than improved the morals of the men.' In one of his ships, the *Asia*, Bechervaise was allowed to borrow books from the cabin of one of the lieutenants. 'This indulgence gave me a pleasure I can scarcely describe.' Sometimes, in the dog-watches, Bechervaise sat at the mess table and read to those around him. 'How different it is now: every one can get a book, and read for himself. He can go to the library, take out a volume from a well-selected stock of books, and one day with another at sea, can have three hours to read and improve his mind.' Many of the men took advantage of the chance. 'We have men now in the service, and I could name more than twenty from one ship, who on entering into her did not know one letter in the book; and now within five years, have learnt to read, write and cypher merely at their spare time.' Speaking with twenty-two years' experience of the lower-deck, Bechervaise thought he could 'see at a glance the vast improvement that has taken place, both in morals and character.'

Now and again, Bechervaise encountered the hidebound voice of reaction. He once heard 'an officer of the Old School observe, that the less of education seamen possessed the better they were fitted for the service; for', continued he, 'when they have much learning they are generally great sea-lawyers, and upon the whole troublesome characters.' Bechervaise answered this with a moderation that does him and the lower-deck of his time the greatest credit. He agreed that the accusation was true in a few cases. But, he said, because a few men were troublesome that was no reason to keep the rest in ignorance and deny them the blessing of being able to read and write.

On the whole, Bechervaise enjoyed his naval service and was proud of himself and the Navy. 'For my part, I never in any one instance had cause of complaint. Sobriety and a desire to fulfil the duties imposed on me carried me through with comfort, and I look back with a degree of pleasure to the day on which I first stood on a ship of war's boards.' Others, he knew, bitterly regretted leaving the Service. 'Not a day passes but I hear seamen deplore their having run away from a ship of war; when, had they not done so, they might now, instead of poverty and rags, have enjoyed a good pension, in respectability and comfort.'

Bechervaise was obviously remembering the Navy through the rose-coloured spectacles of age. But there is no doubt of the sincerity of his pride in himself, in the Navy and in his native land. 'What real seaman is there in the Royal Navy who ever looked at his well disciplined ship without pleasure, and felt the conscious pride of the Briton, that of all ships in the world, those of our beloved country were pre-eminent, and their men the most daring.'

From Burma to Navarino:
the Navy of the 1820s

John Bechervaise heartily approved of the sailor's freedom to choose his own ship. 'A seaman on entering the Navy has every opportunity of choosing his own ship, so that he can have no excuse for returning from it. If he finds his ship different to his expectation, the time is limited; he knows that the end is fast approaching, when he will again be free to seek another.' That was true enough, so far as it went (although the 'limited time' Bechervaise referred to might be as long as five years). But Bechervaise was approving of a state of affairs in which there was no official reserve of seamen for the Navy, nor even such a person as a regular Royal Navy sailor, though from 1831 pensions were granted to seamen who could show twenty-one years' service, and there were to be other improvements in the sailor's health, food and status to persuade men to serve for longer periods. Recruiting for the Navy was still haphazard, depending upon whims and personal fancies. When a new ship was commissioned, her marines came from their barracks and the seamen boys from the port flagship, but everybody else had to be recruited by the captain himself, without the aid of the press gang. The press was still legal, indeed it was to be enshrined on the Statute Book, but it had become socially unacceptable and was almost never used after the end of the Napoleonic wars.

A captain had to find his own crew by using bribery, persuasion, his own reputation, and advertising, by word of mouth, by posting placards, and by setting up recruiting rendezvous in the commissioning port, in London and possibly also in Bristol or Liverpool. The rendezvous was manned by officers and petty officers from the ship, who attracted attention to themselves by posting the name of the ship and the captain prominently, pasting up notices extolling the advantages of service in the Navy, and draping bunting, flags and Union Jacks to catch the eye. A captain could bring a nucleus of men with him from his previous ship. John Cunningham, surgeon of the *Cambridge* (80) commissioning for the Pacific in 1823, noted in his journal that Captain Maling 'claimed' about a dozen men as his 'followers' from his previous ship *Spartiate*; for the rest, rendezvous were set up in London and Gravesend.

A ship with an unpopular captain, or commissioning for an unpopular station (that is, unpopular for deserting), could take months to complete her crew. In June 1818 Captain William Dillon commissioned the frigate *Phaeton* at Portsmouth for service on the Indian station. Having not much success in Portsmouth he sent a midshipman to set up a recruiting station in London. Some sailors signed on, but by October he was still forty short and the port admiral was pressing him. Worse still, he was frustrated by a stream of fine, honest-looking seamen who called at his house at Havant volunteering for *Phaeton* but saying that they had no money to get to Portsmouth. The overjoyed Dillon willingly gave them a shilling for transport, and that was the last he saw of his seamen or his shillings. He did finally scrape a crew together, although he unknowingly signed on soldiers wishing to abscond to India and thus got himself into trouble with the Duke of York, who deprived him of his command when he returned from India, for poaching Army recruits.

Privileged ships had special sources of manpower. When John Harvey Boteler joined the Royal Yacht *Royal Sovereign* at Deptford in June 1820 he found that the crew were 'dockyard riggers, all old men-of-war's men, thorough seamen, of good character, and mostly married men'. In 1822, serving in *Northumberland*, Boteler went up the Thames to a rendezvous at Tower Hill to pick up thirty seamen for the *Gloucester*, commissioning for the Jamaica station. The rendezvous was a public house, with a large Union Jack flying from a window and a notice saying that men were wanted. In December the same year Boteler was appointed first lieutenant of the *Ringdove* brig (18), commissioning for the West Indies. He was delighted. This was his heart's desire and he 'rapidly entered men'. He had the slogan 'Happy, flying, saucy *Ringdove*, she's your chance, good officers' chalked on the long gunwharf wall outside the dockyard gates. Unlike Dillon, Boteler was a popular officer, and a petty officer who had served with him in a previous ship, the *Antelope*, helped him to recruit men. 'If you let me remain on shore for two or three days,' the man said, 'I will pick up some good hands for you. There are several about that want ships, but are looking round for comfortable ones!' 'By his crying me up,' Boteler wrote, 'we soon got many prime seamen.'

The only men who could still be pressed into the Navy were convicted smugglers, who were often sentenced to serve up to five years in a man-of-war. Because of their profession smugglers were quick-witted and resourceful men, expert in boat-handling—excellent seamen, in fact. When Admiral of the Fleet Sir Henry Keppel joined his first ship, the donkey frigate *Tweed* (28), as a cadet in February 1824, he noted in his memoirs many years later that just before they sailed they were supplied with a proportion of smugglers. They were, he said, 'equal to our best seamen'. Robert Seymour, who kept a journal with coloured sketches of a visit to a man-of-war off Spithead and across the Bay of Biscay in the late 1820s, described how, when nearly 300 men were getting up the anchor to the music of fifes and the shouts of the petty officers, 'we were delayed some time before heaving up the anchor—at which time the pushing, fifing and the scolding are at the extreme—waiting the tedious arrival of some smugglers, who were sentenced to three years' service in the Mediterranean. Twenty-four finer seamen never stepped a deck.' One of them, Seymour noted, was a 'gentleman' who had been arrested in his own yacht 'with *doubtful* goods on board; and having refused to pay the fine allotted to him, he was sentenced to serve in the Mediterranean in the same manner as the rest of the prisoners'.

Seamen from ships of the East India Company could be requisitioned for naval service in times of local emergencies and special circumstances. It was not exactly press-ganging, but it was very close to compulsion. In 1824 Mr Billy Layard (afterwards General W. T. Layard) was a guest on board the *Larne* corvette (20), commanded by Captain Marryat the novelist, at Madras when

'Paying Off', by George Cruikshank; a huckster, with all his
wares, is being tipped into the hold.

news of the outbreak of the first Burmese war arrived. He was given the choice
of going back to his home in Ceylon or becoming a Volunteer. As any red-
blooded boy would, young Billy chose to serve. One of his first duties was to
take the captain's gig to a large East Indiaman lying in the harbour, request
her captain to pipe his hands up on deck, and to ask them if any wished to
volunteer to serve in *Larne*. The captain looked at the small figure of young
Billy, dressed in his blue silk camblet jacket, the insignia of his rank on his
collar, dirk at his side and belt round his waist, not yet eleven years old, and
thought he was being hoaxed. 'Aye aye,' he said, 'my men are quite content to
remain where they are and don't want to go to Burma to extinguish
themselves.'

Prompted by the gig's coxswain, who was a bosun's mate, Layard said that
his orders were to ask the men themselves and if the captain had nobody to
pipe up the men his own bosun's mate would oblige. Still more amused and
astonished than annoyed, the captain had 'Clear lower-deck' piped, and very
soon a gathering of fine able-bodied seamen had collected around the capstan.
When Layard asked if any would volunteer, amazingly about a dozen said, 'I
will, I will.' Whereupon the captain said that by law he was entitled to a
certain number of hands for the safety of his ship. Layard pointed out that he
was still three hands over the number. He then selected three of the best, told
them to pack their chests, and took them back in triumph to *Larne*.

A sprightly ballad of the time relates how the fleet assembled in Madras
roads and sailed, in the formation of a 'brilliant line to shew a grand half-
moon', against the Burmese 'to show them British play'.

The main enemy of the campaign was the climate, not the Burmese, but the ballad ignores that and the last few verses wind up the Burmese war admirably. This version gives the fleet as 'sixty-three sail'. *Lilly* should be *Liffey*, and *Leander, Larne*. This extract takes up the story when the ships from Madras have met the 'Calcutta fleet' at Port Cornwallis:

> Our fleet being assembled (the sail was sixty-three)
> A signal gun for sailing was fired instantly;
> When out to sea we bore again, and sailed both night and day,
> And on the tenth of May, my boys, we anchor'd in their bay.
>
> It was early the next morning, the weather being fair,
> We weigh'd our anchors to the bows, and up the river did steer.
> The enemy commenced on shore to put us to the rout;
> But we upon the decks did stand, resolved to fight it out.
>
> The *Lilly* frigate led the way, when clouds of smoke did rise,
> The *Leander* sloop in company, which did our foes surprise;
> The *Sophia* brig and gun boats, their cannon loud did roar,
> Like thunder rent the elements all on the Burmese shore.
>
> 'All hands prepare for landing!' resounded through the fleet;
> 'Let every man have sixty rounds his enemy for to meet.'
> Like lions bold we rushed on shore at ten o'clock that day:
> These cowardly dogs could not us stand, we forced them to give way.
>
> Now Rangoon we have taken, let us drink unto our king;
> May all his loyal subjects fresh laurels to him bring.
> Likewise to General Campbell, who commanded on that day,
> And pull'd their saucy peacock down on the eleventh day of May.

Larne and the other ships provided naval brigades to operate ashore with the soldiers and to assist in such projects as bridge-building, convoyed the troops up the Irrawaddy, and supplied and protected the army from the sea. The Navy had many times sent men ashore to assist the army, but these 'naval brigades' were to be a special feature of the nineteenth-century Royal Navy.

This Burma war was the first in which steam-powered ships took part. Included in the force was the 100-ton paddle-steamer *Diana*, which used to tow other ships up river. The Navy had already experimented with two steamships, the *Comet* and the *Monkey* in 1822, bringing a new breed of men, the stokers, into naval service. The old-fashioned type of naval officer did not regard stokers as proper seamen, indeed they could hardly bring themselves even to look upon them as fellow human beings, but the rate of stokers was officially instituted in 1826, with pay of 46s. 0d rising to 54s. 3d per month; they were paid 50% more when in the tropics with steam up, and this was money well earned.

Steam service had its own special hazards from its earliest days. One morning young Layard went on deck to find a human leg in a bucket. It belonged to *Diana*'s engineer. He had gone to stop the engines suddenly during a squall in the night and, half asleep, had slipped, crushing his leg in the machinery so badly it had to be amputated. *Larne* stayed until the end of the year by which time she had lost thirty of her men from cholera, dysentery and fever. Added to the dangers of disease were the discomforts of constant monsoon rain, heat, poor food, wretched preserved provisions, and a general lack of supplies from India.

The memoirs of the time are full of examples of the determination and ingenuity shown by the sailors in the pursuit of drink. Once, when Boteler was visiting another ship, he looked across at *Ringdove* and saw through a telescope members of his own ship's company hoisting a cask through a port forward in the bows, while the unsuspecting officer of the watch walked the deck aft. In the Hooghly river, young Layard took a boat up to Calcutta to look for recruits. They spent a night in the boat on the way. In the middle of the night Layard awoke to the howling of jackals. To his bewilderment he could not rouse any of his crew, who were sleeping like the dead. Investigating, Layard found that while he had been asleep the crew had removed the side of the locker on which he was sleeping and taken out the keg of rum secured there. It was designed to hold their spirit rations for some days, but they had made short work of it.

On 20 October 1827 the very last sea engagement fought purely between wooden walls took place in the Bay of Navarino, on the south-west coast of Greece. For centuries Greece had been under Turkish domination, as part of the Ottoman Empire, and the Treaty of Vienna after the end of the Napoleonic wars maintained Greece's subject status. However, the Greeks rebelled for national independence (supported by a number of well-known Englishmen, notably Cochrane and Lord Byron). In 1826, when Ibrahim Pasha, son of Mehemet Ali, the ruler of Egypt, had almost defeated the Greeks and put down the rebellion, the Russians decided that they did not want to see Greece wholly back under Turkish rule again. The French and English governments had been neutral, disapproving of the Greek revolt but taking no steps to suppress it. Now they too decided that hostilities must end. In the Treaty of London of 1827, the Russians, French and English decreed an armistice between Turk and Greek. The Turks rejected the armistice, and the navies of the three great powers were called upon to enforce it.

Not for the first or last time in British naval history, an English admiral, Sir Edward Codrington, was placed in a very difficult position. Lacking a clear and unequivocal lead from his government, he was apparently supposed to threaten force without actually using it. He was open to criticism whether he brought the Turkish and Egyptian fleets to action or not.

A truce was agreed but it was loosely framed and Ibrahim soon broke it, by sailing some Egyptian ships out of Corinth to Patras. One night, the English ships actually passed the Egyptian and Turkish fleets at sea. Boteler, serving in the *Albion*, said that his ship 'passed right through the Turkish and Egyptian fleets; all were at quarters, a light showing at each port—it was a very fine sight; we glided silently past, all perfectly still, no sound beyond their boatswain's pipes, and they were rather loud'.

Shortly afterwards, the English ships met the Russian and French fleets. Navarino was the first time in history that these three navies fought together. Boteler compares the seamanship of the English tars with their allies. The fleets had to beat to windward to Navarino. The English ships clawed to windward very soon, but the French and Russians carried full topsails, which was too much. One Russian lost a topmast and fell away to leeward. The French kept up better but then they dropped behind during the night of 19–20 October. On the morning of battle, the English ships had to wait for their allies to catch up.

Night alarm: 'Prepare for Action', *c*.1820.

Serving in *Genoa* at Navarino was a seaman called Charles McPherson. An account of the battle which was published anonymously is almost certainly written by him. He was a Scotsman who ran away to sea against his parents' wishes when he was seventeen, but obviously had a good education and writes in clear, vigorous prose. He had served in *Genoa* for some eighteen months before Navarino; as a member of a gun crew and a foretop man he had an excellent view of the action.

As Codrington took his ship up to Navarino Bay he did not know whether or not he would have to fight. But the sailors in *Genoa* were in no doubt. On the eve of the battle McPherson was roused by a messmate called Ned Lee who asked him, in exchange for a share in a bottle of wine, if he would write a letter to his mother. Together, they drank to the toast 'May we meet again tomorrow!' and shook hands. McPherson borrowed the sentry's lantern, used the crown of his hat as a writing desk and the pile of round shot by the hatch combing as a seat, and after some discussion about what they should say, wrote to Lee's dictation:

Dear Mother and Sister,

This leaves me in good health, and I hope it will find you in the same. Can't say if ever you'll get another letter from me; for we mean to go in tomorrow to Navarino Bay to beat the Turks so, whether I'll be sent to Davy or not I cannot tell: but you must not fret, dear mother, if I should be called away tomorrow, for you know that death is a debt we must all of us pay. If any of your old neighbours are calling on you tell Susan Clare that [here, according to McPherson, Lee paused for a time, and

'Dy'e Mind the Roll She Gave': dinner-time at sea, *c.*1820. Note the crockery racks on the bulkheads, the rum tubs, the capstan amidships and the messdeck decorations.

then went on 'with the manner of one who was accomplishing some finished piece of diplomacy'—McPherson's account is all the more valuable for the air of detached irony he sometimes captures towards his messmates] I have not forgot the little bit of business she knows of, nor the *crooked sixpence*. She will understand what you mean, though you don't. And be kind to her, because as how her father is frail and was an old acquaintance; and tell her I have got some rare shells to bring home.

Now God bless you all, and keep you! I bid you fare well; but I hope to live to see the Turks get a great drubbing, and to weigh anchor again for Old England!

I remain, Dear mother and sister,
Your affectionate Son and Brother,

Edward Lee

McPherson and Lee sealed the letter with a piece of metal, finished the bottle of wine and turned in. McPherson slept soundly for four hours and was roused by the pipe 'Both watches pass up shot'. The men formed a human chain from the shot-locker up to the main-deck and passed shot from hand to hand until all the tubs ranged along the decks at regular intervals were full. The sun was just rising when they were called on deck to make sail. The Russian and French ships had dropped to leeward overnight and, according to McPherson, the English made a stretch out from the land to give the others time to come up.

At eleven o'clock the drums beat to quarters, with the tune 'Hearts of Oak'. The officers mustered the men at quarters. McPherson's lieutenant was Broke, the son of Broke of the *Shannon*. He, too, seemed in no doubt that they would see action that day when he addressed the men. 'Now, my men,' he said, 'you see we are going into the harbour today. I know you'll all be right glad of it; at least, I suppose you would be as much against cruising off here all winter as I am. So, I say, let's in today, and fight it out like British seamen, and if we fall, why there's an end to our cruise. I hope, when the guns are to man, you'll be at your stations.' The drums beat retreat and several men promptly fell fast asleep between the guns.

By the time McPherson wrote his memoirs, which were published in 1829, he must have discussed Navarino a thousand times with his mates on the mess-deck and during the nightwatches. Undoubtedly his account benefited from hindsight. But it does seem that one or two of the sailors prophesied their own deaths. The night before Navarino, a German called de Squaw went up to a man called Tom Morfiet, a Channel Islander and a particular friend of McPherson's, who was playing chequers with another sailor. He grasped Morfiet's arm, lifted him to his feet and gazed intently into his face. 'Morfiet,' he said, 'before tomorrow night, you and I will be playing another game.'

This prophecy had a great effect upon the superstitious sailors' minds. Next day, they went to dinner in thoughtful mood. 'The probability of never meeting again cast a soberness over the mess, which is generally a scene of banter and mirth. One or two tried to raise the spirits of their messmates by the usual sallies of nautical wit, but the effect was only momentary.'

They were within two miles of the entrance to Navarino Bay, all sails set, making about one knot, when their spirits were lifted by the piper playing 'Nancy Dawson', the traditional call for the cook of each mess to go up with his monkey for the mess grog ration. Once again the sailors drank the toast 'May we all meet again tomorrow!' McPherson went on deck with a kettle of pea-soup when *Genoa* was only a quarter of a mile from the harbour entrance. Somebody shouted from one of the forecastle guns, 'There it goes now!' McPherson asked what was the matter and the man said, 'Don't you see those two pieces of bunting at the *Asia*'s masthead? That's the signal to engage, my lad!'

By McPherson's account, *Genoa* was ready for battle. But Boteler, who was following in *Albion*, said: '*Genoa* made no preparation; for the following day when, after the men's dinner and our substantial luncheon, we bore up for the harbour, passing through a continual wreck of men's mess tables, cabin bulkheads, partitions, and what not thrown overboard from the *Genoa*, she not having cleared for action.'

'Casting Anchor': one of a set of eight prints published in 1825
showing men-of-war's men on a run ashore.

The preparations for battle which McPherson described might have taken
place at any time within the last fifty years. 'The word now flew along the
decks. "Stand to your guns there, fore and aft!" "All ready, sir!" was the
immediate reply as the captain of each gun stood with the lanyard of the lock
in his hand waiting to hear the word "fire". This was a period of intense
excitement. A dead silence prevailed and the "boldest held his breath for a
time".'

The pipe went to anchor and furl sails. McPherson went to his place on the
foretop sail yardarm, where he had a grand view of the harbour, and a last
opportunity to speak to Tom Morfiet, who was on the yard next to him, before
they separated, each to make his way to his gun. Lieutenant Broke drew his
sword and told the men not to fire till ordered. 'Point your guns sure, men,' he
said, 'And make every shot tell—that's the way to show them British play!'
Broke then threw away his hat on the deck and told the men to give three
cheers for the Turks, 'which we did with all our heart. Then crying out,
"Stand clear of the guns," he gave the word "FIRE!" and immediately the
whole tier of guns was discharged, with terrific effect, into the side of the
Turkish Admiral's ship that lay abreast of us. After this it was, "Fire away, my
boys, as hard as you can!" '

The handling of the guns was very much left to individuals. They could load
virtually what they liked:

we were ordered to only double-shot the guns, but, in this particular, we ventured to disobey orders; for after the first five or six rounds, I may venture to say that the gun I was at was regularly charged with two 32-lb shot and a 32-lb grape; and sometimes with a canister crammed above all. On being checked by the officers for overcharging, one of the men replied, as he wiped the blood and dirt from his eyes, that he liked to give them a *specimen* of our *pills*.

Aiming, too, was done individually.

'Pelt away, my hearties,' cried the captain of our gun, a young Irish lad, and a capital marksman, 'If they don't strike, we'll strike for them. Oho,' he continued, 'here's a glorious mark—look-out there; we'll load with grape entirely.' The gun was loaded nearly to the muzzle with grape. The Turkish Admiral's yacht, a fine frigate that had been built for him at Trieste, drifted down (her cables being shot away) beside us . . . 'Stand clear there,' cried the captain of our gun, 'she's coming, she's coming! d—— me, if I don't spoil her gingerbread work! Ahah! I'm glad you have come this road at any rate. Now, let's see what I can do for you in a small way!' He pointed the gun and taking aim fired; and when the smoke cleared away, I heard him above all the noise that assailed our ears, vociferating, 'I told ye! I told ye! I've done more than I bargained for; I've carried her spanker-boom as well as her gingerbread work away.' A few minutes after this she caught fire and blew up.

Significantly, the English sailors expected their enemy to give up almost at once: 'we expected them to strike speedily, and many were the enquiries whether they had "doused the moon and stars yet", but the Turks were resolute, and not one of them struck colours during the engagement.'
So the battle went on. An officer who had been wounded came aft to get a drink from the 'fighting water', the cask lashed to the stanchion amidships. De Squaw took a jug and 'skimming back the blood and dirt from the top of the cask, filled it and offered it to the officer' when the wounded man was cut down nearly in pieces by grapeshot. In writing of the battle afterwards, McPherson was able to preserve a detached viewpoint. It was exciting, but it was hideous, and it was not glorious.

We assisted the officer down to the cockpit, where, illuminated by the dim light of a few purser's dips, the surgeon and assistants were busily employed in amputating, binding up, and attending to the different cases as they were brought to them. The stifled groans, the figures of the surgeon and his mates, their bare arms and faces smeared with blood, the dead and dying all round, some in the last agonies of death, and others screaming under the amputating knife, formed a horrid scene of misery, and made a hideous contrast to the 'pomp, pride and circumstance of glorious war'.

It is a measure of McPherson's education and his breadth of reading that he can find here just the right quotation, from *Othello*.

Later, some remarkable anecdotes were told of the fortitude and stoicism of the ships' companies under fire. A marine called Hill serving in *Genoa* had both his arms shot away, but turned to Captain Dickinson standing near him and said, 'I hope you'll allow, sir, that I have done my duty.' He was heard after the battle, singing on the lower-deck. 'I am trying what I can do at ballad singing, now I've lost my arms.' He lived to reach Plymouth but died in the naval hospital at Stonehouse. One sailor, whose name was Neil, behaved with great gallantry, climbing to the fore-royal masthead to nail a fresh Union Jack there after the old one had been shot down. It was the sort of action which, a generation later, would have won the Victoria Cross.

But at least one man was a coward. A big Manxman skulked from his place of duty at his gun and hid in the cockpit until the battle was over. He was discovered and booted up the ladder by the Master at Arms. Later he was given three dozen with the thieve's cat, had the word COWARD sewn on his jacket, and had to mess by himself.

In the middle of the battle *Genoa*'s captain, Walter Bathurst, was mortally wounded and at once 'the whole crew, as if activated by one impulse, set up a cry of dire revenge, and the words 'OUR CAPTAIN KILLED! OUR CAPTAIN KILLED!'' were heard above the roar of the guns.' Bathurst was an extraordinarily popular officer. During the mutiny at the Nore in 1797 the mutineers forbade, on pain of death, any officer to come on board, except Captain Bathurst. Before Navarino, when several men had fallen asleep, the captain did his rounds. Men went to wake those sleeping, but Bathurst said 'Let them lie, let them lie, poor fellows; they have enough to do before tonight.' Bathurst was a very fine officer, an excellent seaman, a considerate man, beloved by his crew. His death stung his ship's company to greater efforts. 'Dreadful as the conflict was before,' said McPherson, 'it now raged with triple violence.'

At last, at about six in the evening, the roar of battle died away. The Turkish and Egyptian fleet had been almost totally destroyed. The Allies had also suffered losses, in *Genoa* in particular. 'Nothing can better show the honourable share the *Genoa* had in the action than that out of 460 men, we had 26 killed and 33 wounded, while the *Asia*, out of a crew of 700 men, had only 19 killed and 57 wounded.'

Amongst those mortally wounded was Morfiet, just as De Squaw had foreseen. He was not present at the roll call held on deck at daylight the next day. McPherson was overjoyed when somebody called out that Morfiet was not yet dead, 'and the mark of red ink was not put down against his name', but when McPherson was going aft he saw two men carrying a purser's bread bag which obviously contained a corpse. He asked whose it was and was told: 'it's just your own messmate, Tom Morfiet—dead at last.' McPherson said that he would bury him himself, and was told he was welcome to the job.

McPherson described his friend's makeshift funeral, in one of the most moving passages of his book:

I went forward to the mess, where they were all at breakfast to get a spare hammock. 'What's the matter?' said one, 'where are you going with that 'ere hammock, and the tear in your eye like a travelling rat?' I made no answer; but having borrowed a sail-needle and some twine, I went off to wrap the lifeless body of my messmate into his characteristic shroud. I undid the mouth of the bag, and cut it down with my knife, for I could not bear my fingers about the body, and I had nobody at this time to help me. The wound on the back of his head seemed to be the only one, but the neat white frock that he had on was sticking to his back with clotted blood. He had his knife with the lanyard round his waist, to which was attached the very thimble with which he had mended his jacket, sitting in the streets of Malta. The thimble I took to keep for his sake; and having stretched the knots out on the hammock, I proceeded to sew it up, beginning at the feet. While thus engaged, I was accosted by someone behind. I did not look up for I was still crying, but I knew the voice to be my messmate's Tom Croaker. When I told him whose body I was enshrouding Croaker offered to get the Prayer Book and read the service for the dead. 'For', said he, 'Tom was always a yonker that I was fond of, and we sailed round Cape Horn and back again in the old Tartar together for three years eight months, and it will go very hard though I am no parson, if my peepers won't do him as he goes to Davy.' Croaker procured the Prayer Book while I finished my work, and having slung two 32-lb shot to the feet, we bore it to the gunroom port. My assistant read the service with a sober, steady voice, and when he came to the words, 'We commit his body to the deep,' I let go my hold and with a gentle push, the body of poor Tom was launched into the water. We looked out, and saw it gradually sinking under the wave; and the hands being lined up, we went on deck to do our duty.

The dangers of battle drew the men together as nothing else could. 'When I came to my berth I was welcomed by the whole mess more like a brother than a shipmate, but this day made us all brothers; feuds and animosities were buried in forgetfulness; and many who had entertained bitter hatred at one another, would be seen shaking the hand of friendship together.'

Boteler's account in *Albion* complements, as well as contradicts, McPherson's story. *Albion*'s anchor did not hold and she drifted down on to a Turkish frigate, which she stormed and captured. The enemy was found to be on fire and *Albion*'s men had to retreat. Before they left, three of the storming party ran up the Turkish rigging and threw three Turks into the sea. One rather simple sailor, the butt of the mischievous ship's boys who used to lead him about the ship by his forelock of hair, surprised everybody by the desperate way he wielded his cutlass in the leading boarding party. The second captain of the foretop, an Irishman, seized a musket, held by the muzzle and used it like a scythe, cutting himself a way through the Turks. By the end of the battle, when *Albion* had twice had to weigh anchor and move off to avoid burning ships, some of the men were so exhausted they fell asleep at their guns and the officers 'had difficulty in rousing them'. Some of them were so deafened by the gunfire that they could hear very little for the next two days.

Boteler was critical of his men's gunnery, and the over-shotting which was ordered in *Genoa* was disapproved of in *Albion:*

> our men were not over well instructed in gunnery, knew how to load and fire, and nothing more in the management and property of the guns. They invariably over-loaded, nearly always with two shot, sometimes with three, and when the gunner on the following day examined the guns and drew the charges, in one was found *four* round shot. The guns, consequently, were very lively, springing back upon their breechings, jumping off the deck.

This recoil was so violent that a midshipman was struck in the stomach, knocked out, and taken below for dead. On at least one occasion, *Albion*'s guns fired on a neighbouring French ship. There was no doubt about it, 'there was our mark on the shot sticking in his foremast'.

The victory was complete, although at home the Duke of Wellington called it 'an untoward event'. Sixty of Ibrahim's ships were sunk, and not one of the Allies'. The Allies lost 174 killed and 475 wounded, of whom 75 and 197 respectively were British. Four days later, the Turkish and Egyptian bodies were floating so thickly in the bay that *Albion*'s boats often had to toss oars to clear them.

In *Genoa*, Bathurst's command was taken over by Captain Dickinson, a man almost as popular. Shortly after he took over, he cleared lower-deck to give a speech which was most unusual for his times. 'If I have ever given you an angry word without cause, I generously beg your pardon, for after your noble behaviour, I must always hold you in respect, and shall be grieved if any of you shall ever forfeit the honourable estimation of you which you have established in my breast.' This was well received by the ship's company, although somewhat incredulously by some of the old tars. One of them, Jack Burgess, according to McPherson, said: 'Damn me, when I was aboard the *Tremendous*, our old shark of a captain would never have axed pardon though he had seen all our back-bones!'

The ship's company signed a 'round Robin' asking that Dickinson command the ship for the passage home. But Codrington refused and Dickinson was actually courtmartialled later for his conduct in the battle. He was acquitted of mishandling *Genoa* in such a way as to endanger *Asia* and *Albion*, and of falsifying the log as to the time of Bathurst's death, but was found guilty of submitting a round robin from the crew. For this, Codrington's reprimand was taken as sufficient punishment. Dickinson later commissioned the *Wasp* and some of the old *Genoa*'s joined him. But not McPherson. He was by that time disgusted with the Navy.

Another man, a Captain Irbey, one of the old school, was appointed to *Genoa* and very soon it was no longer 'happy *Genoa*.' 'So little is mutual attachment and goodwill between master and man studied in the Naval Service,' wrote McPherson. The day after Bathurst's funeral, his old barge's crew went ashore to see their friends. The next day they were brought up as defaulters and

HMS *Genoa* (right foreground) at Navarino in 1827, as depicted
by G. P. Reinagle.

flogged. Nobody else was allowed leave and 'scarcely a day passed but someone underwent the barberous and disgusting operation of the lash'.

Genoa had gone straight home, with Bathurst's body on board, but the other victors of Navarino, including *Asia* and *Albion*, stayed at Malta for three months, repairing battle damage, being fêted and made much of. They arrived off Spithead in March 1828, were inspected by the Lord High Admiral, the Duke of Clarence, later King William IV, and ordered into harbour to be paid off. *Albion* was lashed alongside the hulk *Blake*, the guns hoisted out, the ship unrigged to her lower masts, anchors, cables and all stores returned to the dockyard and *Albion* herself reduced to a 'clean swept hold'.

Boteler does not mention details of the ship's arrival at Spithead but a pamphlet, written by Admiral Hawkins and published anonymously in 1822, entitled *Statement of Certain Immoral Practices in HM Ships*, gives a graphic picture of the typical scene below decks. Every returning ship of war was met by boatloads of prostitutes, taken off by watermen who expect payment from the sailors, who hung around until permitted to come on board:

> The men then go into the boats and pick out each a woman (as one would choose cattle), paying a shilling or two to the boatman for her passage off. These women are examined at the gangway for liquor which they are constantly in the habit of smuggling on board. They then descend to the lower deck with their husbands, as they call them. Hundreds come off to a large ship. The whole of the shocking, disgraceful transactions of the lower deck it is impossible to describe— the dirt, filth, and stench; the disgusting conversation; the indecent, beastly conduct and horrible scenes; the blasphemy and swearing; the riots, quarrels, and fighting, which often takes place, where hundreds of men and women are huddled together in one room, as it were, and where, in bed (each man being allowed only fourteen inches breadth for his hammock), they are squeezed between the next hammocks, and must be witnesses of each other's actions; can only be imagined by those who have seen all this. A ship in this state is often, and justly, called by the more decent seamen 'a hell afloat'. Let those who have never seen a ship of war picture to themselves a very large low room (hardly capable of holding the men) with 500 men and probably 300 or 400 women of the vilest description shut up in it, and giving way to every excess of debauchery that the grossest passions of human nature can lead them to; and they see the deck of a 74-gun ship the night of her arrival in port.

Boteler has left a full and valuable description of paying off *Albion*:

> The ship is made scrupulously clean, decks white and spotless, the officers with cocked hats and side-arms, the men in their 'Sunday best'. The Commissioner comes on board, is received by all the officers, the marine guard presenting arms; he takes his seat in the fore cabin, together with the clerk of the cheque, cashier, and four or five clerks, with the necessary iron-bound cash boxes. In those days, when

seamen's wages accumulated from the time of entry till paid off, the amount required became very large, and in the case of a large ship over two and a half years in commission, reached several thousand pounds. In paying off, the men are mustered aft by open list, *i.e.*, as they stand on the ship's books, a copy of which is always at the navy office in London, and one sent to the pay office at Portsmouth. Then from a string of men on one side of the quarter-deck, three at a time are called into the cabin, and—'William Smith, £34 6s. 8d,' repeated by the clerks from different books, to verify the correctness, followed always by the same question, of—'William Smith, how will you have it, the whole now or part? or you can remit the whole or part to any place in the kingdom, and you will find it there ready for you or anyone you name, for you.' To another, '£57 5s. 6d.'; '£57 5s. 6d.' repeated, and the question again: 'How will you have it?' &c. 'The whole lot, sir, if you please!' Hats are always put on the deck, and into it the money placed, and which the man always stuffs, as it is, into his pocket. Some would say 'Remit every farthing, sir,' and swagger out of the cabin with a defiant air, probably with his pockets turned inside out, knowing whom he was about to face, for there on the gangway the bumboat women who had attended the ship with their account books, eagerly watching the men as they emerged from the cabin; it was no time to squabble, the man would often open— 'You cheated me last paying off, I am even with you this time, my lady'; a number of boats were in waiting, many with persons ready to pounce on the defaulter as he left the ship. Some men would be met with—'Take so-and-so, £3 10s.' 'Eh, what?' 'Mutton so much, soft bread and butter, money lent!' 'Well, all right!' and payment made; at other times a dispute, which we never allowed to go on, but settled elsewhere. On the whole, I imagine bumboat people were amply repaid; all charges high and often false, trusting to the forgetfulness and recklessness of Jack.

While at Malta many of the officers, including Boteler, lent the ship's company small sums so that they could go ashore. Boteler lent a dollar to a black sailor called Hercules Taylor and promptly forgot about the loan. Not so Taylor. Boteler was on the hulk's quarter-deck when Taylor rushed past waving a copper belaying pin and daring anybody to stop him. When Boteler ordered him to put the pin down, Taylor stopped, ran back and pushed a £5 note into Boteler's hand. The last Boteler saw of Taylor, he was in a four-oared wherry racing another wherry manned by the tipstaff for the shore.

Boteler noticed one at least of the traps waiting ashore for the sailor and his hard-earned paying-off money. 'There were two fellows alongside dressed as stage coachmen, in box coats of many capes, voluminous belcher handker-chiefs around their necks, *whips*, and a parchment-covered book in their hands to book men for London by the 'Rocket', 'Nelson', 'Trafalgar', &. I need scarcely add the whole was a fraud.'

'A sailor's the man':
the Navy and the stage 1820–40

Navarino was a popular victory, painted and sung and talked about for years afterwards. The battle confirmed the reputation of the gallant British tar, already high from the French wars. As the last of the wooden wall engagements, Navarino had a special flavour and, being isolated in time from similar battles, was all the more sensational and memorable. Several ballads were composed about Navarino; one of the liveliest expresses very well the image of the Jolly Jack Tar as John Bull's stout representative, ready to knock down all tyrants. But, as Boteler's story of the bogus stagecoach shows, the sailor was still regarded ashore as a gullible innocent, to be duped by anything outside the normal existence of his ship. The popular view of sailors was more complex: he was not only a defender of justice and right and an innocent ashore, he was also a figure of menace, liable to say and do and sing unpredictable things. He was no respecter of property or liquor or the peace of the neighbourhood. There was a traditional version of sailors on a run ashore—frying their watches, eating sandwiches with £5 note fillings, hiring four cabs, putting their bags in the first, their hats in the second, all the Nancy Dawsons and brazen Bêt Monsons in town in the third and bringing up the rear themselves in the fourth. A sailor ashore spent money as though it were no longer in fashion, engaged in day-long drunken carousings, fought pitched fights in the streets with constabulary and watchmen, drove crazy donkey races along the beach, and ended the morning after with a sore and broken head, lost rate and a flogging.

There was a special language, determinedly and exaggeratedly nautical, for describing sailors ashore. Sailors had their own way of life, and their own code of ethics, which made them over-bearing, anarchic, and contemptuous of landlubbers. These are well caught by the prints of the time. A set of eight aquatints showing the adventures of a party of four sailors on shore from a man-of-war were published on 28 March 1825 by John Fairburn, of the Broadway, Ludgate Hill. The first plate is entitled *In Sight of Port:*

> We have here four as tight lads on a cruise as ever stepped between stem and stern, scudding right before the wind, at the rate of six knots an hour, having obtained leave to go ashore. Tom Steady, on the lookout afore, sings out to his shipmates, 'There is a port right ahead.' He is a tough one, has passed many banyan days on board a man-of-war, and weathered many a hard gale in the 'Bay of Biscay, O'. Jack Staysail, on the starboard side, is elated with the prospect, is all life, and capers along to the tune of 'Jack's Alive'. Dick Haulyard, on the larboard side, a real ship-shape tar, on hearing the news, exclaims, 'My eyes! so it is—steady she goes.' The Younker, abaft (coxswain of the jolly boat), is full of joy at the thoughts of being within sight of port.

In the second plate the four, having made the port and found the soundings good, 'cast anchor off "The Ship", Ben Tack, Master. Ben is an old pilot, who after weathering many a storm, has moored his hulk in a snug birth within gunshot of the beach. Our tars are kindly received by his Mate, a well fed landlady, who always has a smile to welcome good customers.'

However, the tars prove not to be such good customers in the long run. Predictably, they get drunk, run out of 'rhino', get obstreperous when refused more liquor, turn nasty, terrorise the other customers, break open the cellar, and retire to drink themselves insensible. The captions tell the story: *Half Seas Over; Run Aground with a Stiff Breeze; An Engagement, with a storm; The Victory; A Dead Calm.* *Performing Quarantine* is the last plate, in which our heroes, completely 'waterlogged', are taken in tow by the enemy (a soldier who has been drinking at the pub) and safely clapped into 'the Bilboes'. The 'half reanimated tars' were compelled to 'lye to, under hatches, till the morn'.

Navarino gave an extra impetus to the early nineteenth-century vogue for nautical drama on the London stage. 'Whoever saw a gallant fight', wrote a poet, 'that never viewed a brave Sea Fight!' The next best thing to a real naval fight was its representation on the stage. One of the leading writers and librettists of the period was Edward Fitzball (1792–1873), whose greatest success was *The Pilot*, based on the novel by Fenimore Cooper, which opened at the Adelphi on 31 October 1825, with an actor called T. P. Cooke in the part of Long Tom Coffin.

T. P. Cooke was to become one of the most famous actors of the early Victorian stage. To the popular mind he came to epitomise the brave British tar. According to Fitzball himself, T. P. Cooke's Long Tom Coffin 'was a masterpiece. He gave a new feature to the sailor's character: that of thoughtfulness and mystery, of deep-toned passion and romance. Long Tom Coffin had beheld the ocean with a meditating eye. He adored it as his element, and reposed upon its billows.'

Cooke was as popular with serving men. Henry Keppel met him at the Beefsteak Club in London in 1829, and once took him to a dinner at the Castle Tavern, Holborn, attended by notable whips and pugilists, including Faulkner of the 'Rocket' and 'Tom Spring.' He was, apparently, 'a great favourite': 'I naturally clung to T. P. Cooke,' wrote Keppel, 'and after a while I drew from him more about himself.'

Thomas Potter Cooke was born on 23 April 1786, the son of a London doctor. He served in the *Raven* when he was ten years old. He was at the siege of Toulon, aged thirteen, and at the battle off Cape St Vincent. Coming home he was wrecked off Cuxhaven, contracted rheumatic fever and was invalided. On his recovery he joined the *Prince of Wales*, under Captain Prowse, flying the flag of Rear Admiral Sir Robert Calder at the blockade of Brest Harbour. He was paid off after the peace of Amiens and made one of his first appearances on the stage as Nelson at the Amphitheatre in 1805 (Keppel says it was at Astley's the year before, and wonders if Nelson ever saw him perform). He played Fid in Fitzball's *The Red Rover, or the Mutiny of the Dolphin* in the Theatre Royal, Adelphi, in 1828 and a contemporary report said that Cooke 'had his hornpipe

T. P. Cooke, one of the most famous actors of the early-Victorian
stage, as a tipsy sailor and as Long Tom Coffin, the epitome of the
brave British tar.

and danced with great spirit'. The same year he was in *Presumptive Evidence,
or Murder Will Out*, by a comic actor and playwright called John Baldwin
Buckstone (1802–1879) who was himself placed on board a man-of-war at the
age of eleven but was brought back and sent to school by a relative. T. P. Cooke
played Duke Dorgan, an Irish sailor who returns to his home in Munster to
look up his friends, relations, and especially his girl friend. In the stage
directions he is described as wearing the Trafalgar medal, which is the
'presumptive evidence', being mislaid by Dorgan and found again tightly
clutched in the hand of an elderly man who has been murdered. Clearly, the
man must have wrenched it from his murderer with his last dying grasp. The
evidence thus points to Dorgan, whose medal it is known to be, and who
denies the accusation in a ringing speech which reflects much of the popular
esteem of the sailor and which must have invariably brought the house down:

I am a British sailor. Is that the character of a ruffian or a traitor? I have
trod the decks of the *Victory*—a deck that was never pressed by a
coward—I laid my hands on the white hairs of my commander, Nelson,
when he lay bleeding on the bed of glory—is it likely I should hack and
hew the hoary head of a defenceless fellow creature? I stood by his side
at Trafalgar, and never shrunk in the daylight from the enemy's
broadside—is it likely that I would stab an old man in the dark? No, I
have served my country faithfully and a felon's death can never be my
reward!

All the same, Dorgan was convicted on the evidence and a felon's death certainly would have been his reward, had not the real murderer been discovered in the nick of time and Dorgan reprieved on the very steps of the gallows.

T. P. Cooke's greatest and most famous role, which he was to play over and over again throughout his career, was William in *Black-Ey'd Susan, or, All in the Downs*, a Nautical Drama in Three Acts, by Douglas Jerrold, which had its first performance south of the Thames at the Royal Surrey on 6 June 1829.

Douglas Jerrold, born in 1793, himself served as a midshipman in the guardship *Namur* off the Nore during the French wars. He took part in theatricals on board and there met Clarkson Stanfield, the marine painter, then a seaman, who painted scenery for him. Jerrold's father Samuel was at one time manager of the Sheerness Theatre, so the sea and the stage were both in his blood (he was reputedly carried on stage as a baby by Edmund kean playing Rolla in *Pizarro*). He had served a long and somewhat unsuccessful apprenticeship writing to order for various theatres including the Coburg (Old Vic) before his and T. P. Cooke's talents exactly chimed in *Black-Ey'd Susan*.

A scene from *Black-ey'd Susan* (1829), one of the most famous of all 'nautical dramas': William (centre) is being arrested after assaulting Captain Crosstree for making advances to Susan.

William was a ploughboy, working on the land, when he married his own true love, the delicate little black-eyed Susan. When the play opens, the couple owe money to Susan's rascally uncle, Doggrass, who intends to use the processes of law to dispossess them of their little house. William has been forced to go to sea in a man-of-war, and Susan to live with an old lady, who also owes Doggrass considerable arrears of rent. Inspired by Doggrass, two smugglers try to deceive Susan and make her unfaithful to William. Despite the best efforts of her friend and adorer Gnatbrain, their schemes are about to succeed when William returns in time to thwart them. He is fighting with the smugglers, when their fight is interrupted by the smugglers' arrest. William's reaction is revealing. 'Smugglers,' he cries, 'I *thought* they were not man-of-war's men! True blue never piloted women on a quicksand.' As was the custom, the smugglers were sent to serve in the Navy.

William is a considerable stage character and has many lines for actor and audience to savour. In one extended metaphor he adroitly compares the Law to a ship.

> His Beelzebub's ship, the Law! she's neither privateer, bomb-ship, nor letter-o-mark, she's built of green timber, manned with lob-lolly boys and marines; provisioned with mouldy biscuit and bilge water, and fires nothing but red hot shot: there's no grappling with or boarding her. She always sails best in a storm, and founders in fair weather. I'd sooner be adrift in the North Sea, in a butter cask, with a 'bacco-box for my storeroom, than sail in that devil's craft, the Law.

William's nautical similes are brilliantly and inventively apt. When he is waiting for Susan to come on board, and every sailor is met by a female except him, William says: 'What! and am I left alone in the doctor's list, whilst all the crew are engaging? I know I look as lubberly as a Chinese junk under a jewry mast. I'm afraid to throw out a signal—my heart knocks against my timbers, like a jolly-boat in a breeze, alongside a seventy-four.' Like every lover expecting a sight of his love, William goes hot and cold, 'as if half of me was wintering in the Baltic, and the other half stationed in Jamaica'. The very mention of Susan's name makes him cry: 'I can feel one tear standing in either eye like a marine at each gangway.' Doggrass's mouth opens, William says, 'like the main hold of a seventy-four'. 'Aren't you a neat gorgon of an uncle now,' he tells Doggrass, 'to cut the painter of a pretty pinnace like this, and send her drifting down the tide of poverty, without ballast, provisions or compass? May you live a life of banyan days, and be put six upon four for't.'

The centrepiece of the play is the singing by a sailor called Blue Peter of the ballad by John Gay from which the piece takes its name; the music was by Dibdin.

> All in the Downs the fleet was moor'd,
>   The streamers waving on the wind.
> When black-ey'd Susan came on board,
>   Oh! where shall I my true love find?
> Tell me, ye jovial sailors, tell me true,
> Does my sweet William sail among your crew?
>
> William, who high upon the yard,
>   Rock'd with the billows to and fro;
> Soon as her well-known voice he heard,
>   He sigh'd and cast his eyes below.
> The cord slides swiftly through his glowing hands,
> And quick as lightning on the deck he stands.

So the sweet lark, high-pois'd in air,
    Shuts close his pinions to his breast
(If, chance, his mate's shrill call he hear)
    And drops at once into her nest.
The noblest captain in the British fleet,
Might envy William's lip those kisses sweet.

O Susan, Susan, lovely dear,
    My vows shall ever true remain;
Let me kiss off that falling tear,
    We only part to meet again.
Change, as ye list, ye winds; my mind shall be
The faithful compass that still points to thee.

Believe not what the landsmen say,
    Who tempt with doubts thy constant mind.
They tell thee, sailors, when away,
    In every port a mistress find.
Yes, yes, believe them when they tell thee so,
For thou art present whereso'er I go.

If to fair India's coast we sail,
    Thy eyes are seen in di'monds bright;
Thy breath is Afric's spicy gale,
    Thy skin is ivory so white.
Thus every beauteous object that I view,
Wakes in my soul some charm of lovely Sue.

Though battle call me from thy arms,
    Let not my pretty Susan mourn:
Though cannons roar, yet free from harms,
    William shall to his dear return.
Love turns aside the balls that round me fly,
Lest precious tears should drop from Susan's eye.

The boatswain gave the dreadful word,
    The sails their swelling bosom spread;
No longer must she stay on board;
    They kiss'd; she sighed; he hung his head;
Her less'ning boat unwilling rows to land;
Adieu! she cries, and waves her lily hand.

William's captain, Captain Crosstree, is infatuated with Susan and, although
he discovers that she is William's wife, attempts to seduce her in a drunken
moment. William, not realising that the assailant is his captain, strikes him
with his cutlass. Though Crosstree admits his guilt—'I deserve my fate'—
William has committed a serious offence against the Naval Discipline Act and is
courtmartialled.

The court scene gives some scope for comments on lower-deck life and
humour. When William is asked if any of his shipmates will speak for him, he

says that he 'didn't think to ask them—but let the word be passed, and may I never go aloft, if from the boatswain to the black cook, there's one that could spin a yarn to condemn me.' One of the character witnesses is a seaman called Quid. He testifies that William is the trimmest sailor as ever handled rope, with the cleanest top and the whitest hammock, the tautest able seaman in the fleet. Yes, says the court, but what about his *moral* character? 'His *moral* character, your honour?' says Quid. 'Why, he plays upon the fiddle like an angel.' Another witness, Seaweed, testifies that William was never known to disobey a command, except once, 'and that was when he gave me half his grog when I was upon the black list'. Seaweed believed that if William did go aloft, there was 'sartin promotion' for him. Did he ever do any great, benevolent action? asks the court. 'He twice saved the captain's life,' says Seaweed, and then, remembering the greatest, most benevolent action he could think of, 'and he once ducked a Jew slopseller!'

The court is sympathetic but there is no legal answer to the charge and William is convicted. The presiding admiral reads out the relevant Article of War, the twenty-second: ' "If any man in, or belonging to the Fleet, shall draw, or offer to draw, or lift up his hand against his superior officer, he shall suffer death." The sentence of the Court is, that you be hanged at the fore-yardarm of this his Majesty's ship, at the hour of ten o'clock. Heaven pardon your sins, and have mercy on your soul!'

The play's dénouement is neatly provided by the villain Doggrass. A letter addressed to Captain Crosstree is delivered by mistake to Doggrass who pockets it 'until William is settled for', i.e. hung. The scene (almost certainly based upon reality) and what happens to Doggrass, are explained to Susan by the faithful Gnatbrain.

Why, the old villain was hovering, whilst the Court-Martial was going on, like a raven about the vessel. The whole sea was covered with boats—there was scarcely room enough to put out an oar. Well, the word was given that the sentence was about to be passed, when old Doggrass, as he would have snuffed up the words of death, as a kite snuffs carrion, sprang hastily up in the boat—she gave a lurch, threw him backward, he went down—not a hand was out to catch him; he went down with the horror of the good and the laughter of the wicked weighing on his drowning head.

William distributes the contents of his chest to his friends, including a bullet which a friend of William's received while defending him from a Frenchman. In a touching farewell scene with Susan, William asks to be buried under an aspen tree by the church porch, where he and Susan played as children; many sailors of the time yearned for their rural childhoods. As they are saying goodbye, a gun fires, and there is a cry of a body overboard.

The stage directions for the last scene are the formal representation of an execution on board.

The Forecastle of the ship—Procession along the starboard gangway; minute bell tolls, Master at Arms with a drawn sword under his arm, point next to the prisoner; William follows without his neckcloth and jacket, a Marine on each side, Officer of Marines next; Admiral, Captain, Lieutenant, and Midshipmen, following. William kneels; and all aboard appear to join in prayer with him. The procession then marches on and halts at the gangway; Marine Officer delivers up prisoner to the Master at Arms and Boatswain, a Sailor standing at one of the forecastle guns, with the lock-string in his hand. A platform extends from the cat-head to the fore-rigging. Yellow flag flying at the fore, colours half mast down. Music. William embraces the Union Jack, shakes the Admiral's hand.

At the last moment there is an interruption. Captain Crosstree rushes on stage with a piece of paper. The body brought to the surface by the gunshot was Doggrass's. A letter was recovered from his pocket. It was William's discharge from the Navy, addressed to Captain Crosstree. At the time of the assault, William was not in His Majesty's service and not subject to the Articles of War. The Admiral reads the paper and says, 'He is free!' There is music, the seamen give three cheers, William leaps from the platform, Susan is brought on by Captain Crosstree. Curtain.

T. P. Cooke was the leading figure of a number of actors, among them Gallot, Munden, Reeve, Yates, Campbell and O. Smith, who played all the Tom Coffins, Jack Junks, Dick Oakhams and Harry Lanyards of the time. O. Smith was Cooke's chief rival. While Cooke was 'celebrated for his bold, vigorous, and romantic pictures, with sudden unexpected dashes of pathos mingled with his good humour and rollicking jollity', O. Smith, on the contrary, 'was notable for his mysterious, abstracted, half-crazed look and manner, for the ominous, hollow voice, stealthy step, and subtle devilry peculiar to him'. He was an ideal smuggler, pirate or mutineer, while Cooke was the rough diamond.

The degree of difference between seafaring men and landlubbers was always good theatre and was exploited in a number of plays. Sometimes the bewilderment of a landsman faced with an authentic sailor and his language could be kept going to the audience's enjoyment for a whole scene. *Gwynneth Vaughan* had its first performance at the Theatre Royal on Easter Monday 1840. It was written by Mark Lemon (1809–1870), co-founder and editor of *Punch* with Henry Mayhew, and editor until his death. The play is set in a small township in Caernarvonshire in North Wales. Morgan Morgan, bosun of the *Telemachus*, has come home to visit his nephew Huw Morgan, teacher at the local school. He first comes on stage in sailor's garb, carrying a bread bag and a small cask of rum. He is a breezy character who, with his experience of life and his £4,000 in $3\frac{1}{2}\%$ Consols providentially left him by a former girlfriend Sally Snouter, acts as a *deus ex machina* for some of the other characters. He is able to solve Gwynneth and Huw's problems; he tells a lover to go to sea to solve his difficulty and the lover does so. He uses phrases like 'tell that to the marines'; to an unusually prim lady, 'you needn't brace your nose up so taut'; calls money 'rhino', but, it transpires, cannot read or write.

Some plays turned on the proposition that a lady of 'quality' could never marry a man on the lower-deck: he must first become an officer. (The same qualification was used forty years later in *H.M.S. Pinafore*). Two plays of this genre provided typical parts for T. P. Cooke. He was Mat Meriton, bosun's mate of the *Ariadne* in *The Ocean of Life, or Every Inch a Sailor*, by John Thomas Haines at the Royal Surrey in April 1836, and Jack Somerton of HMS *Adrastus* in *Poor Jack, or The Wife of a Sailor*, a nautical drama in two acts by John Baldwin Buckstone at the Adelphi in February 1840. Buckstone's piece is remarkably similar to Haines's and both closely resemble an actual incident which happened in 1810 and was published under the title of *The Bride of Obeydah* in 1827.

In both plays Cooke is shipwrecked and cast ashore in the company of a lady of much higher social standing than himself. She is called Eleanor in *Poor Jack*, the Hon. Isabella Morville in *The Ocean*. Jack, or Mat, is played as honest, brave, open-hearted, generous, and chivalrous towards women. Not so the other survivors—two merchant seamen who are represented as shifty, selfish, mendacious and greedy; one of them turns out to be a blackmailer. Both plays use similar bits of stage 'business': a group of survivors cast on a deserted and bleak shore, a cask of rum, a tin of biscuits, and a party of traders who will take the survivors to safety provided the proprieties are observed: Jack, or Mat, though he has no idea of the lady's status, must marry her or he will be left behind to starve.

This ultimatum presents both ladies, who are well aware of social distinctions, with a nice problem. But both rise to the occasion. Neither hesitates. Both make climactic speeches. 'Let me think of his honest heart,' cries Eleanor, 'his manly conduct, his strong feelings, and my lone and defenceless state. Have I no gratitude? Am I the slave of pride—no, no, come to me—come—I—I am yours!' The Hon. Isabella is just as direct. With her the choice lies between Mat and the villainous Hal Horsfield, one of the merchant seamen. 'Not thine,' says Isabella (to Hal), 'anything but that! (Rushing to the arms of Mat) 'I am *thine*.'

In both cases circumstances prevent the marriages being consummated and, in any case, before the couples can *really* be married, the social and dramatic proprieties must be fulfilled and Jack must become an officer. In both cases the promotion is eventually achieved, to similar dialogue. 'Poor Mat,' (says Mat) 'Mat Meriton will mount the white washboards, and the gold swabs for his shoulders already heave in sight!' 'Aye then, it seems poor Jack' (says Jack) 'will walk the white-washed boards and mount the gold swabs on his shoulders at last. So,' (as Jack sings) 'there's a sweet little cherub sits smiling aloft to look out for the life of poor Jack.'

T. P. Cooke played William in over a hundred performances of the original run of *Black-Ey'd Susan* and he played it subsequently at Covent Garden. Douglas Jerrold wrote another nautical play, *The Mutiny at the Nore*, performed at the Pavilion in 1830, and one socially conscious play, *The Rent Day* in 1832. He contributed the well-known series of 'Mrs Caudel's Candle Lectures' to *Punch*. But nothing quite recaptured the success of *Black-Ey'd*

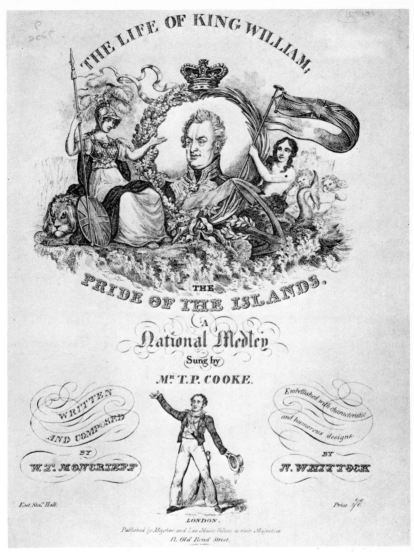

'The Life of King William, the Pride of the Islands'; a patriotic
song of the 1830s, rendered by T. P. Cooke.

Susan. He edited various periodicals, including *Lloyds Weekly Newspaper* from
1852 until his death in 1857. T. P. Cooke's last performance of William was at
Covent Garden on 29 October 1860. He died in 1864 and in his will left £2,000
to the master, deputy master and wardens of the Dramatic College, the interest
to provide a prize for a nautical drama. *True to the Core*, a drama by a Mr Slous,
was duly performed on 8 January 1866, but nothing more seems to have been
heard of the bequest.

'The Origin of Sailors', a popular song of the 1830s; the
illustration shows the typical sailor's clothing of the time.

The accession of William IV, the Sailor King, to the throne in 1830 encouraged nautical drama and nautical songs. The King was popular in the Navy and songs were written about his naval service. A typical one was 'The Life of King William, The Pride of the Islands', published as sheet music and advertised as 'Sung by Mr T. P. Cooke', as an added recommendation. The score was accompanied by charming little line drawings of incidents in William's naval career.

The King was a popular choice as a song subject because the songwriters could laud the British Tar while paying loyal compliments to the Sovereign. 'The Origin of Sailors, or, A Sailor's the Man' ended with a spoken recitative intended to whip up the audience into a patriotic crescendo of approval and cheering. 'Aye! Little England— the country that first gave a genuine sailor to the world—the country whose best and surest defence is her wooden walls now prospers beneath a Sailor Monarch, and while his every action is embarked in the vessel 'Good Intent' may they reach the haven of 'Success' and surrounding nations be taught to acknowledge that for freedom, true bravery, fun, frolic, pretty girls and waving the standard of his country in triumph over the world, A Sailor's the Man!' And so, into the chorus for the last time, with 'A Sailor's the Man, A Sailor, A Sailor the Man!'

While other London theatres purveyed nautical drama, Sadlers Wells specialised in a kind of 'aquatic drama' in which complicated scenic effects were staged, using water. *The Loss of the* Royal George, *or the Fatal Land Breeze*, 'a nautico-domestic drama in two acts' by C. Z. Barnett, opened there in 1840. It loosely follows the well-known story of the line of battleship *Royal George* and her rotten timbers: she was overset by a breeze and sank at Spithead in August 1782, with the loss of Admiral Kempenfelt and several hundred men of his flagship. It was the subject of a poem by Cowper ('Toll for the brave') and several nautical dramas over the years. In the last scene of Act Two of Mr Barnett's work, the stage directions are:

The open Sea. Spithead in the distance. The scene is peculiarly constructed. The waters are seen violently agitated; and are raised about one-third above the level of the Stage; they are transparent. The *Royal George* discovered lying on her side; ships of the fleet seen at short distance from her; loud cries and screams heard from her; guns heard twice from shore; at the second report, she sinks; the swell of the waves etc. becomes terrific; when it begins to subside, the Sailors etc. are seen swimming about in all directions; the masts of the vessel are seen consideraby above the surface of the water, to which many of the sailors cling. From the transparency of the waters, the sunken vessel is distinctly visible.

The cast are saved and are picked up by boats. Kneel and return thanks to Providence for their miraculous preservation. Tableaux.

'Saturday night at sea':
the 1830s

The British tar might be lauded on stage and acclaimed in song as all that was brave and honest and true, but within the Navy there were growing misgivings about his professional skill, and in particular his gunnery. In Nelson's day a British man-of-war simply closed her opponent and fired broadsides into her as hot and fast 'as she could suck it', until the enemy hauled down his flag to three ringing British cheers. This was what the tars of Navarino had expected the Turks to do, but no Turkish ship struck her colours all day. In the War of 1812 the larger, better armed and better fought American frigates had proved too much for their Royal Navy counterparts, with the famous exception of the *Shannon*. The rapidity of the English fire, their superior seamanship and their sheer dogged courage had been too much for their French and Spanish opponents. But they were no longer enough in the nineteenth century.

There was no common accepted gunnery doctrine, no official means of passing round knowledge of improvements. Every captain was left to train his gun crews as often and in such a manner as he himself thought fit, and to exchange information with his fellow captains by word of mouth or by letter, if he wished. Individual captains, such as Exmouth in the Mediterranean and Philip Broke in *Shannon*, might pay special attention to gunnery, carrying out intensive training, with constant drills and repeated firing practice at various targets, but in general the handling of guns was a matter for the gun captains. These, though brave and worthy seamen, took their own time and fired at what they could see through the smoke, almost invariably aiming along the barrels of their guns, always assuming that shot rose upwards, and hardly ever making allowances for the tapering of the barrel, heeling of the ship, over-shooting, different strengths of charge—in fact almost totally ignorant of the science of gunnery.

Concern about the state of the Navy's gunnery began during the French wars. In 1812 Captain Sir John Pechell, an admirer and student of Broke's, published a pamphlet called 'Observations upon the defective equipment of ships' guns'; he published another edition in 1824 and a third in 1828. Pechell was no armchair gunner. As captain of *San Domingo* (74) on the American station in 1814 and of *Sybil* in the Mediterranean a year later, he made both ships remarkable for their gunnery. *San Domingo* could go into action almost as quickly as a frigate. At Spithead, the C-in-C and the captains of ships in company said they had never seen any ship clear for action so quickly or fire guns so rapidly and accurately as *San Domingo*. Pechell introduced a system whereby all the tables, stools, men's bags and officer's trunks were cleared away in less than five minutes and sent below every night; it did not make for easier living, but it was wartime.

Others such as General Sir Howard Douglas also criticised naval gunnery, but still nothing happened until 1829 when a Commander George Smith sent the Admiralty his 'Prospectus of a plan for the improvement of naval gunnery, without any additional expense'. Smith suggested that an establishment be set up for the training of gun crews and for the testing and evaluation of new gunnery equipment. In June 1830, when Pechell was a member of the Board of Admiralty, a Board Minute authorised the establishment of a gunnery school at Portsmouth, with Smith as the first captain. The ship used was the *Excellent*, which was moored in a position in Portsmouth Harbour from which guns could be fired across mudflats without endangering anybody.

'Saturday night at sea', from a print by Kohler.

In 1832 the Admiralty set the gunnery school on a regular footing. Smith was promoted to captain and relieved by Captain Sir Thomas Hastings. Smith was not employed again and he died in 1850. In 1840 he wrote to *The Times* to point out his own share in setting up the *Excellent* (and one senses a feeling that he had not been properly treated). In February the Admiralty addressed a new prospectus to the C-in-C Portsmouth. It was a seminal document and its first paragraph, though nobody realised it at the time, was the dawn of a new era from the bluejacket:

Their Lordships having had under their consideration the propriety and expediency of establishing a permanent corps of seamen to act as Captains of Guns, as well as a Depot for the instruction of the officers and seamen of His Majesty's Navy in the theory and practice of Naval

Gunnery, at which a uniform system shall be observed and communicated throughout the Navy, have directed, with a view to the formation of such establishment, that a proportion of intelligent, young and active seamen shall be engaged for five or seven years, renewable at their expiration, with an increase of pay attached to each consecutive re-engagement, from which the important situation of Master Gunner, Gunner's Mates, and Yeoman of the Powder Room shall hereafter be selected to instruct the officers and seamen on board such ships as they may be appointed to in the various duties at the guns, in consideration of which they will be allowed 2 shillings per month, in addition to any other rating they may be deemed qualified to fill, and will be advanced according to merit and the degree of attention paid to their duty, which, if zealously performed, will entitle them to the important situations before mentioned, as well as that of Boatswain.

A more revolutionary paragraph had never before been published in the Royal Navy. It was studded with key words and phrases—*permanent corps, uniform system*, engaged for five or seven years, *renewable*, increase of pay at each *re-engagement*, advanced according to *merit*—which contained the first seeds of a permanent, professional career for a seaman in the Navy. *Excellent* brought about a revolutionary change in the Navy, almost without the Navy realising it, and certainly without most of the officers appreciating it.

Excellent was therefore established as a sixth rate, with a complement of 200, including Royal Marine Artillery instructors. Hastings was given instructions as to training which were themselves quite unlike anything seen in the Navy before. The officers and seamen gunners who came to *Excellent* were to be taught:

the names of the different parts of a gun and carriage, the dispart in terms of lineal magnitude and in degrees how taken, what constitutes point blank and what line of metal range, windage—the errors and the loss of force attending it, the importance of preserving shot from rust, the theory of the most material effects of different charges of powder applied to practice with a single shot, also with a plurality of balls, showing how these affect accuracy, penetration and splinters, to judge the condition of gunpowder by inspection, to ascertain its quality by the ordinary tests and trials, as well as by actual proof.

They were also to be instructed 'in the laboratory works required for the Naval service, such as making rockets for signals, filling tubes, new priming them, and filling cartridges, precautions in airing and drying powder, care and inspection of locks, choice of flints, correct mode of fitting them &c., &c.' They were to practise as teams, firing all sorts of guns, loaded with all sorts of shot, on a range laid out from *Excellent*.

The old-time sailor needed agility in the rigging, manual dexterity, and little else. The *Excellents* needed these qualities, and very much more. They had to be intelligent and they were encouraged to learn how to read, write and

HMS *Excellent*, on which a gunnery school was established at
Portsmouth in 1830.

cypher. They soon realised that they could not get the most benefit from their
training without these skills, and they were eager to learn. It was quite
common for literate sailors to teach their mates.

Hastings's training methods were also a surprise. He did not simply give
orders to a sailor, under threat of the lash, but showed him which method was
best. One visitor to *Excellent* noticed how Hastings handled a sailor who had
got into the habit of using the handspike lever to train a gun in a most
awkward and inefficient way. 'Now,' said Hastings, 'take notice how *I* use the
handspike, and you shall try the difference yourself.' The sailor watched the
process with great attention, then resumed the handspike, and found, to his
great surprise, that the gun now moved about with as much ease as if the 32-
pounder had been changed to a 12-pounder. 'What think you now?' asked
Hastings. 'I'll never use the other way as long as I live, sir,' came the pithy
reply.

Excellent was also used as a boys' training ship, and a mizzen mast was kept
rigged for sail training until as late as 1869. But the main practical training was
firing the guns. A red flag was hoisted in *Excellent* to show that firing was
about to start; none took place until the mud flats were uncovered by the
ebbing tide. The shot was recovered by 'mudlarks', many of them from the
splendidly-named local family of Grub, who sold the shot back to *Excellent*.
The Grubs used to 'ski' about the mud with wooden boards strapped to their
feet, had special implements for extracting shot from the mud, and on a good
day could earn as much as eleven shillings.

The sailors who trained in *Excellent* liked it. In a letter dated 15 December
1838, a young seaman wrote to his father in Worcestershire:

I suppose by this time you have received my last letter. I shall endeavour to give you an idea in this of my different duties. They pipe up hammocks at 6 o'clock in the morning, we then clean ourselves and the mess tables till 7 o'clock. We are then piped to breakfast, which consists of Cocoa; at half past 7 o'clock, I go to the rigging loft in the dockyard till 12 o'clock; which is very good of Captain Hastings to put me there, being the only one in the ship that goes there. At 12 o'clock on board again and piped to dinner. At 1 o'clock the drum beats to quarters where we are instructed in the great gun exercise; after that the sword and musket exercises, the boats are hoisted up and our days work is nearly done. At half past four o'clock, tea, and the liberty men are piped away.

I am a mizzentop man. No. 86 at instructions. I shall have to buy a set of instruments before long, as soon as ever I get out of the second instructions, because I shall be put in the schoolroom and shall not be able to do without them. I have had to buy several things already; a set of cards of instruction I have also bought, 3/6 the set, and a few clothes as we must dress all alike, when we are mustered which is every morning and must not dress in white in the winter. I pay 2/- per month for washing, subscribe twopence per month to an excellent library and 1/- entrance money. I shall have to buy a fresh monkey jacket as mine is so very shabby and you *must be clean and neat* and if you are always so, you are sure to be taken notice of. I am afraid I shall not be able to do without that money that Uncle John Jukes was so kind to give me. I do not like to draw any money here, at all events not for this five or six months; if you send it be sure to pay a penny with it and direct to me as J. Burnett Seaman-Gunner on board H.M.S. *Excellent* Portsmouth. I am very comfortable and happy here and quite well; what time I have to spare is fully taken up in learning my cards of instruction. Let me know when Sam comes home that I may write, and let me know how you all are and how everything goes on. I must now conclude for they are piping for Hammocks to be slung.

John Bechervaise also went to *Excellent* after his Arctic voyage. He had thought that an injured eye might count against him but when Hastings heard what ship Bechervaise had served in and saw his papers he entered him immediately. 'Of all the places presented by Her Majesty's naval service for the good of seamen,' wrote Bechervaise, 'I deem *Excellent* the very best.'

Under an enthusiastic captain, the training showed results afloat. One well documented example of gun drill was in the 28-gun frigate *Andromache* (Captain Henry Chads), lying at anchor in Madras roads in 1836. In a fresh breeze, with a heavy swell running, the guns were cast loose and a whole broadside fired at a buoy 600 yards off in one minute twenty-five seconds, with most of the shots observed to fall round and close to the target. The ship's company fired four broadsides in three minutes and twenty-two seconds; they actually loosed away the guns, fired the broadsides and secured the guns for sea again in six minutes fifty-nine seconds from beating to quarters.

Chads himself became captain of *Excellent* after Hastings in 1845. Life under

Chads was described by John Moresby who qualified as a gunnery lieutenant in 1849 and later became an admiral. There were some 600 men under training living on the lower deck, messing between the 32-pounders as in a sea-going ship. Once a week, at 'first quarters', the officers and men competed against each other at great-gun drill. (This in itself was a revolutionary innovation in the Navy's life.) Then, 'as the stirring drums beat to quarters with a rush that made the old ship tremble, each crew took up its station, and proud was the one which, after loading and running out, first stood to attention. Generally, but not by any means always, this would be the officers' gun, and so also in the following evolutions.'

Excellent proclaimed the word of naval gunnery, but for years it fell on stony ground in some quarters. When Astley Cooper Key, also a future captain of *Excellent*, was gunnery lieutenant of the frigate *Curaçao* (24) at Rio in 1843, he asked the captain to let him exercise the men firing at a target. The ship had been in commission eight months, and this was the first gunnery practice on board. A target was anchored 500 yards away and, though the ship was rolling heavily, Key was pleased with results. 'The firing was excellent,' he wrote. 'We were obliged to send out four new targets during the forenoon. But what pleased me most was that the *Excellent* men we have on board were the four best shots in the ship. I may say, I had a good laugh at the fellows who run them down.'

The original *Excellent* had been Collingwood's ship at St Vincent. She was broken up in 1834, and replaced by the *Boyne* who was herself replaced by the *Queen Charlotte* in 1859. But they were all named *Excellent*, as was the shore establishment on Whale Island which replaced them and which was enlarged and extended by spoil and waste brought by convict labour later in the century. The first building, 'The *Excellent* House that Jack Built,' was erected in 1864. In July 1861, when *Punch*'s 'Naval Inspector' was sent to the training ship *Excelsior* at Sherrymouth, as he termed it, he found the same balance of physical work and mental training. 'One stares at first to see big horny-fisted fellows ciphering like schoolboys with slates upon their laps; and one stares still more to hear that trigonometry, perhaps, is the study over which those brown-faced heads are scratched. In big gun work it seems that trigonometry is somewhat of a help to triggernometry. . .'

That there were only four *Excellent*-passed men in *Curaçao*'s crew (of 240 men) and they obviously had their critics, shows that it was many years before the *Excellent* training had its effect on the Navy at large. The memoirs of William Petty Ashcroft, beautifully written out in a flowing copper-plate hand when the writer was an old man, at the end of the century, hardly mention gunnery at all, although they do give an evocative picture of a commission of the 1830s.

Ashcroft was born in February 1823 at Pembroke. In 1833 his father was carpenter on board the *Asia* (of Navarino fame), flying the flag of Admiral Sir William Parker, at Lisbon. The ship was refitting, with her lower yards and topmasts struck. Ashcroft Senior had told the Sergeant in H.M. Schooner *Pike* that he might bring young William out to Portugal, and when *Pike* left

Falmouth that November with mails for Vigo, Oporto and Lisbon, young William was on board, delighted to be there and bringing with him a basket of fruit and other things that his mother had prepared for his father. His father was 'vexed' that William had left school and would have sent him back had it not been for the ship's gunner who persuaded him to let the boy stay. So William stayed, 'and very soon became a favourite and likely to have been spoiled, but I was kept at my studies under the Naval Instructor with a run ashore two or three times a week'.

The *Asia* paid off at Chatham in July 1834 but moved to Sheerness early in 1836 to recommission. Ashcroft rejoined her as the master's boy, first class. Of manning, Ashcroft said 'the Marines were easy enough to get from Barracks, the first class boys came from the Marine Society or from shore, and the second class boys from the Greenwich School. Rendezvous were arranged at three places, Tower Hill, Liverpool and Bristol, with a Lieutenant and Petty Officer at each. I don't think anyone was refused so long as he could pass the doctor.' At this time, when one ship returned from a foreign commission, the Admiralty recommissioned another, so that sailors might have a chance of signing on again. In September 1846 another reform was introduced: seamen as well as petty officers could go to the flagship, have six weeks' leave, get their time and pay whilst on leave, deposit hammocks and clothes at dockyards while they were ashore, and on return enter any ship they chose. But in 1836, the system was still in a transitional stage and once the men were on board *Asia*, although they were ostensibly volunteers, they were not allowed ashore again, nor any money nor clothes, for fear they would desert. Some of them had high top-hats and long-tailed coats, others had scarcely a shirt to their backs, so it was a motley crew that mustered by open list on the first Sunday.

At the muster, one man said that he had never served in a square-rigged vessel before, only fore-and-afters, so he was told off to be cook's mate. But the second lieutenant recognised him as the chief bosun's mate of *Asia* at Navarino. His real name was Ingle but he had deserted from the *Victor* brig in the West Indies and now called himself by the 'pusser's'—a corruption of 'purser's', meaning naval issue—name of George Bolt. The commander told him to take his old berth again. 'It made some of the "greenhorns" stare,' said Ashcroft, 'to see the "cook's mate" rated chief boatswain's mate.'

After fitting out and hauling into the stream, they bent on sails and anchored at the Nore. All hands were paid two months' advance pay. The ship was at once surrounded by bumboatmen, and the main-deck filled up with sharks, hucksters and Jews trying to sell their wares. At five o'clock, when the ship was cleared, two men managed to escape by dressing up as women. One man disguised himself and came on deck shouting, 'Any more for the shore?' The commander kicked him over the side, not realising he was one of the crew. After 'Beat to Quarters', the ship was searched for liquor. Very little was found. Ashcroft thought that was because it had all been drunk.

George Bolt was already emerging as a ship's character and at Spithead he asked if he could have his wife on board. The woman he pointed out was not the same as his 'wife' at Sheerness and the Commander asked him how many wives he had. 'Five,' he said, 'one in Plymouth, one at Portsmouth, one at Sheerness, and two in Cork.' This, as Ashcroft could confirm, was quite true.

Asia had been built in Bombay of best teakwood and once out in the Mediterranean she proved the best sailer of all the ships of the line, outsailing the flagship *Caledonia* with topsails to her studding-sails. One afternoon the *Thunderer* signalled: 'Be cautious. Your masthead man is asleep on your foretopsail yard.' The captain of the top took two steady men to seize the sleeper before waking him. He protested he had not been asleep, but still got fourteen days' 'black list'.

When *Thunderer* and *Edinburgh* sailed for England, *Asia* took over a hundred of their best men and gave them in return a hundred of her worst. *Asia* took men from every ship leaving for England and before they had been in commission twelve months she had the finest crew on the station and the captain was very proud of them. But, of course, this system penalised the best, keeping them on station, while the worst went home.

There were twenty men in Ashcroft's mess, with two boys to clean the messtraps, scrub out the mess, and fetch food from the galley and breadroom. Having been to school, Ashcroft was of above average education for the lower-deck of his time. He was one of only about fifty (he reckoned) who could read out of the total complement of 700 on board. Because of his education and quickness, he was transferred to signal duties. When mail left for England, he had some thirty or forty letters to write for his messmates, and he was engaged to read their letters for them when they came on board. Men would bring books on board, such as Marryat's novels (a son of the novelist was serving in *Asia* at the time) and Ashcroft sat on the capstan, reading, while the men sat around listening. If he said he could not read because he had clothes to make or mend, there were always volunteers to do those chores for him. Ashcroft's own mentor and 'sea daddy' was the captain of the foretop, Harry Tongue. In return, Ashcroft taught him to read, whereupon Tongue was promoted to bosun's mate and later to bosun.

There were two boys on board, twins, from the Greenwich School. Joe, the old bosun's mate of the lower-deck, looked after them. One day, when the hands were all at exercise, the master-at-arms 'had one of the boys seated on the breech of a gun with his hands tied up to two hammock hooks above and a shin bone hung in front of him. Every time he passed he gave him a stroke with his cane.' When Joe heard of it, he told the commander, who came down and caught the master-at-arms in the act.

The master-at-arms's punishment was draconian. Lower-deck was cleared to witness his disrating. The corner of his service certificate was cut off to denote a dishonourable discharge. His jacket was turned inside out. The ship's corporal put a rope round his neck and he was led all round the decks. As he was going over the side, the captain said to him, 'You blackguard, you are leaving the ship with a halter round your neck and that is the way you will go out of the world!'

Asia was a good, taut ship. On the lower-deck, the messes competed to 'cut each other out' for smartness. *Asia*'s main topgallant yard was always the first across at 8.00 a.m. every morning. The whole fleet envied *Asia* the man who rigged it, a very smart black man, but one of the foretopmen, a white man, claimed he could rig the upper yardarm of the fore topgallant yard faster than the black man could rig the main. There was a race one evening after quarters and heavy bets were struck. Other ship's companies climbed their riggings to watch. On the fore-rigging Jack, the white man, won. But when they shifted to the mainmast the black man was first by about the same margin. So it was declared a draw and the two men were ordered to shake hands and go ashore together in Malta for forty-eight hours.

Asia's company spent the first Christmas in Malta. The captains of tops took the boys' places for the day, each mess had its own decorations and its pudding duff. At dinner time the band played 'The Roast Beef of Old England' and the captain and officers walked round the lower-deck. Ashcroft's mess had a decorative banner spelling out the letters of *Asia*'s name:

> Another Christmas Day we greet
> Success attend our noble Fleet
> In Friendship let us all be seen
> And united sing 'God Save the Queen'.

As so often in memoirs of Christmas Day, it came on to blow later. Hands were piped to hand down the topgallant mast, and one man fell overboard and was drowned. They had five Christmases that commission, and lost a man each time.

That summer *Rodney* came into Grand Harbour to hang a marine, Thomas Sweeney, who had thrown a sergeant down a hatchway and killed him. The question of who should man the hanging rope was solved when a signal was made for all boats to be armed and rowed alongside *Rodney*. As each boat came alongside the bowman was ordered out and told to go down on the main-deck. It so happened that all *Asia*'s were black men, except for the bowman of the captain's barge. Every ship in harbour had her marines fallen in on the poop, topmen in the topmast rigging, forecastlemen, gunners and afterguard in the lower rigging. *Rodney* had a spring on her cable to bring her broadside on to the other ships lying close to her. The rope was rove to the main-deck so that the men on it could not see the condemned man. At 8.00 a.m. *Rodney* fired a gun and the men ran away with the rope with such force than a toggle about a fathom from the man's neck carried away and the rope stranded. He hung for an hour and then, because he was a Roman Catholic, his body was taken away by monks from Floriana.

Russell, in harbour at the time, laconically recorded the execution in her log. '7.20 a.m. Sent boats manned and armed to H.M.S. *Rodney* to attend the execution of marine for murder. At 7.30 turned up the hands and manned the rigging to witness the punishment. Read the articles of war. 8.30. Boats returned.' There had been an American frigate in harbour. She put to sea a day before the execution and returned the day after.

Leave in *Asia* depended almost wholly upon the captain's personal view of a man. A few were never allowed ashore, because they would sell their clothes, break their leave, and 'return in Maltese dress with their feet blacked'. These men had to go below for as long as the watch had leave, and could not show themselves on deck; they called this punishment 'a lower-deck cruise'.

Life was hard for the boys. They were cuffed and kicked if the mess traps were not clean, they had to 'marry the gunner's daughter'—strapped to the breech of a gun and flogged—for misdemeanours. But they had fun, too. In Malta they went riding on shore, or drove out to Civitta Vecchia—'Shiver the Week' as they called it—or visited the underground catacombs of the Hypogeum. Every night after quarters, at sea or in harbour, 'Hands to dance and skylark' was piped. The fiddlers played on the main-deck, or the band played on the quarter-deck, and sometimes the drum and fife band as well until 9.00 p.m. On the forecastle and down the gangways the men and boys played games such as 'Beat the bear', 'Sling the monkey', 'Hunt the slipper', 'Jump-back leapfrog', or 'Follow my leader' up and over the rigging. The officers had their own games on the quarter-deck. When King William died and Queen Adelaide embarked in *Hastings* and visited Malta, the ships had a two-day regatta and other sports.

Asia anchored at Spithead five years to the day since the commissioning pendant had been hoisted. They had orders for Sheerness but the captain went to Portsmouth so that Codrington could inspect his old ship. After his inspection Codrington had the men aft to speak to them, but his feelings overcame him and he broke down. There were still about thirty men on board who had served at Navarino, fourteen years before. Codrington asked if there was anything he could do for them. George Bolt told the admiral he had run from the *Victor* brig and lost seventeen years' service. 'Why were you so foolish as to do that?' Codrington asked. 'I got in tow with a lass and she jilted me.' Codrington had his daughter with him, and he turned to her and said, 'See what you ladies bring the men to.' But, according to Ashcroft, Codrington got the Navarino survivors all they asked for.

They got under way again and anchored in the Downs. They met the *Salamander* steamer sent to tow them but the captain would have none of it. To be towed was a slur on one's seamanship.

Asia paid off on 10 April 1841 at Sheerness. Ashcroft and some other West Countrymen hired a four-wheeled covered wagon, 'victualled' her for the voyage, and got to Plymouth four days later. Ashcroft found that his father was serving in the *Bellona* and his younger brother in the *San Josef*, the prize taken by Nelson from the Spanish in 1797.

On paying-off day, the sailors used to sing:

> God bless the old Commissioner,
> And his pay clerks also;
> And may they come alongside soon,
> And cry, 'Tis time to go.'

Paying-off was a nostalgic pause in a sailor's life, a time of hard work and

'The Signal for an Engagement' – at home and abroad – by
J. Fairburn, 1838.

soft hearts, when old scores were forgotten and old ships remembered. No
matter what hardships the commission had brought, a sailor felt that he was
leaving a part of himself behind. In an article published in the *United Service
Journal* in 1838 a sailor wrote of one paying-off in a ship coming home from the
West Indies. The captain had promised a leg of mutton and turnips, with a
bottle of rum, to the first man to sight England. They anchored at Spithead on a
beautiful morning in May, and made preparations for the admiral's inspection.
On the morning, the deck was as white as holystone and sand could make it.
Not a stray yarn was to be seen, not a rope's bight slack or an Irish pendant
dangling. The men mustered on deck in their white frocks and trousers. The
side boys had on their best looks and handed out their best ropes bound with
red bunting for the day. The marines stood as fierce as yellow soap and
pipeclay could make them, while the drummer had his sticks ready crossed.
The officers paraded on the quarter-deck in their best uniforms, with cocked
hats and swords. As the admiral's barge came out, the pipes shrilled, the order
'away aloft' was given, the yards were manned, the drummer drum-rolled, off
went the cocked hats and up went the muskets in salute.

The men were recalled from aloft and mustered in ship's book order. There
were drills, exercising the guns, manning, arming and sending away the boats.
Next morning a powder hoy came alongside and the powder was taken out.
The same day they went alongside a hulk in the harbour and on completion of

the day's work a certain number were allowed to go ashore. Those left on board could only go ashore if everybody returned promptly. When one failed, he was summarily punished on the mess-deck. One man with an old cocked hat from the midshipmen's gunroom represented the captain while another read a mock sentence from a book. The offender was sentenced to be 'cobbed'—laid over a table or cask while every man in the mess gave him a whack with a cook's ladle.

The writer was a sentimental man. 'I have been a wanderer now upon the face of the deep for many years, and during that time many acquaintances have come into my ken; yet never having any avowed enemies I never parted with one but with regret. As with messmates so with ships. In the present instance I was doomed to see the home in which I had been domiciled for several years broken up, and every tie that bound me to it shattered before my face.'

A ship ready to be paid off presented an unusual sight, with her masts reduced to stumps, the decks cleared from end to end and great gaps where the guns used to be. Most of the men lashed up their bedding ready for the morning and slept on bare boards. Some did not sleep at all, but pooled all their candles and danced to a Jew's harp or a fife and fiddle. In the morning every man received his due in pay. According to the writer, three cheers were given, and then, with a shaking of hands and exchange of 'God bless you's', each one took his separate road, with a neat parody of *Paradise Lost*, 'The world before them—Henry Hase their guide' (Henry Hase being a celebrated bank director of the time).

Despite the low level of literacy in the Navy—*Asia* was typical of her time—the contrast between the 'old' Navy and the new 'edificated' Navy was already great enough to be pointed out in an article published in the *United Service Journal* in 1837. 'Ben Brace,' (sic) once Nelson's coxswain at Trafalgar but now a Greenwich pensioner, meets some of the ship's companies of the *Magicienne* frigate, the *Mosquito* and the *Queen Charlotte* drinking ashore in the Jolly Sailor on Portsmouth Hard. He is first struck by their strange appearance. In Ben's day they wore pigtails and every boy in the ship greased his skull twice a day to give him a chance of getting 'a tail' and a tidy set of ringlets. But *now*, he tells his friend and fellow pensioner Bob,

> all that's altered; the head is cut as round as a skimming dish, there is not a fid of grease used in a twelve-month; and if a man has a curl he has nursed for his sweetheart, the ship's barber cuts it off and gives it the quartermaster, to make the fly of a dog-vane, then, bless your heart, the petty officers have got things on their arms like our porters wear, only one is in the shape of an anchor and the other like a plate; and, Bob, would you believe it? these new-manufactured seamen wear braces, have trousers cut close to the leg, and work in pusser's shoes, which are large enough for jolly-boats for ten-gun brigs.

Through the article breathes the old-timers' conviction that their successors are pampered and somewhat effeminate, in short, that 'it don't blow like it used to blow'. These new-fangled chaps drink *tea*—'Hyson mundungo, three halfpenny a cartload, stuff they used to dunnage an Indiaman's hold'. Ben can read, but his hosts apologise to him, in case he cannot—'when you went to sea edification was not a general thing'.

In spite of himself, Ben is impressed by the handy way the new boys get their frigate to sea: 'Everything, like the treadmill at Maidstone, was on the silent system; you could not hear a word; and when the lads went aloft, "loose sails", there was no manning rigging, as in our time, but up they shinned as fast as possible, and I heard "all ready on the foretopsail yard" before it would have been "trice up and lay out" in 1806. Thinks I this is doing it properly . . .'

Everywhere Ben looks, change and decay. Living conditions are positively sybaritic: 'messes all fitted out with tea-cups and saucers, and are classed in a row like soldiers on parade'. After a fight between a quartermaster and a marine corporal, old Ben fully expects the cat of nine tails to be brought out. But no: the ship's company mustered by divisions while the articles of war were read out. Petty officers could not be flogged, so the two were disrated.

It is Saturday Night at Sea, and after a pipe of tobacco (not the proffered cigar which disgusts old Ben) Ben sings a song about Nelson, and is appalled to find himself answered by sailors called 'Tom Gingerbread' and 'John Tendersides' who sing songs about 'How sweet to walk by the streamlet's side' and 'I'd be a butterfly born in a bower'. 'I'm ashore, Bob,' says Ben, 'and if ever they catch me afloat again amongst your Tendersides and Gingerbreads, may I be kicked to death by cockroaches, or sucked to death by mosquitoes.'

Although Captain Fisher in *Asia* only flogged once, for drunkenness, Bathurst and Dickinson in *Genoa* flogged once each, for theft and for cowardice, and the combatants Ben saw in *Magicienne* were disrated instead of flogged, this did not mean that flogging was obsolete in the Navy. The quota men, the convicted criminals, and the pressed men of the French wars had gone (although the press gang was put on the statute book in 1835), and the crews of the Royal Navy were all officially volunteers (except the smugglers), but in some ships flogging went on very much as it had in the eighteenth century. Everything depended upon the personality of the captain.

Joseph Hume MP, a tireless campaigner for naval reform, successfully moved that naval punishment returns for 1845–6 be laid before the House, and from 1853 punishment returns were regularly submitted to Parliament. In 1839 2,007 men were flogged; in 1847 the number had dropped to 860, but individual ships still went far above the average. In 1849 Commander John C. Pitman made his ship *Childers* such a floating hell that she was a scandal throughout the Navy. An attempt was made to conceal the suicide of a young seaman. A marine went insane after four dozen lashes. Two of Pitman's officers, one of them his first lieutenant, deserted rather than go to sea with him. Pitman was tried by court-martial for cruelty and oppression to officers and men, found guilty, and discharged from the Navy.

In 1835 there was a Royal Commission on punishment; Hume kept up his campaign for reform, and most important of all, there was a feeling inside the service, slow at first but gaining ground all the time, that flogging was

Princess Victoria visiting Eddystone Lighthouse during a cruise
in the yacht *Emerald*, 1833.

degrading and unnecessary. The Admiralty did in time respond to public and professional pressure, but it was a slow process. In spite of the improvements, it was still a Navy in which midshipmen could be sixty years old, and captains could go without promotion for half a century; a midshipman in *Albion* in 1852 reported that a week rarely passed without the gratings being rigged for punishment and after a time he became so used to seeing what was called 'scratching a man's back' that he could watch the whole spectacle from start to finish without a qualm. Men could still be spreadeagled in the rigging, lashed hand and foot to the shrouds and left hanging for three or four hours, sometimes with a gag in their mouths. Another midshipman saw a troublesome man put in a little cage made of gratings. He could not stand up or lie down, but only crouch. The owner of a bumboat, which had been found bringing spirits alongside, was hoisted up to the main yardarm, still in his boat, and left dangling there for hours.

The main fault of flogging was, simply, that it was inefficient. In time, as for a marine in *Russell*, it lost its power to terrify and 'the young and plucky used to consider it a feather in their caps to be able to undergo a flogging without uttering a cry, and advanced themselves considerably in the estimation of their shipmates if they took their "four bag" like a man.'

'Bound Over to Keep the Piece': an illustration from Anthony Crowquill's *Com* *Album*, 1835.

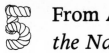 # From Acre to Borneo:
the Navy of the 1840s

The 1840s was a busy decade for the Royal Navy. There was a war in Syria, in the vital strategic theatre of the Mediterranean, another in China—the beginning of a protracted campaign there—and a third in New Zealand, the first of several against the war-like Maoris. The Navy maintained ships on over a dozen stations at home and abroad, each with its Commander-in-Chief, and was fully engaged in patrols against piracy off Borneo and Malaya, against slavery off the West Coast of Africa and in the West Indies, besides mounting explorations to polar regions and continuing surveys of the seas, rivers and coastlines of the world. In 1847 another Naval Discipline Act (more familiarly known as the Articles of War) reconstructed and revised the laws relating to the government of the Navy. In the technical field, the most significant event of the decade was the trial between *Alecto*, a paddle-ship, and *Rattler*, a screw ship, off the Nore in 1844. Both ships had identical hulls and similar engines, but when they were lashed stern to stern and the engines set going, *Rattler* was able to tow *Alecto* backwards at a speed of about two knots, thus proving the advantages of screw over paddle once and for all.

The Syrian War of 1840 was the first occasion on which the Navy really felt the lack of manpower, when ships had to be manned rapidly in times of emergency. There was no crisis as there was to be on the outbreak of the Crimean War, but still, this was the first practical proof that the old methods were no longer enough. It had to a certain extent been foreseen. In 1835, the then First Lord Sir James Graham introduced a Register of Seamen which was virtually a gigantic roster for service in the Navy. Those who reached the top of the list were required to serve for five years, after which they would be released and replaced by others on the Register. This was, of course, essentially a short-term proposition; there were still no such things as long-term engagements, no barracks to house men ashore, no means in fact of holding men permanently. Men lodged in hulks until their ships were ready. In practice, the period of five years' service was very seldom kept to; normally it was three or four years, the length of the ship's commission, just as it had always been. In 1846, when Lord Auckland was First Sea Lord, a naval reserve was created from the Dockyard Service and the Coastguard, but it provided very small numbers of men compared with the nation's total need.

The Syrian War was yet another consequence of the decline of the Ottoman Empire. The great European powers, Russia, Austria, France and Great Britain, hoped to obtain a part of the decadent carcass for themselves, but watched each other jealously, meanwhile maintaining the Turkish *status quo*. Russia particularly coveted Constantinople and for that reason, if no other, the other three powers were interested in preserving the Turkish Empire intact. Mehemet Ali, ruler of Egypt, had once been a soldier in the Turkish army but

HMS *Powerful* at the bombardment of St Jean d'Acre by British
and Allied squadrons, November 1840.

by ability, intrigue and applied murder, had risen to be independent ruler of
Egypt, though nominally he still owed some allegiance to the Sultan. Sure of
his power in Egypt, Mehemet Ali considered he might well become Caliph
himself. He assembled a large army and sent it into Syria under his son Ibrahim
Pasha. Ibrahim took the fortress of St Jean d'Acre and when the Turks sent an
army against him he defeated them in a bloody battle at Nesib in June 1840.

The Turkish fleet then defected and sailed to join the Egyptians at
Alexandria. In a period of increasing tension, it appeared that France had
secretly encouraged Mehemet Ali and for a time in 1840 it seemed that war
with France was not impossible. The other great powers issued Ali with an
ultimatum which Ali unsurprisingly rejected, saying that what he had won
with the sword must be taken with the sword. Admiral Sir Robert Stopford
then blockaded Alexandria with three ships of the line (including *Asia* with
Ashcroft on board), a frigate, and two steamers; the Austrians provided two
frigates and a schooner. The Turks fitted out another small fleet under the
command of a Royal Navy officer, Captain Baldwin Wake Walker. A fleet of
transports was assembled, to take over 5,000 Turkish troops to Syria. The
British contribution to the land actions in the Syrian War was made entirely by
seamen and marines from the fleet.

At home, Captain Charles Napier was ordered to hoist the broad blue
pennant of a commodore in *Powerful* (84) and to take under his command
Ganges, *Thunderer*, *Edinburgh*, the frigate *Castor* and steam-frigate *Gorgon*.
Napier was then fifty-four, a dashing, brave and brilliant leader, and a much

more charismatic personality than the seventy-two year old C-in-C Stopford, whose best years were long behind him in the French wars.

The fleet's gunnery during the campaign was quite outstanding. One officer, writing from a ship off Beirut on 1 October 1840, described how a deserter from the enemy was trying to get on board the ships while being chased by Egyptian soldiers. 'A nice little 32-lb shot fired just over the head of the victim put to rout his pursuers.' On another day, 'three guns were ordered to be pointed at a hole in a castle, not more than four feet in diameter, through which three fellows were looking out, to fire upon our boats inshore; the whole went off as one gun, and every shot went slap into the hole.'

The climax was the bombardment and capture of St Jean d'Acre on 3 November. Ali had not completed his improvements to the defences by that time, but it was still a formidable fortress with over a hundred heavy guns.

Stopford flew his flag in *Princess Charlotte* (104) though shifting to his son's ship, the steam-frigate *Phoenix*, to get closer to the action. Napier flew his flag in *Powerful* and led the northern division of *Princess Charlotte*, *Thunderer* (84), *Bellerophon* (84) and the frigate *Pique* (36) towards the fortress guns facing west. Captain Collier in the frigate *Castor* (36) led the southern division of *Benbow* (72), *Edinburgh* (72), *Carysfort* (26), the frigate *Talbot* (26), the sloop *Hazard* (18) and the brig *Wasp* (16) to attack the guns in the southern embrasures. *Revenge* (84), the Austrian and Turkish flagships, and the steam-frigates *Gorgon*, *Vesuvius* and *Stromboli* were also engaged.

Because of light winds, it was 2.00 in the afternoon before the ships got into action. After two hours' steady battering, they suddenly had a dramatic success, hitting the main magazine in the fortress. According to Lieutenant Kerr in *Gorgon*, the explosion 'was the most awfully grand sight I ever saw, equal for the time, I should say, to any eruption of Vesuvius. Immense stones came tumbling down upward of a minute after it occurred, and an immense cloud of earth and dust, about four or five hundred feet high, moved slowly with the breeze, completely hiding the ships as it passed them.' By about 5.00 p.m., when the signal to disengage was made, the accurate gunnery of the ships had reduced the main wall of the fort to a state 'like a large bit of plum pudding with the plums picked out'.

The steamships were in action for the first time, coming under fire themselves and returning it, while towing the line-of-battle-ships clear. Because their paddles were vulnerable they had to be kept at a distance.

When the troops and landing parties from the ships got ashore they found a demoralised enemy already evacuating Acre. The main explosion had killed or wounded two or three thousand people and devastated a wide area. There were always risks in ships engaging powerful forts but the Allied losses were only fourteen English and four Turks killed, and forty-two wounded. Buoys had been placed overnight off the forts, which the defenders thought were anchoring marks and so ranged their guns accordingly. However, when the Allied ships arrived they sailed right over the buoys, which may have disconcerted the defending gunners for the first vital minutes. To quote from Lieutenant Montagu Burrows, lower-deck battery officer in the *Edinburgh*,

'the very first broadsides were murderous, and the smoke very shortly
enveloped all of them as there was very little wind.' So the first salvoes from
Acre went over and damaged only the ships' rigging and the fortress's gunners
had no further chance to correct their aim.

For the Navy and especially for *Excellent*, the bombardment of Acre could
not have come at a better time. It served to silence the rumblings of criticism
about the need for a gunnery school, by politicians who complained of the cost
(about £35,000, a year in 1835) and by conservative officers who abhorred all
the new-fangled technical nonsense and loudly proclaimed that any time not
spent in seamanship (which meant handling ships under sail) was sadly
wasted. In 1834, when Admiral Sir Charles Rowley read one of the
examination papers of a gunnery lieutenant, he found he could not understand
the words 'impact' and 'initial velocity'. He asked another member of the
Board, Sir John Beresford, who said, 'I'll be hanged if I know, but I suppose it
is some of Tom Hastings's scientific bosh; but I'll tell you what I think we had
better do—we'll just go at once to Lord de Grey and get the *Excellent* paid off.'
However, de Grey told him he could not sanction it, 'for you have no idea how
damned scientific that House of Commons has become'.

While sailors such as Bechervaise and Ashcroft set down their memoirs in
the leisure of retirement, other educated members of the lower-deck kept
diaries or logs. There must have been hundreds of them in the nineteenth
century, mostly now lost—either discontinued by their writers or discarded
by their heirs. Generally they make dry reading, being little more than a
record of places visited, watches kept, sails worn, salutes fired, and the
occasional accident, man overboard, storm or fall from aloft. The writer seldom
had the imagination to breathe life into the bare bones of a commission, and if
he had any private feelings about his officers or his fellows he lacked the
ability (or, quite possibly, on an overcrowded and overlooked mess-deck, he
thought it too dangerous) to write them down.

William Sharlock, ship's painter of HMS *Scout*, kept a journal of their
commission 'Up the Mediterranean, from 16th June 1841 to 20th June 1845'.
Whatever Sharlock lacked in erudition he made up for in application. His
journal is beautifully written in immaculate handwriting. The frontispiece
alone must have taken him many hours of loving effort. The title and subtitles
are neatly hand-printed and ornamented with a watercolour painting of *Scout*
herself. The text includes several carefully executed watercolour *vignettes*, of
'leaving England', a Malta *dghaisa*, 'manning the yards', Mount Etna in
eruption, and Greek peasants in national costume.

Scout (Captain Larcom) was a three-masted corvette armed with eight guns,
sixteen carronades and two long guns, and a crew of 125 officers and men.
Sharlock records that they 'bent sails' for the first time on 12 August 1841, and
four days later sailed to embark powder at Gillingham. On 23 August he saw
men working in diving bells on the *Royal George* at Spithead. On 1 September
they reached Plymouth; two days later they sailed for the Mediterranean. The
journal is a list of places visited rather than a narrative, but Sharlock records
the major incidents of the commission. On 7 January 1842 *Scout* ran aground at

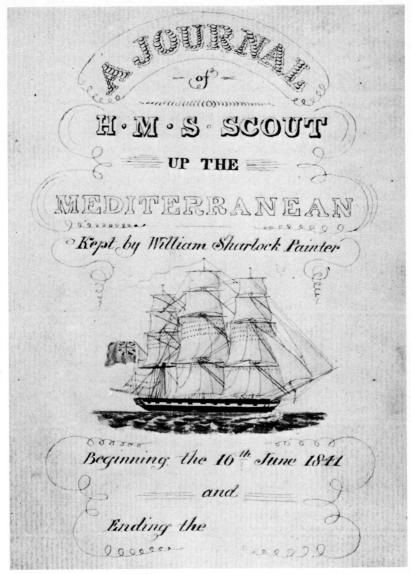

The frontispiece of William Sharlock's *Scout* journal, 1841.

Larnaca in Cyprus. The ship's company hoisted out the guns and sent them ashore on rafts. The sails and the anchor cables were sent to the *Inconstant* frigate who was in company. Divers went down and found that the false keel and rudder had gone. They got her off on 23 January, to three cheers from *Inconstant*, and when they arrived in Malta on 11 February the captain, ironically, left on promotion. When *Scout* was hove down they found a large hole in her bottom and it was a surprise to all that she ever reached Malta.

Scout's commission was one of routine, cruising round the coasts of Italy, Syria, Spain and Greece. The ship was dressed overall and fired a Royal Salute on 20 June to celebrate the anniversary of Queen Victoria's accession. Salutes were fired on 19 November 1842 in honour of the victories in China and on 19 December, at Piraeus, in honour of the King of Greece. At Barcelona a salute was fired and yards manned with blue lights for Isabella, Queen of Spain. Again at Barcelona, another salute was fired and the ship was dressed overall in commemoration of the anniversary of the French Revolution of 1830 which placed Louis Philippe on the throne of France.

Leave in *Scout* was granted fairly freely to men of good character; Sharlock himself went on a very pleasant walk through vineyards in Corfu. There was a boat accident during a regatta at Gibraltar and a sergeant of marines was drowned; the ship's company and troops ashore raised a handsome subscription for his widow. William Burrell, a private of marines, vanished one night, 'after appearing in very low spirits'. Christmas was celebrated, according to Sharlock, 'in the usual way'. He laconically notes other events: rebellions at Barcelona and at Alicante, an earthquake at Joppa, the night *Scout* was fouled by a Spanish brig and was towed out of Barcelona by the *Locust* steamer, the garland hoisted to celebrate the marriage of the master and a Gibraltarian lady.

There is no record of *Scout's* ships company being exercised at quarters, or of the guns ever being fired (except for the interminable Royal Salutes). It was a quiet, utterly normal commission, in which *Scout* kept the seas and the peace, typical of hundreds in the nineteenth century. Nothing much ever happened, although life was seldom dull for those on board. Sharlock's little book has several pages sewn in, possibly by a later descendant, and it concludes with some recipes for cough mixture.

At the time Sharlock was writing, ships were being withdrawn from the Mediterranean to take part in the war in China, which he mentions. The first China War, which began in November 1839 and lasted until the Treaty of Nanking in August 1842, was not one of the most creditable episodes in British history. For many years, opium grown in India had been imported into China in British ships. The Chinese government, understandably, objected to the import of the drug (and to the export of massive amounts of silver to pay for it). In 1839 the Chinese reacted by damaging British property, ill-treating and insulting British citizens, locking British merchants in their factories, firing on the British flag, breaking up the British Trade Commissioner's luggage, delivering cases of poisoned tea to British officials, burning large quantities of confiscated opium, judicially strangling convicted Chinese opium smugglers, detaining British ships by force and demanding the delivery of all the opium in all the ships in the Canton River.

To Captain Elliott, the trade commissioner, these actions were tantamount to a declaration of war and hostilities began on 3 November 1839, when the *Volage* and *Hyacinth* inflicted casualties and damage upon about thirty Chinese junks and fireships in an action off the Bogue forts in the Canton river. The Chinese were driven upstream of the forts and the ships retired, whereupon the Chinese claimed a victory and redoubled their efforts to re-arm and re-equip their war junks.

The pattern of the war, as it ebbed and flowed along the coastline and the great rivers of China, was one of furious activity followed by a trucial lull. The guns of the ships would batter into subjection the forts at the Bogue and at Tycock Tow, bluejackets and troops would be landed to seize islands and strongholds at Amoy, Chusan and Macao, and the Chinese would capitulate, call for negotiations and promise to return hostages. But once the landing parties had been re-embarked and the ships had retired, negotiations broke down, fresh hostages were kidnapped, trade was not reopened, forts were re-armed, fireships were prepared, embankments and fortifications were dug, booms were stretched across rivers, and large rewards offered for the capture of English ships or officers, the size of the reward increasing with the rank of the captive. The Chinese exercised their troops in action against specially built 'mock' English ships, whose companies wore red, the colour of foreigners. Foreigners and Chinese considered each other barbarians.

For the ordinary bluejacket, the Chinaman was a somewhat unnerving opponent. He would ambush his enemy, shamming dead or wounded, and then spring up when his opponent had passed. He would undermine the ground in front of his positions by burying hollow bamboo tubes filled with gunpowder. He kept up an intense psychological pressure: sailors would lie awake in their ships, out in the stream, listening all night to a barrage of gongs and bells and shouts, with an occasional cock crow. A stray shot would be answered at once with a great ripple of fire all along the shore forts, where whole village populations were labouring to throw up fresh embankments.

The Chinese war junks were an amazing sight. Their main armaments were ancient guns and gingals, aged firelocks loaded with bric-a-brac and fired from a stand. Stink-pots filled with sulphur were hurled from mastheads upon the unwary. The junks were decorated with streamers and dragon banners, with ornate carved poopdecks and the muzzles of the guns painted a bright intimidating red. The flagship was larger, had more and bigger banners and streamers, and three tigers' heads painted upon her stern.

William Petty Ashcroft arrived on the China Station in *Cornwallis* (72) in March 1842, in time to take part in the assault and capture of Chung Hai, at the mouth of the Ningpo River. Ashcroft had joined *Cornwallis* as an ordinary seaman in May 1841, along with six other men, only two of whom ever got back to England again. He was not yet nineteen but as Captain Peter Richards had said that he intended to try every man and boy in the ship and give them the rate they deserved, Ashcroft hoped that he might be rated AB. *Cornwallis* sailed with over 1000 men on board, many of them supernumaries, and including 125 marines who messed on the main-deck.

On passage it was clear that *Cornwallis* was going to a war theatre. They had plenty of drills, on the great guns and with small arms and cutlasses, and exercised landing parties, stretcher parties, scaling parties with ladders, and field-piece crews. They also had boats specially fitted with paddles, like canoes, for going up narrow creeks. After weathering a typhoon off the

Philippines, they arrived at Hong Kong on Christmas Eve, sailing almost at once for Chusan, a dead beat against the monsoon, to relieve *Wellesley*. Admiral Parker had already come out by land, his predecessor having been invalided.

The attacking squadron for Chung Hai was *Modeste* (18), *Clio* (12), *Columbine* (12) and *Algerine* (10), with the two East India Company steamers *Phlegethon* and *Nemesis*, and the boats of the squadron with soldiers from the 18th, 26th and 49th Regiments, making a total of some 1,500 men against about 8,000 Chinese troops ensconced in the heights above the city. *Cornwallis* and *Blonde* lay at the entrance as there was not enough water for them to go up river.

Cornwallis's sailors embarked in *Nemesis* and amongst them was Ashcroft, equipped, as they all were, with musket, bayonet, 40 rounds of ball cartridge, a blanket, a water-bottle and a haversack with provisions for two days. In his account Ashcroft simply says 'we took the place' (Chung Hai), and they camped there for the night. The sailors all filled their blankets with booty of silk and syce silver but the next day they marched so far and hard that Ashcroft cut the strings of his blanket and let all his prizes go. When he got back on board *Nemesis* at 9.00 p.m., he was unfolding his blanket when out rolled a five dollar piece. He gave it to a young man for a Navy gill of rum.

The Chinese were full of resource and liable to attack at any time. 'One night after "Pipe Down",' said Ashcroft, 'when all hands were in their hammocks, the Chinese sent over a hundred fire rafts down on the fleet. All boats were sent away to grapple them and the ships opened fire to sink them. It was a fine sight, but many a Chinaman lost the number of his mess that night.'

The climax of the war came in the summer of 1842, with the assault and capture of the walled city of Chin Kiang on the Yangtse in July and the advance to Nanking, 150 miles from the sea, in August. But first the forts of Woosung and Shanghai had to be reduced. They were bombarded by the ships, which had been towed into position by East India Company steamers lashed alongside them, and then stormed by sailors, soldiers and marines.

Ashcroft landed at Woosung. His narrative is unemotional and fragmented, noting what happened immediately next to him but unconcerned with the battle at large. He is clear on remarks spoken to or near him, but most of the events were literally hidden from him by the smoke and fog of war. 'One of our men saw a Chinaman running and broke ranks to take a shot at him. The mate in command of the party said, "If you shoot that man I will shoot you!" "I don't care if you do," said the man, "I came here to shoot a Fukee and I am going to have this one." He fired and the Chinaman fell; the mate, who had only a sword, grabbed a musket out of another man's hand and fired at the sailor but missed. The 18th Royal Irish were passing at the time; a sergeant called out, "Officer, if you had shot that man I would have shot you dead," and another said, "I have a ball in my pouch with your tally on it." '

Dido was part of the assault force of nearly eighty sail which weighed anchor on 6 July 1842 to go up the Yangtse to Nanking. Keppel, who commanded *Dido*, wrote that 'it was a beautiful sight. On a signal from Flag for fleet to weigh, in a few minutes you would see a white cloud, three miles in extent, moving up the river. While the seamen went aloft to loose sails, troops manned sheets and halyards. Wind heading, the reverse took place, and a forest of masts succeeded the white cloud.'

The fleet was headed by the *Plover* brig and the *Starling* schooner as surveying vessels, and sailed in five divisions including men-of-war, Company steamships, troopships carrying infantry, artillery, sappers, miners and rifle companies, store ships carrying horses, and colliers.

The river current was so strong that *Cornwallis*, every stitch of canvas set, could hardly make headway upstream. The Chinese called *Cornwallis* the 'two-eyed ship' because of her double row of gun-decks, which they thought unfair, and they followed her along the banks, keeping up with her and shouting and jeering. Sometimes the fleet stopped for a couple of days, to allow *Plover* and *Starling* to do their work and to give lame ducks a chance to catch up. On one occasion *Cornwallis* went aground, so it was 'down yards and topmasts, disembark stores and shot into lighters, start water casks, lay out anchors and shore up the ship so that she would not fall on her side'. With the crew at the capstan and a steamer lashed on each side full astern, *Cornwallis* eventually came off.

The attacking force for Chin Kiang was about 7,000 men of all arms. The naval brigades were not at first intended to take part. However, the seamen and marines did land to play their part in storming walls, dislodging the defenders with rockets and gunfire, and blowing open the city gates. The ships had several casualties, from Chinese fire and from heatstroke. Ashcroft, once again, was in the thick of it, going ashore with the admiral.

Soon we opened fire; that day I carried the Admiral's flag in place of his coxswain who usually did it. We were on a hill from which we could see all that was going on. Here also was the General, Sir Hugh Gough, giving orders to his staff: 'Send the 18th here and the 26th there, with the marines and the flatfoots' (this was what he called the sailors). The Admiral's boat's crew were acting as his bodyguard but he sent them, under the Flag Lieutenant, to try and stop the Chinese from killing their women and children, which he had heard they were doing. We came to one place where one of the steamers had been shelling and there were many dead, but the survivors were lying down among the dead and after we had passed they gave us a volley. The Flag Lieutenant said, 'You treacherous rascals. Fix bayonets, men, and if you pass anyone that looks as though he is going to fire on you, give them the steel.' We had some fairly hard fighting and lost several men.

On 9 August the ships anchored in the river, with their nearest guns only 1,000 feet from the walls of Nanking. At this, the Chinese government agreed to parley. The ships stayed in the river while the treaty was negotiated and signed, when *Cornwallis* was 'full of head mandarins and it was quite a gay turnout with lots of saluting and chin-chinning'. But it was also the height of the Chinese summer and the day temperatures soared to 110 degrees

Fahrenheit in the shade. Cholera broke out in the troopship *Belleisle* and soon spread to other ships. In *Cornwallis* they had epidemics of dysentery and 'ague', as Ashcroft called it, as well as cholera. Ashcroft, who had cholera himself but recovered, noted that it seemed to be the healthiest men who were struck down. They buried an average of three men a day, but it was even worse in the merchantmen. They had lost so many men that *Cornwallis*'s sailors, having furled their own sails at the end of the day, had to send a party across to the nearest storeships and troopers to help furl theirs.

Having emptied the casks holding all their water, they had to drink the river water (which accounted for the cholera). Their food was very bad indeed, 'beef like old horse,' said Ashcroft, 'biscuits full of maggots and weevils; you had to get into a dark corner so as not to see what you were eating!' *Cornwallis* had three anchors down and the foretopsail set, with men steering at the wheel, to try and keep the ship steady in wind and current. Even then she sometimes took such a 'big yaw you thought she would tear her bows out'. She left two anchors behind her in the mud when she went, as did several other ships.

The treaty was signed on terms advantageous to the British and the ships could disperse. *Blonde*, *Modeste* and *Columbine* sailed for England and HM Steamer *Driver*, the first man-of-war steamship on the station, arrived. Some new midshipmen joined *Cornwallis*: 'puny, sickly-looking Middys sent out from England', Ashcroft called them. The sailors soon summed them up, with a savage sense of humour: 'His father is one of the pillars of the nation,' Ashcroft heard an old salt say of one, 'and he has come to sea to revenge the death of Nelson.'

Cornwallis's last year was unhappy and a textbook example of how discipline and morale could crumble if the sailors were not properly led. *Cornwallis*'s commander went home, taking copies of the Treaty with him. The first lieutenant was promoted in his place. Here was a change for the worse. 'I'll die a lieutenant and I'll die a tyrant,' the new commander used to say; 'I'll make her as hot as hell.' The first half of his prophecy was wrong, but the second was accurate. In general Ashcroft had a poor opinion of the officers: he called them a 'poor lot'. 'They must have scoured the Navy to get hold of them all. There was a saying: "the biggest scamp for the Army, the biggest rogue for the Navy, and the biggest fool for a Parson!" It was hard to believe that some of ours were gentlemen's sons.'

Back in Hong Kong, *Cornwallis* still lost men through sickness. They would go out to Green Island in seventeen fathoms of water to bury the bodies, but the shot used to work out of the hammocks and they had to send away a boat to sink them again. Ashcroft could never eat his dinner on these occasions. *Cornwallis* also lost as many men by desertion; men 'ran' and joined merchantmen about to sail.

Ashcroft was now an able seaman and an experienced signalman, with a chance of being rated yeoman of signals when he was older and, as the captain said, he 'had got some hair on his face'. He was an intelligent, keen and conscientious rating, who should have been a prospect for warrant rank. But he would never volunteer for that. At Trincomalee, their last port of call in

Ceylon, the ship landed all the stores she could spare, including a waist anchor which had to be hoisted out with sheerlegs by the bosun and his party. While the sheerlegs were being dismantled a rope jammed and was cut free with a knife. When the commander noticed the cut rope he was furious, put the man who cut it in irons, put the captain of the forecastle in cells, and sent the bosun to his cabin under a sentry's charge. Ashcroft watched and noted this—'that was the first thing that put me against taking a warrant.' By such behaviour a few stupid officers discouraged sailors from advancement. There was another serious grievance: from 1830 a warrant officer's pension was not paid to his widow after his death. It was no wonder that as the 1830s and '40s went on, promotion to warrant rank became less and less attractive.

On the passage home, lower-deck feeling against the commander mounted. When the ship was lying in the Calcutta river, a letter addressed to the admiral had fallen out of the admiral's valet's hammock. It mentioned the rascally usage meted out to the ship's company, and it was signed 'a broken-hearted seaman of HMS *Cornwallis*'. Unfortunately, the admiral and the captain were in Calcutta and the letter was given to the commander.

So the commander knew the ship's company's feelings and he had confirmation at Cape Town when he went on board another ship and heard from her captain that *Cornwallis* had quite a reputation back home. He came back on board and was heard to remark: 'So some of you have been writing to England painting the ship black. Not half so black as she will be by the time we arrive there.'

One of the afterguard was a coloured man called Joe Coglin, a very good seaman. He had been one of the boats' crews who had manned the execution rope in *Rodney*. After a mishap on deck the commander called him a 'black dog'. Joe said, 'I black but my heart white, you white but got black heart.' This was a foolhardy epigram for a commander RN. Joe was nearly 'started'—made to pass round all the bosun's mates who thrashed him with their rope's ends—but the commander thought better of it. He thought better of flogging him, too. Joe had already been flogged five times and as the commander said, 'We may as well flog the mainmast.'

So Joe went scot-free, another sign that discipline was crumbling. When the ship sailed from the Cape the commander's fine cat went missing. He offered fifty dollars reward, with no result. Then his mongoose disappeared, followed by 'Jack', a sheep they had brought out from England. The admiral received three more anonymous letters signed by 'broken-hearted seamen of *Cornwallis*'. One night the commander smelt burning and found a rocket in the magazine below, lit with a slow match and pointed at his bed. No culprit was discovered although the gunner, the gunner's mate and the whole gunner's party were put under arrest. A seaman missed his muster for the morning watch at 4.00 a.m., and when the decks were washed down at 6.00 a.m. he was found lying drunk on the main-deck. He had got the liquor from a steward. The man got three dozen lashes, the steward four. Afterwards somebody stabbed the drunken man in his hammock, but fortunately mistook the head for the foot, although cutting the calf of his leg to the bone. When asked who his assailants were, the man gave several names and all were given four dozen lashes on suspicion. Two collars were then made of heavy wood, one weighing 42 lbs and the other 28. They had a hinge and a padlock and men had to wear them as punishment. But, as Ashcroft said, 'some men became so hardened by this sort of treatment they were past caring.'

Cornwallis reached Spithead on 4 November 1844, eleven months and four hours from Hong Kong. The admiral went ashore and the ship turned back to Plymouth, discharged powder and went up harbour. No leave was allowed for the first two days—no bumboatmen, no Jews, tailors, or relatives, although ten men at a time were allowed to go down into the boats alongside to see their friends and relations. This was particularly galling for the *Cornwallis*, because *Nimrod* had also returned from the Far East and gave leave right away. As a special favour, and as a sign of Ashcroft's personal standing, his father was one of the very few visitors allowed on board.

At last, paying-off day came. The captain promised them all a medal and battle money. Back in India, the commander had once told a man, 'I suppose you are one of those who are going to give me a hiding when we pay off. I do not fear any dozen of you as you are a set of cowards.' Now was his chance to make good his words.

Anticipating the fun, Ashcroft landed at North Corner and watched from an upstairs room. 'When the officers landed they got it from the women and some of our men dressed in women's clothes. Our only "good" lieutenant was carried into the town to an hotel.' Nearly all the officers had their epaulettes and clothes torn from them and, in spite of a police guard the ship's company 'caught the commander the same night in Plymouth, getting into a cab, he got it the worst of the lot'. The newspapers printed the story and when the Admiralty enquired about the disgraceful behaviour of the *Cornwallis*'s sailors the captain explained that so many men had been killed, had deserted or been invalided that he had had to ship runaway convicts from Sydney to get the ship back to England. There was probably some truth in this but, all the same, as Ashcroft said, 'there were not many wet eyes on leaving her.'

It was by no means uncommon for unpopular officers to be assaulted after paying off a ship. William Kennedy, when he joined as a midshipman in the early 1850s, heard of a ship a few years before which paid off at Devonport after a commission in West Africa in which nearly every man on board had been flogged. The captain was walking along a street in Devonport when an old woman came up and accosted him.

'Be you Captain——?'

'Yes, my good woman,' he said, 'what can I do for you?'

'Take *that*, for flogging my son,' she cried, whipping out a hake-fish and 'letting him have it' across the face.

After the China War, Keppel sailed *Dido* across the South China Sea to Sarawak, whose ruler James Brooke had just been to Singapore to ask for assistance in the task of suppressing, or at least curbing, the piracy which was rife along the shores and rivers of Borneo and Sarawak.

In May 1843 *Dido* arrived in a theatre of war where her bluejackets and

The attack by two pirate *prahus* on the *Jolly Bachelor* off
Borneo; from a picture by Lieutenant Hunt of the *Dido*, 1842.

marines took part in battles fought almost entirely in small boats, in ship's
launches, cutters and gigs, where the largest vessel was a pinnace armed with
a 6-pounder gun, along waterways narrow enough for a man to throw a
spear across. The dense jungle undergrowth came down to the water's edge.
Any bend in the river might reveal a waiting ambush, or a line of armed war
prahus each with a score of yelling Dyak natives on board, or a Dyak village
festooned with shrunken heads and the spoil of a hundred war raids. The
sailors spent nights standing upright in drenching tropical rain storms, with
their muskets hidden under their coats to keep them dry. At night the
menacing noises of the jungle were shot through with the terrifying war yells
of the Dyaks, which were enough to shrivel an unwary man's heart. In those
waters a small cut could lead to crippling sores or gangrene. A chill could
quickly turn to fever or pneumonia—one doctor who fell overboard caught a
chill and died of fever in two days. Drinking unboiled water could lead to
cholera. The food, as so often in naval expeditions, defied rational description
except where it could be supplemented with fruit or fowls bought locally.

The raiding parties were often of mixed race, exhibiting a fine range of
motives. The British wanted to suppress piracy. The Malays sought loot, while
the Dyaks were after tribal revenges. One incident was pure adventure story.
Dido's largest boat was under repair and Brooke lent Keppel a boat he had had
built at Sarawak. She was called the *Jolly Bachelor* and she was armed with a 6-
pounder and a volunteer crew of a mate, two midshipmen, six marines, twelve

seamen and a fortnight's provisions. She was under the command of *Dido's*
second lieutenant, Mr Hunt. They had been ordered not to close the land, but
after five days all hands were so fatigued that they anchored close in shore.
Exactly as Keppel had feared, they all fell asleep.

Just as the moon was rising, Hunt awoke to see a Dyak savage brandishing
his *kris* and dancing in triumph at the ease with which he had apparently
captured this fine trading vessel. But the sight of 'Jim Hunt's round fat face
meeting the light of the rising moon' disabused the man and he immediately
plunged overboard. Before Hunt was properly awake, *Jolly Bachelor* was
swept by four cannon shots from two war *prahus*, one moored on each bow.
The sailors sprang up, now wide awake, cut the anchor cable, manned the oars
and backed *Jolly Bachelor* out of the anchorage. Our men, said Keppel, 'fought
as British sailors ought'. The deadly accurate fire of the marines prevented the
enemy reloading. The *prahus* had stout grape-proof barricades along their
bulwarks and these had to be knocked away by *Jolly Bachelor's* 6-pounder
before the musket fire could take effect. But when this had been done, musket
and 'grape and canister told with fearful execution'. The work, according to
Keppel was 'sharp and short, but the slaughter great'. One pirate *prahu* was
captured, with three feet of blood and water in her, and the other escaped.

The gun-deck of HMS *Leander, c.*1850 (from a coloured
lithograph by T. Lee used as the frontispiece for *Remarks on
Directing Ship's Broadsides,* Cdr. Arthur Jerningham R.N.).

A series of punitive raids was carried out against individual pirate leaders,
or 'sheriffs' as they were called. The tactics were generally the same:
reconnaissance from the sea, an assault landing by bluejackets and marines,
and the capture and burning down of the pirate village; the sheriff was either

killed or turned out into the jungle, and his plunder recovered, while he suffered loss of face in his tribe's eyes.

One major operation was carried out on 19 August 1845 against Sheriff Houseman, a particularly brutal and atrocious pirate whose stronghold was at Malluda Bay. The attacking force was 530 seamen and marines, from ships of the squadron, embarked in twenty-four boats, nine of them gunboats, commanded by Captain Talbot of *Vestal*.

There were between 500 and 1000 pirates, in two forts, armed with about a dozen heavy guns. The entrance to Malluda Bay was narrow, and flanked by dense woods. Inside, the land was flat and covered in mangrove trees. The water was shallow, though several rivers ran into the bay. The approach to the pirates' village was guarded by a strong protective boom, made of three large tree-trunks, bolted and chained together.

When the attacking boats were within a hundred yards of the boom, the pirates sent a flag of truce. Talbot thought it a device to gain time. But he sent a message offering to convey Sheriff Houseman to James Brooke. The offer was derisively refused and the pirates then opened a heavy fire. Their guns were laid on the boom and they kept up their fusillade for over an hour while the sailors struggled to cut the boom with axes, whilst returning the fire vigorously with guns and rockets. Eventually the boom was sufficiently cleared to allow the smaller boats to cross it and the marines got out of the larger boats, crossed the boom and embarked again in the smaller. They were then able to land near the village. The pirates immediately fled.

The huts in the village and some *prahus* drawn up on the bank were burned. It was found that the cable on the boom was the anchor cable of a ship of some 300 to 400 tons and there were many other signs of pirate's plunder in the village, such as a ship's long boat, two ship's bells, one of them ornamented with grapes and vine-leaves and marked 'Wilhelm Ludwig, Bremen', and every kind of ship's furniture. Twenty-four brass guns, which Keppel said 'were as good as money', were captured. The iron guns were spiked and destroyed. Sheriff Houseman escaped into the jungle where it was thought he died.

The casualties were high for this kind of operation: six killed, including the mate of *Wolverine*, killed on the boom, and seventeen wounded, two mortally and the others very severely. The pirates carried off many of their dead into the jungle but Talbot in his report said, 'some of those left on the field we recognised as persons of considerable influence.'

The fight at Malluda Bay was one of the best known of many such incidents, and it was the subject of a ballad, 'The Borneo Heroes':

Come, all you jolly sailors bold, the truth you soon shall know
Concerning of a glorious fight on the Isle of Borneo.
As we were cruising off the coast we heard the dreadful news
How the pirates they had massacred our merchants' crews.
 *Huzza! huzza! huzza! huzza! with Captain Talbot, boys, we'll die or
  win the day!*

When we came up to the boom we found it so secure,
The cannon from their batteries on us poor lads did pour;
But soon we cut our way through, like lions sprang on shore,
And soon five hundred pirates lay bleeding in their gore.
  Huzza, etc.

While they were bleeding in their gore we rushed into their town,
And there the produce of many a gallant ship we found;
For plunder and distribution, boys, it was our whole intent:
In one hour and twenty minutes the town to ashes sent.
  Huzza, etc.

Now we have returned to England, to let our friends all know
How we destroyed the pirates on the coast of Borneo;
For we left the flag of England by all nations to be seen:
And for our reward we'll boldly go, boys, to our gracious Queen.
  Huzza, etc.

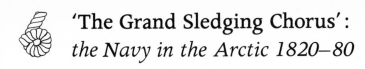

'The Grand Sledging Chorus':
the Navy in the Arctic 1820–80

Life on board was always hard, but life in the Arctic was especially demanding. However, in the 1820s John Bechervaise in *Blossom* wrote with a patriotic flourish that 'there, even there, the indefatigable Englishman has found his way'. It was a victory for the Navy, not this time over barbarism, but over cold and loneliness.

Officers and men in *Blossom* were thrown together to an unusual extent. At one time they all shared the same 'eight on four' rations—eight men on food for four. A ration consisted of eight ounces of bread (which was baked on board every day), six ounces of beef or pork on alternate days, six ounces of flour for dinner one day, a gill of peas the next; in addition to the daily ration of rum. Bechervaise used to dream of food, of 'mutton stew and dumplings (vulgarly called doughboys) gracefully floating on the top, and shewing their white tops in beautiful brown liquid'. The officers shared the cold and the hunger with the men. They also very occasionally shared a meal; on one run ashore, Bechervaise and some of his mates were joined by the master of the ship, a well-liked officer, for a meal of fried salmon and birds' eggs. This would have been an unheard-of proceeding later in the century, or away from the Arctic.

The difficulties of preserving food and preventing illness were of vital importance to the great programme of polar exploration on which the Navy embarked in the nineteenth century. In many ways it seemed that the commissioning, storing and routine of naval ships had remained the same for forty or fifty years—the Navy appeared eternal, unchanging, conservative— but in fact changes were there.

On 24 September 1847, the three-decker sailing line-of-battle-ship *Bellerophon* commissioned at Portsmouth for the Mediterranean Station. The next day, a manning rendezvous was set up at Portsea and two days later fifteen petty officers and one seaman joined. Meanwhile the warrant officers, the gunner, the carpenter and the bosun all joined, as did twenty-two boys first class and nineteen second class from the flagship *Victory*. A captain of marines, a lieutenant, two sergeants, two corporals, one fifer and sixty-two privates joined from barracks on 28 September. The following day the master joined.

The ship was rigged, one mast at a time. Several dockyard artificers were employed on board, including fourteen shipwrights, nine joiners, two caulkers, two painters and two plumbers. On 4 November the guns were got into their places and on 10 November the ship was stored (between 500 and 600 lbs of fresh beef were being received on board every other day, but this was the official storing day). 2,630 8-lb pieces of beef and 5,280 4-lb pieces of pork were embarked, together with flour, suet, raisins, peas, oatmeal, sugar, chocolate, tea and vinegar. The rum had already been drawn.

By 27 November the ship was fully rigged and the ship's company moved out of the hulk. The lieutenant of marines came back from volunteering men at Portsea, and on 30 November the ship was towed out to Spithead, where Sir Charleş Ogle, the C-in-C, inspected her on the following day. The ship's company were mustered, and yards manned. Ten days later the ship sailed for Corfu. She could make nine or ten knots with a good quarterly breeze and she arrived at Corfu on 11 January 1848, having called at Plymouth and Gibraltar on her way.

The commission was spent partly in the Mediterranean and partly at home. Several floggings were logged, from one to three dozen lashes, for offences such as drunkenness, uncleanliness, disobedience of orders, and drinking by a sentry of spirits put under his charge. The log never mentions leave but in one week of May 1848 four men were entered as 'run'. On 1 July, at Spithead, a court-martial sentenced John Macdonald, marine, to be transported beyond the seas for the term of his natural life for striking the captain. On 21 September, the ship's company were exercised at quarters, firing at targets; 106 rounds of 32-pounder shot and twenty-five rounds of 68-pounder were expended.

The target practice showed the influence of *Excellent*. In earlier years John Macdonald would have been flogged round the fleet, perhaps hanged. The fifteen petty officers and the one seaman who joined at Portsea were volunteers after leave from a previous commission. *Bellerophon*'s stores included tea and sugar; sugar had been available in ships since about 1815, but in 1847 sailors were able to draw tea and sugar at their discretion in lieu of their spirit ration.

The scale of rationing in *Bellerophon* was typical of her day. The standard diet of the bluejacket was $\frac{3}{4}$ lb of salt beef and $\frac{3}{4}$ lb of flour one day, $\frac{3}{4}$ lb of salt pork and $\frac{1}{2}$ pint of peas the next. Banyan (or meatless) days had been abolished. The scale was improved again in 1851.

Layard in the Irrawaddy, Ashcroft in the Yangtse twenty years later, and a score of other campaign accounts of the time all complained about poor food and rampant disease on board. *Bellerophon*'s stores, with their preponderance of salt beef and pork, suggested that the seaman's diet had not changed since the wars. This was partly the seaman's own fault: always conservative and never more so than over what he ate, he fiercely resisted any change in his diet.

The problem of providing edible preserved food was not just a question of the sailors' likes and dislikes. It was also a strategic matter: anything that improved the range and efficiency of fighting ships was devoutly to be wished. In 1795 Napoleon offered 12,000 francs to whoever devised a reliable means of preserving food. The prize was won by a Monsieur Nicholas Appert, who bottled meat, vegetables, fruit and milk by compressing them in glass bottles, sealing the mouths and heating them until the air inside was driven out. His *boeuf bouilli*—'bully beef'—was tried out and approved by the French Navy in about 1803.

In 1810 Appert's results were published in a book which was read and enthusiastically followed by Mr Bryan Donkin, a Fellow of the Royal Society and the 'father' of the modern canning industry. Donkin, with John Hall who bought the patent and founded the Dartford Iron Works in London, and John Gamble who owned a sheet metal business, used iron containers instead of glass; they were better for stowage and improved the preserving process. As early as 1813 the firm of Donkin, Gamble & Hall offered trial samples of their preserves to the Commissioners for Victualling.

The response from the fleet was enthusiastic, particularly from Cochrane on the North America Station. Mr Grimstone, surgeon of Cochrane's flagship *Tonnant*, reported that the 'bully beef' appeared to him to be 'infinitely superior to anything I have seen in use, particularly in large ships, where a sick mess is established'.

Donkin, Gamble & Hall became regular contractors to the Navy and by January 1817 their preserved meat had replaced as medical comforts the old 'portable soup' (glue-like slabs, marked with a broad HM Service arrow, a relic from the days of Captain Cook) which Grimstone, who tried it in 'every form I could', said was 'invariably rejected, both by the convalescent and those labouring under complaints'. In 1818, despite the initial hostility of the sailors, the Admiralty bought 46,000 lbs of comestibles, packed in 23,779 containers. In 1831 tinned provisions were added to the medical comforts for ships all over the world. In 1847, tinned beef became part of the general service provisions and appeared on the mess-decks as bully beef.

The 'bully beef' story was not of course, an unblemished path to success. In 1816 Donkin & Co. were being asked to explain the failure of some bottles of preserved soup in *Asia*, which were 'wholly defective and extremely offensive'. The corks had been damaged in the rough handling on board. A much more serious scandal occurred in 1845 which concerned Donkin's rival Stephen Goldner. Goldner tried to make bigger and ever bigger cans, some of them up to 32 lbs in weight and one of them containing a whole sheep. The sterilisation methods of the time were not up to this increase in size. Many more tins were condemned and there was a general distrust of canned food on the mess-decks.

But in the long run nothing could detract from the success of bully beef. In 1840 Captain Basil Hall wrote 'how astonishingly good the preserved milk is' and tinned meat, he said 'eats nothing, nor drinks, it is not apt to die, does not tumble overboard or get its legs broken, or its flesh worked off its bones by tumbling about the ship in bad weather, it takes no care in the keeping, it is always ready, may be eaten hot or cold'.

In 1866 the Admiralty began preserving meat in the Royal Victualling Yard at Deptford. The first issue of 'pusser's' boiled beef was in 1867, and it so happened that a woman called Fanny Adams was murdered at Alton in Hampshire in August of that year. Her body was hacked into pieces by her murderer, one Frederick Parker, who was hanged for the crime at Winchester Gaol on Christmas Eve 1867. The bluejackets inevitably called the new meat 'Fanny Adams'. The tins were often used as mess utensils and the general term for them became 'Fanny'. The last known tin from Deptford, which ceased preserving in 1871-2, was opened in 1922. One of Donkin & Co.'s cans, from

1818, was opened in 1938 and the contents found perfectly fresh and edible, though rather leathery and almost flavourless.

The provision of drinking water at sea was also a strategic problem, which the Admiralty were not as enterprising over solving. Sir Richard Hawkins had a 'still' at sea in 1594, as did Sir Walter Ralegh in *Warspite* on the 'Islands Voyage' of 1596. Captain Cook had a still, and there were a number of eighteenth-century working models. In 1815, most of the wooden water casks in ships were replaced by iron tanks, filled by hoses. Until then, water casks had had to be manhandled out of the ship, filled ashore and stowed again. The full casks were extremely heavy, and ruptures were amongst the most frequent occupational diseases of the Navy. With the coming of steam, more ships had distilling apparatus, although in March 1854 in the Baltic, Keppel noted that *St Jean d'Acre* was 'one of the few ships fitted with distilling apparatus, we were constantly supplying other ships with pure water'.

The dangers of the constant washing down of decks with water, leading to chest complaints, rheumatism and tuberculosis, were realised early in the nineteenth century. In 1824 Robert Finlayson, surgeon in the Royal Navy, published a pamphlet addressed to captains in the Navy concerning the health of their crews. He warned of the dangers of men sitting or lying in a damp atmosphere, having been paddling about in ankle-deep water for some four hours before, with their clothes and bodies soaking wet. From his own experience Finlayson knew of a line-of-battle-ship in which the surgeon recommended dry holystoning, while the captain favoured the usual washing. When, the next year, a captain was appointed who favoured dry holystoning, 'not a single case of acute disease occurred for several months; and the medium number on the sick-list did not amount to one third of that the previous year.' Many surgeons agreed with Finlayson that much disease in the Navy was caused by men getting drunk and then sleeping on damp decks, or failing to change their wet clothes when they went below, and generally living in a constantly damp and humid atmosphere.

On some mess-decks the atmosphere was not only humid: it was actually close to lethal. The hammocks were slung some seventeen or eighteen inches apart. At sea one watch was on deck but in harbour, with no shore leave, five hundred men slept cheek by jowl, in foetid heat, with body odours and the dangers of contagious disease. Until the end of the wars men slept over what was virtually an open drain. The ballast was sand or shingle, tightly pressed down. Over the years, bilge water, urine, excrement and liquid waste of all kinds soaked into this mass, which was hardly ever disturbed, let alone cleaned or disinfected. The substitution of pig-iron blocks and some of the freshwater tanks for sand as ballast did help the situation but the smell was often indescribably abominable. Sometimes the air was actually toxic, with a mixture of sewer gas, methane and carbon dioxide. In the old 74-gun *Minden* in 1820, a party of a dozen men sent down to clear the pump-well in the bilges lost consciousness and would have died had not a quick-thinking petty officer noticed them. They were all hauled to safety, and survived. Spencer Wells, surgeon in the *Modeste* sloop in the Mediterranean in 1852, wrote that 130 seamen had to sleep in a space of fifty-four feet by six feet, which was less breathing space 'than is enjoyed by the inhabitants of the lowest lodging houses in the narrowest alleys of London; still further less than is secured to the felons condemned to imprisonment in any gaol in Britain'.

A Mr Perkins invented an experimental ventilator which was quite well spoken of by surgeons, and various ingenious captains and first lieutenants tried out methods of ventilation using wind scoops, tunnels, wind pumps, bellows or socks. Setting a fore-sail so that it gave a steady draught below was also a common practice. But none of these methods gave a constant or indeed any supply to some of the obscurer parts of the lower-deck.

Just as the knowledge of distillation of fresh water was gained only to be discarded and not pursued for many years, so too was the cure for scurvy found and then lost again. Scurvy was the disease which carried off thousands more seamen than were ever killed by any enemy. The key was simple. Those who had enough ascorbic acid in their diet did not suffer scurvy. Those who had not, did (although the disease did not normally occur until about four months after the cessation of a normal diet so that symptoms of scurvy appeared, with monotonous regularity, four months after a voyage began). The symptoms were: horny patches on the skin, which turned to pimples which bled; sore and swollen gums, ultimately with teeth falling out; old wounds breaking out, and new ones failing to heal; inability to work for more than short periods due to rapid exhaustion; and, in the end, death, usually of a heart attack. James Lind, a Scots naval surgeon, a great doctor and an expert on the disease, published his *Treatise on Scurvey* in 1753. Though another great naval doctor, Gilbert Blane, carried on Lind's work, the Navy delayed any general action against the disease, partly because of ignorance and partly because the recommended antiscorbutic, lemon juice, seemed too primitive and 'not scientific enough' as medicine. In the early nineteenth century the issue of lemon juice became general throughout the fleet, the lemons coming from Malta, except in the West Indies where the squadron used limes from Montserrat. The limes were four times less effective against scurvy than lemon juice (the Admiralty, for reasons of economy, changed to Montserrat limes in 1865) and in fact were not sufficient to prevent the disease on their own. Nevertheless, scurvy did decrease in the nineteenth century for a number of reasons: more fresh vegetables and a generally improved diet for the sailors, shorter voyages, and less frequent wars. Only in some of the voyages to high latitudes did misunderstandings about the disease and misplaced confidence in preserved foods as antiscorbutics lead to serious outbreaks of scurvy.

In 1814 Sir John Ross took some of Donkin's new meat to the Arctic and his men all liked it. Edward Parry took it on all four of his northern expeditions and wrote on his return from one trip in 1820 that he felt it 'impossible to speak too highly of the preserved meat and soups'. It was Parry whom Beechey in *Blossom* (with Bechervaise on board) was to try to meet in 1825. John Bechervaise mentions that *Blossom* carried preserved meat and provisions— 'pickled cabbage, sour crout, pippins, portable soup, preserved meats in tin cases'.

Bechervaise stressed the difficulties and dangers of the journey and was pessimistic about their chances. He went because he had to, but many others were volunteers. Some went on more than one voyage. Expedition leaders said that men-of-warsmen made easily the best personnel for these voyages. When, in 1824, Captain George F. Lyon sailed in *Griper* for surveys of north-east America, he attributed their survival to naval discipline. *Griper* was an old tub and a bad sailer and at one time nearly ran aground on a lee shore. But nobody lost their heads and eventually the ship escaped, after everybody had been working for twenty-four hours without stop. 'Noble as the character of the British sailor is always allowed to be in cases of danger,' wrote Lyon, 'yet I did not believe it possible that among forty-one persons not one repining word should have been uttered'.

The Arctic journeys brought out the best in the sailors. In 1827 Parry made a boat and sledge journey to the latitude of 82°45′N, although he had hoped to achieve 83°. The men worked with tremendous cheerfulness and goodwill, drawing their sledges across the floes at least eleven miles a day in spite of exhaustion. But the floes were themselves drifting south at about seven miles a day. As one sailor innocently remarked 'we're a long time getting to this eighty-three degrees!'

The first steam ship to be used in Arctic discovery, the paddle-steamer *Victory*, left England on 23 May 1829 and did not return until 18 October, 1833—four years and five months later. The great success of the voyage was the discovery of the magnetic pole by James Ross (Sir John's nephew) on 1 June 1831. The pole was confirmed by the 'absolute inaction' of several horizontal needles, which were suspended in 'the most delicate manner possible, but there was not one which showed the slightest effort to move from the position in which it was placed'. Afterwards a ballad was composed. One verse commemorates the cairn and the canister containing a record of their journey which Ross's party erected:

> 'Twas thought that no one since Creation
>   . Would find it until time did end;
> But King William's name of this nation
>   So proud on that magnet does bend.
> So build for bold Ross a fine pillar,
>   And cast it with gold letters o'er;
> Bold Ross brav'd the Wave, ice and billow,
>   In triumph reached Old England's shore.

A picture of the bluejacket in the Arctic is given by Captain Back, who sailed in the *Terror* on 14 June 1836 for a surveying voyage north of Repulse Bay. The expedition did not achieve much, but Back left some revealing comments about his crew. They were a motley collection, 'hastily gathered together, and for the most part composed of people who had never before been out of a collier. Some half a dozen indeed, had served in Greenland vessels', but according to Back the discipline in those was as lax as in colliers. 'A few men-of-warsmen who were also on board were worth the whole put together.' Although the first lieutenant made strenuous efforts to get the crew to pull together 'though nominally in the same mess, and eating at the same table, many of them would secrete their allowance, with other unmanly and unsailorlike practices'. They were a well educated crew. There were only three or four in the ship who could not write. 'All read, some recited whole pages of poetry, others sang French songs. Yet, with all this, had they been left to themselves I verily believe a more unsociable, suspicious, and uncomfortable set of people could not have been found. Oh, if the two are incompatible, give me the old Jack Tar, who would stand out for his ship, and give his life for his messmates.'

The Medal for Arctic Discoveries, 1818–1855.

Like every other commander in the Arctic, Back had the problem of keeping his crew amused. They had a 'general masquerade' which gave them a lot of fun, and later some theatrical entertainments were organised.

Terror, too, was several times in great danger. One night she was caught in ice that opened and shut several times, threatening to crack the ship like a nutshell. Revealingly, Back held divisions at 8.00 a.m. next morning, 'I thought it necessary to address the crew, reminding them, as Christians and British seamen, they were called upon to conduct themselves with coolness and fortitude, and that independently of the obligation imposed by the Articles of War, every one ought to be influenced by the still higher motive of a conscientious desire to perform his duty.' The men did perform their duties and *Terror* came safe home, after many more perils.

The most famous polar voyage of the first half of the nineteenth century was Captain Sir John Franklin's, on which he and the officers and ships' companies of *Erebus* and *Terror* were lost. They sailed from Greenhithe on 26 May 1845 and were last seen by the Hull whaler *Prince of Wales* on 26 July, moored to an iceberg in the upper part of Baffin Bay. They had provisions for three years, even four, but when by 1847 no word of any kind had been heard, uneasiness

The reverse side of the Naval General Service
Medal, first issued in 1847. Over 200 different bars
were issued with this medal, covering actions from
1793 to 1840.

'Christmas at Sea' in Jack's mess on board a man-of-war; from a
picture by E. T. Dalby.

about the fate of the expedition turned to foreboding. Many search expeditions were mounted, some privately, some by governments. The private enterprises tended to do rather better. An expedition sponsored by the Admiralty and commanded by a whaling captain called William Penny sailed in 1850 and found storehouses, meat tins and coal bags marked *Terror* in a remote bay of Beechey Island. They also found the graves, each with a neatly carved oak head-board, of an able seaman and a marine of *Erebus* and a sailor of *Terror*.The Arctic was strewn with sailors' gravestones; most anchorages and wintering places had a small cemetery, set apart. William Domville, surgeon in HMS *Resolute* (Captain Henry Kellett), came upon one on Kron Prinz Island in 1852. The epitaph which he noted in his journal is evidence of the lapidary taste of the bluejackets' funerary memorials and one of the commonest industrial accidents of the Victorian Navy.

> You mariners that pass by here
> Upon my grave let fall a tear
> Henry Mackinson is my name
> In the Albion Captain Hill I came
> It was the month of April I came here
> But did not think death was as near
> On the fifteenth day of April
> It was my lot to have a fall
> From the crosstrees of the maintopmast
> I on the quarter-deck was cast
> And so was hurted by the fall
> My life soon after God did call.

The fate of Franklin's party was discovered by McLintock in *Fox* in 1859. A small cairn was found at Point Victory on the north-west coast of King William Island. Franklin had died in June 1847. The ships had been beset in the ice from September 1846 until April 1848, when the survivors under Captain Crozier abandoned the ships and tried to march overland to Hudson's Bay. From the relics and equipment lying all around there could be no doubt that this was Franklin's expedition.

One of the ships searching for Franklin was HMS *Plover* (Commander Thomas Moore) which left England in January 1848. Fortunately a full account of the voyage was written in a journal by William Simpson, a sergeant of marines. He writes fluently, authoritatively and, so far as is known, accurately. He was a versatile man, having not only his regulating duties as master-at-arms but also being the ship's steward, ship's schoolmaster and part-time taxidermist—the captain gave him the task of skinning and preserving the birds caught by the expedition.

Living conditions were arduous. It was so cold on board that when the men woke in the mornings they found icicles four or five inches long hanging from the deck-heads. Simpson had two men constantly employed sweeping, scraping and wiping up as the condensation turned to ice. Nevertheless they made themselves as comfortable as they could, with an outside temperature of 21° below. They played football on the ice and, like Back's men years before, they passed the time with what Simpson called plays and masquerades, in which the captain and officers took part. Some of their characters 'would not have disgraced the boards in some of our minor theatres at home'. At one performance of a piece mysteriously called *How to settle accounts with your laundress*, the audience was augmented by about forty or fifty Eskimos who greatly applauded the incomprehensible entertainment.

Simpson took part in the football matches but he suffered badly from rheumatism and was eventually invalided home, arriving in the spring of 1851. His journal shows him as an intelligent and able man, with many talents, but apt to cut corners and a bit of a 'sea-lawyer' who always knew what was in the small print. He could not have been easy to serve with and occasionally he seems to have been more lenient with the ship's company than a master-at-arms should be. However, his allusive narrative shows a more heightened, sympathetic relationship between officer and man.

Some of *Terror*'s ship's company had set out for their last journey in their best clothes, as though going ashore in England. McClintock found several skeletons, one in particular lying face downwards in the snow, on the south coast of King William Island, about 135 miles from where *Terror* and *Erebus* were abandoned. The man was wearing trousers and a jacket of fine blue cloth, with a blue greatcoat and a black silk neckerchief. He had on him the pocket book, service certificates and other private papers of Harry Peglar, captain of the foretop in *Terror*. But the dress was unusual for a seaman and was more suitable for a steward and the man could well have been Peglar's friend Thomas Armitage, gunroom steward of *Terror*, who was about the same build as Peglar. Peglar may have entrusted his documents to his friend because he was unable to go on any longer himself. The man either pitched forward, exhausted, or sat down to rest on a stone and fell forward when he got up, never to rise again. One of the papers on the body looked as if it had been written by two people as a joint effort, the words forming a circle on the page. Many are now illegible but they do clearly begin: 'O Death, whare is thy sting . . .'

Edward Parry's latitude record of 82°45' lasted for nearly fifty years, until Captain George Nares's expedition which sailed from Portsmouth in *Alert* and *Discovery* on 29 May 1875. *Alert* was a 750-ton steam sloop specially strengthened for polar service. *Discovery* was a Dundee steam whaler bought by the Government and commanded by Captain H. F. Stephenson. A store ship *Valorous* followed them. After a stormy passage across the Atlantic, the two ships parted company in August, *Discovery* remaining in a bay of Grant Land, named Discovery Bay, for the winter, while *Alert* pressed on northward.

Discovery was embedded in the ice for ten and a half months. The ship's company placed six months provisions in a store ashore, in case of accident to the ship. They shot thirty-two musk oxen, and at one time had 3,053 lbs of frozen meat hanging up. As the Arctic winter went on, snow piled up outside the ship fifteen to twenty feet thick. A layer of snow mixed with ashes was laid on the upper-deck, which gave a kind of 'macadamised' walking surface, provided good insulation and kept the lower-deck temperature between 48° and 56°. The sun left *Discovery* on 10 October and it was dark for the next 135 days.

Meanwhile, on 31 August, *Alert* passed into latitude 82°24′N, higher than any ship had done before. In September, as soon as the ice was strong enough, sledge parties were sent out to try (unsuccessfully) to make contact with *Discovery* and to place a cache of stores to the north-west. On 27 September this party reached 82°48′, breaking Parry's record.

Examining a 'haul' on board the *Challenger*, 1876.

The party was led by Commander A. H. Markham, *Alert*'s commander, using eight-man sledges, one of which he named 'Challenger' after his previous ship. In temperatures ranging from 15° to −22° the sailors manhandled their heavy sledges over wet soft snow, weak ice, and between patches of open water and awkward snow hummocks. It was often misty, and the wind blew from the north constantly. Of the party of twenty-four, seven men and one officer returned very badly frost-bitten; three men had to have limbs amputated and all had to stay in bed for the rest of the winter.

Daniel Harley, one of the petty officers in *Alert*, kept a diary of his experiences and wrote a clear account of life in a sledge party:

About 9.30 p.m. as we were rather tired and it would of been no good of trying to bring the boats up that night, we pitched our tent on a nice piece of floe under the lea of some large hummocks. As we were pitching them Lieutenant Parr arrived with his sledge and hitched their tents alongside of us. The cooks then set to work getting the supper ready which is a very unthankful billet as it takes a long time to thaw the snow and condense enough of water for the tea and rum, as we have our rum at night. And the cook being cold and hungry himself into the bargain makes it not a very pleasant job especially as he has to serve everybody else before he serves himself, but he has to rub over it as cheerfully as he can as it only comes to his turn once in six days. While the cook prepares the supper the remainder of the men brush the snow off their boots and clothes before getting into the tent. After getting inside they take off their snow suits and boots and boot hose and blanket wrappers which are wet and frozen and putting on a dry pair of blanket wrappers and a dry pair of stockings and a pair of moccasins for sleeping in, these things being carried in the canvas knapsack. After that they get into their sleeping bags and settle down in their allotted sleeping place for the night. The snow suits and bags have to be put under one while asleep to keep them from freezing or else you would not be able to put them on next morning. For some to have the weather below zero, they would be pretty stiff. Stockings and wrappers are taken in the bag with you to insure their being thawed by the morning because they have to go on again wet or not and the dry ones that are taken off are placed in the knapsack again. After settling down in your bags the topics of the day goes around or a talk about home or something else until the poor cook cries out 'supper', when in comes the allowance of Pemmican through the small windows of the tent in his panicans. Every man carries his own spoon which is made of horn. After the Pemmican is disposed of the tins are passed out again; then the tea is passed in in the same tins just as they were passed out, as the cook cannot make hot water to wash them out so that the tea slips down pretty well as it is nice and greasey; but a tin of hot tea is prized too much to take notice of that. After the tea is passed in, the cook manages to get his supper while the water is condensing for the rum and to put in the water bottles. After that the cook clears up a little and gets the cooking apparatus ready for the morning, but his trouble is not over yet; brushing himself and taking off the necessary clothing he settles down in his bag, his billet being close to the door or porch which is not a comfortable place and is colder than the remainder. The cook being settled, the grog is served out and then around goes the songs and stories until getting sleepy the coverlet is spread and the bags buttoned up; it does not take us long to fall into the hands of murphy. Next morning the cook has to be up some two hours and a half before the remainder, to prepare the breakfast. After breakfast the bags are rolled up, and the snow suits and boots and everybody dresses. The tent is struck and rolled up and the sledge packed all ready for a start.

Nares, too, had the problem of keeping his expedition amused and content during the winter. Again, it was an unusually literate ship's company. Only two could not read, so a school was set up, and a printing press for printing bills of fare and theatre programmes. Once a week, in what Nares called the Thursday 'Pops', there were lectures, concerts, readings or theatrical performances. On the opening 'night'—in a land of eternal night—the programme commenced: 'The Royal Arctic Theatre will be re-opened next Thursday night, by the powerful Dramatic Company of the Hyperboreans, under the distinguished patronage of Captain Nares, the Members of the Arctic Exploring Expedition and all the Nobility and Gentry of the neighbourhood.' On 2 March 1876, the Pal-O-Christy Minstrels ('This Troup Never Sings in London' was their slogan) sang a Grand Palaeocrystic Sledging Chorus, which went:

> Not very long ago,
> On the six foot floe
> Of the palaeocrystic sea,
> Two ships did ride
> Mid the crashing of the tide—
> The *Alert* and the *Discovery*.
>
> The sun never shone
> Their gallant crew upon
> For a hundred and forty-two days;
> But no darkness and no hummocks
> Their merry hearts could flummox:
> So they set to work and acted plays.

In *Discovery* they had a bonfire on 5 November, burned a guy, fired rockets and blue lights. They made a skating rink and a walk a mile long, keeping the snow shovelled away from it. As soon as the ice was strong enough they built houses, an observatory, a smithy and an ice theatre which opened on 1 December. Men and officers produced plays alternately, with songs and recitations. A hole in the ice was kept free as the winter drew on by blasting and by ice-saws. The dogs lived on the ice all winter. On Christmas Day the sergeant of marines, the chief bosun's mate and three others, went round the ship singing Christmas carols. They had a church service, dinner with plum duff, and opened the presents they had brought with them from England.

There was a tremendous variation in temperature. The chaplain recorded a change of 60° in the outside temperature in a few hours. The sun returned on the last day of February but the weather went on getting colder. One night in March *Alert* recorded a temperature of −73.7° or 105 degrees of frost. It was so cold that the barrels of shotguns contracted and the cartridges would not go in them. But still, *Alert*'s game bag for the winter and early spring was six

Alert in the Arctic: Sunday morning service, and on the
northern march; from *Polar Sketches* by Dr Edward Moss.

musk oxen, twenty hares, seventy geese, twenty-six ducks, ten ptarmigans
and three foxes.

With the coming of spring, the sledging parties set out again. Three main
parties were dispatched, one to the north under Markham towards the Pole, a
second east towards Greenland under Lieutenant Beaumont, and a third west
over the 'roof' of North America led by Lieutenant Aldrich.

Markham set out with thirty-three men on 3 April. He had four sledges, named Marco Polo, Victoria, Bulldog and Alexandra, each with a crew of an officer and seven men, and two boats, provisioned for seventy days. Each sledge weighed 1,700 lbs, so that each man had about 230 lbs to drag. The tents were eleven feet long, and gave each man a width of about fourteen inches to sleep in. They wore clothes of duffle, like thick blanket, with a duck suit outside as a 'snow repeller'. They had blanket wrappers, thick woollen socks and mocassins on their feet. They also wore snow spectacles, which proved very efficient in preventing blindness. They had three meals a day, eating breakfast of cocoa and pemmican with biscuit in their sleeping bags. After five or six hours' marching they had dinner of hot tea, bacon and biscuit. Often they had to wait an hour and a half for the kettle to boil for the tea. Supper was taken in their sleeping bags again; tea and pemmican, mixed with preserved potatoes, the day's grog ration, and a pipe of tobacco.

In spite of all the knowledge gained about scurvy, Nares had omitted to provide enough antiscorbutic acid in the diet, and very soon men began to show the symptoms. In Aldrich's party, Sergeant William Wood, Royal Marines, was the first, on 30 April. Aldrich noted: 'The Sergeant Major has just shown me a very ugly-looking red patch or blotch above the ankle; the limb is slightly swollen.' The leg gave him no pain but the redness spread. By May, some of Markham's party were suffering so badly they were almost useless. A camp was made on 12 May and, leaving the cooks to look after the invalids, Markham himself and a small party pushed on northwards. At noon they got a good altitude of the sun and Markham calculated that they were at latitude 83°20'26", 399½ miles from the Pole. Markham's account gives a curiously vivid image of his little party standing utterly alone in a bleak landscape, surrounded by a totally hostile environment, thousands of miles from home. There was a stiff south-westerly wind so their flags and banners fluttered out bravely enough although it was very cold and unpleasant. When Markham announced the altitude, they all gave three cheers, sang 'The Union Jack of Old England', the 'Grand Sledging Chorus', and ended with 'God Save the Queen'. They then went back to camp and were joined by the invalids for a second celebration of whisky and hare, with some cigars to smoke. They ended the day with songs and 'general hilarity'.

They had a very difficult journey back. Gunner George Porter RMA died of scurvy and towards the end only Markham and a handful of men were still on their feet. The rest were incapacitated and being carried on the sledges. *Alert* eventually had thirty-six cases of scurvy on board and at one time her lower-deck resembled a naval hospital. Nares was forced to recast his plans because of the enfeebled state of the crew: they returned early, reaching England on 27 October 1876.

Nares had been leading another scientific venture before going to the Arctic. He had left the *Challenger* at Hong Kong in January 1875 to come home and join *Alert*. *Challenger* was a three-masted, ship-rigged steam corvette of 2,300 tons and 1,200 horsepower. Besides her officers and ship's company of about 240, she also had three naturalists, a chemist, a physicist, and a photographer, led by Professor Wyville Thomson. She was fitted with laboratories, a dark room, a special chartroom and an analysing room, and carried thousands of fathoms of rope and lines of all sizes, weights, thermometers, winches, trawls, dredges and sounding apparatus.

Challenger sailed from Sheerness on 7 December 1872 for an epic voyage of oceanographic and scientific research which took her across the Atlantic several times, to the Pacific and down to Antarctica, and eventually right round the world, before she returned to Spithead on 24 May 1876. She steamed 68,890 miles, set up 362 observing stations, plumbed sea-depths miles deep, and sent home hundreds of specimens. The notes of the voyage filled fifty volumes and took ten years to publish.

Challenger's voyage was a high point in the great and continuing Royal Navy tradition of scientific research. The Arctic voyages were more spectacular, but the ordinary humdrum work of surveying and charting went on all the time. It was unselfish work: the results of the surveys were not kept for private use, but available to all. The brunt of the work fell on the bluejacket who had to spend hours away in small boats, laying buoys, heaving a hand lead-line, hauling up anchors and rowing on to another position, all for a scientific purpose largely incomprehensible to him. Not for him the reward of seeing the pieces of hydrographic data fitting into the larger chart, as though in a satisfying jigsaw puzzle solution; he was not even mentioned in the fifty volumes.

In *Challenger*, the sailors' quarters were necessarily more cramped, to allow for the scientists' rooms and equipment. The discipline did not seem to be harsh but the scrubbing of decks went on: Herbert Swire, one of the ship's officers, noted that decks still had to be scrubbed in a latitude of 50°S when many of the men were suffering from coughs, colds and rheumatism. The mess-decks had no chance to dry in that climate and the sailors suffered severely in spite of warm clothing and hot stoves. As the ship was at sea for long periods, leave was generous. The sailors went ashore to drink in a tea-house in Yokohama, and to get drunk on threepenny porter in the Falkland Islands. Of the 243 who left Sheerness, only 144 returned to Spithead. Seven had died, five had gone with Nares to the Arctic, and twenty-six had been invalided out of the Navy or left behind in hospitals. But sixty-one men deserted, most of them attracted by the gold fields of Australia or the diamond mines of South Africa.

Challenger had one outstanding ship's pet. His name was Robert, a grey parrot whom the naturalist Henry Mosely acquired at Madeira early in the voyage. Robert had something wrong with one of his legs, and his feathers never grew properly, but he was perfectly happy on board, normally perching on a hat-peg in the wardroom, where he braved heat and cold, gales and the roughest seas. Many parrots can talk but Robert was something of a prodigy. He knew his name and could be heard calling 'Robert, Robert' rather plaintively when the furniture was falling about his ears. He could also say, many times, 'What! two thousand fathoms and no bottom? Ah, Doctor Carpenter FRS.'

'Three cheers for the red, white and blue': *the Crimean War*

In the 1850s the Government at last made an attempt to face the long-standing problems of how to man the Navy properly in peacetime, and how to increase the Navy's strength rapidly in wartime without, if possible, resorting to the press gang. It was high time something was done. For most of the 1840s the Navy's manpower had been in a state of chronic imbalance between the number of men available and the number the Navy required at any given time. Sir James Graham's Register had some 175,000 names on it by 1839, with about 22,000 apprentices. In 1852 the figure had dropped to 150,000 but over 50,000 of those were exempt, and in any case not much more than about one man in twenty-five on any of the lists had ever seen service in the Navy. Throughout the 1840s, men were leaving the Navy at the rate of over a thousand a year. *Excellent* had been in existence over twenty years but fewer than 3,000 men had passed through it.

In 1852 Lord Derby's government appointed a committee of naval officers, with Admiral Sir William Parker, home from the Mediterranean, as chairman, to examine the question of recruitment and to report. The committee met after a decade of inefficient naval manning, in which the general position had deteriorated because of the repeal of the navigation laws, the last bastions of protection for British shipping, in 1849. There was also the question of defence against the French who had shown themselves much more energetic and imaginative at sea in the previous decade, concentrating upon steam ships and improving their big gun ammunition, by replacing solid shot with explosive shell. The French caused periodic palpitations in Whitehall. Wellington genuinely believed that Britain was vulnerable to attack at any time, at any state of weather, wind or tide. Palmerston said that steam had thrown 'a passable bridge' across the Channel, over which 20,000 to 30,000 Frenchmen could pour overnight.

When the Manning Committee reported in 1852, Lord Derby's government had fallen and Lord Aberdeen was in power. It was his First Lord, Sir James Graham, and Rear Admiral Berkeley, one of the great reforming figures of the Victorian Navy, as Second Sea Lord, who put the recommendations of the report into effect.

An Order in Council of 1 April 1853 and the Continuous Service Act of the same year embodied the main recommendations of the Committee, which were very largely formulated by the clerk of the committee, C. H. Pennell. The Committee's opinion of the old manning schemes was given in the preamble to the Order, that the old 'desultory mode of proceeding is a cause of great embarrassment and expense in conducting the ordinary duties of the naval service. It creates uncertainty as to the period when ships may be expected to be ready for sea; and the evil becomes one of great magnitude, and a serious danger, when political considerations demand the rapid equipment of Your Majesty's ships.'

From 1 July 1853 all new boy entrants to the Navy engaged for ten years' continuous service, their 'time' to start from the age of eighteen. Boys and seamen already serving were encouraged to transfer to the new continuous service. Standards of entry were tightened up. The chances of promotion from boy to ordinary seaman were improved. The pension was now payable after twenty years from the age of eighteen, instead of the old 1831 period of twenty-one years from the age of twenty. Pay in general was increased, ordinary seamen from £1 6s. 0d to £1 13s. 7d a month, able seamen from £1 14s. 0d to £2 1s. 4d. A new rate of leading seaman carried an extra 2d a day, and senior ratings could go on to become chief petty officers, at an extra 3d a day. Men who had passed the *Excellent* could qualify for warrant gunner, or for 'captains of guns'. There was now paid leave between commissions, sick pay conditions were broadened and improved, and, most important for the older sailors, their right to choose their ship was still preserved. As for discipline, the Act stipulated a more uniform and temperate scale of punishments, urging captains and officers once again to moderate their language and their behaviour, and to employ corporal punishment with more restraint. The 1853 Act laid down, in fact, foundations of the system which is in use in the Navy of today.

The secret was to 'catch them young'. Training brigs had been in commission for many years: they went on training cruises in home waters and did some discreet but useful recruitment. The Committee extended the principle of training afloat. The old two-decker *Illustrious* was established as a training ship for boys at Portsmouth in 1854, followed by the *Implacable* at Devonport a year later. The *Illustrious* was commanded by a very able officer, Captain Robert Harris, who instituted a year's course of seamanship instruction, with some general education. Harris thought so highly of his system that he had his own son do the same course as the boy seamen. This led to officer training afloat and the first course joined in August 1857. The old rank of first class volunteer had been abolished and the rank of naval cadet instituted in 1843. It was soon clear that the training of naval cadets needed special facilities and personnel. By 1858 it was necessary to provide another, larger, ship for officers' training. This was the start of the old *Britannia*.

The new boys, known as 'Jemmy Graham's Novices', grew up in time to prove themselves in the Crimea, China and the Indian Mutiny by the end of the decade. One man who trained in the 'old Guardho' *Illustrious* has left an account of his experiences in *A Sailor Boy's Logbook, from Portsmouth to the Peiho*, published in 1862. He does not give his full name but simply refers to himself as 'John'. He joined in 1855, against the will of his family, who tried hard to dissuade him. But, he said, 'I had devoured *Robinson Crusoe* and not a few books of travel and wild adventure, and thought ploughing the main and seeing foreign countries would suit me much better than learning how to sell locks and hinges, kettles and scythes.' On a very cold winter's day he travelled down to Portsmouth by train. *Illustrious* was moored half a mile from the shore. It was growing dark when he got on board, and nobody about. When the old quartermaster of the watch came up and accosted him, he said he wanted to be a sailor. 'The old fellow chuckled at my answer, as though he said, "Another simpleton caught by a biscuit!" and bade me come below.'

When a lieutenant eventually arrived he asked John if he could read.

Most certainly I could. 'Well, then, look at that,' and he handed me a bill, pasted on a board, stating the advantages of serving one's country in the Royal Navy, scale of wages, provisions, and a list of necessary clothing. I read the bill, and gave it back, telling him I fully understood it: 'Then you'll enter for ten years' continuous service, will you?'

'Yes, sir,' I unhesitatingly answered.

John was given a handkerchief full of 'good sound Clarence-yard biscuit' which he liked much better than the bread he had at home or at school. He was also given a bed and blanket, so he spread the mattress bed on the orlop deck, took two shot from a rack, put his coat and trousers over them for a pillow and slept soundly, except that he awoke once during the night, 'and for a moment forgot that I had left home, till the melancholy rippling of the water against the bends, and the striking of the bell, recalled me to a sense of my new situation and my future prospects'.

He woke to the 'unmelodious pipe' and shouts of 'Rouse out, here! rouse out! Show a leg and a purser's stocking! Rouse and bit: lash away! lash away!' The wash-house was on the main-deck, with forty zinc bowls set out. All hands had a sluice and then wiped themselves on their own towels, if they had them.

After breakfast, which was half a pint of cocoa (very good, John said it was, much better than his *last* cocoa in the Navy which was full of 'horribles'), he was medically examined. The dispensary was a small cabin on the lower deck where the 'man of medicine looked first at my mouth and teeth, then felt the muscles of my arms and legs, telling me to make one step backwards or forwards; then, "Cough, will you? but don't do it in my face. Cough again— again. Were you ever ill? Did you ever break an arm or a leg?" and "Have you been vaccinated?" '

John gives a detailed account of his training syllabus, showing exactly what a seaman of the 1850s was required to know. His 'First Instruction' was three days of elementary knots and hitches, and the proper way to lash up a hammock. 'Second Instruction' was boat pulling, how to dip, toss and feather oars. John was issued with his clothing: one pair of blue cloth trousers, two blue serge frocks, two pair of white duck trousers, two pair of white jumpers, two pair of stockings, two white frocks, three flannels, two caps, one knife, and a marking type, all of which cost £3 10s., including bed and blanket. John's 'shoregoing togs' were made up into a neat bundle. He was offered sixpence for them by a shark from shore, so he gave them away.

After ten days, John went to cutlass drill, in a class of twenty, taught by Jim

Clements, an old marine. He was 'not choice in his expressions when any one blundered'. After three days they went on to rifle drill, how to march and present arms and finally how to aim and fire; they fired at some old stakes in the mud when the tide was out, firing over the ship's quarter in the direction of Porchester Castle, at ranges of about two hundred to two hundred and fifty yards.

'Fourth Instruction' was exercise on the big guns: the different parts of the gun, its weight, the different charges, the uses of the train and side-tackle, and how to dismount a gun. The drill was 'four rounds quick firing, second and third round sponge, load and shift breechings'. John thoroughly enjoyed this drill, which was much better than handling a musket all day.

'Fifth' was more rope work under 'Old Pipes' the bosun: all sorts of splices, short-long, long-short, eye, left-handed, and complicated knots such as 'shroud', 'man rope', 'Matthew Walker' and 'Turk's Head'. After three weeks, they went on to 'Sixth', under a very good-tempered middle-aged seaman who gave them instruction with a model-rigged ship in the schoolroom, to learn the names and uses of all the ropes, and 'such things as putting an eye into a hawser, making sword, thrum, and paunch mats, and turning in a dead eye'. The seventh and last instruction was in handling the lead-line and learning the points of the compass, after which they were passed as boys. They had spent six months under instruction and were now sent to the training brig *Sealark*, which made short cruises in the Channel.

Life was brisker and harder in the *Sealark*. 'I was made a "maintop-gallant-yardman", No. 60, and for a long time my elevation was a source of discomfort. Having to run aloft without shoes was a heavy trial to me, and my feet often were so sore and blistered that I have sat down in the "top" and cried with the pain; yet up I had to go and furl and loose my sails, and up I did go, blisters and all.'

After three months in the brig, John went back to *Illustrious* where he and his mates were now of some real use, given some responsibility, were exempt from all drills, and 'were allowed to improve ourselves in our profession in any way we pleased'.

In December 1855, John joined the steam corvette *Highflyer*, commissioning for the China Station, as a boy first class. He and his mates had been given a good grounding in seamanship. There was no question of their having to 'pick it up as they went along'. Their syllabus had been well thought out and taught by men who knew their business.

The reforms of the 1852 Committee went some way to solving the Navy's manning problem in peacetime, although the committee did not address themselves to the question of wartime manning. All their solutions were overtaken by events when the war in the Crimea broke out in 1854.

In the 1850s, just as in the 1820s, Russia craved Constantinople and in the summer of 1853, without first declaring war, Russian forces occupied the Danubian Principalities, which were then governed by Turkey. The Tsar intended to use these territories as levers to force Turkey to recognise Russia as the protector of the Greek Church in Turkey. The Turks replied with an

'The Naval Brigade at Sebastopol': a late-Victorian painting by
R. Caton Woodville.

ultimatum that the Russians must evacuate the captured territory by 23 October. The day before the ultimatum expired, the British and French governments put pressure on the Tsar by sailing their combined fleets through the Dardanelles, to anchor off Constantinople.

The Tsar retaliated by ordering his Black Sea Fleet to begin operations against the Turks. On 30 November 1853, the Russian Admiral Nachimoff with eight sail of the line bore down on a Turkish squadron of seven frigates, two corvettes, and two steamers, in the Bay of Sinope on the northern coast of Asia Minor. The Russians rounded to, anchored some 500 yards away from their opponents, and opened fire. Two Turkish ships blew up, one ran ashore, and only one, a steamer, survived. It was the first time that incendiary shell had been used in action, and although its actual effect was less than had been expected, a great cry of: 'for God's sake keep out the shell!' went up in naval circles; this undoubtedly hastened the coming of the ironclads.

This so-called 'Massacre of Sinope' had an electric effect upon British and French public opinion. Anti-Russian feeling intensified during the winter and in February 1854 Great Britain and France demanded, on pain of war, that Russia evacuate the Danubian Principalities. The Tsar refused and so, on 13 April, Britain and France declared war on Russia.

The same month Russian troops besieged the town of Silistria on the Danube, but the Allies had complete control of the sea. Steamers bombarded Odessa on 20 April and captured twelve merchant ships. In May Allied troops for the coming offensive began to assemble at Varna, and in June an Austrian army of 50,000 men was massing on the borders of Transylvania. By 23 June the Russians had raised the siege of Silistria and began to evacuate their troops. By September, when there were some 63,000 Allied troops in Varna, the Russians had withdrawn and the ostensible reason for the war had disappeared. The object had been achieved. However, public opinion at home, fanned by a succession of inflammatory articles in *The Times*, demanded the destruction of the Russian fleet and the harbour of Sebastopol which protected it.

The mounting of the expedition was delayed by an epidemic of cholera at Varna. Some ships lost as many as a hundred men and the fleets at one time had to put to sea to get clear of the disease. The 26,000 British, 30,000 French and 7,000 Turkish troops embarked in a huge convoy which set sail in two parts, the French first and the British later, on 7 June 1854. There were eighty-two British troop transports, formed in six columns, in groups of three ships, with two sail being towed by one steamer. The close escort were four ships of the line and twelve frigates, with eight ships of the line and nine frigates as a covering squadron. The French had fifty-two troopers but so many troops had embarked in their eighteen warships that they would have been unable to fight. Fortunately, although the Russians had fourteen ships of the line, seven frigates and eleven steamers at Sebastopol, they made no attempt to molest the convoy, which reached Kalamita Bay, thirty miles north of Sebastopol, on 14 September, and began to disembark the troops. It says a lot for the organising ability of the C-in-C Mediterranean Sir James Dundas, and the dockyard at

Malta, that nearly four hundred boats and launches of all kinds had been assembled for embarking and disembarking the troops. By 18 September the entire force had been safely landed, with rations and supplies for three days.

The march on Sebastopol was begun on 19 September; the next day was fought the battle of the Alma, where a Russian army of nearly 40,000 men was defeated. Now, with the Russians in disarray, was the time to take Sebastopol. Lord Raglan, the British C-in-C, wished to do so. But the French demurred, on the ground that their troops needed rest. The Allied army remained in camp for two more priceless days, while the Navy cleared the battlefield of wounded and embarked them in the ships. By 23 September the Allies had advanced to a point on the heights of the bank of the river Belbek from which the fortress of Sebastopol could be seen. With hindsight, it can now be said that had the Allies attacked then, Sebastopol must have fallen. Instead, a flank march was made to Balaclava, on the southern coast of the Crimean peninsula, which was reached on 26 September. Even now, an attack could have been made, but once again there was delay. It was decided to land the siege trains from the ships. Not until 17 October was a bombardment opened on Sebastopol—later by twenty days, in which the defenders had had time to improve their positions.

Lord Raglan had asked for the assistance of the Navy, and on 1 October the first of the naval brigades mustered and began to land their guns and stores at Balaclava. The total strength was eighteen lieutenants, eighteen mates (midshipmen) and 1,000 seamen, under the command of Captain Lushington of *Albion*. *Britannia, Agamemnon, Albion, Rodney, Queen, Trafalgar, Bellerophon, Vengeance, London* and *Diamond* each provided a contingent. 1,400 marines also landed and encamped on the heights above Balaclava. The men were armed with cutlasses, one man in three having a pistol with ten rounds of ammunition. They each had a change of clothing, a monkey jacket and two blankets, a haversack, and a water-bottle.

The sailors had already been hard at work landing the Allied siege train and stores. They were now called upon to provide extra guns from the ships. Six 32-pounders usually carried on the upper-deck, each weighing about forty hundredweight, were landed from *Britannia, Albion, Queen, Rodney*, and *Trafalgar*. Twenty guns were taken out of *Diamond* (Captain W. Peel) and the ship was secured inside Balaclava harbour and prepared as a hospital ship. 150 rounds of shot and thirty common shell were landed for each gun, with seventy rounds for the field pieces. Four of the *Terrible*'s 68-pounders (each weighing ninety-five hundredweight) and two of the *Beagle*'s Lancaster guns were also landed; later, four more 68-pounders from *Terrible* and six 32-pounders from the other ships were added. By 7 October, the sailors had constructed the first Lancaster Battery ashore, and a second battery, of one Lancaster and four 68-pounders, was ready on the evening of 9 October.

Everyone noticed the sailors' cheerfulness. In those early days of October 1854, wrote Kinglake, 'whilst our soldiery were lying on the ground weary, languid and silent, there used to be heard a strange uproar of men coming nearer and nearer. Soon the comers would prove to be Peel of the *Diamond*, with a number of his sailors, all busy dragging up to the front one of the ship's heavy guns.' The 'sailors used always to find their own way of evolving their strength. This this they would do by speaking to the gun as to a sentient, responsible being, overwhelming it with terms of abuse.' If the sailor had a fault, it was that he was

> too strong. He pulls strong carts to pieces as if they were toys. He piles up shot-cases in the ammunition wagons till the horses fall under the weight, for he cannot understand 'the ship starting till the hold is full'. He takes long pulls and strong pulls at tow ropes till they give like sewing silk; and he is indefatigable in 'rousing' crazy old vehicles up hill, and running full speed with them down hill till they fall to pieces. Many a heap of shot or shell by the roadside marks the scenes of such disasters; but Jack's good humour during this 'spree on short' is inexhaustible, and he comes back for the massive cargo from the camp with the greatest willingness when he is told it must be got up ere nightfall. It is most cheering to meet a set of these jolly fellows 'working up a gun to the camp'. From a distance you hear some rough, hearty English chorus borne on the breeze over the hill-side. As you approach, the strains of an unmistakable Gosport fiddle, mingled with the squeaks of a marine fife, rise up through the unaccustomed vales of the Crimea. A cloud of dust on the ascent marks their coming and tugging up the monster gun in its cradle with 'a stamp and go', strange cries, and oaths sworn by some thirty tars, all flushed with honest exercise.

Having neglected to intercept the troop convoy, the Russians then feebly failed to sally out of Sebastopol harbour and harry Allied shipping. Instead, on 23 September they sank seven of their ships of the line as blockships across the mouth of Sebastopol roads, and used some 18,500 disembarked seamen and all the guns and resources of the fleet as land forces, in defence of the city.

At the request of the army, it was decided (against the advice of Dundas, many of whose guns and men were already ashore with the Naval Brigade) to bombard the fortress of Sebastopol from the sea on 17 October, the attack from the sea being supposed to begin with the opening barrages on land. The allies were constantly bedevilled by the difficulties of a divided command and this showed itself particularly in the deployments for the bombardment. The French, who believed in long-range attack, were allocated forts which had enough water near them to be approached closely; while the British who traditionally preferred close quarters had to attack Fort Constantine, which could not be approached within much less than 1,000 yards because of shoal-water.

The land bombardment began at 6.30 a.m. but for various reasons the first ships were not in position to open fire until 11.00. Twenty-five British, twenty-seven French and two Turkish ships took part, the sailing line-of-battle-ships being towed into action by steamers lashed alongside the port, or disengaged, side. The ships bombarded for nearly six hours but did the forts very little damage. The ships were badly knocked about, with casualties of

'Sebastopol', by Captain M. A. Biddulph.

forty-four British killed and 266 wounded. The French had 212 killed or wounded, the Turks five. Two batteries placed 150 feet up on the cliffs, where the ships' guns could not be elevated enough to reach them, did particular damage with red-hot shot and explosive shells. *Albion* and *Arethusa* were forced to retire to Constantinople to refit. In *Rodney*, Midshipman Kennedy noticed that the upper-deck was unusually clear because so many men and guns had been landed to join the naval brigade. The ship ran aground under fire and was damaged but the steamboats *Spiteful* and *Lynx* very gallantly towed her out of danger. *Sans Pareil* was hit many times by shot and shell and she had eleven killed and fifty-nine wounded; she herself fired between 1,400 and 1,500 rounds in reply. *Britannia* was set on fire, as was the *Agamemnon*, and by the close there were very few ships left undamaged. As Dundas himself said, the bombardment was 'a mere diversion in which an imminent and fatal disaster was risked for little or no adequate advantage'.

The bombardment on shore had also failed to reduce the city and it was becoming clear that Sebastopol could not simply be taken by storm. Both sides were beginning to settle down for what was to be a long and cruel winter. On the Allies' side, the inefficiencies of the campaign planning were showing themselves. The troops had been landed without haversacks, and the tents had been sent back on board the ships when the army set out from the Alma. They were not sent ashore again until 10 October. Several ships laden with haversacks and other stores sailed to Constantinople or even to Marseilles, or went two or three times across the Black Sea, without landing them. The soldiers had no change of clothing, and were on short rations. Cholera was breaking out again in the encampments.

At home, patriotic feeling against the Russians still ran high. A magazine called *The Anti-Russian*, a weekly journal 'for the diffusion of Sound Information regarding the Dangerous Designs of Russia', was published; the first issue appeared on 16 January 1855. Patriotic fervour even permeated *Black-Ey'd Susan*, still running in London with Mr E. L. Davenport as William. Included in the performance was Mr Davenport's rendering of the song 'Britannia the Pride of the Ocean' (The Red, White and Blue), with the chorus:

> Now the grog, boys, the grog, boys, bring hither,
> And fill, fill up true to the brim:
> May the mem'ry of Nelson ne'er wither,
> Nor the star of his glory grow dim.
>
> May the French from the English ne're sever,
> But both to their colours prove true
> This Russian bear they must thrash now or never,
> So three cheers for the Red, White and Blue.

Songs might reflect the patriotic need for Jack Tar to serve his country, but the truth was that the war against Russia revealed the crisis in the Navy's manning. The Russians could be engaged at sea in the Mediterranean, the Baltic, the White Sea and in the Far East. The ships already in the Mediterranean could be moved east to the Black Sea, and operations in the Arctic and the Far East were only peripheral (in the Far East the main event was an abortive and unwise British attack on Petropaulovski, which was made even more difficult by the suicide, just before the attack, of the commanding Admiral, Rear Admiral Price). But the Baltic was a different matter.

For the Baltic, the Navy had to create a fleet out of virtually nothing. In 1853 the Russians were reported to have a fleet in the Gulf of Finland of some twenty-seven sail of the line, besides frigates and smaller vessels, and a large disposable army at St Petersburg. Vice Admiral Charles Napier had warned Lord Aberdeen's government as early as July 1853 of the danger of the situation in the Baltic but nothing was done until the end of the winter when, on 23 February 1854, Napier himself was appointed C-in-C of the Baltic Fleet (although no such fleet existed). He urged Graham to authorise a bounty, to help recruiting. The Government had recently passed a Bill authorising a bounty for all volunteers in time of war, but Graham refused to issue the proclamation: there was a loophole in the Bill's wording, by which all the men already serving could also claim the Bounty at an estimated total cost of half a million pounds. The Navy had to fall back, as in the past, on anybody they could recruit. At Tower Hill, where Rear Admiral Berkeley, the senior Sea Lord, set up a recruiting post, the only volunteers were riff-raff, landsmen who thought they might try a little sea adventure, debtors escaping from their creditors, and criminals or near-criminals.

By March Napier had scraped a fleet together, of eight screw ships of the line, four screw frigates and three paddle sloops. He flew his flag in *Duke of Wellington* (131). The ships were only got to sea through the efforts of a small

Men-of-war's men leaving Portsmouth for the Baltic Fleet, 1854.

nucleus of trained men on board, many of them coastguards. They were elderly, by lower-deck standards. At the first Sunday church service in the *Nile*, 'off caps' revealed many balding heads, and there were a good few pairs of spectacles adjusted. But without these men, the fleet could not have sailed.

The coastguardmen did not react kindly to naval discipline. *Cressy* (81) joined the fleet in a state close to mutiny; already aggrieved at being sent back to sea, the coastguardsmen on board objected to wearing 'pusser's slops'— service issue clothing—instead of the clothes they had brought with them. Napier himself had to come on board to address them. He took the coastguardmen's side.

A second squadron, under Rear Admiral Corry, was assembled in an even more parlous state of manning: 'I warn you,' Napier wrote to Graham, 'to beware that, if accidents happen to us from want of men, it will be no joke.' Almost as an afterthought, he added, 'Be sure you send us powder and shot.'

Napier was accused of being 'defeatist' about his fleet, but misgivings were being expressed on all sides. Graham proposed to reinforce the fleet with men from *Cumberland*, just back from three years on the North American station. He would dispatch her to the Baltic (needless to say, without consulting or informing her officers or men) because 'many of her men would be found qualified for higher ratings, in which case they might be distributed as petty officers amongst the ships in want of them'. Graham and Berkeley both said in Parliament that they were satisfied with the state of affairs, and *The Times* wrote eulogies about the fleet, but privately Berkeley was saying that the Navy had 'come almost to a dead stand as to seamen', and after it was all over admitted that 'we had got to the end of our tether'. The shipowner William Lindsay said: 'The Lord have mercy upon the British Fleet should we again have the world in arms against us!'

On 10 March 1854, the Queen reviewed the Baltic fleet at Spithead in her Royal Yacht, the paddle-steamer *Fairy*. Next day, when the fleet sailed, *Fairy* accompanied them, leading the way as far as St Helens in the Isle of Wight. The Queen, the Prince Consort and members of the Royal Family, somewhat curiously wearing kilts, could be seen standing waving on the *Fairy*'s deck as the cheering ships passed.

The Baltic Medal, 1854–1855.

With Napier that day sailed the new screw liner *St Jean d'Acre*, (101) with Keppel in command. She had commissioned at Devonport in May 1853, when Keppel noted in his diary that there were already 'warlike rumours'. The crew, with officers and men, was 900 strong. Marine artillerymen and seamen gunners joined from *Impregnable*, marine infantrymen from barracks. On 15 June they coaled for the first time, taking five days to embark 509 tons. During steam speed trials the engineers complained about the quality of the coals. *St Jean d'Acre* joined the Channel Squadron under Corry which was to provide the bulk of the Baltic Fleet. In December 1853 they went down to Portugal for a month's cruising off the mouth of the Tagus to 'train newly-raised men'. So not all of Napier's fleet consisted of raw or elderly men. By the time war broke out, *St Jean d'Acre* (and other ships such as the screw corvette *Amphion*, with Cooper Key in command) had been in commission for a year and were reasonably well worked up.

The fleet was short of warm clothing, ammunition, and competent Baltic pilots. When eight Baltic pilots did arrive, they were seen to be a 'rough lot, with huge pipes, wearing sealskin caps and waistcoats'. Keppel said that his pilot was on board for nine months at *fifteen shillings a day* and was eventually landed in the Downs in December 1854 without having been of the slightest use.

At Vinga Sound Napier left the fleet and went on to Copenhagen, returning on 19 March, Keppel noted, 'bringing lots of cherry brandy'. On 23 March the fleet sailed for the Great Belt and anchored in Kioga Bay where, on 4 April, Napier made his rousing signal. 'Lads! war is declared, with a bold and numerous enemy to meet. Should they offer us battle, you know how to dispose of them. Should they remain in port we must try and get at them. Success depends on the precision and quickness of your firing. Lads! sharpen your cutlasses, and the day is your own!'

Napier was still the most charismatic of all the Navy's admirals. He was the hero of the Syrian War and all the earlier deeds of valour going back to the French war. He was sixty-eight, although that was not old by the standards of the Navy of the time, with a slouching slovenly gait, a lame foot, a large round face, black bushy eyebrows, and thinning hair. His double chin, his ugly old shoes, his trousers hoisted above his ankles, and above all, his waistcoat front perpetually snuff-stained, were well-known. He was extraordinarily popular, and many ballads were sung about him, with titles such as 'Bold Napier', 'We're off to the Baltic with Charley Napeer', 'Give it to him, Charley', and 'I am Baltic Charley and no mistake'. Specially composed pianoforte pieces, such as the Baltic and Napier Polkas, were sold in sheet music form. His quarrel with Sir James Graham also found its way into ballads:

> Now Jemmy, you shall see by-and-by
> I will make you open your weather eye
> And like a pig for quarters cry
>   For insulting Baltic Charley.
> Boatswain's mate, come quickly, jump,
> Seize old Jemmy up to the pump,
> And give him a dozen over the rump
>   To the tune of Baltic Charley.

In spite of the ballads, Napier was not the dashing force he had been. His orders, too, were cautiously phrased. He was not to allow any Russian ship of war to slip past him into the North Sea, but he was not to run his head against any stone walls, or stone forts, either. In any case the Russians preferred to stay inside their fortresses at Sveaborg and Kronstadt, and refused battle. As summer went on, there was a general air of disappointment in the country about the Baltic campaign, and Napier himself was criticised in Parliament. It is difficult to see what else he could have done. To take his ships inshore to attack heavily defended forts would have been extremely dangerous. Tactically, therefore, the most noteworthy actions were planned and carried out by individual commanders in single ships or small squadrons. Nevertheless, the

Baltic Fleet tied up a very large standing Russian army in the north and had an immeasurably important strategic effect.

Patriotic ballads may have reflected the feelings of voters and taxpayers, but many of the sailors' feelings were more accurately expressed in a bitterly resigned little poem by William Pegg called 'On leaving for the Baltic Squadron, April 1854':

> So into war they drag us, willy nilly,
> Oh! I've no patience with 'em—they're so silly,
> Bringing upon us such expense and trouble,
> Already there's the Income Tax made double:
> No hides—our boots and shoes will soon be frightful,
> Oh! I declare it makes me feel quite spiteful:
> Our pitch and tar will be dear as leather,
> Tar?—Yes I'd tar him—that old Czar—and feather!
> From being feathered, guards and gates may bar him
> But let Jack Tar pitch into him, he'll tar him
> Oh the abominable nasty Bruin,
> I hope and trust we're paying for his ruin.

Meanwhile, in the Crimea both sides were settling down to a war which was to be much longer than either had expected. On 26 October the Russians made a very determined sortie against the Allied positions, which the Naval Brigade helped to repulse, and on 5 November the battle of Inkerman was fought. Some six hundred sailors fought in the field, the rest manning the gun batteries. At Inkerman and in the actions leading up to it, the naval brigade suffered many casualties. William Russell of *The Times* wrote that the 'Sailors' brigade suffered very severely; although they worked about thirty-five guns in the various batteries, they lost more men than all our siege train, working and covering parties put together'.

All observers noticed Jack's excellence as a campaigner and his extraordinary, almost touching, sense of propriety under stress. Evelyn Wood, later a field marshal and a VC, but then a midshipman in *Queen* and serving with the naval brigade, lent a handkerchief to Able Seaman Simmons of *Diamond*, to tie up a dangerous wound in his thigh. When Simmons returned to the battery six months later he brought the handkerchief and gave it back to Wood, with many thanks for the loan.

The Crimean winter was very severe and its effects were doubly harsh upon the troops in the trenches because of the general lack of transport, roads, storehouses and equipment of all kinds. The naval brigade did not suffer as badly as the soldiers: their tents were in more sheltered positions, and the sailors were able to return for twenty-four hours' rest on board the ships, with comparatively good food, after every four days in the batteries. Their officers, such as Captain Peel, paid special attention to sanitation, cooking facilities in trenches, warm clothing, the use of sails and tarpaulins for waterproof shelters, and rotation of duties through a strict watch bill. Every sailor could look forward to regular relief and a chance to eat properly, warm himself and change into dry clothes. But even for them, the campaign was terribly hard. On the night of 14 November a violent storm blew from the south-west. Tents and bedding were whirled away in the gale. The countryside became a muddy morass, ravines were filled with raging torrents of water, waist-deep. Twenty-one storeships in or waiting to enter Balaclava were lost. The most unfortunate loss was the 7,000-ton storeship *Prince* loaded with medical stores, food, 35,700 woollen socks, 53,000 woollen frocks, 17,000 flannel drawers, 2,500 watch coats, 16,100 blankets and 3,700 rugs. The warships lying off Katcha were on a leeshore but none was lost, although the seas running were so great that line-of-battle-ships were pitching their bows under, with their rudders out of the water and their anchor cables tautening and stringing up into view for many fathoms ahead. One heavy sea shipped over *Rodney*'s bows, swept her upper-deck clean and flooded the captain's cabin aft. Of the storeships which parted their cables and were driven ashore, all were lost except the *Lord Raglan*, whose master kept his wits about him. He ordered the main and mizzen masts cut away, so that the remaining foremast acted as a kind of sail and pulled the ship round so that she flew before the wind. The master steered for a sandy beach and drove his ship up high and dry and safe, instead of slewing broadside on like the others. She was successfully pulled off a month later. The paddle-wheel frigate *Samson* was steaming ahead to her anchors, when she was hit by two storeships and dismasted. She held on, while the other two disengaged and drove ashore. A few days after the gale had died down the *Ganges* transport caught fire at her anchorage and blew up. To acts of God were added the inefficiencies of man. One ship arrived from Varna with her upper-deck piled with cabbages but the authorities had forgotten to address them to anyone in particular. Nobody was willing to take the responsibility for them so they eventually went rotten and were thrown overboard.

All the sailing ships were sent home for the winter except *Rodney* and *Vengeance* who were moored head and stern in a creek where they acted as 'rest centres' and living accommodation for men out of the trenches. The weather was bitterly cold, with snow falling several feet deep over the battlefront. Evelyn Wood went to sleep at about eight o'clock one evening in December in the sailors' battery, when it was freezing hard. At daylight he was literally frozen stiff and he had to be carried back to camp and revived with hot-water bottles packed around him. One morning Captain Lushington ran to help a soldier he saw come staggering out of the trenches, but the man fell dead before he could reach him. His heart had given out under the cold and the exhaustion.

The battlefield was a mass of frozen mud, shell holes, wrecked huts and fortifications, and dead animals. When Keppel arrived he found his way to the naval encampment by using the trail of dead horses as signposts. *St Jean d'Acre* arrived off Balaclava in the early hours of 30 January 1855. She had sailed from Cork with 645 troops, drafts of different regiments for the Crimea. During the passage the Irishmen amongst the recruits ate half a ton of raw turnips which had been brought on board to feed the Southdown sheep Keppel took with him.

The health of the bluejackets was in general very good, much better than the soldiers who seemed less able to look after themselves, poorer improvisers, poorer *scroungers* than Jolly Jack. But in March there was an outbreak of smallpox amongst the naval brigade. Keppel had his midshipmen and youngsters vaccinated. On 4 April there were thirty-nine smallpox cases and Keppel went ashore to visit them. A small site had been selected on Kazatch, a small uninhabited island, two houses were erected, yellow flags hoisted and a 'regular lazaretto established'. It was airy and clean, and Keppel was pleased with it, but the smallpox room was 'a trial'. He had got the sailors' names beforehand and he tried to say something consoling to each of them. 'Their heads were swollen into the shape and appearance of huge plum-puddings; eyes closed—their mothers would not have recognised them.' All they could do was to move their heads slightly to show that they were pleased to have a visitor. Keppel had the ship's band landed to play to them.

In April the battle flared up again. On 11 April a fresh contingent of one lieutenant, two midshipmen and 200 bluejackets, most of them from *Rodney*, were landed as reinforcements. Captain Peel was wounded, and Keppel noted that 'seventy-six seamen were *hors de combat* and Lord Raglan asking for more. They are decidedly the best shots, but take no care of themselves.' Many of the sailors' casualties in action were caused by failure to take proper precautions. The ordinary bluejacket seemed to think it beneath his dignity to shelter behind a stone defence for the Russians or anybody else. Stray shots wounded many a sailor who should have been taking proper cover.

The sailors were capable of incredible stoicism in action. On 8 April Evelyn Wood was in command of an 8-inch gun, with one of *Queen*'s able seamen, Michael Hardy, as 'No. 1' on the gun. Another member of the crew, Boy First Class Charles Green, also of *Queen*, was just drinking a pannikin of grog which had been served to the crews at the guns, when a shot from the Redan took his head clean off. Michael Hardy was at that moment 'serving the vent', which meant sealing the gun's vent with his thumb, to stop stray currents of air entering the barrel. The gun-barrel was hot, and air might cause sparks which would ignite the fresh cartridge just being loaded.

Hardy had turned up his sleeves and trousers, and his shirt being open low on the neck and chest, his face and body were covered with the contents of the boy's head. Now, if he had lifted his thumb from the vent the results might have been fatal to Nos. 3 and 4, who were then ramming home the next charge; but Hardy never flinched. Without moving his right hand, he wiped with his left the boy's brains from his face. Those sitting at my feet were speechless, being startled, as indeed I was, for I had felt the wind from the Russian shot which had passed within an inch of my face. We were brought back to a sense of duty by Hardy's somewhat contemptuous, 'You —— fools, what the hell are you looking at? Is he dead? Take his carcass away. Ain't he dead?

Take him to the doctor. Jim, are you ar home?' he asked of No. 3 the Loader, who was in the act of giving the final tap, after having rammed home the charge, and seeing him nod, without bestowing another look on us, or possibly even thinking of me, he gave the order, 'Run out. Ready.'

As always, the only thing that could upset the sailor was a bad officer. On 3 February, Wood was given charge of a party of 150 seamen who had turned sulky and, just as they were dragging some guns to the Left Attack trenches, dropped the drag-ropes and returned to camp. They were employed 'Watch and Watch'—four hours on, four hours off—for a week as punishment. They were then, in Wood's word, 'forgiven'. It was all due, he said, to 'injudicious treatment by the officers'.

At dawn on 18 June, the anniversary of Waterloo, the guns of the British batteries opened a two-hour bombardment. An attempt was to be made to storm the strongpoint of the Redan, on the outskirts of Sebastopol fortress. The Russian batteries replied with shot for shot, shell for shell. When the barrage lifted the valley between the guns was shrouded in a thick fog. Presently, the firing slackened and eventually stopped. Midshipman Kennedy was watching from the sailors' battery.

By degrees the fog lifted when, to our intense sorrow, we discovered that our people had been repulsed. There was the Redan looking as grim as ever, its slopes dotted with many a redcoat, with here and there a bluejacket beside him, the sailors having been told off to carry the scaling-ladders. At 8.00 a.m. we returned to camp to learn the melancholy news. About ten officers and sixty of our bluejackets were killed and wounded. I saw the last of a fine young fellow, Lieutenant Kidd: he was shot through the lungs, and lived for an hour after we carried him to his tent. The *Rodney* had suffered severely, several of our best men being killed with the scaling-ladders, and also in the trenches. One of our guns burst in the battery, killing every man at the gun. The captain of the gun lay dead at his post, and round about were the mangled and blackened corpses of his crew.

Evelyn Wood's charmed life continued. He was with the scaling parties and when a sailor was killed, took his place on the ladder. By the time they got to the wall there were only three of them left.

The man in front was only a few years older than myself, an Ordinary seaman, but he had shown no other feeling than the desire to be first up. I had not carried it far when the man alongside of me was killed, and then the Ordinary seaman in front, feeling no doubt that he was bearing an undue share of the weight, not knowing I was under the ladder, turning his head as far as he could, addressed me as his messmate. 'Come along, Bill; let's get our beggar up first.' Before he recognised me, while his face was still turned backwards, he was killed, and with him tumbled the ladder.

Staffordshire pottery of the 1850s: 'The Wounded Soldier' is
helped by a sailor friend, while 'The Rammers' depicts two
sailors manning a gun during the Crimean War.

The sailors' assault on the Redan was watched with admiration by a soldier
of the Greenjackets who wrote home that half of his own company were killed
or wounded, 'and I am sorry to state, a number of the sailors were killed. God
bless them! They are England's bravest men.' He added that 'the Jack Tars are
curious animals in camp'. Keppel took over the command of the naval brigade
in July 1855 and he, too, wrote in a letter:

> Find our Jacks queer fellows; they deal in horses or anything else, and as
> soon as they come out of the trenches they are all over the soldiers'
> camps, doing work for the officers, repairing tents and that sort of thing,
> receiving part payment in grog, and then share it with the first 'soger'
> they meet.
>
> I avoid too many restrictions, as long as men appear at the 10 a.m.
> muster, properly dressed, with their arms cleaned and correct, with
> correct numbers of the men and battery they have to relieve. They are
> then dismissed, and find their own way by trenches or over the open. In
> a body they are pretty sure to draw the enemy's fire.

It was not only in a body that the sailors drew the enemy fire. They positively invited it. One army officer noticed 'a recklessness about the seaman's courage. For instance, whenever a particularly effective shot issued from one of their embrasures, the tars would leap *en masse* upon the parapet, wave the Union Jack and cheer like devils. A defiance that had the effect of bringing upon the brave but thoughtless fellows, an augmented dose of iron.'

In the Crimea the Navy experienced, very probably for the first time in its history, the attentions of the accredited war correspondent. An artist for the *Illustrated Times*, who gave his piece the by-line '*Walmer Castle*, Balaclava Harbour, 18 August 1855', described a visit made to the 21-gun battery manned by the sailors. It was a day when according to the sailors, 'the Rooshians must have had a fresh stock of ammunition in', because they were returning fire more freely than usual. The reporter, writing when things were fresh in his mind, noted that the sailors were much more circumspect under fire than later, perhaps legendary, accounts suggested. 'The moment a shot is seen to leave the Russians there is a cry to look out and when a shell is seen whizzing through the air, the cry is "look out a mortar" and everybody not only gets out of the way of the direct line of fire but stops behind any object in the way or if the shell is very near, falls on his face.'

After the deplorable muddles of the first winter, the Allies did succeed in organising some measure of logistical efficiency out of the chaos in the spring. The Allies had the advantage of communications. There were very few roads in Russia and no railways. The main routes to the Crimea were down the great rivers, Dnieper and Bug to the Black Sea, and the Don to the Sea of Azov. The Navy successfully transported a Sardinian army to the Crimea and a Turkish army across the Black Sea. In May 1855 a squadron was sent to seize the Straits of Kertsch and to operate in the Sea of Azov.

On 16 August 1855 was fought the battle of Tchernaya, the last attempt by the Russian field army to break the Allies' grip on Sebastopol. It failed, and on 5 September the final bombardment of Sebastopol began. On 8 September the French at last took the great Malakoff Redoubt. The Russians evacuated Sebastopol and withdrew to the north side of the harbour. The naval brigade were re-embarked at the end of September. The fleet sailed to bombard the fortresses at Kinburn, on the estuaries of the Dnieper and Bug. Troops were landed virtually unopposed on 16 October. Gunfire from ships of the line, gunboats, mortar vessels and three French armoured monitors, reduced the defending forts to ruins. The French monitors lay only 800 yards off the forts for six hours without sustaining any damage, and had a dramatic effect on naval thinking, seeming to show that armour could defeat the gun.

After the operations at Kinburn there was a pause. The forts were never used in anger. In January 1856, there came the Armistice.

The most accurate reflection of the sailor's view of the Crimean War was recorded by John C. Sabbens, surgeon of *Sphinx* from 1854 to 1857. In his diary he notes several examples of lower-deck verse, such as 'Sing a Song of Mockery, a Fleet without a Foe'. The most biting commentary is called 'Cui Bono? or, The Fleet's Statistics'. 'Two hundred and forty-three ships, 3,172 guns, and 32,810 men, compass this mighty armament':

> Two hundred and forty-three vessels of war!
> What did we build this big fleet for?
> To go to the Black and the Baltic main
> And what did it do? It came back again!
> Three thousand, one hundred and seventy-two.
> What in God's name did these great guns do?
> Oh, they drilled with shot, and they practised with shell,
> And saluted on Wednesday wonderfully well.
> Thirty-two thousand, eight hundred and ten!
> What have they done—all those Englishmen?
> They pottered at Sveaborg and fished in Azoff
> And can man their yards without tumbling off.

The last line glosses over the high casualty rate of falls from aloft in the fleet, but the meaning of the whole verse is plain enough.

In the Crimea, the Naval Brigade had an average strength of about 1,200 men. Eight officers were killed or died of wounds, another three died of disease and forty were wounded. Of the men, 116 were killed or died of wounds, forty-one died of disease and 431 were wounded. Their graves lay on the bleak hillside above Balaclava, some marked with stone but the majority with wooden crosses, commemorating the men of *Queen, London, Wasp, Albion* and *Leander*. One in marble, behind the 21-gun battery of the Right Attack where the sailors fought for so long, was 'Sacred to the Memory of Many British Artillerymen, Seamen, & Sappers who were Killed near this spot and buried here during the siege of Sebastopol A.D.1854 and 1855'. The memorials survived until most of them were destroyed in the battles of another siege of Sebastopol, when the German XI Army took the city in July 1942.

At home, Captain Lushington persuaded the directors of the Kensal Green Cemetery in London to donate the site for a memorial to the Naval Brigade. Dedicated in 1858, it was made of white Carrara marble; on its top, carved in solid marble, were representations of the men's tents, and on the front was a group of flags, with a broken cannon. The sides of the monument were made to represent broken masts, with the names of the ships who took part inscribed on them. With the names of officers and men who died was the inscription: 'To the Memory of the undermentioned officers and men of the Royal Naval Brigade, who fell at the siege of Sebastopol A.D. 1854 and 1855, this is erected by the surviving officers'; and a text from Isaiah 43:5–6: 'Fear not: for I am with thee. I will bring thy seed from the east and gather thee from the west. I will say unto the north, Give up; and to the south, Keep not back; bring my sons from afar and my daughters from the ends of the earth.' Ironically, this monument too survived until a Luftwaffe land-mine in 1941 destroyed the memorial chambers in which it was housed.

The Victoria Cross

'Among the various changes introduced since the Peace,' wrote John Bechervaise, 'for the benefit of the seamen of the Royal Navy, there is not one that has been so useful, or tended to so much good, as the medal and gratuity money, given for long service and good conduct.' The medal was introduced in 1831, having a dark blue ribbon, an effigy of William IV, and a ship on the reverse. It was changed in 1848 to a blue and white ribbon, with the sovereign's head, and a full-rigged ship on the reverse—the same design used today.

Campaign medals were also struck. There was one for the Burma War of 1824–6, with on the obverse an attacking party advancing towards a pagoda, Sir Colin Campbell directing operations underneath a palm tree in the foreground, and a steamer in the left background. The reverse had a white elephant of Ava, kneeling before a victorious lion. Ashcroft got a medal for the China War, with a crimson and yellow ribbon, an effigy of Victoria, and a palm tree, an oval shield with the Royal Arms, a trophy of weapons and the motto *Armis Exposcere Pacem* ('Vehemently to entreat Peace by the use of Force', a succinct statement of British foreign policy at the time).

Medals were struck for the Baltic, 1854–5, and for the Crimea, 1854–6, with the bars of 'Sebastopol', 'Alma', 'Balaclava', 'Inkermann' and 'Azoff'. Both had blue and yellow ribbons. The reverse of the Crimea medal showed Victory crowning with laurel a Roman warrior, while the Baltic medal had Britannia seated holding a trident before the fortress of Bomarsund on one side and Fort Sveaborg on the other.

For some time, Queen Victoria had herself been thinking of a new medal. It was to be named after her, and to be awarded for acts of extreme gallantry in action. It was to be open to all ranks, and take precedence above any other order of chivalry. The Queen herself chose the design of the medal, a cross *patté* in bronze, showing a crown surmounted by a lion and the motto 'For Valour'. The ribbon was crimson for Army winners, blue for the Navy. The medal, the Victoria Cross, was first instituted by Royal Warrant on 29 January 1856, and the first awards announced in the *London Gazette* of 5 February 1856. The awards were made retrospectively, based upon recommendations in the dispatches of the campaign.

The heroic act for which the first Victoria Cross was awarded happened during Napier's campaign in the Baltic in 1854. In June, Captain Hall of the sloop *Hecla*, with *Valorous* (Captain Buckle) and *Odin* (Captain Scott) reconnoitred the defences of the fortress of Bomarsund, in the Aland Islands, in the Gulf of Bothnia. At 4.30 p.m. on the afternoon of 21 June, the three ships entered the channel of the Ango Sound, leading to Bomarsund. They had Finnish pilots on board, because it was a difficult passage. Not only were there the dangers of red-hot shot and rifle fire from shore, but the channel itself was only one to two cables (two to four hundred yards) wide and only five fathoms deep at the most.

The ships fired on the woods along the bank as they went, to prevent surprise by riflemen. At about 5.35 the largest shore battery, which Hall described as 'a casemated battery of two tiers, mounting between 70 and 80 guns', returned the ships' fire and a live shell landed on *Hecla*'s upper-deck. With great coolness and bravery, a nineteen year old mate, Charles Lucas, picked up the shell and threw it overboard, where it detonated. He saved the ship considerable damage and many casualties, and was promoted lieutenant on the spot. He was also mentioned in Hall's and Napier's dispatches, and awarded the first Victoria Cross. Lucas, an Irishman from County Armagh, married Captain Hall's daughter, became a rear admiral and died a few days after the opening of the 1914–18 War. (The Royal Humane Society also awarded Lucas their medal—a curious award, since he was engaged upon destroying life at the time.)

Captain Hall was not so honoured. Although Sir James Graham praised the action in Parliament, privately he wrote a strong letter of protest to Napier, as did Admiral Berkeley. Hall reported that the shore forts were ablaze and must have suffered greatly, and that large bodies of riflemen and horsemen had been dispersed, but in fact his bombardment had risked his ships to achieve very little. Hall might write about 'the awfully grand appearance of the flames' when his squadron left, but the fact was that his squadron had used all their ammunition and could get no more until it could be sent out from England. Five men had been wounded and the ships had been damaged. All *Hecla*'s boats were unserviceable. The action had a welcome propaganda value at home, showing that Napier's ships were not totally idle, but it did prove once more that in general it was not wise to take ships close inshore to attack forts. Admiral Chads, a notable gunnery officer, carried out a second and rather similar attack at the same place in August and the lesson was relearned.

The earliest act by a sailor to gain the Victoria Cross was performed by a man almost certainly not a British national, who was not a seaman or gunner but a stoker. In June 1854 the paddle-steamer *Porcupine* was dispatched to Stockholm to enter any able-bodied Swedes or Norwegians who wanted to volunteer for the fleet. ('Try and recruit Scandinavians,' was the advice that Graham had given Napier.) One of them so recruited could have been Stoker William Johnstone, of HMS *Arrogant* (Captain Yelverton). Some mystery surrounds him. There was no William Johnstone on the ship's books of *Arrogant* or any other ship at the time. There was a Leading Stoker John Johnstone, in *Arrogant*, who was born in Hanover, Germany. His age was given as thirty-two, and he had seven years' service in at the time, and one good conduct badge.

In August 1854 the fleet lay off Wardo Island in the Baltic. On 7 August Captain Yelverton returned from a visit to Napier and remarked to the officer of the watch in *Arrogant* that the admiral had learned that important despatches from the Tsar were being landed at Wardo and then forwarded to the commanding officer at Bomarsund. The admiral had said he was surprised that nobody had sufficient enterprise to put an end to this traffic.

The officer of the watch, Lieutenant John Bythesea, went down to the ship's office after his watch was over and enquired if anybody in the ship's company spoke Swedish. He was told that Stoker William Johnstone did, because he was a Swede by birth. Bythesea suggested to Yelverton that he and Johnstone land ashore and intercept the Russian mails. Yelverton was doubtful about sending only two men on such a mission, but he was persuaded that a larger party would be more liable to attract attention.

The Victoria Cross: the Naval ribbon was blue, and the Army ribbon red

On 9 August, Bythesea and Johnstone rowed themselves ashore to a small bay, and walked to a nearby farmhouse, where Johnstone got into conversation with the farmer. All his horses had been 'hired' by the Russians and he was only too glad to give information. He said that the mails were so important and were delivered so regularly that the Russians had just improved nine miles of road to carry them. He gave his visitors food and lodging and when a Russian patrol called at the farm, his daughter successfully dressed Bythesea and Johnstone as Finnish peasants.

On the morning of 12 August, Bythesea learned that the mails were to be landed and passed to Bomarsund that night. He had reconnoitred the route thoroughly beforehand, and by midnight he and Johnstone were in position to ambush the Russian mail as it was brought ashore. Unknowingly, he had chosen a hiding place also used by the Russians and, with a touch of comic opera, at one moment Bythesea found himself only an elbow's length away from an unsuspecting Russian courier. Bythesea and Johnstone drew their pistols and challenged the Russians, whereupon two of the carriers dropped their mailbags and ran. The other three were captured, and taken down to their own boat. Bythesea made the prisoners row the boat back to *Arrogant*.

Just as the party embarked, a Russian patrol came down the road, looking for the mails. They saw nothing and went away, singing, to report that all was well. The mails and despatches were taken to Admiral Napier.

For this extraordinary 'cloak and dagger' affair, Bythesea and Johnstone were both awarded the Victoria Cross. It was so extraordinary that one senior French officer, General Baraguay d'Hilliers, would not believe what he had been told until he actually had the captured despatches in his hands. Even today, the story is difficult to believe.

Of the nineteen Victoria Crosses won at the battle of Inkerman, the Navy gained six and the Royal Marines one. One of the winners, Acting Mate William Hewett of HMS *Beagle*, had already distinguished himself a few days earlier, on 26 October, when the Russians attacked the Right Lancaster Battery where Hewett commanded a gun crew. Hewett disbelieved, and consequently disobeyed, an order to spike the gun and retreat, saying that Lushington could never have given such an order. Instead Hewett trained the gun round and drove the Russians off with grape and 68-lb solid shot. He was also recommended for his gallantry during the battle of Inkerman and was awarded the Victoria Cross for his behaviour on both days.

Another Victoria Cross awarded to a naval officer was actually won three times. Captain William Peel, of HMS *Diamond*, third son of Sir Robert Peel, was one of the most talented and brave men who ever served in the Navy. On 18 October, when the Naval Brigade were in the trenches before Sebastopol, Peel took up a live shell which had just landed outside a powder magazine and threw it over the parapet. It actually exploded as it left his hands, but nobody was injured. At Inkerman, Peel joined the officers of the Grenadier Guards and helped them to defend their regimental colours at a time when they were hard pressed. At the assault on the Redan in June 1855 Peel led the first scaling party to the foot of the wall where he was hit and severely wounded in the arm. He was led back, half-fainting from loss of blood, by his aide-de-camp Midshipman Daniel who, according to Evelyn Wood, also Peel's aide-de-camp, was the only one of seven naval officers in the assault unwounded. Wood himself was wounded in the arm by a musket ball which struck his sword from his hand and twisted the blade.

Peel recommended both his young midshipmen for the Victoria Cross but only Daniel was awarded it (Wood's VC came later during the Indian Mutiny, when he had transferred to the army). Like Peel himself, Daniel was decorated for three separate actions: for volunteering to bring in powder to Peel's battery from a wagon in a very exposed position under destructive fire, for his general behaviour as Peel's aide-de-camp at Inkerman, and for accompanying Peel and applying a tourniquet to his arm during the assault on the Redan, while both were under heavy fire.

The Russians' great effort to take the commanding heights of land above Sebastopol failed at Inkerman, after a day of heavy fighting. For the marines from the fleet, attached to the Light Infantry Division near the Lancaster Battery, it was a day of fog, smoke and confusion, of unexplained firing heard in front and in the rear, of contradictory orders, first to advance and then to hold their position. At one point the marines came under accurate fire from a frigate in Sebastopol harbour and from Russian snipers hidden in caves. A platoon under Sergeant Richards and Corporal Prettyjohns, of HMS *Bellerophon*, moved out to clear the caves. In doing so they exhausted almost all their ammunition, and then found fresh parties of Russians creeping up the hillside toward them in single file. According to a marine who was there, Corporal Prettyjohns, 'a muscular West Countryman', said, 'Well, lads, we are just in for a warming, and it will be every man for himself in a few minutes. Look alive my hearties, and collect all the stones handy, and pile them on the ridge in front of you. When I grip the front man you let go the biggest stones upon those fellows behind.' When the first Russian appeared on the level ground in front of them, Prettyjohns seized him in a wrestler's grasp, 'gave him a Westcountry buttock' and threw him down the slope. The other Russians were knocked over by a shower of stones. 'We gave them a parting volley and retired out of sight to load ; they made off and left us, although there was sufficient to have eaten us up.' Corporal Prettyjohns was awarded the Victoria Cross, but Sergeant Richards, according to the account, got nothing. Another NCO, Colour Sergeant Jordan, got a medal for distinguished conduct in the field, and a pension of £20 per annum.

During the battle of Inkerman, the Russians made a very determined attack upon the Right Lancaster Battery, where many of the soldiers were killed or wounded. Five members of the Naval Brigade were there and, as one of them said, he 'wouldn't trust any Ivan getting within bayonet range of the British wounded', so the five sailors mounted the banquette (defence works) and kept up a 'rapid repulsing fire'. The wounded soldiers, lying in the trenches, reloaded the Minie rifles and passed them up to the sailors, until eventually the Russians 'fell back and gave no more trouble'. Two of the sailors were killed by the withering enemy fire which constantly swept the top of the parapet but the remaining three, James Gorman, Mark Scholefield and Thomas Reeves, all from HMS *Albion*, survived to be mentioned in Lushington's despatches and, in February 1857, gazetted for the Victoria Cross.

At that time there could be no posthumous awards of the VC; the other two sailors who were killed got no mention and are now forgotten. There must have been scores of heroic actions well worth a posthumous VC. One such 'Divine-like act of self-sacrifice' was described by Evelyn Wood.

On 3 June 1855, some sailors were going down to the battery to relieve others and, ignoring safety regulations, were walking in the open instead of by the covered way. Suddenly the sound of an enormous shell, known as a 'Whistling Dick', was heard and everyone ran to take cover. They all reached the safety of the trench except John Blewitt of *Queen*.

Blewitt, as he bent forward to run, was struck immediately at the back of the knees by the mass of iron, 13 inches in diameter, and fell to the ground crushed under its weight, in sight of his horror-stricken messmates. He called out to his chum, Stephen Welch, 'Oh, Stephen, Stephen, don't leave me to die !' The fuse was hissing, but Welch,

A special Victoria Cross supplement was included in the *Illustrated London News* in June 1857

CECIL W. BUCKLEY (COMM.) AND HENRY COOPER (BOATSWAIN) FIRING THE RUSSIAN STORES AT GENITCHI.

THOS. REEVE, JAS GORMAN, AND MARK SCHOLEFIELD, BRING ON AN ATTACK WITH THE GUNS OF THE DISABLED SOLDIERS AT INKERMAN.

R. J. LINDSAY (BREVET MAJOR) AT THE BATTLE OF THE ALMA.

THOMAS WILKINSON, R.M.A., PLACING SAND BAGS TO REPAIR DAMAGES, UNDER A GALLING FIRE.

LUKE CONNOR, (LIEUT.) WHEN SERGEANT, TAKING THE COLORS FROM LIEUT. ANSTRUTHER, AND THOUGH SEVERELY WOUNDED, CARRYING THEM, TO THE END OF THE DAY AT ALMA.

WILLIAM PEEL, (CAPTAIN,) THROWING A LIVE SHELL OVER THE PARAPET

HONOUR TO THE BRAVE

jumping up from under cover of the edge of the trench which must, humanly speaking, have ensured his safety, called out, 'Come on, lads; let's try,' and running out, he had got his arms round Blewitt, and was trying to roll the shell from off his legs when it exploded, and not a particle of the bodies or of the clothes of the two men could be found.

The Naval Brigade won another Victoria Cross in the spring of 1855. The winner was Bosun's Mate John Sullivan, of HMS *Rodney*. Like a very high proportion of *Rodney*'s ship's company at the time, Sullivan was an Irishman, born in Bantry, Co. Cork, in April 1830. In the Naval Brigade he was captain of the crew of one of *Terrible*'s 68-pounders and he had already distinguished himself in action: his gun was credited with making the first breach in the Malakoff redoubt, and with blowing up an important magazine at the start of the siege of Sebastopol. He and his crew were noticed by Lushington and were transferred to No. 5 Greenhill Battery, where on 10 April 1855 a volunteer was called for to go forward and place a flagstaff on a mound, to act as an aiming point for some troublesome Russian guns which were concealed from the direct view of the sailor's battery.

As captain of the gun, Sullivan considered it was his duty to go. Although he was in plain sight of the enemy and under constant fire when he reached the mound, Sullivan took his time, looking carefully both ways to make sure that he was on the straight line between the naval guns and the target. Reassured that he was, he scraped a hole with his hands, planted the flagstaff and collected stones and earth to bank it up securely. The Russian snipers had seen him and the bullets were whistling around him, but he gave the flagstaff a final shake to test its firmness before coming back to shelter. His bravery was reported by Commander Kennedy, who observed that Sullivan's 'gallantry was always conspicuous'. He was mentioned in Admiral Lord Lyons's despatches and gazetted for the Victoria Cross on 24 February, 1857.

The assault parties attacking the Redan on 18 June suffered terrible casualties. The attackers were exposed to fire for too long and the walls were too formidable an obstacle to be mounted by scaling ladders under fire. But, as so often in British military history, a gloomy tactical situation was brightened by acts of superb individual bravery. Besides the feats of Peel, Daniel and Wood at the wall, the Naval Brigade won three more Victoria Crosses. After the attack had been repulsed, a soldier of the 57th (Middlesex) Regiment was shot through both legs and could be seen from the sailors' trenches, sitting up and calling for help. At once, Lieutenant Henry Raby, of HMS *Wasp*, with John Taylor, Captain of the Forecastle of HMS *London* and Bosun's Mate Henry Curtis of HMS *Rodney*, left their battery and ran across some seventy yards of open ground towards the salient of the Redan to help the wounded man. He had been shot in both legs and could not assist himself, so he had to be carried. Though the enemy's fire was intense—Curtis had a shot pass actually between his legs—none of them was hurt, and they got the soldier back to the safety of the trench. All three were mentioned in Lushington's despatches and all were awarded the Victoria Cross.

Raby was promoted Commander in September 1855 for his services in the trenches. As senior officer present of the Senior Service, he was the first man to be invested with his Victoria Cross by the Queen at the 1857 Investiture.

Some of the Victoria Cross citations read rather baldly now. Bombadier Thomas Wilkinson, Royal Marine Artillery, of HMS *Britannia*, won a VC 'for gallant conduct in the advanced batteries, 7 June 1855, in placing sandbags to repair the work under a galling fire'. The Russian fire that day had been so heavy that it had demolished most of the earthworks in the most forward British positions. Wilkinson leapt up on the parapet, and rebuilt the works with sandbags handed up to him. It took him some time to go from place to place and put the bags in position. Eventually, both the enemy and his British mates in the trenches noticed what Wilkinson was doing. The former fired, while the latter replied with volley on volley of cheering. Wilkinson was commended by Colonel Wellesley, Deputy Adjutant General, Royal Marines, and awarded the Victoria Cross.

The last Victoria Cross for the Naval Brigade at Sebastopol was won by a most unusual man in a most unusual manner. He was John Sheppard, bosun's mate of *St Jean d'Acre*. Born in Kingston-upon-Hull in 1816, Sheppard was in his fortieth year when he won his Cross and might have been thought a little too old for the hectic adventures leading up to his award.

The Russians had sunk several blockships across the mouth of Sebastopol harbour early in the war, but there were still some line-of-battle-ships moored further up harbour. On 23 June 1855, Keppel noted in his diary that Shepherd (the spelling varies) was preparing 'to destroy, alone, a Russian three-decker'. He showed Keppel his contrivance which 'appeared simple enough' and the next day Keppel took him with his apparatus to see Admiral Lyons who 'was amused and approved, leaving the time for the experiment to me'. Sheppard planned to 'prepare a light iron case a foot long by eighteen inches, with a loop at each end. The case to be fitted with a Bickford's fuse, which burns under water. A sort of canvas duck punt was to be fitted to exactly hold the case amidships. The after part was to hold one sitter, who could easily steer with a canoe paddle without noise.' Sheppard would paddle silently up to a Russian man-of-war, fix his explosive charge to her side, and paddle away again.

There was some understandable scepticism in the fleet about Sheppard's weird and wonderful scheme, but he proved it worked. General Sir George Higginson wrote in his memoirs years later:

> This petty officer offered to blow up any one of these ships they (the Russians) kept afloat further up the harbour out of range of our batteries, by means of his own devising if given a free hand to use a special canoe he had constructed. Being allowed to explain his purpose, he said that if allowed to choose his own time he would place a bag containing one hundredweight of explosive powder in such a position against the forefront of any ship of the Allied fleet as would, when exploded, sink it. He was allowed to try the experiment 'in dummy' on the British Fleet. A sharp lookout was kept by patrol boats but one morning at daylight a

dummy bag, big enough to hold one hundredweight of explosive, was found screwed to the forefront of the British admiral's flagship. Clothing himself entirely in white with the canoe covered all over in white canvas, the adventurous youth had started out by night noiselessly from his own ship, unseen except by a confederate, with the bag attached to a large auger. Paddling stealthily through the fleet, he then slipped close past the side of the flagship, with two turns of the auger fastened the bag to the forefront and adjusted what would represent a fuse.

The General was writing from hearsay many years later (it was unlikely that Sheppard and his canoe would be all *white*, and Sheppard might have been adventurous but he was certainly no youth) but the account is still probably accurate on Sheppard's method of attack.

Sheppard made his attempt on the night of 15 July. Keppel and his coxswain went with him. It was a very dark night, specially chosen, and 'the spot for embarkation was only separated by a spur of land covered by thick scrub and bush, but the darkness of the night enabled our guide to take us to the water. At half-past twelve the punt left the rough slips and was immediately lost to sight, nor was there the slightest sound.' The canoe floated only three inches above the water, and on such a night it must have been invisible to the enemy. They were within range of the Russian sentries, but they waited for three hours, until there were signs of daybreak, without any signs of Sheppard's return. Keppel was afraid he had been lost, 'as, if caught he would be shot as a spy'. However, an hour after they got back to camp, they were delighted to hear of Sheppard's safe return. 'The plucky fellow had pulled past and between a number of Russian steamers and was within 400 yards of the three deckers, when a whole string of Russian boats pushed off from the western shore to convey troops across. For an hour he lay in his little punt hoping for an opening to pass through. Daylight came and he had not time to return the distance to where we were; he therefore struck at once for Careening Bay, one side of which he knew was in the possession of the French.' Apparently a new plan of night attacks and bombardment by the British had made the Russians change their troop convoy routes across the bay.

Because of that failure, Sheppard apparently had to demonstrate again what the press called 'his atmospheric boat, capable of being guided when sunk beneath surface and supplied with a reserve of air to last a given time for the support of its adventurous owner'. The *Illustrated Times* of 11 August 1855 reported that on 19 July Sheppard 'announced to the officers of HMS *London* that he would come in the course of that night and chalk up the ship's name on the side just above the watermark, do what they might to prevent him'. Double sentries were posted, officers kept special watch that night, and everybody was satisfied that nobody had come near the ship. 'Daylight however showed the letters conspicuously chalked on the ship's side as the sailor had said they would be.'

Sheppard made a second attempt, from the French side of Careening Bay, on 16 August, but with no more success. The whole exploit, however, had been well worth a Victoria Cross. Keppel and Lyons had no hesitation in mentioning Sheppard in their despatches and Sheppard's Cross was gazetted with the first awards announced on 24 February 1857.

Sheppard's VC was sent abroad, because he was serving in *Highflyer* on the China Station. There is no record of who presented the medal or where.

The Russians had their own 'devilish inventions', in particular a kind of floating mine which they used against the Baltic Fleet. They were described by Able Seaman William Puxty, who was in *Cressy*, as 'crude and primitive inventions, like a sugar loaf. The cones were made of galvanised iron, about twenty inches long and sixteen in diameter; each held about ten pounds of powder which was fired by sulphuric acid.' Some of these mines were hauled in and one actually exploded, seriously injuring the men standing by.

Cressy was part of the great fleet which sailed for the Baltic in 1855, this time under Admiral Dundas. It consisted of some eighty ships in all, mounting more than 2,000 guns. The French contributed sixteen ships with 400 guns. On 9 August 1855 the combined fleets began one of the longest ship-against-shore actions in naval history—the bombardment of Sveaborg, which had been unsuccessfully attacked the year before. According to Puxty, 'the drums beat to quarters, the gunners stripped to the waist and took their positions beside the muzzle-loading guns'. The scene below decks had hardly changed since Navarino, or Trafalgar. The bombarding ships were 'like circus horses running round the ring, going round and round the first delivering their broadsides, with the forts blazing back. The sailors became black with smoke and sweat and utterly exhausted as the fight dragged on, hour after hour, for two days.'

Puxty complained of 'too much time for brooding and not enough fighting in the Baltic'. He blamed brooding for much of the disease on board. Cholera broke out, brought on board by two Finnish prisoners. *Cressy* was burying seven or eight men a day at one time. It was a sailor of *Cressy* who wrote 'The Russians Won't Come out':

What can we luckless sailors do? no fun comes to our share;
The enemy keeps out of view—to meet us they won't dare!
In avain our pennants fly so gay, our cruisers roam about,
We might as well in Portsmouth lay—the Russians won't come out!

In Helsingfors they lay quite close; 'neath Cronstadt mole they
    crowd;
They'll not come out and meet the foes whom once they dared so
    loud.
Like to some worn-out batter'd hulk each gallant ship so stout
Behind the batteries does skulk—the cowards won't come out!

The *Arrogant* and *Hecla*, too, gave them a lesson rough;
Tho' fighting to our lads was new they proved both smart and tough;
They strewed the ground with soldiers gay, their batteries knocked
    about,
And brought their merchant ships away, yet still they won't come
    out!

While in the Baltic we deplore our idle time at sea,
Our comrades on the Turkish shore are as badly off as we.
Though many ships they've made their own, ta'en many a strong
    redoubt,
And batter'd half Odessa down, the Russians won't come out!

That mighty man, Prince Menschikoff, in harbour still does lie,
And at the Allied Fleets does scoff as they are sailing by.
'Don't think,' says he, 'that I'm a fool, a valiant, headstrong lout;
I'm safe and snug in Sebastopol, and be hanged if I'll come out.'

Oh! would they but their anchors weigh and boldly put to sea,
With joy to see a sight so gay how full each heart would be;
But oh! such wishes are in vain: they know there's little doubt,
They never would get in again if once they venture out.

However, there were still chances for individual heroism in the Baltic. On 13 July 1855 the boats of *Arrogant* were engaged against enemy boats and batteries at Viborg when the second cutter was hit and swamped. The powder on board her blew up and the wrecked boat drifted inshore under the guns of a Russian battery. George Ingouville, captain of the mast in *Arrogant*, saw the boat's plight, and though wounded in the arm he jumped overboard, swam round to catch hold of the boat's painter and began to tow her away. He might still have drowned and the boat's crew killed, had it not been for Lieutenant George Dare Dowell RM, who was in the *Ruby* gunboat while his own boat was being loaded with a fresh supply of rockets, and noticed what was happening in *Arrogant*'s boat. Calling for three volunteers, he took away *Ruby*'s quarter-boat, pulling the stroke oar himself. The Russians ashore and in the boats tried to prevent him but Dowell rescued three of the crew of *Arrogant*'s boat and brought them back to *Ruby*. That might have been enough, but he went back again, rescued Ingouville and the others, and towed the sinking cutter out of gun range. Towards the end, even the Russians are said to have joined in the cheering. Dowell and Ingouville were both awarded the Victoria Cross and were present in Hyde Park to receive them from the Queen.

The expedition of May 1855 to seize the straits of Kertsch and to operate in the Sea of Azov consisted of some 15,000 infantry and fifty-six ships: frigates, light draught steamers, gun and rocket boats, augmented later by twenty line-of-battle-ship launches armed with 24-pounder howitzers and rockets. The Russians blew up their forts and retreated from the straits so that the objectives were captured without the loss of a man. A steam flotilla under Captain Lyons (the C-in-C's son) went through the Straits and within a week had sunk four steamers of war and 246 merchant ships, captured corn, flour, and powder magazines to the value of £50,000, and taken over 17,000 tons of coal. There was a good deal of looting at Kertsch. Victor Montagu, as a midshipman of *Princess Royal*, led a patrol ashore and arrested many soldiers and bluejackets but, he said, 'fair and square looting seemed to be winked at'.

By the middle of June the main force had retired, leaving a garrison of some

The first Victoria Cross investiture, which took place in Hyde
Park on 27 June 1857.

7,500 men. The Azov operations had no seaborne opposition and the actions
were mostly daring ventures by small parties, much like commando raids, to
destroy the enemy's *materiale* ashore. On 29 May, Lieutenant Buckley of
Miranda, Lieutenant Burgoyne, senior lieutenant of *Swallow*, and Gunner
John Robarts of *Ardent* landed on a beach near the town of Genitchi, out of
gunshot of the Allied squadron and in the teeth of enemy opposition. They set
fire to corn and stores, and destroyed enemy equipment before embarking
again. On 3 June Buckley landed again, this time with Bosun Henry Cooper,
also of *Miranda*, in a four-oared gig manned by volunteers, at the town of
Taganrog which was at the time under bombardment by the Allied squadron.
The town was garrisoned by some 3,000 Russian troops but Buckley and
Cooper fired government buildings and stores, landing several times under fire
wherever they saw a likely target. Buckley, Burgoyne, Robarts and Cooper
were all awarded the Victoria Cross. Buckley, being the first alphabetically,
was the first name to be gazetted in the list of 24 February 1857.

For some holders of the VC, their last days were a decline into sadness after
the triumphs of their youth. A classic case was that of Able Seaman Joseph
Trewavas, known as 'Long Joe'. His picture shows him as a handsome young
man, with flowing, curly hair, a broad chest and clear grey eyes. He was born
in Mousehole, Cornwall, in December 1835 and joined *Agamemnon* as a boy in
October 1853. He did not volunteer for continuous service, although it turned
out that he served for nearly ten years. He landed with the first of the Naval
Brigade in October 1854, and was lent from *Agamemnon* to *Beagle* for duty in
the Sea of Azov.

Beagle was commanded by Lieutenant 'Bully' Hewett, who was himself to
win the VC. In July 1855, Hewett was ordered to destroy a pontoon bridge
between the mainland at Genitchi and the long Spit of Arabat, forming part of
the Russian supply convoy route to the south. Two unsuccessful attempts had

Bosun Joseph Kellaway, VC.   Bosun Henry Cooper, VC.   Bosun John Sheppard, V

Gunner John Robarts, VC.   Bosun's Mate John Sullivan, VC.

Able Seaman Joseph Trewavas, VC.

Quartermaster William Rickard, VC.   Colour Sergeant John Prettyjohn, RMLI,

already been made, so the garrisons were thoroughly alert when on 3 July a party from *Beagle* approached the pontoon in a four-oared boat, covered by a small paddle-boat armed with one gun in the bows. The gun fired one round and then seized up, but the boat's crew rowed on. They had been told by Hewett not to return until they had cut the pontoon bridge; they took this to mean that they would be courtmartialled if they failed. As one of them said, 'we might as well be killed by Russian bullets as have the fore-brace block for an awning' (i.e., be hanged). The shore was lined with Russian riflemen. Every window in every house had its marksman. The Russians held back until the boat touched the pontoon and Trewavas jumped out with an axe, whereupon they opened a tremendous fire on the pontoon, on Trewavas, and on the boat and its crew. Trewavas was wounded but succeeded in chopping through the rope hawsers that held the bridge. Then, as he said himself, 'By coolness and pulling for dear life and by the Russians' shocking aim, we got back, the boat being completely riddled and up to the thwarts in water.'

Trewavas received his VC from the Queen and was also awarded the Conspicuous Gallantry Medal. Later, in 1857, he went to the East Indies; he served in Burma during the Indian Mutiny and in New Zealand for the Maori wars in 1860. He left the navy in December 1862 to become a fisherman in Penzance, married in 1866 and became a member of the Penzance Board of Guardians and a respected member of the community, who told *Who's Who* that he had no hobbies, being much too busy getting a living. At the beginning of 1905, Trewavas suffered a stroke which left him partially paralysed. The change from an active and responsible life to one of dependence upon others evidently preyed on his mind. On 20 July 1905 he died of shock and haemorrhage, two days after he had inflicted a throat wound on himself with a cheese knife (the second naval Crimean VC to take his own life); the coroner's verdict was that he had committed suicide whilst of unsound mind.

The first naval VC to become a prisoner of war was Bosun Joseph Kellaway, of HMS *Wrangler*. On 31 August 1855, Kellaway, Mr Odevaine, the mate, and three seamen of *Wrangler* landed at a place called Marienpol to burn boats, some fishing stations and hay stacks which were on the opposite bank of a small lake. They had nearly reached their objectives when they were fired upon by a party of about fifty Russian soldiers who had ambushed them by slipping round behind them and cutting off their retreat. One sailor was captured but Kellaway, Odevaine and the others were managing to escape when Odevaine slipped and fell. Kellaway thought he had been wounded and came back to rescue him. The delay caused Kellaway himself to be captured; he and Odevaine were surrounded, and had to surrender after a gallant but hopeless resistance. Lieutenant Burgoyne, who was then *Wrangler*'s captain, had watched the incident and afterwards reported: 'I was myself an observer of the zeal, gallantry and devotion that characterised Mr Kellaway's conduct.'

Kellaway and the other prisoners were exchanged by the Russians at Odessa on 20th October, being released for two Russian officers and the wife and child of one of them. Boats put out from shore and from the ship and the exchange was made at sea between them.

The last VCs for these night raids were awarded to Commander Commerell and Quartermaster Rickard of HMS *Weser*. Commerell, Mr Lillingston, the mate, and three seamen—Rickard, Milestone and Hoskins—left *Weser* in a boat at 2.30 a.m. on 11 October 1855. They hauled the boat over the Spit and rowed across the Putrid Sea, reaching the other side at about 4.30. Mr Lillingston and Hoskins were left in charge of the boat while Commerell and the other two went inland. They walked about two miles, using a compass to get their bearings, and having to wade two canals neck-deep in water. They reached their objective, a store containing about 400 tons of corn and forage, and were just setting fire to it when the Cossack guard came streaming out of their guardhouse and began to pursue them. Milestone was exhausted by the chase and begged to be left, but the other two removed his boots and half carried him. Assisted by Lillingston and Hoskins who fired from the boat, the three managed to escape and embark in time, although the Cossacks were only sixty yards away when the boat left the shore and Commerell killed the nearest horseman with his pistol. The look-out watching from *Weser*'s masthead reported that the corn store had burned to the ground. Of the three, Milestone was the only one who did not receive the Victoria Cross; for every Rickard awarded the Cross, there were thousands of Milestones returning to oblivion.

On 27 June 1857 a vast crowd of over 100,000 people gathered in Hyde Park to see the Queen present the first Victoria Crosses to some of the heroes of the Crimean War. It was a fine day and people began to arrive soon after dawn. The troops began to fall in, facing Park Lane, at 8.30 a.m. The parade was commanded by Lieutenant-General Sir Colin Campbell, who had led the Highland Brigade up the Heights at Alma. The cavalry was commanded by the Earl of Cardigan, of the Light Brigade, and the Royal Artillery was under Major-General Sir Fenwick Williams. There were also companies from the Royal Engineers, the Royal Marines and the 79th Cameron Highlanders, three battalions of the Foot Guards, and the 2nd Battalion of the Rifle Brigade. The Navy was represented by a hundred men from *Excellent* and *Osborne* (this led to complaints in Parliament, some saying that there should have been at least a thousand bluejackets present).

The Queen arrived to a royal gun salute just before 10.00, riding up in a glittering cavalcade of splendid uniforms, tossing helmet feathers and jingling harness. The VC winners formed up in single file and marched in front of Her Majesty, where Lord Panmure handed each Cross to the Queen, who stooped from her saddle and fixed the medal to a loop on the winner's breast. Twelve naval VCs were there: Commanders Raby, Bythesea and Burgoyne, Lieutenants Lucas and Hewett, the warrant officers Mr Robarts, Mr Kellaway and Mr Cooper; and Trewavas, Reeves, Curtis and Ingouville. Lieutenant Dowell and Bombardier Wilkinson of the Royal Marine Artillery were also decorated that day, with forty-eight officers and men of the Army.

Of the absent twelve naval Crimean War VCs, Taylor was already dead and the majority of the others were serving on the China Station, where another war was in progress.

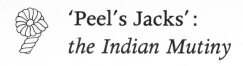

'Peel's Jacks':
the Indian Mutiny

In October 1856 the British *lorcha* (or cutter) *Arrow* was seized by the Chinese authorities on a charge of piracy. Her crew were returned, at Britain's request, but no apology was made (understandably, since the crew were undoubtedly pirates) and the incident led to a second Chinese war in which, once again, the Navy was involved.

Late in October the Bogue Forts in the Canton River were taken and the city itself was entered in November. Much of the work was done by parties of bluejackets in ship's boats. Midshipman Kennedy was in command of one of the flagship *Calcutta*'s pinnaces for over three months without returning to the ship. He lived as the sailors did, in the clothes he stood up in, and existing on the same diet of salt pork, biscuit and a ration of rum. Kennedy had the greatest respect for his coxswain, Jim Parnell, who was *Calcutta*'s captain of the foretop, and for the rest of his crew.

> I often think that it is on detached service of this sort that bluejackets show to advantage—always cheerful and contented and respectful at a time when it is not easy to enforce the discipline of a man-of-war. No matter whether the pork was rancid or the water stank, I never heard a murmur of discontent: they knew that what did for them did for me. One day our copper—the only cooking apparatus we had—was lost overboard, and it could not be replaced for some days, so we had to eat our pork raw, but we all shared alike. I had no medicines in the boat— we couldn't afford to be sick—but I told the men that if any of them were really ill they should have an extra glass of rum from our limited store, and some of us would go without it. I never had a single application, nor did I have a case of sickness in the boat, although we drank the river water, about the same colour and consistency as that of the Thames at London Bridge; and at this very time the *Calcutta*'s men were dying in the hospitals at Hong Kong from dysentery, caused by drinking impure water.

But Kennedy, like everybody else, had the problem of keeping his crew sober. At Christmas 1856, when they were guard-boat in the river, Kennedy went down to his boat at midnight to find his crew 'all helplessly drunk, excepting the coxswain and one other. What was to be done? I dared not report them unfit for duty, as I should have been punished for not looking after them; so, making the two sober ones take an oar, and taking the helm myself, I pushed off into the stream, having first refreshed the rest of the crew by a few buckets of water thrown over them.' They 'rowed guard' by anchoring unobtrusively in the river, where the two sober men took a couple of oars each and kept dipping them in the water until daylight, when they returned to the camber. Afterwards Kennedy was sent for, and complimented upon the admirable way his crew had kept guard during the night!

Later, in a foolhardy episode, Kennedy took his pinnace armed only with a 12-pounder gun and fourteen men down river to attack the main fleet of Chinese junks. He was egged on by another midshipman, Mathew Byles, and in a moment of madness he agreed. They were in action when one of those panics occurred which sometimes take place even with the best men. One fellow threw his oar overboard and lay down in the bottom of the boat, and,

> to their shame be it said, nine others followed his example, only leaving their oars in the boats. In vain I ordered, entreated, and even threatened them with my revolver. Byles gallantly supported me, using the boat's tiller on their heads with good effect, and so did the coxswain and three brave fellows who were helping me with the gun. The boat meanwhile was drifting helplessly to destruction, and we could hear the yells of the Chinamen as their prey seemed within their reach.

Very fortunately for Kennedy, and for themselves, the men returned to their sense of duty, picked up their oars and began to row. The steam-paddle gunboat *Coromandel*, flying the flag of Admiral Sir Michael Seymour, came to their assistance, and all was well. Kennedy said nothing, but there must have been gossip, for a few days later the Admiral and Kennedy's own captain, William King-Hall, asked him what had happened and he had to give them the whole story. King-Hall was so indignant he seized by the throat the man who had thrown his oar away and swore he would hang him at *Calcutta*'s yardarm. Those who had panicked were disrated on the spot, while the faithful four were promoted. Kennedy went back to the ship to pick another crew and, 'I was not long . . . as the whole ship's company volunteered.' In spite of the physical hardships and the occasional dangers, detached service in small boats was much preferred by the ordinary bluejacket to life on board ship.

Seymour had too small a force to occupy Canton permanently, so in January 1857 the city was evacuated, although the Bogue Forts were still garrisoned. The following May reinforcements arrived from England, including Keppel, who had commissioned the frigate *Raleigh* at Portsmouth in September 1856. (William Pegg saw her going out to Spithead in November under sail 'which is quite a novelty nowadays'.) Her commissioning pendant had been hoisted by the bosun's wife, 'a handsome-looking woman' according to Keppel, and it should have brought the ship luck. Unhappily it did not, for *Raleigh* ran aground and became a total loss off Macao in April 1857. But Keppel was present to take a leading part in the action in Fatshan Creek, a branch of the Canton River, on 1 June 1857.

Reconnaissances were carried out of the Chinese position on Sunday 31 May. In fact, an attack could have been launched that day but Admiral Seymour, not wishing to desecrate the sailors' Sabbath, deferred the attack until the next day. The sailors were called at 3.00 a.m. for a basin of ship's cocoa and a biscuit, and by dawn they were ready.

The Chinese position was formidably defended by batteries of heavy guns on either side of the creek. Some seventy or eighty junks, the pride of the Imperial Navy, were moored in a line abreast the creek, with banners and streamers flying, guns run out to cover the approaches to the creek, stink-pots at every masthead, and boarding nettings triced up ready to drop on the bluejackets as they got alongside so that the Chinese could spear them through the meshes. The Chinese mounted some 800 guns, many of them European 42-pounders, manned by about 6,000 fanatical Chinese braves.

The battle began at 3.30 a.m. Admiral Seymour led the attack in *Coromandel*, with other gunboats including *Haughty* and *Plover*, the steamers *Hong Kong* and *Sir Charles Forbes* and all the available launches, pinnaces, gigs and jolly-boats of the fleet, with about two thousand bluejackets embarked. *Coromandel* had hardly entered the river when she ran aground. Seymour transferred to his galley and the advance went on, though all the gunboats went aground at some stage in the operation. But the tide was flooding and they were able to get off and go further upriver. Bluejackets and marines stormed and took a strong battery on the bank, but the Chinese fire from the junks was heavy, sustained and accurate. One of *Calcutta*'s pinnaces, with Kennedy in command, was badly holed below the water-line. Her two stroke oarsmen were wounded. A round shot passed right through the boat, smashing into the magazine but happily not exploding it. They plugged the holes with seamen's frocks and went on. They were even able to reach *Calcutta*'s launch just as she was sinking, and take off her crew and gun.

Keppel's galley was hit and sunk, and he and the survivors of his crew were rescued by one of *Calcutta*'s boats commanded by Mate Michael Seymour, the Admiral's nephew. The steamer *Hong Kong* was hulled twelve times in a few minutes, and her decks were covered with wounded, brought in from the various boats. The Chinese saw their success, redoubled their fire, gongs and chanting, and for a time it did seem that the attack was going to fail.

However, Keppel had only retired *pour mieux sauter*. Somebody tore off a piece of blue bunting for use as a commodore's broad pennant and hoisted it, while Keppel called out, 'Let's try the boats once more. boys!' 'At this moment,' Keppel wrote in a letter shortly afterwards, 'there arose from the boats, as if every man took it up at the same instant, one of those British cheers, so full of meaning, that I knew at once it was all up with John Chinaman.'

And so it was. At this renewed attack the line of junks wavered, broke and retreated. The boats pursued some of them for as much as seven miles and all but eight were captured. The jubilant sailors went on the rampage in the junks, catching up armfuls of silks, brocades, and fine clothing. They dressed themselves up as mandarins in full costume and began to dance on deck. The junks were swarming with bluejackets, silk-clad and smoke-blackened, quite intoxicated with their victory (and with palm spirit which was also among the booty). The fleet losses were thirteen killed and forty wounded. There would have been much more had the Chinese stuck to their plan to hold their fire until the fleet's boats were alongside, and had they used their boarding nets properly.

In the middle of this campaign in China news arrived of the outbreak of the Indian Mutiny. Troops *en route* to China were diverted to India and Admiral Seymour sent reinforcements from the China Station, consisting of the 50-gun steam-frigate *Shannon* (Captain Sir William Peel), which had just arrived from England, and the 21-gun steam-corvette *Pearl* (Captain E. S. Sotheby), diverted from the Pacific Station.

The reverse side of the medal for Indian Mutiny service, issued in 1858.

As in the Crimean War, no first-hand bluejacket's account of the Indian Mutiny seems to have survived. What the sailors did and how they lived and what they thought about it all, have to be deduced from the accounts of their officers. Captain Peel was ordered to place himself under the orders of Major General Sir James Outram, and when the ships arrived at Calcutta in August 1857 his first action was to form a Naval Brigade, to go inland to serve with the army in quelling the mutiny. Twenty-three officers, 329 seamen, two officers and fifty-four privates of the Marines, with a siege train of ten 65-cwt 8-inch naval guns, embarked on 18 August in the steamer *Chunar*, towing a flat, for the passage up the river Ganges.

It was, as Peel remarked, a long and anxious voyage. The engineer was drunk and the stokers mutinous, the feed pump was out of order, and *Chunar* could not stem the tide, so they had to come back. The next day they started again but the feed pump still gave trouble and the steamer had the greatest difficulty in making headway. On 21 August they changed to another steamer, the *River Bird*. One of the able seamen had an attack of mania and was sent back to *Shannon*. Fresh beef was embarked on most days, and the ships anchored every night, but other difficulties mounted up. It was the hottest time of the Bengal summer and the weather was very unpleasant for Europeans. They all suffered from heatstroke, boils and mosquito bites. The number of sick rose to five, to nine, and then to fifty, who were all landed on 29 September. Nine men died, of cholera or typhoid. There was the usual trouble over drunkenness. The petty officers, due to a misunderstanding, complained about the way the rum was issued. Thomas Oates, captain of the maintop, was picked out as leader of the disaffection and was summarily disrated to AB, also losing two good conduct badges. Boy First Class Isaac Ambrose was punished with thirty-six lashes for theft. Able Seaman George Sutherland was punished with twelve lashes for drunkenness and excessive abusive language, but the sentence was remitted. On 13 September they changed to yet a third steamer, the *Coel*, and arrived at Allahabad on 3 October, taking over garrison duties in the fort three days later. The sick who had been disembarked rejoined on 10 October.

On 20 October, Peel was reinforced by the arrival of Lieutenant Vaughan of *Shannon*, with five officers and 121 men, most of them merchant seamen whom Vaughan had recruited in Calcutta. Peel was very pleased with their fine appearance, good behaviour and excellent discipline, and thought that their volunteering 'showed the fine spirit of the Merchant Service, as these men entered on board the *Shannon* without any conditions and against six pounds per month wages offered by the shipping'.

With a total force of over 500 men (although he still had a long sick list) Peel was able to begin operations. On 23 October he sent Vaughan to Cawnpore with a small arms company under Lieutenant Salmon, a field piece party of 100 men, with four siege-train 24-pounders. Four days later, another party of 170 men under Lieutenant Young, *Shannon*'s gunnery officer, left for the same purpose, with another four 24-pounders, two 8-inch howitzers and a large amount of ammunition. The rest of the Naval Brigade—about 240 officers and men, of whom more than sixty were sick—were left at Allahabad under Lieutenant Wilson. Midshipman Daniel VC, Peel's aide-de-camp from the Crimea and his companion now, had been sent to Cawnpore on special service on 16 October.

Peel himself went with Young's party and they were joined on the way by men of the 53rd Regiment, some sappers and the Highlanders. It was not long before 'Peel's Jacks', as they were called, proved their marching and fighting powers. They marched seventy-two miles in three days with one day for rest and on 1 November, after marching sixteen miles since dawn, they fought a battle at a place called Khujwa, a fortified village defended by some 4,000 mutineers. In the middle of the action the commanding colonel was killed and Peel took charge. Under his leadship the Naval Brigade outflanked the sepoys, stormed their guns and forced them to retreat with great loss. Peel's force themselves lost nearly a hundred killed or wounded. Sepoy losses were estimated at over 300. The bluejackets returned with the colonel's body on a captured gun carriage, after chasing the enemy eight miles up the road.

'Peel's Jacks' were gaining a reputation amongst the mutineers, or 'Pandies' as the sailors called them. The local Indian press reported that the sepoys regarded the sailors with almost superstitious awe, and attributed to them fantastic and supernatural powers. The mutineers apparently believed that the Jacks were cannibals who ate as much of their victims as they could at first sitting and then salted down the rest for later consumption; that they went on all fours, were only four feet high, and measured five feet from snout to tail. The Pandies were especially recommended to avoid such monsters, who could carry 9-pounder guns over their heads with ease and were very terrible in battle. On 27 October, before the battle at Khujwa, Lieutenant (later Field-Marshal and VC) Roberts wrote home from Cawnpore that the '93rd Highlanders marched in this morning, looking so nice in their kilts. The natives think they are the ghosts of the murdered women, but the sailors astonish them most. 4 ft. high, 4 ft. broad, long hair and dragging big guns!! They can't make them out . . .'

On 14 November, Peel's Jacks took part in the attack on Lucknow. *Shannon*'s brigade was then about 200 sailors and marines strong, with six 24-pounders, two 8-inch howitzers drawn by bullocks and two rocket tubes mounted on hackeries (two-wheeled carts drawn by bullocks). The sailors and the marine rifle companies made up the infantry escort. At noon they were under fire, from round shot and muskets, and they had to evacuate the compound where they had halted. According to the Reverend Bowman, who kept a diary, the sailors moved their heavy guns into a position from which they could reply and some of the troops were ordered to charge; 'the enemy were repulsed and the sailors returned and bivouacked for the night. During the day one of their guns went off whilst being loaded, probably on account of not being properly sponged, which resulted in one seaman being killed, and two wounded.' The man killed was Francis Cassidy, captain of the maintop.

After a pause on the 15th, because no reserves of ammunition or stores had been brought up, the Naval Brigade went into action again on the 16th, advancing on a high, walled enclosure made of thick masonry, known as the Secunderabagh, which was some 120 yards square and very strongly defended by the mutineers. The guns of the Navy and the Royal Artillery bombarded the place for an hour and a half before a small breach was made and the fortress was stormed and taken, over 2,000 mutineers being killed inside. With the same guns and some mortars, the Naval Brigade then went on to attack an even stronger fortress, which was a domed mosque surrounded by a masonry wall with loopholes cut for muskets. It was called the Shah Nujef.

Although Peel led his guns up to within a few feet of the Shah Nujef wall and, as Sir Colin Campbell wrote later in his despatches, 'behaved very much as if he had been laying *Shannon* alongside an enemy's frigate', the Shah Nujef resisted the attacks. Peel called for volunteers to climb a tree, whose branches touched the nearer angle of the Shan Nujef wall, to direct fire against the enemy. Lieutenant Salmon, although already wounded in the thigh, and Bosun's Mate John Harrison, responded. They both climbed the tree to dislodge, as ·Salmon put it, 'some ruffians who were throwing grenades'. Salmon called his injury a slight flesh wound, 'with not the slightest danger attached to it'.

One of the guns nearest to the wall was served by Lieutenant Young and Able Seaman Hall. They ran their 24-pounder up so close that its muzzle almost touched the brickwork and they continued to fire in spite of enemy grenades and musket balls. At one time the smoke and dust were so thick that Young, Hall and the gun were completely hidden from view. Hall himself said later that 'after firing each round we ran the gun forward until finally the crew were in danger of being hit by splinters of brick and stone torn from the wall by the round shot. Lieutenant Young moved from gun to gun, giving calm encouragement.' When Hall was left the sole survivor at his gun, Young took the last gunner's place and helped him to load and serve the gun.

After about three hours' hard pounding the Shah Nujef still looked untouched except for one very small breach. But when some of the 93rd Highlanders went round the corner they entered the wall and found the place partially deserted. They called up reinforcements and in a few minutes the stronghold had been captured.

Next day, the naval guns were again in action against a building called the Mess House which was stormed and taken that afternoon. The troops went on to reach and relieve the Residency, which had been very capably defended by Sir James Outram. Three more of the Naval Brigade were killed, making the total casualties five killed and fiteen wounded. Salmon, Harrison, Young and Hall were all awarded the Victoria Cross.

On 22 November 1857 the bluejackets in Lucknow were completing a three-day bombardment of the Kaiserbagh fortress to cover the evacuation of European women, children, stores and wounded from the Lucknow Residency. They were brought safely out on the night of 22–23 November, with the naval guns and rocket tubes keeping up their fire to the last moment, and two naval guns remaining behind to cover the retreat the next day. (The women and children did eventually reach Calcutta safely, after an eventful journey. Pearl's log for 8 January 1858 records: '5 PM. Dressed ship in honour of the arrival of the Ladies from Lucknow. 7. Undressed ditto.')

In March 1858 some four hundred officers and men of the Naval Brigade formed a small element of Sir Colin Campbell's force (small compared with the total of nearly 20,000 officers and men) which took Lucknow. The final advance began on 2 March and the sailors assisted with the bridge building for the crossing of the Gumti river on 6–7 March. Naval guns bombarded the strong points of the Martiniere on the 9th and the Begum Cotee on the 11th. By 13 March the sailors were defending earthworks in the grounds of the Begum Cotee, with troops occupying nearby houses and a garden, exchanging fire with sepoys in the houses opposite. During one skirmish a house on the sailors' left was set alight. The naval guns opened fire and during the action some of the sandbags and brushwood protecting the gun battery caught fire. Able Seaman Edward Robinson brought up waterskins to douse the flames inside the battery and then climbed over the top of the breastworks to do the same

'Man Overboard' from HMS *Shannon*: Able Seaman William Hall, the black sailor standing up, won the VC during the Indian Mutiny.

Able Seaman William Hall, VC.

outside. The sepoys were only fifty yards away and at once fired at him. Robinson was hit in one collar-bone and fell back into the battery unconscious. He was dragged to safety by his mates in the gun crew. He was awarded the sixth naval VC of the Mutiny.

While *Shannon*'s brigade served in Lucknow, the *Pearl*'s fought in open country warfare in north-west Bengal. They won no VCs although they served

The Naval Brigade at Lucknow.

Able Seaman
Edward Robinson, VC.

longer in the field than *Shannon*'s, from October 1857 until returning to Calcutta in February 1859. At the outset of the Mutiny there were so few British troops in India that *Pearl*'s were the only white troops in that area and were responsible for the defence of a huge stretch of the sub-continent from the Ganges northwards to the Nepalese border.

The first party from *Pearl* started up the Ganges on 12 September 1857, under Captain Sotheby himself. It comprised 158 bluejackets and marines, a 24-pounder howitzer, a 12-pounder howitzer, four light field guns and a 24-pounder rocket tube. With them went Chaplain Williams and Midshipman Victor Montagu, who both wrote accounts of the campaign. A second *Pearl* party followed, under Lieutenant S. W. D. Radcliffe, with seven officers and ninety-four seamen and marines. The officers included Midshipman Henry Stephenson who kept a diary of events.

The bluejackets covered great distances by route marches. At every halt, they exercised firing ball cartridges at target marks, gun drills and battalion exercises. They lived in the open air, sleeping under canvas, serving side by side with Gurkha and Sikh soldiers with whom they soon established a warm relationship. Sometimes they stayed for several days at a village, while they sent out punitive detachments to find parties of mutineers and burn down their villages. Convicted mutineers were hung, shot or blown from guns. Most of the time, according to Williams, 'no enemy showed himself, but occasionally a Brahmin, a spy or *budmash* would be captured and executed'. When they did fight a pitched battle they were almost always outnumbered by well-armed mutineers, well supplied with guns and ammunition, some of them mounted on elephants.

'The Royal tar', as Montagu called the men of the Naval Brigade, made a very good campaigner, as he had done in the Crimea. 'We had our horsed battery and companies of infantry; and it was really astonishing how soon the sailors learned to ride and gallop their horses and guns about, very often like horse artillery. We picked out the most horsey bluejackets for our battery: some that had had in their boyhood to deal with horses, or at any rate, who knew something about them.' What a novelty it was, Montagu wrote, all trained to the sea as they were, to be suddenly turned into soldiers!

And they were excellent soldiers. On 2 March, Stephenson put in his diary, the sailors 'marched in company with 500 Goorkhas and 35 Seikhs to attack the Fort at Belwah. 4.30: Opened fire on the fort and took possession of two villages. The fort immediately returned the fire with guns and rifles. After two hours' firing, the night coming on we retired and buvouacked.' At a larger engagement at Amorha, Lieutenant H. D. Grant, Third Lieutenant of *Pearl*, with Shearman the Engineer, Midshipman Lord Charles Scott, Able Seaman Ward and another sailor, captured one of the mutineers' guns and loaded it from its own limber. Having no port-fire, they discharged a rifle with its muzzle to the vent instead, and so they were able to carry on firing the gun at its previous owners. Victor Montagu said of this incident that 'there is no doubt that they won the Victoria Cross. Somehow this event was never represented.'

As the hot monsoon weather of the summer of 1858 drew on, the Naval Brigade were quartered at Bustee, a town some miles north of the river Gogra and in the general centre of the area where they had been operating. It was too hot for operations but there were still occasional alarms caused by raiding parties of mutineers on the move, and the sailors mounted several flying columns to seek out isolated parties of sepoys in the surrounding villages.

Some of the men suffered severely from the heat and many fell ill with fever. Several died of dysentery. But in the cool of the day, they kept themselves amused with athletics, cricket matches, pony races, *dhooley* races and even elephant races. The sailors ran and jumped and threw shot. Sometimes the Jacks dressed up as ladies of the eighteenth century and rode about on ponies, with their bare feet touching the ground. They had theatricals in the evenings, and a reading room, with a portable library, in a special tent.

After their last major battle, at Tulsipor in December, the *Pearls* came back to the ship, marching most of the way and arriving in Calcutta in February 1859, having, as Montagu said, 'stayed up country until the whole neck of the Mutiny was broken'. *Pearl* anchored at Spithead on 6 June 1859.

Captain Peel was never to receive his Victoria Cross. It was sent out to India, but on 9 March, at Lucknow, Peel was hit in the thigh and badly wounded by a musket ball. It was cut out by a surgeon, but Vaughan had to take over command of the Naval Brigade. Peel then contracted smallpox on 20 April when he was returning with the rest of the Brigade to Cawnpore, and he died on the 27th. Midshipman Edward Daniel, Peel's companion in so many adventures, was presented with his Cross by Captain Marten, Peel's successor, on 13 July 1858. But he too came to a melancholy end, forfeiting his Cross for desertion two years later.

Shannon anchored at Spithead on 29 December and paid off on 15 January, amidst a certain amount of controversy. Somebody had been writing to the papers about the indiscipline of *Shannon*'s crew and Marten's tyranny. A writer in the *United Service Magazine* complained that 'the major part of the crew of the *Shannon*, it should be observed, is composed of very young men who volunteered chiefly from merchant ships in Calcutta. The life they led in the Naval Brigade was the reverse of disciplined. They were the terror of friends as well as foes. No orders restrained them, and the loot they acquired was considerable.'

Various distinguished gentlemen wrote to *The Times* to refute the accusations, which were libellous on both points. Victor Montagu certainly shared Peel's high opinion of the merchant seamen who joined in Calcutta. He had to recruit about a hundred of them for *Pearl* and it took him four days to induce enough of them to volunteer. But, though they had to be fitted out with clothes and taught how to use firearms, 'curiously enough, they turned out some of the best men in the Brigade'. As for Marten's tyranny, no punishments were recorded while the Brigade were in the field. Six seamen were imprisoned for three weeks for robbery in Calcutta. On the voyage home, four men were each punished with four dozen, two for drunkenness, one for theft and one for insolent conduct. At home, two men were punished 'per warrant' and in the last five days of the commission, five men were sentenced to fourteen days in Winchester gaol.

But the best tribute to Peel's Jacks and the other bluejackets was paid by Mr Ritchie, Advocate General at Calcutta:

Of the events of the late mutinies, I know no single one which can be viewed with more unmixed satisfaction than the conduct and behaviour of the Naval Brigades, formed of men of Her Majesty's and of the Indian Navy. Conspicuous among those brave men were the crews of the *Shannon* and the *Pearl*—names that never will be forgotten in Calcutta. It is not their prowess in the field to which I allude, though this has never been surpassed, even by British sailors, but their admirable steadiness, good conduct and humanity throughout a most trying campaign, and under circumstances of great temptation. No single instance of outrage to unoffending man, woman or child has occurred in either case.

'Stakes and Stinkpots': the China War 1859–60

Understandably, after their ship's companies' exertions in the Mutiny, *Shannon* and *Pearl* never returned to the China Station, but the war in China went on and gave some of the best war reporting from the lower-deck since Navarino. After the capture of Canton and the destruction of its forts in December 1857, Lord Elgin submitted the British government's demands to the Chinese. They were ignored or evaded; the main difficulty when dealing with the Chinese was in meeting anybody who had the authority to negotiate. It was decided to press the demands at Tientsin or at the capital itself, Peking. The fleet moved up to the Peiho river in May 1858, when a joint force of British and French gunboats took the Taku forts guarding the river entrance, in an action lasting only two hours, with casualties of under a hundred killed or wounded. The way was now open to Tientsin, where a treaty was signed in June.

But, once again, the Chinese agreed to treaty demands only to ignore them once the attacking force had retired. In June 1859, under a new C-in-C, Rear Admiral James Hope, the fleet was back off the Peiho once more, to find that the Taku forts had been tremendously strengthened in the past year. The forts were protected by enormous dykes, bristling with sharp wooden spikes. The channel had been sown with tripod-shaped iron stakes, weighing several tons each and placed so that their points were a couple of feet below high-water level. Across the river were stretched two huge booms, made of iron and wood lashed together with hemp ropes; the gap between the booms was too narrow and awkward for a warship to pass through. However, in spite of or perhaps in ignorance of these formidable defences, the sailors in the fleet were delighted when they heard that negotiations with the Chinese had broken down again and they were to attack the forts.

The British and French, with the help of an American steamer *Toeywan* whose captain had decided that 'Blood was thicker than water', arrived off the Peiho on 24 June. That night, sailors in two white-washed cutters with muffled oars tried unsuccessfully to cut the booms. The next morning, according to John in *A Sailor Boy's Logbook*, 'dawned brightly and summer-like, and so calm that not a ripple stirred the water. At seven o'clock we had breakfast, laughing and joking the while. Old Archie "know'd they wouldn't fight, and we'd have our suppers inside them forts"; and so, indeed, many of us thought. The meal over, most of the blue-jackets were distributed to the different gun-boats, to man and fight the bow-guns.'

With *Opossum* leading, the Admiral flying his flag in *Plover* next, followed by *Cormorant, Lee, Nimrod, Banterer, Kestrel* and *Starling*, the force advanced upon the booms, but as the water shoaled they ran aground, one after the other. The morning went by, and hands went to dinner. Shortly afterwards,

Ready to fire ten-inch guns at the Ty-Cock-Tow forts along the
Canton River, February 1858.

Opossum carried the boom and *Plover* was just following when the masks fell
from the forts' embrasures and the Chinese guns, which had been silent the
whole day, opened fire. John and about a score of the *Highflyers* were sent
across to *Starling* to work her gun but unfortunately she ran aground in a
position from which she could not fire. They tried everything to get her off,
jumping up and down on the quarter-deck, rolling shot about, shifting the
heavy pivot gun, but she would not budge. The sailors were ordered to get
down into the boats on the sheltered side of *Starling*, away from the Chinese
gunfire. The Chinese shooting was very good and 'it was somewhat laughable
to see how we—British bluejackets—ducked when a ball chanced to whistle
close over us. However, this paying of respect to the swift iron bullets saved
many a life that day.'

With some others, John had climbed back on *Starling*'s upper-deck to watch
the action.

> I can hardly tell how I felt; for after the firing began such a state of
> excitement possessed me that I could scarcely contain my feelings, and I
> caught myself several times singing out and clapping my hands, keeping
> my eyes all the while rivetted on the forts. With what a burst of savage
> joy did I see the enemy's walls shattered by our shot, and 'Well done,
> *Cormorant!*' 'Bravo, *Lee!*' 'Pretty firing!' were cries in which my
> emotions found vent. Others exclaimed, 'It can't last long, the Chinese
> rascals won't stand to their guns long. Smart work.'

As at Navarino, the British tars could not believe that their opponents could

The ship's company of a gunboat in the Canton River at
prayers.

resist for so long, and again they were surprised. 'But they did stand, as shot
after shot testified, tearing away our bulwarks and splintering spars,
scattering death on all sides, or sullenly plunging beneath the water-line of the
vessel. So it went on; furious uproar—frightful crashing—smoke—
groans—and death; neither side showing the least signs of giving in.'

One shot struck *Starling*'s pivot-gun, knocked away the trunnion,
overturned the carriage, scattered splinters all around and finally lodged
between gun and carriage, where it was firmly wedged. The admiral had
shifted his flag to *Opossum*, where John and his mates were now transferred.
The first thing they saw on board was the admiral himself, 'sitting on the
gunwale, looking very pale, and bleeding from a wound in the thigh; yet
refusing to go below or have it attended to'.

John joined the crew of *Opossum*'s pivot-gun:

We fired away briskly, with very good effect. And so did the enemy for
the matter of that. A sapper who stood next to me was cut in two, and fell
at my feet. Then and at such-like times it was that I felt more fearful than
before. So long as I was not close to the wounded, or one who fell killed, I
kept my courage, and could do my share of duty at the gun; but it made
me wince to see the man whose shoulder rubbed mine picked off so
suddenly. However, it was for this I had gone through my drill in the old
Illustrious, and now or never we had to put our lessons in practice.

Opossum hauled out of range, giving the sailors a chance to catch their
breath, before closing the forts again, bow first, so that the crew of the pivot

The landing to attack the Taku Forts on 25 June 1858.

gun aft had nothing to do but stand and watch the firing. The flag captain came aft and ordered them, 'For God's sake men, lie down! You are too valuable to be shot now. Besides, we can't go twenty-two thousand miles every day for men like you.' It was sound advice, of which the Admiralty Board would thoroughly have approved. Highly-trained bluejackets were so valuable on foreign stations that the Admiralty jealously watched their employment, especially in naval brigades ashore.

The Chinese firing slackened and then stopped and the admiral, mistakenly as it proved, decided to launch an assault on shore to take the forts. Boats full of marines, and British and French bluejackets, were towed upriver. John was amongst them with his musket, water-bottle, empty haversack, and sixty rounds of ammunition in his pouches. As the boats came near the landing-place (selected, according to John, by an officer who did not have to land himself) the Chinese opened a tremendous fire.

The nearer we came to the landing place, the nastier it looked. However, as soon as our boat touched the ground we jumped out, and found

ourselves up to the waist in water and slime; and, what was worse, our
ammunition was rendered useless by the soaking it got. Some poor
fellows lost their footing, and went down so deep into the mud that they
were drowned by the jump from their boat. Others seemed petrified, and
crouched into the very bottom of the boats, so terrible appeared the iron
storm that we had to face.

We were under the charge of an old petty officer. He was addressing
an order to one of our party, when a shot struck him, and he fell dead.
We moved on: might as well advance as to stand there to be killed,
especially as the forts were passing on us a murderous fire of grape-shot
and all other conceivable missiles. The sight was sickening to see so
many falling around, and yet no one able to stretch out a helping hand to
save. All at once I felt a sudden numbness in my head, and my cap was
knocked off. I instinctively put up my hand, but felt no blood, and
fortunately kept my footing. My impression was that I had been
accidentally hit by a Frenchman behind me who was firing at the forts.
Dreadful was our struggle through that greasy mud. At length we
reached the outermost trench, where about half of our number, having

spoilt their ammunition, could not molest the enemy; so we halted under cover, looking on, and wishing the Chinese, the forts, and the officer who selected the landing-place, at the devil; anywhere but in the place they happened to be.

I fired my musket once after landing, and then, in consequence of my plunge and many falls, which choked the barrel, I could only stand by, ready for whatever turned up.

Presently we made a push for the inner trench but had not gone very far when I saw an officer lying half-buried in the mud, which was by this time pretty well sprinkled with dead and dying. I went to his assistance, and found he was wounded in the throat, or I fancied so, and managed, in spite of balls and bullets, to drag him down to the water's edge, and place him in the bottom of a boat.

I once more trudged along in order to regain the mass of seamen and marines who were struggling gallantly onwards, returning but a feeble fire to the storm from the walls. I came on the way to a small patch of rushes, and pretty firm ground: how blessed did it seem to one's feet, although sodden! While I stayed here a little to get breath, three or four bluejackets and marines approached, one of whom came by my side and halted, as I had done, to recover breath. I turned to ask him for a drink from his water-bottle, when a shot struck him in the heart: 'Get you out of it,' he said to me, and fell dead. Another, while advancing to speak to me, was cut in halves by a ball, and I felt his blood bespatter me.

And now again that fierce don't-care feeling came over me. I sprang up, and tore across the open space, from the rushy patch to the second trench which was lined with our men; shaking my musket in impotent defiance, as it were, against the yelling Chinese, who now swarmed at intervals upon the settlements. The trench was full of water, but I ran recklessly in, and swam, and waded to the opposite side; still clutching my musket. Then I sank; but felt someone grip hold of me by the collar of my frock, and haul me into soundings; at the same time a shipmate's familiar voice said, 'Nearly gone that time, John! Stand on that big stone, you won't be out of your depth.' On looking round, I found my preserver to be 'Snarley-Yow' so called and that I was standing close to Captain Shadwell, our own captain, who, though up to his armpits in water, kept up his spirits wonderfully, and now and then spoke a word of encouragement to the men, who in their turn gave a hearty reply.

After one attempt to raise scaling ladders had failed, the attack was called off and the sailors 'had the mortification of doing that which few Englishmen like to do—namely, turn our backs upon the enemy':

No sooner did the Chinese see us begin the retreat, than they raised such a succession of fearful yells, as I shall never forget; the sky above was black, the water we were in was black, and the very Chinese on the battlements above seemed like black devils, as they uttered yell after yell, at the same time sending after us a withering fire.

In the darkness, with mud and water up to their armpits and still under

Chinese fire, John and the others struggled back to the boats. They threw aside their arms and haversacks, and made the best way they could. Many of them were wounded, and many who were untouched during the battle drowned on the way back. John himself was hit by a spent ball and might have given up, but he met a marine officer who gave him a reviving drink from his flask. When the boats came, the sailors were so eager to get into them that there was some overcrowding. Some officers, once their boats were full, had to beat off the men or threaten them with pistols. The French, John noted, took anybody and crammed their boats as full as they could.

The Royal Naval Rendezvous on Tower Hill, hoping
to attract and recruit 'bounty men', May 1859.

At last, John got back on board the *Banterer* and threw himself down,

wet clothes and all, by the warm funnel, and soon slept the deep sleep of fatigue and exhaustion. Few of us cared whether tomorrow's sun rose upon us dead or living. Not one of us had tasted food since noon. It was six in the evening when we landed, and two in the morning of the 26th before the last of the survivors were brought off from the mud; no wonder, therefore, that the combined effect of hunger, toil, disgrace and disaster produced such a feeling of utter indifference and dejection. But for that nip of brandy from the marine officer's flask, I, too, might have given in before the rescue came.

The sun rose next morning on *Banterer*'s upper-deck, where

lying in groups round the deck were the seaman and marines, bedaubed with mud; their hair all tangled; some shoeless, some without caps; few had retained their belts, and all looked miserable even in sleep. And to match the heap of men, there lay in ugly confusion broken muskets, spoiled and wasted ammunition, belts, pouches, cutlasses and all the disheartening signs of a retreat; while from below came the groans of the wounded, and in many cases dying.

Highflyer had lost twenty-eight killed or wounded; the total casualties were 464 killed or wounded. Characteristically, the bluejackets thought that the fort guns must have been manned by 'more than Chinamen'. Some thought the Russians were there. There was talk of another assault, but it never came off. After smashing the machinery in *Cormorant* and setting fire to *Plover*, both hopelessly damaged and aground, so that the Chinese could get no advantage from them, the fleet sailed back to Shanghai.

Twelve months later, the ships were back again for the third time, carrying the troops and stores for an assault on the Taku forts which finally succeeded. The ships carried the army upriver to Peking, which was entered on 13 October, 1860.

Fortunately, an accurate account of this 1860 assault on the forts exists, also written from the lower-deck. The writer's name was Walter White, an eighteen-year-old ship's painter (his nineteenth birthday, he said, was the day after the forts were taken) who was serving in the 21-gun wooden screw corvette *Scout* at the time:

21 August—As soon as it was daylight we got the guns into position and directly the Chinese saw us a bright flash and a heavy gunfire gave us to know they meant business. They had it all their own way for 20 minutes or so, when we joined in. The gunboats opened fire from the river and what with their guns and we on shore and the Chinese in the Forts, you may imagine that there was a pretty high row on. About an hour after starting hostilities we were almost deafened by a terrific explosion and could see that the upper North Fort was obscured by a dense smoke cloud. When it had drifted off the Fort was observed to be a mass of ruins and we quite thought that this had decided the question for them, but to our great surprise they started to fire as briskly as ever. Ten minutes after another Fort magazine blew up, but nothing daunted by the catastrophe, they kept right up with the fire with what guns remained. It was seven o'clock before the fire slackened and by this time we had knocked a large breach in the wall. We had left the guns to storm the Forts; the sappers and Marines were told off to carry pontoons to lay in the water ditch, the 44th Regiment meanwhile covering them with a very hot rifle fire. We all made a rush, but when we arrived at the margin of the ditch we had no cover and men began to roll about in every direction, until every man carrying the pontoons was either killed or wounded. I saw fifteen men go down in less than 10 minutes. At last Lieutenant Rogers and some of the 67th men swam the ditch, pulled up

A bluejacket of the landing-party guards one of the Taku Forts
taken by assault in August 1860.

some of the bamboo stakes with which the ground was planted, and got
up under the corner of the wall. We crossed the ditch a few at a time in
the same manner, many being shot in the water. When we were strong
enough we attempted to storm the walls, but the first time we were
driven back. Eventually more of the 67th and 44th storming parties
reached us and after a fierce hand-to-hand fight in which soldiers, sailors
and marines, French and English, were all mixed up together, we drove
the Chinese from the casements. Still they would not give in, but
maintained a heavy fire at us until nearly all were shot down or
bayonetted. Lieutenant Rogers of the 44th, Lieutenant Burslem of the
67th, Lieutenant Chaplin of the 67th and Private John Lane, also of the
67th, were the first in the Fort. In this engagement, we had had 25
Officers wounded, 17 men killed, 162 wounded. The French had 15
killed and 160 wounded. All around the parapet were planted sharp-
pointed bamboo sticks. The ground was strewn with crow's feet of iron
spikes constructed so that whichever way they lay two spikes pointed
upwards. On these the Chinese were in several instances impaled
through being thrown over the walls. In one corner of the casement I
counted 23 bodies bayonetted round a gun and in the ditch lay 32 more
men dead, in fact the ground was thick with dead and dying Chinese
soldiers. After disarming all that were left, we had orders to leave the
Fort as a rumour was current to the effect that the Fort was mined. We all
fell in and piled arms outside with all our own dead in a row in front of us
and everybody was covered with mud and thoroughly worn out. Sir
Robert Napier was lying on the ground, exhausted, his hand I noticed

was bleeding and I heard him telling another officer that a gingal bullet had knocked the telescope out of his hand and another had cut open his boot.

Walter White may have read John's book (published in 1862, when White was still serving) or he may even have met him personally. There are numerous resemblances between John's published account and Walter White's stories which he collected and wrote out in 1870 or 1880. For example, the Taku forts were, according to White, 'nearly all silenced as we thought, the setting sun shone through the embrasure of the walls and gave them the appearance of being on fire'. According to John,

> I sat in the stern-sheets of the boat, and as we were pulling inshore, one of our party said to me, 'Hurrah! John, the forts are a-fire!' 'Can't be,' says I; 'they were as black as ever ten minutes ago!' It was the setting sun which, throwing out the forts in strong relief, and shining through loophole and embrasure, had produced the appearance which deceived my mate.

Walter White also had a story how he was hit and wounded during the Indian Mutiny, 'after the fight of Kiedjura' (probably he means Khujwa, in November 1857, which was before he joined the Navy). But though he was not there himself, Walter had talked to a seaman who certainly was. His account has the feel of an eye-witness's. In the Mutiny story, '. . . the bullocks were unhitched from the guns and sent down to the tank under escort, sentries being thrown out as usual. It was Sunday evening, very hot, with darkness just closing down . . .'

But, although there are anecdotes which (from the ship's log) are plainly untrue and some which are highly unlikely (for example, the day Walter was bailed out of prison in Rio by his captain), Walter also describes crossing the line, a burial at sea, concert parties, general quarters, and Christmas Day on board, all clearly from his own experience.

The explanation for the discrepancies in Walter's tales lies in the sailors' main pastime on board which was, simply, yarning. Squatting on deck in the waist during the long watches, or sitting below in their mess-decks, the sailors had hours in which to swap yarns, of past ships, past shipmates, past officers, past wars and storms and shipwrecks. Books of reminiscences such as John's were read, or read aloud, and added to the store of common experience. Walter White, who was born in 1845, joined the Navy in 1859 and left in 1864, was an intelligent and imaginative man, who studied art and became an interior designer much influenced by William Morris. He had seven children, one of whom kept his memoirs in manuscript after his death in 1912. His tales are a typical selection of the sort a mid-nineteenth-century sailor would accumulate during his service: he would understandably tell them in the first person, as though they had happened to him, and would not neglect to accentuate the part he personally had played. Thus his tales are a mixture of fact and fiction, of conjecture and personal experience, of truth and hearsay, myth and theory. They may be factually wrong on many points, but they are right in a deeper, more subtle sense.

John Highflyer bought himself out of the Navy when the ship got home to Portsmouth in May 1861, after five years away from England. By July he was a free man, having had to pay £12 16s. to get out because he had served only five of his ten years' engagement. A day or two later he went up to Somerset House to collect his share of the £30,543 15s. prize money for the operations in Canton. He was paid 28s. This, he said, 'apart from the glory, was all I got for my fortnight's hardlying and the chance of being shot by the Provost Marshal'.

John had been something of a misfit on the mess-deck. He was an unusually well-educated man for the lower-deck who must have attracted the officers' attention. One of the midshipmen on board, Jackie Fisher (the future admiral and First Sea Lord), must have noticed such a man. The ship's chaplain once asked John what his occupation was before he came to sea. The answer, which John does not give, caused the padre to exclaim: 'Whatever could have possessed you? Surely you do not mean to continue a sailor?' He had books sent to him from home, including '*Airy's Astronomical Lectures, The House with the Seven Gables*, and other works of pleasant reading'. During the trip out he said that he had 'very gloomy and dissatisfied thoughts, getting very sick of the company I was in, and my mode of life'. He wrote of mess-deck life with the faint irony of an outsider, as, for instance, about dinner time:

Fancy to yourself a lower-deck mess-table!—time a quarter to eight bells in the forenoon—presently I heard the bugle playing up cheerly 'The Roast Beef of Old England', and aft to the galley rush the hands whose turn it is to do duty as cooks to draw the day's allowance of meat.

It is drawn and on the table, and my messmates sit round, and are soon busily engaged in criticising. No matter for dirty hands or tangled hair: it doesn't do to be particular on board ship. 'What won't poison will fatten,' is a sea proverb. 'Well,' says Bill, nicknamed the Calf, 'if that's dinner, God send supper! Here's for a smoke;' and off he goes. Presently, Joe, who has eaten his share, gets up, and after belching rudely in his neighbour's face, exclaims, 'I'd like to have Mr Somerset, or whatever they call him, just to taste this here meat; I'm blest if it wouldn't make him stare! Beef, they call it; I'm glad they've found a name for it. It beats the tea, so called. I s'pose the Admiralty gets the pair of 'em cut out by the law of economy, don't they?'

John describes his messmates, very probably a typical cross-section of a mess-deck of the time, with a clear, even bleak eye:

First in order comes the caterer, generally a steady-going petty officer, who is considered responsible for the orderly state of the mess, and any faults committed by his messmates. Harry B. is an open-hearted, intelligent man, fond of reading, and very well informed; he is tolerably lenient and impartial in his judgement. He and I often used to have a romp together.

Then there's Mikey, a real broth of a boy; good-tempered when sober, but inclined to liquor, and when so, extremely wild and racketty. He has read a great deal, and is pretty intelligent and thoughtful, in fact, quite a step above the common herd. He is greatly incensed at the abuses which are creeping into the service, and vows when paid off he will join the Yankees: 'something like, their service is!'

J.W. comes next, commonly called West-Country. An old Arctic man—he has been out with Captain Kellett in two expeditions, searching for Sir John; he is generally light-hearted and cheerful, full of curious yarns. For example: 'I was once,' said he, 'along with a first lieutenant, and he was everlasting picking his nose; he was always a-finding fault; he'd stop p'raps at the cable-tier, or the shot-locker, then he'd begin at the nose again: "Dirtiest hole in the ship, master-at-arms! dirtiest hole in the ship!" How the chaps used to laugh at him!' He used to say also, that he was once towed six miles under water by a whale, and only came up once to breathe. He has in common with the rest, one sad failing: whenever he can he gets drunk, and firmly believes it does him good.

Bill is the next one, a young fellow who has served most of his time in big ships, and considers small ships to be a bore 'cause they ain't half manned, and wants the work done big-ship fashion all the same, 'little big-ships I call 'em'. He growls tremendously, and says Andrew won't catch him in a small craft again; and when his time's up he'll have a slap at the Yankees.

Young Joe comes before us next, looking dissipated but has a redeeming blue eye, and an amiable temper; he is very ignorant of books, but eagerly listens to folks who know more than he does; is quick and handy at his work, but knows too much of what is no good to him.

Who next? Quimbo, born in the West Indies, very good-natured and simple. He has, though, a wicked temper; he also greatly affects the dandy; hence he is the general butt of the mess. I used to write his and young Joe's letters—love letters and all. They would bring the paper to me with the request; and the, 'You know what to say well enough; I'm going to have a smoke,' and I was left to concoct the letters alone; and so great faith had they in me that when I read it to them they would say, 'Oh, that'll do fizzin'.' In fact, I was letter-writer for many a shipmate.

The carpenter, or wood-spoiler, comes next; a disagreeable fellow, and to use the men's favourite expression, 'He's a big eater, and his shipmates don't like him.'

I come next—but I trust the reader will be able to describe me without any further help on my part.

Now for the last and youngest in the mess, Dick, a fine sprightly little fellow, with a good elementary education, and a fair stock of commonsense; not a bad seaman, and one day will do some good for himself.

Unlike the Army, the Navy won no Victoria Crosses at the Taku Forts, but the Taiping Rebellion of the 1860s in China did provide some action, and one more bluejacket VC, won in an almost forgotten incident.

The winner was Able Seaman George Hinckley, who was serving in HMS *Sphinx*, commanded by another VC winner, Captain G. F. Day. On 7 October 1862, a party of sailors from *Sphinx* was landed to attack the fortified town of Fung Wha, ten miles below Shanghai. The sailors marched thirty miles, carrying three days' rations of biscuit and salt pork. The road was very bad and rain fell incessantly until, as the sailors said, 'the only dry thing about us was our ammunition—seventy rounds of ball in our pouches'. The sailors camped in the rain, and took breakfast, of biscuit and a tot of rum, at four o'clock in the morning. By eight o'clock they were in front of the gates of Fung Wha which was strongly defended by the Taipings. One dash was made for the main gate but it was repelled by a tremendous fire of muskets, gingals, stinkpots, slugs, nails, and great jagged lumps of iron, fired from loop-holes and turret-slits cut in the walls. The ground in front of the gate was very soon strewn with dead and dying. Mr Croker, assistant master of *Sphinx*, and Mr Browne, an army officer, were both badly wounded and lay out in the open.

Able Seaman George Hinckley, VC.

Meanwhile the sailors had retired under cover, where they could hear the ground and gravel being scored and raked by hundreds of shots and slugs. Getting permission, Hinckley ran out, lifted Mr Croker in his arms, threw him over his shoulder face downwards, and ran for the safety of a josshouse about 150 yards away. When he came back, Hinckley volunteered again, ran out a second time and carried Mr Browne to safety, for which he was quite rightly awarded the Victoria Cross.

'Boys, see my back?':
naval discipline of the 1850s

Just before he left the Navy, as almost his last act as a sailor, John *Highflyer* was persuaded by his friends, much against his will, to have his photograph taken in uniform. The picture appears as a frontispiece to his book and it shows a typical sailor of about 1860, dressed in the uniform the Admiralty had laid down, for the first time in the Navy's history, in 1857. John wears a floppy blue hat, with a gold cap ribbon with *Highflyer*'s name. He has a blouse-like blue frock, tucked into blue serge trousers, with baggy sleeves and broad-banded cuffs, a very large black or dark blue scarf tied round his throat and a lighter blue collar. He has a thin beard, or Newgate fringe, from ear to ear.

In the first half of the nineteenth century, captains were free to dress their ships' companies much as they liked. In *Tweed* in 1827 Keppel saw the men in 'petticoat trousers' manning the ship's side for the arrival of *Royal Sovereign* flying the Duke of Clarence's flag. When Captain Walpole commissioned the frigate *Vernon* in 1840 he dressed the men in red frocks. Afterwards he found these difficult to replace and they had to use blue serge from the ship's stocks. Eventually one watch wore red, the other blue. In 1845 Captain John Washington dressed the crew of *Blazer* in guernseys with vertical blue and white stripes, possibly the origin of the word 'blazer'. Captain Wallace Houston, in *Tourmaline*, had his crew in red shirts and fancy caps. Thus the naval novelist Captain M. H. Barker was not so fanciful when he made the commander of the *Tulip* in his book *The Naval Foundling* have his crew dressed in green with an imitation of the flower reversed in their caps, and his boat's crew in tiger skins, resembling Indians, with short paddles instead of oars. Captains were often particularly fussy over their gig's crews, whose adornment reflected their taste, wealth and idiosyncrasy. Commander Wilmot of *Harlequin* dressed his gig's crew as harlequins. The captain of the *Tiger* had them in jerseys with yellow and black stripes. Admiral Dundas put his barge's crew in Dundas tartan (men of the Naval Brigade in the Crimea are often shown with tartan Kilmarnock or Tam O'Shanter caps). But times changed: when Captain Courtenay of the frigate *Constance* arrived in Rio in the 1860s, the C-in-C would not receive him on board the flagship because he disapproved of his boat's crew's dress of dungaree suits with red sashes and long sheath knives in their belts.

In 1850 Captain Blackwood of the *Victory* dressed his ship's company in a Sunday best uniform of a short blue jacket, with double rows of mother-of-pearl buttons sewn very close together, a white frock with a blue jean collar worn outside the jacket, and wide blue cloth trousers. This was very similar to the official sailors' rig, announced in the Regulations of January 1857, which, for the first time, gave the sailor a standard dress. The introduction of a uniform was a matter of prestige, showing that a permanent standing force

'John' of *Highflyer*, as he was photographed for the frontispiece of his memoirs *From Portsmouth to the Peiho*, in the sailor's uniform of 1860.

now had a permanent recognisable uniform, and it was also an improvement in personal hygiene. There was now a regulation standard of appearance and cleanliness to be maintained.

From 1857 the issue of clothing was: a blue cloth jacket, a pair of blue cloth trousers, a blue serge frock, a duck frock, a pair of duck trousers, a black silk handkerchief, a pair of shoes, and one collar which originally had only two rows of tape. The sailors continued to wear black straw hats known as tarpaulins, which often had the ship's name in gold letters, but most wore a blue peakless cap with a ribbon. Occasionally an old sailor could be seen with a 'glazed' tall hat, often daubed with tar until it was hard and heavy and shiny. From 1859 a free kit on entry was authorised, and men were permitted to buy their uniforms from non-service sources, if they wished, when the cash value of the clothing would be paid to them instead.

Although John Highflyer gives tantalisingly few facts about himself, merely saying (wrongly) that the reader can deduce them from his book, he is much clearer about life on board. This is the daily routine at sea:

Four a.m., 'Watch and idlers to muster' (cooks, stewards, and boys, are termed idlers). Five a.m., 'Watch and idlers coil up ropes; wash and scrub upper deck.' Three-quarters of an hour, 'Coil down ropes.' Then, if all plain sail were on the ship, 'Reset sail; take another pull of all halyards; *sweat* the light sails up *taut*.' Seven a.m., breakfast. Half an hour, 'Call the watch; watch below clean lower-deck.' Watch on deck as requisite. 'Divisions;' prayers. Twelve noon, dinner. Two p.m., 'Call afternoon watch'; employed on deck. At four, 'Call the first dog-watch.' And so on, with but little variation from day to day; nothing meeting one's gaze but the boundless waste of wild blue water, enlivened now and then by a sail.

In heavy weather, when it came on to blow harder, the order was: 'Hands reef topsails!' which was followed by

a tremendous rush, each one of us striving to be in the rigging before his fellow, treading on one another's fingers, hustling, and well-nigh capsizing a shipmate out of the shrouds. Then holding on by the yard, we get out on the foot-ropes, and gather up the sail as far as the reef-band, and hold it firmly in our grasp, ready to tie the points, while the captain of the top is hauling out the weather-earring, which must be always secured first. All this time it may be raining hard, pelting into your ears and eyes, running in a merry stream down your back; and the yard strains and jerks with the furiously flopping sail till you are all but knocked off. As soon as the weather-earring is hauled out, 'Haul out to leeward' is the cry, and the lee-earring is tied; then the impatient officer below sings out, 'Sheet home,' 'Hoist away,' and before you are barely clear of the yard, the 'sheets' are close 'home' and the sail rehoisted. You descend to the deck again, the ship staggers on under her lessened canvas, the rain still pelts down upon you, and the loose bottoms of your trousers carry off little rivulets of water. Such watches as these did not tend to make us amiable; and look out for squalls if you put a messmate out in dirty weather. We used to stand pretty much as a donkey does in the middle of a field, silent and sullen; and when the watch was relieved we were always ready to dive below, and get a shift of dry clothes.

In the heyday of sail, the topmen were capable of astonishing feats of agility and daring. Familiarity bred a contempt which made many men fall to their deaths, but the survivors seemed to have no fear of heights, no sense of vertigo whatsoever. When manning yards, or even when merely skylarking, men used to stand with their arms folded on the trucks of royal masts, at least 220 feet from the deck. Evelyn Wood, in *Queen*, noted that when Queen Victoria inspected the fleet off St Helens, Isle of Wight, on 4 August 1853, a Private Buckle of the RMLI removed the fore-royal-mast lightning conductor and, with folded arms, *balanced on his head* on the bare truck, 147 feet from the upper-deck. One of the *Marlborough*'s bosuns used to dive off the main yard, a hundred feet above the water, swim under the ship and come up the other side; one day he evidently dived too deep and failed to emerge on the other side.

Crews were so disciplined that they worked sails in silence, except for the occasional word of command or note of a pipe. Victor Montagu was greatly impressed when he was alongside the *Marlborough* in his boat and the order was given to 'cross royal yards and loose sails'. The ship had been refitting, her topmasts were struck, the yards were down and stowed across the hammock nettings. So the evolution, as Montagu said, 'was a very big business'. But 'no sooner was the pipe given than 1,300 men forming the crew were rushing to their stations up ladders and hatchways; and beyond the pit-a-pat of feet, not a sound was to be heard.' The captain, Houston Stewart, said to Montagu: 'Can you hear a pin drop?' Most of the orders were given by flag signals. 'If any voice was heard, or the slightest confusion arose on any part of the deck, or aloft, the bugle immediately sounded the "Still"; and not a soul moved.' It was like a children's game of Grandmother's Footsteps, played by men aloft. As Montagu said, 'It was curious to see the strange positions of arms and legs at such moments.'

The handling of such a ship needed men, hundreds of them. The watch in a line-of-battle-ship 'would be 350 men or thereabouts', according to Montagu, 'and the wretched mid was nearly choked before he got half-way through the muster'. The midshipman had to call out these hundreds of names as quickly as possible because the old watch was not free to turn in before the muster was over.

Silence aloft was enforced with the cat. Henry Capper, who later became a lieutenant-commander, first joined the Navy as a boy seaman in the training ship *St Vincent* in 1869. One afternoon, he and his fellows were, they thought, unjustly deprived of leave and made to learn knots and splices instead of going ashore on a Wednesday afternoon. Their instructor, Petty Officer Pontin, a man of some twenty years' service,

> seeing we were seething with a sense of wrong, he kept us in hand until the officers had gone away; then, to our amazement, instead of giving us knots and splices to make, he very deliberately commenced to take off his jumper, white frock and flannel, and thus stripped to the waist, he suddenly turned round, with his back to the unruly class. Across his back, and particularly on the right side, were livid blue stripes from the shoulders to the waist with scarcely an inch here and there of healthy skin.
>
> 'Boys', he said, 'see my back? That is where I was twice flogged with the cat. The first time because I told an officer he was unfair to me, *and he was*; the second time because I would not give a messmate away who had made a noise aloft. Now, take an old man's advice and while you are in the Navy do as the printed rules tell you; obey all orders implicitly.' No one replied, but a very chastened group was afterward sent aloft to see how sails were bent and furled; nor did I, for one, ever forget that practical lesson in discipline.

Sometimes the discipline enforced and the daily routines to which the sailors had to submit were senselessly harsh. Victor Montagu was mate of the

main-deck in the battleship *Algiers* in the Channel Fleet during the
exceptionally hard winter of 1859–60. At times the rigging and sails were
frozen. But,

> twice a week the ship's company had to wash their clothes, which
> generally took from an hour to an hour and a half. Consequently, the
> routine was put a little out of joint. Time had to be made up somehow.
> The usual hour to turn out was at 5 or 5.30 a.m., to wash decks; but on
> washing mornings I have seen the men turned out at 7 bells in the middle
> watch (3.30), on a freezing morning, to scrub hammocks and wash
> clothes, with nothing but a wretched lanthorn and a farthing dip to see
> by; and this was the only light for ten or a dozen men to wash their
> clothes by. After this the decks had to be washed in icy cold water, and
> at 6.30 these wretched frozen men consoled themselves with breakfast of
> cocoa and ship's biscuit—possibly with bread and butter, if the bum-
> boat had come alongside.

As mate of the main-deck Montagu had to be present at what he called 'these
remnants of barbarism', to see them carried out.

At about the same time, another line-of-battle-ship put into Falmouth for a
short time on a Saturday and gave leave from half-past three on the Sunday
afternoon until the next morning. Very few of the men who went ashore had
any money and no boats were sent ashore to bring them off, but only six of
them deserted. One of those who did return was the captain of the forecastle, a
regular old salt of thirty years' standing, who was brought on board hopelessly
drunk. The commander had him placed between two guns on the main-deck
under the eye of a sentry and mustered all the first and second class boys in the
ship to jeer and laugh at the old sailor in his disgusting and degraded state. Yet,
when Henry Capper was a boy in the *Inconstant* in the 1860s, it was a regular
thing for men to come off senseless with drink; a whip was rigged on the
mainyard to hoist them on board and they were left in the scuppers to sleep it
off for five or six hours; if they then turned to their work, nothing more was
said.

After the end of the Russian War, the Navy had increasing difficulty in
manning its ships and there were more and more deserters. The reasons were
the old ones of the rival attractions of the Merchant Marine and the foreign
navies, especially the American Navy, compounded by poor food, poor pay
and harsh treatment. But all discontents were aggravated by the main problem
of leave. Until the Navy gave leave on a more regular and more humane basis, it
did not even begin to approach a solution to what amounted to a crisis of
discipline in the service at the end of the 1850s.

In April 1856, after the Russian war, there was a fleet at Spithead of some
twenty-five sail of the line and some 200 other classes of ships. Their combined
ships' companies totalled more than 26,000 men. Within two months more
than half of those ships had been paid off and 15,000 men had been discharged
to shore. But when the screw line-of-battle-ship *Princess Royal* (91)
commissioned in August, she was three months getting a crew and she was

eventually manned by so poor a lot of seamen that the Parliamentary Returns of punishment in the Navy showed that *Princess Royal* had more floggings *per capita* each quarter than any other ship in the Navy. Captain George Giffard was requested to resign and the commander was relieved of his appointment. A more lenient captain, Thomas Baillie, was appointed but the crew, if anything, became more mutinous. In the Mediterranean, *Princess Royal* was caught in a storm on her way to Alexandria and the sailors refused to go aloft. Had it not been for the officers, the ship might have been lost. The C-in-C relegated the ship to trooping duties, which were always unpopular, and often sent her to sea while other ships were in harbour. *Princess Royal* was eventually sent home first, after serving barely three years on the station, although *Conqueror, Brunswick* and *Centurion* had all been out months longer. So, once again, the system penalised the good sailors, sending home the bad before the good.

Princess Royal's manning difficulties had had some excuse, because she was commissioning at the same time and place as the frigate *Shannon* under the popular and competent Peel, and small ships were always more popular than big. But there was no such excuse for *Ganges, Boscawen* and *Cumberland*, all paid off in 1857 and all taking four to five months to complete with crews which were described as very indifferent. *Orion* (91) paid off at Devonport in October 1857. *Renown* (91) commissioned at Sheerness the following November. She took six months to get her crew and not one man from *Orion* joined *Renown*. *Monarch* (84) paid off in the summer of 1858, when several large ships were commissioning, but the majority of her seamen left the Navy and many of the new continuous service ratings bought their discharges.

The Admiralty themselves took advantage of this situation in May 1857 by inviting all petty officers, seamen and boys in ships in home waters or arriving home from foreign service to take their discharge, without payment, from their continuous service engagements. Of men on non-continuous engagements, only petty officers and able seamen were allowed to re-engage. All continuous-service men of poor character or poor physique, together with boys who were judged unlikely to make good seamen, were compulsorily discharged. This was a return to the atmosphere of the bad old days of casual recruiting and 'hand-to-mouth' manning, and it was bitterly resented, especially as many sailors, typically, took their tickets and then regretted it. It seemed that the Admiralty had learned nothing: after all the fanfares for a new deal for seamen, after all the promises of a permanent career, their thinking had progressed little beyond the press gang stage.

The 1853 Committee had by no means solved the long-term problems of naval manning. However, some measures were taken. The Coastguard, founded in 1831, was transferred from the province of the Board of Customs to the Admiralty in 1856 and the emphases in its recruiting were placed on forming some kind of war reserve. Entry was restricted to men under thirty-seven years of age, with seven years' active service as seamen. They were called 'Fleet men' and they began to train at guardships placed at convenient ports round the coast. By 1859 there were about 5,600 coastguards. At the same time more attention was given to recruiting for the Royal Naval Coast Volunteers, but these were for the most part the fishermen and longshoremen who were traditionally difficult to recruit and hostile towards the Queen's service. There were consequently never very many of them, and neither they nor the Coastguard could possibly provide the large pool of men required.

In June 1858 the First Lord Sir John Pakington set up a Royal Commission on Manning, which reported in January 1859. They recommended more training brigs for boy seamen. They also recommended the issue of free bedding and mess utensils to new recruits and free uniform for continuous service entrants. An improved scale of victualling was introduced. They suggested improved pay for seamen-gunners; the Admiralty went further and doubled their pay, and also allowed them to count five years as six towards their pensions. Even this had little effect on the shortage of seamen-gunners and in January 1860 a class of 'trained men' with more pay was established, and above them an even higher rate, with higher pay, called 'gunnery instructors'. But the Commission's most important recommendation was the setting up of a Royal Naval Reserve.

In 1846 Lord Auckland, then First Sea Lord, had had the notion of creating a naval reserve from the Dockyard Service and the Coastguard. The men were to live at home but be taught gunnery and be available for call-up in time of national emergency. But the Navy's reputation was against it, and after five years of keen recruiting fewer than 2,000 men had signed.

The government changed while the 1859 Commission was rendering its report, and it was Lord Palmerston's administration which passed the Statute authorising the Royal Naval Reserve in August 1859. Its intention was to make use of the thousands of sailors of the merchant marine who made comparatively short voyages, returning to home ports three or four times a year. The scheme's author was Commander J. H. Brown, registrar general of seamen, and it concentrated on quality rather than quantity. The new reservists had to be of British descent; physically fit; under thirty-five years of age (although they were allowed to join up to forty until 1860); with five year's sea service in the previous ten, at least one year with the rate of AB; if possible of fixed abode; personally known and selected by their shipping master; and approved by their local coastguard officer. They had to report to their shipping master once every six months or obtain special leave of absence if they had to go on a longer voyage.

The reservist's training was twenty-eight days a year (which could be split into weekly periods if preferred) in a ship or hulk, or at a shore battery under the local coastguard commander. He was paid naval rates during his drill and at the end of it he was paid £6 as a year's retaining fee, paid quarterly by the shipping masters. He enlisted for five years' service to begin with, but he could qualify for a pension after fifteen years' service (if he was over thirty when he first enlisted) or twenty years' (if he was under thirty); the pension was at least £12 a year, from the age of sixty. The Navy tried to make it easier for him to serve, but harder for him to join a foreign service. Commanding officers were cautioned to 'conciliate the feelings' of the reservists during their service. But the pensions were only payable to men in the British Isles.

Reservists could only be called out by a Royal Proclamation and in times of 'sudden emergency'. They would be called up for three years, which might be extended to five, with extra pay. They had the same pay, allowances, food and living conditions as continuous service men, and the same prospects for promotion. The railways were asked to co-operate in getting men to the ports quickly, route lists were written out, and instructions prepared beforehand. Commander Brown expected about 20,000 men to join the scheme; a third would be ready in a week, the next third in a month, and almost all the rest inside two months.

In theory, Brown's scheme was splendid. It was well advertised with notices, placards and booklets. But when the lists were opened in January 1860, the response was almost nil. The merchant seaman still suspected the Admiralty. He still had thoughts of the 'press'. He wanted to know what sort of 'sudden emergency' would qualify. He was afraid he would be, literally, shanghaied to join the war in China. The Admiralty's stupid and reactionary behaviour in discharging continuous service men in 1857 was still remembered. In any case, there was a shortage of skilled able seamen.

By the end of 1860 only about 3,000 men had joined. The *Trent* incident in 1862, when a British ship was stopped on the high seas by an American warship whose captain was publicly encouraged by his government, gave the scheme a much-needed boost and by 1865 there were 17,000 men in the RNR.

But in the meantime, in 1859 as in 1853, the Admiralty's plans were somewhat overtaken by events. Recruiting was still poor when there was another 'anti-French scare' in 1859 and a bounty had to be offered to men who enlisted: £10 for able seamen, £5 for ordinary seamen, and £2 for landsmen. Energetic recruiting efforts were made in Newcastle and Liverpool and especially in London, where the Admiralty hired a large van, drawn by four greys, with a band of musicians and outriders. The cavalcade toured the streets of the East End, the roof covered with volunteers, the Union Jack flying bravely above, the interior of the van crammed with warrant officers from the receiving ship *Crocodile*, moored off the Tower. Wherever the van stopped, the band struck up 'Rule Britannia', 'Hearts of Oak' and other stirring airs. A Mr Ward, keeper of a celebrated lodging house for sailors, the warrant officers, and anybody else who had a fancy to stay there, addressed the crowds who gathered, urging able-bodied sailors to bestir themselves and join, and induce others to volunteer also to serve the Queen and Old England. The Queen's special proclamation, authorising the bounty, was read out to deafening cheers. A steamboat, profusely decorated with Union Jacks, ensigns and other national colours and manned by a crew of dashing bluejackets, left London Bridge for a cruise down the river. As she passed through the Pool of London, the crews of nearby ships waved their caps and cheered and shouted. The steamer reached Gravesend, where the bluejackets paraded their colours through the streets of the town followed by a vast crowd. More volunteers were welcomed, and the whole party re-embarked at the Town Pier to the strains of 'The Girl I Left Behind Me'.

The recruiting razzamatazz certainly worked up to a point. It brought into the Navy what became known as the 'Bounty crews', which did contain some skilled and valuable merchant seamen, but were mostly men who could never adjust to naval discipline, a rag-tag and bobtail gallimaufry of criminals, ne'er-do-wells, mentally deficients, unemployables, debtors, and family black sheep, reminiscent of the old days of the press. When Captain Phipps Hornby joined *Neptune* in 1861 she had what he called 'the last and worst of the bounty crews'. They appeared to him 'a rough-looking lot' and indeed they proved to be 'shameful riffraff'.

In many ships there were virtually two ship's companies, the regulars and the bounty men. The regulars did not like it. A petty officer in *Brunswick* wrote to the *Daily News* that 'the good seamen in the ship dislike being mixed up with a lot of tinkers and tailors who have lately been entered as ordinary seamen, and they murmur and say, "We have our own duty to do, the duty those men ought to do, and to teach them into the bargain, for the same pay that we should have supposing that every person did his own duty": and it makes them dissatisfied.'

The Admiralty had given instructions in June 1859 that merchantmen should be broken into the Navy gently, and that officers should be 'firm but patient and forebearing' but the bounty crews very soon exacerbated an existing disciplinary problem.

The basic grievances, about leave, were aggravated by harsh, old-fashioned or downright stupid handling by the officers, for the Navy was still suffering from the long stagnation of the officers' promotion lists. A 'purge' of captains was held in 1847, another in 1851, and again in 1864, but it was not until 1870 that the Navy List was properly divided into 'active' and 'retired' officers.

The screw frigate *Liffey* (Captain George W. Preedy) commissioned at Devonport in November 1858, when no other large ship had commissioned for some months so that Preedy was able more or less to pick his own crew. After a short Channel cruise, *Liffey* was ordered to Liverpool to enter seamen for the Navy, and then suddenly received orders to go to Plymouth Sound before foreign service. In the Sound the ship's company asked for leave to see their families and friends before going abroad for several years. Preedy refused. That evening there was a disturbance on board, with parties of men in a state of insubordination, refusing duty and rolling shot about the deck. When the Admiralty heard of the mutiny, or 'emeute' as it was then called, they ordered leave to be granted, whereupon the ship's companies of other ships also mutinied for leave. There were incidents in the *Hero* at Portland, and in *Caesar*.

In August 1859 there was a 'disgraceful disturbance' in the *Marlborough* (121), flagship of Admiral Fanshawe Martin, C-in-C Mediterranean (and the very ship whose drill Montagu so much admired). She had been fitted out at Portsmouth in February 1858 when there had been complaints about the severe discipline meted out by the captain and the commander. Very large ships were unpopular with seamen anyway, and *Marlborough* was a long time completing, eventually having to make up from the flagships at different ports.

When *Marlborough*'s crew heard about the *Liffey*, they broke into open mutiny. They had been particularly exasperated at being ordered to change their clothing three or four times a day, and with this as the pretext, sailors refused duty, and threw shot down the hatchways. Four men were put in irons and later tried by court-martial. Three were sentenced to fifty lashes and two years' imprisonment, the fourth to one year's imprisonment. The Admiralty thought the sentences too lenient.

However, their Lordships took a different view of the case of *Princess Royal*, which was an almost classic example of how not to handle seamen. The ship had come back from her unhappy Mediterranean commission and at Spithead the Admiralty announced that her crew would be transferred to the *Queen*. The men objected, the proposal was withdrawn and the ship was paid off.

The mutiny in *Princess Royal* arose over leave, compounded by the vacillations of the officers. One Saturday, when Queen Victoria was in Portsmouth to launch the screw three-decker *Victoria*, the crew of *Princess Royal*, then alongside in the dockyard, asked the commander for leave to go ashore. After consultation between the commander, captain and admiral, leave was granted to half the crew. But there was a squabble over *which* half. Unusually, it was decided that one half of each watch should go (instead of the more normal whole of one watch). But this too caused an argument. The admiral thereupon cancelled leave for all, and the men who had reached the dockyard gates were turned back. Some of the men, drunk and disappointed, became angry. Fights broke out. The men took over the lower-deck and attempted to strike their officers. The marines were summoned to disarm the mutineers. A total of 119 men were charged with being present at a mutiny and not suppressing it. Two men were sentenced to two years' imprisonment and hard labour, five to eighteen months, and two to six months. However, the Admiralty eventually pardoned, released, reimbursed and granted leave to all the accused. Captain Baillie, the officers and the ship's police were censured. The admiral, Bowles, was also criticised.

New regulations in April 1860 authorised captains to grant regular leave, of forty-eight hours or four days, depending upon the recipient and the circumstances. The first experiments were watched 'in an agony of suspense' by senior officers.

In the winter of 1860/61, *Edgar, Trafalgar, Algiers* and *Diadem* of the Channel Fleet gave leave at various times. *Algiers* lost sixty men through desertion, *Edgar, Trafalgar* and *Diadem* lost a hundred (which, in *Diadem*'s case, was a fifth of the ship's company). By the end of the decade, desertions from the Navy had reached almost epidemic proportions. In 1862, less than one man in a hundred deserted on the West African Station, for obvious reasons of climate and opportunity. But this rose to four per cent in the Channel Fleet, to a surprising five per cent for the coastguards, to nearly ten per cent in Australia and the Pacific, and to nearly fifteen per cent on the south-east American station. Halifax, Nova Scotia, was notorious for its attractions, as were the gold fields of New Zealand and the wide open spaces of Australia. Men also deserted because of the abusive and offensive language and behaviour of some officers. William Petty Ashcroft was coxswain of the pinnace of the *Siren* brig for their whole commission in South America from 1855 to 1860 and lost two boat's crews and a few petty officers because, he said, of the tyranny of the first lieutenant. Ashcroft himself, as a continuous service man, did not desert.

A deserter forfeited all pay, prize money, bounty, annuities, pension, medals, decorations, clothes and any effects left on board. Yet, most years, between 2,000 and 2,500 men were formally noted as deserters and, if caught, were prosecuted, although many men deserted more than once in the same year. In 1859, 2,338 men deserted, of whom 712 had received bounties which had cost the country £4,571. Of these, eighty-six were apprehended. The Naval Discipline Act of 1860 formally defined desertion for the first time: a man was marked as 'Run', with an 'R' in the ship's books, after twenty-one days' unauthorised absence from the ship. The naval police advertised for deserters, giving particulars of their appearance, and offering rewards, in the *Police Gazette*, sometimes even providing a photograph. Ships had to keep a Description Book, and an Open List of every man on board. Prosecutions were brought against anybody who harboured or assisted a deserter in any way; the penalty on conviction was a fine of £30, which many magistrates were loth to impose because they thought it too high.

In 1866, leave was granted in three categories. There was a 'Special' class for men of good character, 'Privileged' for less reliable men who were given leave when convenient, and 'Regular' for anyone else, especially men in the Second Class for Conduct. Not until 1890 did leave become a right and not a privilege. The trend was to punish men for leave-breaking through their pockets rather than on their backs. Elaborate formulae were drawn up and promulgated, to be 'rigidly adhered to', for computing the amount of pay a man forfeited as punishment for overstaying his leave. There was provision for especially punitive action against those who returned on board unfit for duty through drink.

Largely through the exertions of Joseph Hume, MP for Montrose, who spoke longer and more often than any other private member, Parliament had regular returns of punishment in the Navy and kept a sharp eye on the numbers of men flogged. The Admiralty, too, strenuously issued strict injunctions to captains to restrain from excessive punishment, and, sometimes, if they thought the sentences excessive or unjust, stepped in to redress the situation. In 1859 the First Class for Conduct was introduced. No sailor or marine in this class could be flogged except by sentence of court-martial. Some captains, like McClure in *Esk* on the China Station in 1860, were well known for awarding the maximum penalty of forty-eight lashes for almost every offence. But a captain could only go so far. In 1861, Captain C. F. Hillyar in *Queen* was censured for flogging a man in the First Class for Conduct. In November of that year, Commander B. G. W. Nicholas of the *Trident* was courtmartialled for flogging two boys, second class, who had returned on board forty-three hours adrift on their leave. They were asked no questions but flogged at once, one of them until he was insensible. Nicholas admitted

ADMIRALTY.

Description of Deserters and Stragglers from Her Majesty's Sea Service.

Although £3 reward is offered for the apprehension of Deserters at the time, £2 only is payable at the expiration of 3 months, and £1 only at the expiration of 6 months from the date of desertion, and after the expiration of a complete year, no reward will be paid, except under special circumstances.

No reward will be given in these cases if apprehended within the precincts of a port where a regular Police is organized, but all reasonable expenses will be paid.

NAME.	SHIP DESERTED FROM.	DATE.	RATING.	AGE.	SIZE.	WHERE BORN.	HAIR.	EYES.	FACE.	MARKS AND REMARKS.
William Sutton	*Agincourt*, deserter	26 July	butcher	39	5 5	Plymouth, Devon	brown	blue	dark	£3 reward
Benjamin C. Gage	*Swiftsure*, straggler	6 Aug.	private, R. Marines	18	5 8	Stratford	brown	hazel	fresh	£1 reward
L. Bovill	ditto	6 Aug.	gunner, R. M. A.	18	5 9	Norwich	dk. brn	hazel	fresh	ditto
James H. Costellon	ditto	6 Aug.	ditto	22	5 8	Norfolk	dk. brn	blue	fresh	ditto
John MacNally	*D. of Wellington*, deserter	27 July	ordinary, 2nd class	18	5 5	Dublin	lt. brn	blue	fair	£3 reward served in *Boscawen*
John Maslen	ditto	2 Aug.	ordinary	20	5 5	Bexhill, Somerset	light	blue	freck.	£1 reward burn on right cheek; served in *Spartan*
William Lippett	ditto	2 Aug.	ditto	19	5 4	Holy Cross, Worcester	dark	brown	dark	ditto served in *Swiftsure*
George Gray	ditto	2 Aug.	ordinary, 2nd class	18	5 3	Bethnal-green, Middx.	brown	grey	fresh	ditto served in *Excellent*
Joseph Shell	*Pembroke*, deserter	22 July	stoker	28	5 6½	Deptford, Kent	brown	grey	fresh	£3 reward
Michael Deedy	*Diamond*, deserter	1 Aug.	boy, 1st class	17	4 10	Bristol	sandy	brown	fair	£1 reward served in *Victory*
Robert Tom	*Simoom*, straggler	5 Aug.	stoker, 2nd class	21	5 4	Hove, Sussex	lt. brn	blue	fair	served in *Indus*
Edward F. French	*Excellent*, deserter	5 Aug.	A.B.	23	5 8	Southampton	lt. brn	blue	fair	£3 reward scar on right side of left eye
James Abbott	ditto	26 July	ditto	23	5 6	London	lt. brn	hazel	fresh	ditto
William John Dixon	*St. Vincent*, straggler	2 Aug.	boy, 2nd class	16	5 3¾	Bermondsey, Surrey	brown	blue	pale	£1 reward served in *Fisgard*
Charles Richardson	*Triumph*, straggler	4 Aug.	private, R. Marines	24	5 6¼	Bradford, Yorkshire	auburn	grey	fair	10s. reward served in *Royal Adelaide*
George Doughty	ditto	4 Aug.	ditto	28	5 7⅛	Manchester	black	hazel	dark	ditto
William H. Knowles	ditto	4 Aug.	bandsman	41	5 7	Roscommon	black	grey	dark	ditto served in *Bellerophon*
William J. Stewart	ditto	4 Aug.	stoker	21	5 2	Plymouth	lt. brn	blue	fair	ditto served in *Indus*
Henry Kelly	ditto	5 Aug.	A.B.	—	—	—	—	—	—	ditto served in *Royal Adelaide*
George Smith	ditto	5 Aug.	ordinary	—	—	—	—	—	—	ditto ditto
John Mason	ditto	5 Aug.	ditto	—	—	—	—	—	—	ditto ditto
John O'Sullivan	ditto	5 Aug.	A.B.	—	—	—	—	—	—	ditto ditto
Samuel Satterly	ditto	5 Aug.	ditto	—	—	—	—	—	—	ditto ditto
Josh. Woods	ditto	5 Aug.	ditto	—	—	—	—	—	—	ditto ditto
Robert Lyons	ditto	5 Aug.	ditto	—	—	—	—	—	—	ditto ditto
Richard Moon	*Swiftsure*, straggler	5 Aug.	ordinary	22	5 5	Devonport	light	grey	pale	£1 reward ditto
Charles J. Bicknell	ditto	5 Aug.	ditto	19	5 7½	London	brown	hazel	—	ditto ditto
Jonathan Lowry	ditto	3 Aug.	ordinary, 2nd class	20	5 6	Modbury, Devon	brown	grey	fair	ditto ditto
James Lee	ditto	4 Aug.	gunner, R. M. A.	24	5 7	Gloucester	brown	grey	—	ditto pockpitted
William G. Rolf	ditto	4 Aug.	ditto	25	5 7	Portsmouth	lt. brn	blue	fair	ditto
William G. Bowden	ditto	4 Aug.	ditto	25	5 6	Stonehouse, Gloucester	dk. brn	hazel	fair	ditto
J. H. Wright	ditto	3 Aug.	boy, 1st class	18	5 5	St. Andrew's	black	dark	swrthy	ditto
Samuel Davis	ditto	3 Aug.	ordinary	19	5 5	Gloucester	dk. brn	hazel	fresh	ditto served in *Royal Adelaide*
Robert Hudd	ditto	3 Aug.	ordinary, 2nd class	19	5 3	Essex	brown	grey	fair	ditto ditto
Wm. G. Millard	ditto	3 Aug.	ordinary	19	5 4	Shoreham, Kent	dk. brn	brown	dark	ditto ditto
Edward Haynes	*Sultan*, straggler	3 July	gun-room servant	18	5 8½	Plymouth, Devon	dark	dark	dark	ditto
John Brockington	ditto	4 July	A.B.	27	5 6	Portsmouth	brown	dark	dark	ditto coat of arms on left arm
James Howie	Naval Barracks, deserter	20 July	ordinary	19	5 0¼	Dundee, Forfar	light	blue	fair	£3 reward served in *Magpie*
Henry Still	*Favorite*, deserter	1 Aug.	ditto	20	5 5	Plumstead, Kent	brown	brown	fair	ditto served in *Endymion* and *Excellent*
Henry Howe	*Active*, deserter	9 May	ditto	20	5 5	Hemel Hempstd., Herts	light	grey	fair	ditto

Descriptions of 'Deserters and Stragglers from Her Majesty's Sea Service', as advertised in the *Police Gazette*.

sixty to seventy strokes, but one of the boys said it was over a hundred. They were given no food but kept on the quarter-deck holystoning from noon to midnight. They were flogged again two days later, and a third time the day after that. Nicholas admitted that he had 'committed a grave and serious error of judgment' and was sentenced to be discharged with disgrace.

In 1862 William Hickman, Clerk to the Admiralty, recommended captains to use a Table of Summary Punishments composed by Captain A. P. Ryder of *Hero*; 2,000 copies were printed and distributed to the fleet. Between 1860 and 1866, five Naval Discipline Acts were put on the Statute Book. The number of capital offences was reduced to four: murder, treason, piracy, and destruction of arsenals and dockyards. The number of offences liable to corporal punishment was reduced to eight: mutiny, desertion, repeated drunkenness, smuggling liquor, theft, repeated disobedience, desertion of place of duty and indecent conduct.

As in the past, everything depended upon the personal whims of the captain, and the memoirs of several admirals show that flogging was still commonplace when they were midshipmen in the 1860s. Sydney Eardley-Wilmot, in the screw wooden two-decker *Duncan* (90) on the North American Station in 1864, wrote that 'flogging was pretty frequent in those days. I witnessed many in the *Duncan*.' One man in *Duncan* said he would rather drown than have the cat. The captain at once had the gangway cleared away and told the man he was free to go—overboard. The man looked down at the sea, came back and took his flogging without another word. Henry Lewis Fleet, in the steam-frigate *Constance* (35) in 1864, saw half a dozen floggings. Some of the best men in the ship, notably the sergeant major of marines, 'a fine specimen of a man who would have been ruined by prison life', had their 'four bag'. One man, a bad character, 'richly deserved his fate', and Fleet thought the bosun's mates liked flogging him. They began laying on 'fancy strokes', at which he shouted 'that's my bloody liver!' and 'that's my bloody lights!' and 'hit fair you swine!' after every stroke. The captain had to stop the flogging and tell the bosun's mates to flog 'fairly'. Boys were birched, and when one boy's punishment was over he sang out 'Domino'. The commander asked what he had said. On being told, he said 'Give him three more on his *domino*'. Apparently the men all said 'Domino' at the end of their floggings, and the boys were copying. Percy Scott, in his first sea-going ship, the steam-frigate *Forte* (50) in 1869, suffered under a martinet of a commander. Masthead for the midshipmen and the cat for the men, was this commander's motto. Scott saw one man take four dozen on Monday and another three dozen on Saturday, without a murmur. But Nemesis caught up with the commander. He was eventually courtmartialled and dismissed the ship for flogging a man less than twenty-four hours after the offence, contrary to regulations.

The *United Service Magazine* scrutinised punishment returns closely, and kept its lines of communication open with the fleet, commenting upon the capabilities of serving naval officers with a freedom that seems incredible today. When Captain H. Cockburn took over command of the *Diadem* in 1861, the *Magazine* noted that he had 'not the happy knack of making his men contented'. Rear Admiral Robert Smart, commanding the Channel Fleet, 'is said to bear such a name at Plymouth, that he would not be able to get his flagship manned at that port'. From the general character Admiral Smart bears in the Navy, the *Magazine* said, 'we do not think he will bring the crews of the ship forming the Channel fleet into that contented and efficient state that is to be desired'. On Christmas Day 1860 there was a riot on board *Orion* in the Mediterranean. The captain had assembled the crew on the evening of Christmas Day and kept them on deck for two hours while he tried to find out if any of them were intoxicated. Almost the whole ship's company took part in acts of insurbordination and it was impossible to find out any ringleaders. *Orion* was put on the 'black list' by the admiral and ordered to sea so that none of the crew could have leave. The *United Service Magazine* made no bones about where the blame in *Orion* lay: 'since Captain Frere has joined her, there have been constant complaints made by both officers and men, as to the annoying mode of discipline carried on, and she is now looked upon as an uncomfortable and badly managed ship'. When Captain Moorman of the *Cossack* was tried for tyranny towards one of his men on the West Indian Station, the *Daily News* blamed the Admiralty for ordering *Cossack* home to try Moorman, and sympathised with him for being tried. On the contrary, said the *Magazine*, 'we consider that the Admiralty were to blame for not trying Captain Moorman for disobedience of their regulations, and so far from sympathising with the captain, we pity the officers and men who have to serve under such an eccentric officer. That every man on board the *Cossack* would be glad if Captain Moorman was superseded by a more consistent officer is a real fact.'

In its own way, the *Magazine* was a very good advocate for the lower-deck, pointing out the shortcomings of officers in such a way and in such a publication that was bound to be read and noticed. It printed what amounted to 'league tables' of flogging ships and did not hesitate to chide officers and to give the Admiralty advice. After a long list of ships and the floggings on board them in 1860, the magazine said:

> Special enquiry ought to have been instituted by the Admiralty into the discipline carried on in some of the above ships. The *Basilisk, Vesuvius, Spy* and *Swallow* are known to have been uncomfortable ships during their late commission. Discontent is also reported to prevail on board of the *Arachne, Iris, Lyra,* and *Simoom*. The average amount of flogging in the *Lyra*, 16 out of 78 men, is far beyond what ought to be necessary, and we think it would be better if the ship was recalled to England, and an investigation made into the cause of this excessive punishment.

To prove the point, the *Magazine* published a list of forty-three ships in commission in which there had been no flogging at all.

At last, the publicity, constant pressure and surveillance in Parliament, urgings by a (sometimes) reluctant Admiralty, and a changing social attitude towards flogging, had their effect. Returns of punishments to Parliament were discontinued in 1867. The Army suspended flogging in 1868 and abolished it

Drafting coastguardsmen to their ships, on board the flagship
Duke of Wellington.

altogether in 1881. The Navy suspended flogging in peacetime in 1871 and
altogether in 1879. But the punishment is still suspended to this day, and
theoretically the cat, like the press, could be reintroduced in wartime. As late
as 1880 a marine in *Mosquito* was sentenced to twenty-five lashes and two
years' prison at hard labour. The Admiralty ordered the flogging to be
cancelled.

Unofficial floggings, such as mess-deck 'cobbings' for theft, were always
frowned on, but difficult to suppress. In the gunboat *Fly*, on passage to the
West Coast of Africa in February 1868, the petty officers carried out their own
flogging on a careless look-out; on a clear and moonlit night, the man had
allowed another ship to approach so close that she almost ran *Fly* down. Under
the 'new regulations' the captain was only empowered to administer what the
ship's company thought was too light a punishment. So the petty officers
administered a dozen with hammock clews on the culprit.

The last execution under the old law, before it was changed in 1861, and the
last time a man was hanged at the yardarm of one of Her Majesty's ships, was
the hanging of Marine John Dalliger on board HMS *Leven* in July 1860.

Dalliger had joined *Leven* in February 1860. She was a 500-ton gunboat,
barque-rigged, and principally a sailing ship, although she was fitted with an
auxiliary steam engine. She was on the China station where the war was still
going on, and together with *Actaeon* was carrying out surveys of likely
anchorages for the fleet.

John Dalliger was known as a bad hat with an unsavoury reputation, but the
commanding officer, Lieutenant James Hudson, made attempts to rehabilitate
him. He even made him his own personal servant. On 8 July, Hudson
discovered that some wine and brandy were missing from his cabin. He told
Dalliger that he was satisfied that he had stolen it. He does not seem to have
used threatening language. He seems in fact to have treated the offence rather
lightly. But Dalliger, because he was mad, or drunk, or for whatever reason,

took his revenge. The next morning at 8.30 he came into Hudson's cabin, where he was sitting on a sofa after breakfast, and shot him in the back of the neck with a pistol, wounding him very badly (although Hudson did not die). Dalliger then went on deck and told the second master, Mr Ashton that the captain wanted to see him. He followed Ashton to the ladder and shot him, too, wounding him slightly. He was overpowered, arrested and put below in irons. *Leven* had no medical officer and a boat was sent to *Actaeon* for help.

At 10.45 that morning both ships weighed and went round to Ta-lien-wan, where the fleet was lying, with Rear Admiral James Hope flying his flag in *Chesapeake*, arriving on 10 July. A court-martial was held two days later. The evidence was clear; Dalliger was sentenced to death and the sentence was carried out within twenty-four hours. He was guilty only of attempted murder, but the fact that the ships were virtually in a theatre of war, thousands of miles from home, may have influenced the sentence.

On 14 July *Leven* put to sea and Dalliger's epitaph is in the ship's log: '4.30 a.m. Weighed and proceeded out of harbour. 6.40 a.m. Committed the remains to the deep. Cape Rock bearing S.E. $1\frac{1}{2}$ miles. Expended hammocks, two in number, round shot ten in number.'

'Six men flogged before breakfast':
signs of reform in the 1860s

In the decade of the 1860s, the contrast between reform and reaction in the Victorian Navy was particularly striking, especially in the matter of crime and punishment. Some captains were still inflicting the lash with almost the old freedom and Captain Chads in the Mediterranean might often flog six of *London*'s 'Bounty' crewmen before breakfast, but at home William Hickman was pioneering the use of social statistics to justify changes in the Navy.

In January 1862, as well as revising the Table of Summary Punishments and the Index of Offences for the Navy, Hickman prepared a new form for the Defaulters' Book and the Quarterly Return of Punishments. Hickman, at that time Secretary to the C-in-C Portsmouth, wrote of his form that 'it would save a great deal of writing, that the punishments would be more correctly recorded, and that keeping a page or half a page for each man and boy's name would render the book easier of reference than Defaulters' Books usually are.' Of the Quarterly Return, he said : 'I have devoted the greatest possible attention to this form, with the view of making it the basis of some statistical facts applicable to the whole Navy.'

Hickman urged the Admiralty to keep statistical information for three main reasons. First, he said,

> that we should, by comparing the amount of Crime in the Navy with that committed in other classes of Society, composed of people in the same condition of life, know whether the vast expense incurred with the view of improving the moral and social condition of the Petty Officers, Seamen and Boys of the Fleet, has been attended with the results that might be expected, or whether on the contrary it has been money thrown away; in other words, whether Badge Pay, Continuous Service Pay, Gratuities, Early Pensions, the employment of an increased number of Chaplains and a better description of Schoolmasters, as well as the establishment of carefully selected libraries in each Ship, have been adopted in vain, or led to improvement in the Conduct of those for whose benefit they were intended. Secondly, that we should know whether the mild system of discipline of the present day is sufficient to keep crime within ordinary bounds. And thirdly, and above all, that the circumstances would be known, under which particular crimes prevail, which knowledge would be a sure basis whereon to legislate for their prevention.

Many sailors of his day would have disputed Hickman's use of the word 'mild' to describe naval discipline but, nevertheless, here at last in nineteenth century naval administration was an intellect willing to question old beliefs about crime and punishment and willing to suspend judgment until some data had been gathered.

Shortly afterwards, Hickman was appointed to the Admiralty and undertook the work he had himself suggested. Nearly every flag officer and captain serving afloat took part in an inquiry into the workings of the new Naval Acts. Their replies were edited by Hickman and printed in 1867 under the title 'Reports and opinions of officers on the Acts of Parliament and Admiralty Regulations for Maintaining Discipline and Good Order in the Fleet, passed and issued since the year 1860'.

Some of the captains' opinions seem startlingly modern.'I think it would not be money ill spent,' wrote Captain Wilmshurst, of HMS *Fisgard*, 'or beneath the Admiralty, to have a well-salaried correspondent, not only to answer the press, but to tell the country the truth, and to undeceive people as to the condition of the Royal Navy . . . I think that in most naval questions the Admiralty allow judgment to go by default. I don't think the Admiralty can afford to treat the Press with contempt.'

Many captains thought that the 'new' punishment regulations, though more lenient, marked a man's career for good. There was no way of erasing the record of a punishment from a man's papers. A flogging, at least, was quickly over and done with, and no more said. 'I think', said Captain Houston Stewart in *Wellesley*, 'every captain should be authorised when he thinks proper . . . in the presence of the men, to strike his pen through the records against an offender, and commence afresh.'

Drink, always, was a matter of concern, but here again there were some sensible suggestions. Commodore A. P. Ryder recommended 'that beer should be issued in lieu of spirits whenever practicable'. Captain Johnson of *Pembroke* wondered whether 'a gill of wine might not be advantageously substituted for spirits; several means might be adopted to render the change less unpopular at first', and here Johnson showed a nice knowledge of sailor's psychology, 'such as serving out the wine at the same time that the men are piped to dinner, by allowing the full savings value to those who did not care for it, and by allowing a ration of beer (say a pint a man) in the home ports instead of the wine'. Captain Miller of the *Royal George* thought that 'the men who prefer to remain on board, in lieu of going ashore, might be allowed each an imperial pint of beer during the evening'.

The privileges and responsibilities of petty officers were also considered. Commodore Dunlop said that no mutiny, no combination of disaffected sailors or any other unrest, could ever happen on the lower-deck without the petty officers' knowledge. It was the petty officers' duty to discourage any such feelings and, if they were not successful, to report the likelihood of trouble to the officers. Dunlop was stating a proven rule of naval life; it has been demonstrated again and again, up to modern times, that as Dunlop said, 'no outbreak would I feel convinced ever take place if the petty officers as a body did their duty.' If they failed, then 'I would therefore upon every such occasion inflict some severe punishment on the petty officers, either by loss of all time served and disqualifying them for pensions, or by some other punishment that will affect their future prospects so seriously that it cannot fail to be deeply and lastingly felt by them.'

Captain Wilmshurst, who seemed a very enlightened man in many ways, had another point to make about petty officers, just as valid, but on their side. When petty officers broke their leave, 'no punishment should be authorised, but deprivation of badges for a first time offence, and "disrating" if they repeat it; indeed punishing petty officers in any other way, lowers and degrades the position, and weakens their influence over the ship's company.'

The trend of sentencing in the 1860s was already towards confinement rather than corporal punishment. The Admiralty were considering the question of cells on board ship (an Order of 1862 prohibited the use of *coal bunkers* as cells). Men were sentenced to military prisons where they were available. There were military prisons at Gibraltar and at Corfu and a naval prison at Corradino in Malta. The governors were nearly always retired officers. At Corradino in the early 1860s the governor was remembered as 'an old nut of a retired naval officer, quite a character. The men did not like being sent there much, he used to work them hard.' Jackie Fisher's commander in the *Victory* when he first joined the Navy 'afterwards became a phenomenal Governor of a prison. No man ever went to that prison a second time!'

The prison mentioned might have been Lewes, which became a naval prison in 1862. The building was originally the county gaol of Sussex and was bought by the Government during the Crimean war to house Russian prisoners-of-war. Later, it was a marines' barracks and a convict hospital, before becoming a special prison for sailors and marines, to 'save our seamen from the contamination of prisoners in civil jails'. The population varied, depending upon whether the Channel Fleet or the Flying Squadron were in harbour, but an average of about five hundred men were admitted every year, for sentences of twenty-eight days and upwards. Part of every sentence was served in solitary confinement, and there were 120 solitary confinement cells. The offences were nearly all connected with leave-breaking or absence without leave, and almost all of them had their root in drunkenness.

Lewes was a grim place. A visitor in 1874 'was struck with the good order and dead silence that prevail, broken only by the monotonous voice of the warder conducting the shot drill'. On admission, a prisoner was strictly searched and relieved of any 'contraband'—money, pipes, tobacco, and everything he had on him being taken away and placed with his own clothing in a depository, to be returned to him on his discharge. Every article was noted in a register which was signed by the governor and a warder. Prison clothing was issued, 'more useful than ornamental'. Prisoners' hair was close-cropped, but a man within one month of release was allowed to grow his.

Life was hard for all, but there were degrees of hardness. A man in the first class was allowed a bed and bedding, and after the day's labour, drill and prison duties were over, could 'associate' and talk to other first class prisoners from six until eight in the evenings. Second class prisoners slept on bare boards every third night and were allowed to read or receive instructions between six and eight, but in strict silence. Third class prisoners kept silence all the time, slept on bare boards every other night, and picked oakum every evening. All prisoners did their daily labour, shot drill and prison duties in silence.

The prison was supervised by a board of visitors, consisting of the C-in-C Portsmouth, his flag captain, two of the chief magistrates of Lewes, the Speaker of the House of Commons, and one or two more selected people. The governor was a retired naval officer and the visitor of 1874 remarked that it was because of this officer's judicious firmness and method of carrying out the prescribed discipline in the prison 'that very few men return a second time within its walls'.

The Navy paid rather more attention to housing sailors in prison than out. In the 1860s there was still only one naval barracks, at Sheerness. At all the other ports seamen were lodged in hulks, often moored as much as a mile out in the stream. The men had to have an early breakfast to let them get ashore to the dockyard to draw stores, fit rigging or do any other work. At a quarter to twelve they stopped, to catch a boat back to the hulks for their dinners. At three bells (half past one) the working parties mustered again to go back ashore. At the end of the day, the sailors again caught a boat out to the hulks. A married man had to report back on board the hulk after work and *then* go ashore again. If he had leave all night he had to turn out at 3.00 or 4.00 a.m. to catch a boat. Any sailor who wanted to go ashore after work could find a libertymen's boat, but coming back was another matter: he had to pay a waterman sixpence to ferry him out. Men did not normally join ships until they had spent all their money and they would borrow, sell their clothes, do anything for a run ashore. The need to find and pay for his own boat, perhaps on a rough and rainy night, must have tempted many a man to break his leave and stay ashore. Barracks would be cleaner, healthier, would save time, labour and money. In short, hulks were unsatisfactory and insanitary, they bred disease and disaffection, and there was nothing to be said for them.

Yet, amazingly, there were officers who recommended hulks and gave evidence in favour of them to the Royal Commission on Manning in 1859. Captain Hewlett, of *Excellent*, said, 'I am entirely in favour of hulks for seamen. I think they would get into longshore habits in barracks and be, perhaps, less willing to go to sea, from a barrack than from a hulk'. He thought sailors should be 'habituated to wet and dry'. Commander Bickford of *Victory* said that a sailor 'shook down' better into his place in a hulk than he would do in a barrack. Captain Preedy said he doubted whether men on leave would return to the barrack if allowed to go ashore for a run outside the yard, and he believed a hulk the only fit place for a seaman to live in. Although one would have thought the case for barracks so strong it hardly needed arguing, the reactionary view prevailed. No more barracks were built for many years, and the hulks stayed.

One of those who argued most strongly against hulks was Admiral Sir William Fanshawe Martin, C-in-C of the Mediterranean Squadron. 'Fly' Martin was a true reforming spirit, but almost all his proposals were ignored. He recommended sailors' homes, and recreational facilities for sailors ashore, without any official response. But he did have one success—in the prevention of venereal disease—where events proved him right.

There had been very little venereal disease in Malta where examination of prostitutes had been compulsory for years. But in 1859 it was found that these examinations were illegal. Prostitutes refused to be examined, and so, in 1860 there was an alarming increase in venereal disease in the island. Admiral Martin recommended compulsory examination, regulation of premises, regular inspection of sanitation, and closer oversight of prostitutes. The rate fell dramatically to nil in 1861.

Venereal disease was one of the most common sailors' diseases and its incidence was, of course, closely linked to the number of prostitutes ashore and to the ease with which women could be brought on board. Conditions had improved since the Napoleonic Wars and the 'Immoral Practices' Statement of 1822, but it was not until 1869 that a circular letter excluded women from warships at all times without express consent. Ashore in Portsmouth, the police reckoned in 1861 that there were 1,791 known whores in the town, or nearly one in fifty of the whole population. There were over a thousand known prostitutes in the Chatham-Woolwich area and about 18,000, one in three of them diseased, walking the streets of London.

In 1864 a Parliamentary Committee was set up to enquire into the treatment of syphilis and ways of reducing the chances of infection. That year the first Contagious Disease Act was passed, making it compulsory for women in specified areas to submit to medical examination if information had been laid against them. The 'specified areas' were towns such as Portsmouth, Plymouth, Chatham, Woolwich, Sheerness, Aldershot, Windsor, Colchester, Shornecliffe and Londonderry. The scope of the first Act was widened by two more, in 1866 and 1869. But in 1869 Mrs George (Josephine) Butler and the Ladies National Association began to campaign for the repeal of the Acts.

The degree of disease in the Navy shows a close correlation with the effective enforcement of the Acts. The rate of venereal disease per thousand men in the Navy sank from 170 in 1850 to 53 in 1868, after the Acts had been passed. But in 1882, when enforcement lapsed, the rate soared to 183, and to 316 the following year, when the Acts were repealed. (But by 1913, improved naval hygiene and social living conditions for seamen had been largely responsible for bringing the rate down to 22 per thousand.)

The presence, or absence, of women on board had a predictable effect upon that shadowy area of naval social history, buggery on the lower-deck. Homosexuality was not an offence under English law until 1885, but the Navy always took a severer view of the practice. Until 1829 sodomy on board was punishable by death. In 1842 two seamen convicted of buggery were flogged round the fleet, sentenced to a year's imprisonment and discharged with disgrace. A marine in 1859 was sentenced to death, later commuted to two years' imprisonment, and discharge with disgrace. In *Leander* in 1861 a man convicted of indecency was towed ashore on a grating and landed on the beach.

Such draconian punishments showed that the Navy knew that homosexuality was perilous to discipline on board, and corrupted youth. But conditions in ships often encouraged sodomy: not only lack of women, but lack of leave and privacy, long sea passages, very crowded lower-decks and the close proximity of older men to young boys. In some ships there is no question that sodomy was rife and openly accepted. Officers, warrant officers and senior ratings had their special 'boys'. The offences were variously phrased in the charges as perpetration of lewd acts, gross indecency, scandalous and unclean conduct, indecent assault, indecent acts to boys, uncleanness, nasty acts, disgraceful conduct, scandalous action, filthy conduct, and indecent liberties. Occasionally drink caused a man to expose himself. Very rarely, there were acts of bestiality, committed with the livestock kept on board.

But once women were available, on shore, the clock seemed to run back and the sailors of the 1860s seemed to behave much as the sailors of the 1760s. As a young boy in Portsea in 1864, Henry Capper watched the antics of sailors discharged from a ship which had just paid off. The sailors engaged every available cab in the town and formed them up in procession on Common Hard. Each man had his 'long-haired chum'—generally a woman of the town. The cabs were decorated with flags and pennants, each box seat held one or more sailors and women, with more inside and on the roof. A few men were astride the horses and two of them, to show their independence, sat facing the tails of their animals and were towed by lines to the horse or cab next ahead. Off they all went, with a tooting of horns and a roaring of chanties, with drum and fiddle accompaniment, on a grand tour of the villages surrounding Portsmouth, Fareham or Botley, 'where unreportable orgies took place'.

Part of the trouble was the old custom of paying the men in one huge sum. In 1860, ship's companies could be paid yearly instead of at the end of the commission. But even this could lead to trouble. When the crew of *London* under Chads arrived at Gibraltar with a year's pay burning holes in their pockets, there was naturally a great deal of drunken rioting. There were many brawls with the soldiers of the Rock garrison, who used to sponge on the sailors and marines. One of *London*'s seamen, a negro with the 'Pusser's name' of Tom Dollar, stabbed and killed a soldier in a fight. He was tried ashore and sentenced to ten years' imprisonment, the chief witnesses against him being a corporal and a sergeant. After a few months, the two witnesses fell out, and the corporal shot the sergeant dead. He was duly sentenced to be hanged, but no hangman could be found, nor anybody else willing to undertake the job. At last, Tom Dollar volunteered, on condition he was given a free pardon. He hanged his man, got his pardon and went back to England on a free passage. (He actually went on board *London* when she arrived at Devonport to pay off.) Thus, the story worked out to a dreadfully neat solution: all three of Tom Dollar's enemies died, two of them by his own hand, and Tom himself suffered very little.

'Hoisting the ruddy old twiddler':
life in the early ironclads

'Ding, Clash, Dong, Bang, Boom, Rattle, Clash, Bang, Clink, Bang, Dong, Bang, Clatter, bang bang BANG! What on earth is this! This is, or soon will be,' wrote Charles Dickens in *The Uncommercial Traveller*,

> the *Achilles*, iron armour-plated ship. Twelve hundred men are working at her now; twelve hundred men working on stages over her sides, over her bows, over her stern, under her keel, between her decks, down in her hold, within her and without, crawling and creeping into the finest curves of her lines wherever it is possible for men to twist. Twelve hundred hammerers, measurers, caulkers, armourers, forgers, smiths, shipwrights; twelve hundred dingers, clashers, dongers, rattlers, clinkers, bangers bangers bangers!

In his description of the building of the *Achilles* in 1863, a novelist of genius captures exactly the excitement, the novelty, the sheer inventive industry, of the coming of the ironclad. In the late 1840s, as an experiment, the Admiralty had ordered six iron frigates. Firing tests against their ships' sides showed that even the very best rolled and wrought iron of their day was still so brittle, so full of carbon, that it shattered into a million lethal shrapnel fragments on the impact of shot. Men might as well have gone into action behind sheets of plate glass. The six frigates were disarmed and converted into transports, and the Admiralty went back to wood. However, the iron masters improved their processes and built rolling mills to produce plate thick enough to break up the heaviest solid shot and explode harmlessly the heaviest shells, without itself being shattered. The French used this plate on the 'floating gun batteries' which bombarded Russian forts towards the end of the Crimean war, with sensational success. The French naval architect Dupuy de Lome then went a step further and laid some of the new plate on the sides of an already half-built wooden three-decker, removing her upper tier of guns to preserve stability. This ship, launched in 1859, was *La Gloire*, the world's first ironclad.

Goaded by Parliament, press and public, the Admiralty responded to the French challenge with one of the boldest and most imaginative advances in warship construction in the Navy's history. Designed by Scott Russell and Isaac Watts, the new ship was built of iron throughout, in her frame structure and her hull plating. Her ratio of $6\frac{1}{2}$:1 of length to beam was greater than any warship before her, and her length between perpendiculars of 380 feet was longer by 120 feet than any of her predecessors. Her hull was armoured with plate $4\frac{1}{2}$ inches thick for 208 feet of her length, and the armour extended over the central gun battery as well as along her sides. Internally, she was subdivided into separate watertight compartments for greater protection against

In the engine-room of HMS *Warrior*, 1860.

flooding, each compartment having its purpose, to hold machinery, stores, ammunition, or coal. Her 1,250 horsepower engines gave her a top speed over a measured mile of 14.3 knots, which left all her contemporaries out of sight. Her coal bunkerage of 850 tons was the largest in the world at the time. She was launched in 1860 and named *Warrior*. With her almost identical sister ship *Black Prince*, completed two years later, *Warrior* was one of the most revolutionary warships of all time.

Through the use of forged iron and steel instead of cast iron, the weight of the largest naval guns increased by nearly three times between 1860 and 1865. *Warrior*'s forty-one guns were a transitional outfit, of 68-pounder smooth bores and rifled Armstrong breech loaders. One 100-pounder Armstrong was mounted on each bow on the upper-deck, and a third on a turntable at the stern. Four 40-pounder Armstrongs were mounted on the quarter-deck. The remaining eight 100-pounder Armstrongs and twenty-six 68-pounder smooth bores were carried on the main gun-deck, all except six of them mounted inside the central armoured 'citadel'. *Warrior* was the first vessel with a single gun-deck on which the ship's company also had their messes. With all stores and weights on board, *Warrior* had a calculated displacement of 9,140 tons.

By 1870 the Royal Navy had some thirty ironclad ships of the line and all of them, because of the sheer rapidity of technological changes, were unintentionally experimental. Not all were made of iron: in 1862, the Admiralty decided to use up half-built wooden hulls, cladding them with armour, cutting down their top hamper and altering their lengths; this produced *Caledonia, Royal Alfred, Lord Warden, Lord Clyde* and others. Of the iron-hulled ships, some like *Warrior, Black Prince* and the three five-masted 10,000-ton giants *Minotaur, Agincourt* and *Northumberland,* fired their guns in a broadside, just as in Nelson's day. Some were central battery ships, like *Bellerophon* and the four *Invincible* class. Some were turret ships, like *Monarch* and the ill-fated *Captain,* launched in 1869. There were eighteen different hull shapes, eight different thicknesses of armour, and five designs of bow: *Warrior* and *Black Prince* had the old-fashioned knee bows; *Achilles* and her sisters had stems with a slight outward curve; the five-masted ships, *Defence* and some others, had rounded underwater rams; *Captain* and *Favorite* had straight stems; and the rest had pointed wooden rams. There were three types of stern: *Warrior, Black Prince, Resistance, Defence* and the *Invincible* class had regular frigate sterns, with wide taffrails, quarter galleries and ornamentation; the five-masters and *Achilles* had plain round sterns, rising vertically from a low counter; the rest had a blunted form of the modern so-called 'cruiser' stern. Some ships had trunk engines, some direct acting engines, some return connecting-rod engines, with single screws, twin screws, disconnecting screws, or hoistable screws.

There were twenty different scales of armament. Breech loaders were discarded, and by 1870 the Navy had reverted to rifled muzzle loaders, of up to six different calibres. Most ships mounted guns of two calibres, some even three. There were 6-inch guns mounted on wooden trucks and trained by handspike; 7-inch guns on iron carriages and slide mountings, trained by tackles; 8, 9 and 10-inch guns trained by winches; and 12-inch guns in turrets trained by steam. 6 and 7-inch projectiles were lifted to the muzzles by hand, the larger calibres by shell whips. 10 and 12-inch calibre shells were rammed home by the whole gun crew manning bell-ropes on the rammer staff, the smaller calibres rammed home by the loading numbers only. All calibres were laid for elevation by hand-lever, and fired by lanyard and friction tube.

Externally, the early ironclads were all painted a solid, unrelieved black, except for a narrow white strip of boot-topping or band running round the ship outside the hammock nettings. Masts and spars were painted buff, or stone colour, or light brick-red. Bottoms were oxide or copper. Funnels were black or buff. Boats were black, with occasional smaller ones white. In one aspect, all ships were the same. They all carried a full outfit of masts and sails. The shortage of coaling stations across the world, and the low endurance under steam, made it necessary for ships to go on long passages under sail alone. However, the five-masters were quite unmanageable except under steam, so never served further afield than European waters. *Black Prince, Warrior* and *Achilles* were very difficult to tack (bring their bows through the wind) because of their length. But once properly on a port or starboard tack, they moved well because of their beautiful hull lines. *Achilles* was the best ship of the three in a seaway, gliding easily over waves when *Warrior* and *Black Prince* would be shipping water green. The two best twenty-four hour sailing performances by early ironclads, with fires drawn and propellors discon-

HMS *Warrior*, the Navy's first ironclad, was launched at
Blackwall on 29 December 1860 with her sister ship *Black Prince*
(on the right).

nected, were the 243 miles run by *Ocean* (wooden-hulled) on passage from Rio
to Singapore in August 1867, and the 242 miles by *Monarch* returning to
England from America in March 1870. *Monarch* touched eleven knots for four
hours, with a wind of force 6–8.

Life in the early ironclads had its own special flavour. The ships had much
less 'tumble home' than the old wooden liners, and their upper-decks were
much more spacious. The flush-decked *Achilles*, for example, had an upper-
deck like a parade ground, with very little reduction in width from forward to
aft. A battery of field guns and their limbers could be marched round *Achilles*'s
upper-deck from the foremast to the skylight of the captain's after cabin.
When making sail, hoisting boats or catting the anchor, the men hauling the
topsail halliards, the boats' falls or the yard tackles had a clear run from the
order 'hoist away' to 'high enough' and when drilling in competition with other
ships, *Achilles*'s officers had to take care that check-stoppers were properly
manned and looked after, or the men could do a great deal of damage in the
rush of their enthusiasm. One remnant of traditional thinking remained: the
ships all had 7-foot-high bulwarks which shut out the view and made the
upper-deck as enclosed as a prison yard. In the old days of sail, these had been
needed to protect the crews on deck in an action, but in an ironclad the deck
was almost deserted at general quarters, except for a small steering and
navigational party. However, tradition demanded bulwarks, so bulwarks
were provided.

Most ironclads had only three decks, upper, main and orlop. With watertight compartments and wing passages on the orlop decks, the ship's company berthed and slung their hammocks on the main-deck, except in a few ships of the *Caledonia* class where there were no wing passages and consequently more room on the orlop deck. In the ships with 'broadsides', the mess tables were hung between the guns for as far as they extended. In the ships with central batteries, the battery itself was not normally used as a mess-deck; the sailors messed forward of the battery, on the main-deck. The officers' accommodation was generally very poor, with small, badly lit wardrooms, and cabins opening out of them, with no daylight except through small hatchways two decks above.

Forward of the wardroom in a typical ironclad was a space known as the steerage, where the midshipmen kept their chests and slung their hammocks. This was normally bounded on its forward end by a transverse watertight bulkhead extending the width of the ship. Forward of this, again, was a series of compartments known as 'the flats' which extended along the orlop deck right up into the bows of the ship. In the first of these compartments was the large open hatch leading down to the engine room; two equal sized hatches above, in the main and upper decks, admitted light to the engine room. As the hatches only had coamings, heat from the engines spread through the whole ship. Here the engineer officers had their chests and hammocks. Next were two lengthy compartments over the boiler rooms, with the funnel and ventilator casings amidships and shell lockers and the ship's company bag racks on either side. Forward of these were the fore holds, tank rooms, magazines, shell rooms and lower store rooms. The orlop flats also contained the stokers' mess-deck, the sail room, the hawser tiers, the cells and upper storerooms. Aft, the wardroom had small plug scuttles, six inches wide, pushed by an iron bar and screw nut into place. These were only four feet from the waterline, never opened at sea and only rarely opened at anchor at Spithead or the outer Nore. In ships with wing passages there were no scuttles on the orlop deck forward of the wardroom and, as the engine room hatches were the only ones opening to the upper-deck, all the forward compartments of the orlop deck were lighted by candle lanterns.

The main-deck messes, being one deck up from the orlop messes of the wooden liners, were better lighted and ventilated and more healthy than in the old days. But the men got all the light and fresh air they needed aloft and preferred their mess-decks 'snug'. Life on board was in a constant state of tension between the desires of the men to have cosy, enclosed mess-decks, and the design and routine of the ship which favoured open spaces and continual upheaval. Mess tables hung between guns were always having to be cleared away, not only for the weekly general quarters which involved everybody, but also for battery divisional drills, which disturbed the watch below. The five-masters *Minotaur* and *Agincourt* were peculiar in having no transverse battery bulkheads on the main-deck, giving one clear sweep from forward to aft. It was possible to stand right up forward by the hawse-pipes and look along the whole length of the ship where seven hundred men were eating, or sleeping, or chatting amongst themselves.

In spite of the hundreds of men on board, the early ironclads suffered a shortage of men, caused by the refusal of a conservative Admiralty to recognise that ironclads were new and needed new manning scales. From time immemorial in the Navy, ships had been graded in 'rates' and their complements fixed rigidly, assessed on the watch and quarter bill of a ship of that rate. But rates did not apply to ironclads. To count the number of guns, as in the old days, was absurd. That would put *Warrior* down among the frigates. The Gunnery Branch calculated that *Warrior* needed 740 men, which was close to that of a third-rate ship of the line (which had 705 men). So the Admiralty, for manning purposes, classed *Warrior* as a third-rate. Once the figure of 705 had been settled on, it was then applied to all ironclads, regardless of their size. *Minotaur*, for example, had an official complement of 705 but always carried supernumaries and seldom had fewer than 800 officers and men on board. *Warrior's* quarter bill was the first to be drawn up on the principle of a full gun crew to each gun, instead of a gun crew to every pair of guns. In *Minotaur* the watch and quarter bill for a three-masted ship obviously was not appropriate and she had to have a special watch bill made out, whatever the Admiralty might lay down officially.

The ironclads forced some new thinking about sanitary arrangements. The heads on board the old ships had not changed much for centuries. In ships with a knee bow, the head was usually a pair of latrine troughs, with lids drilled with holes, lying fore and aft on either side of the bowsprit. The soil pipes ran down to the waterline. The troughs were sheltered by canvas head screens normally painted black, but were open above to the sky and the winds of heaven, and men using them were exposed to rain, snow or, in rough weather, spray. If the ship was pitching into a heavy head sea, the forward heads were abandoned and a makeshift rigged in the lee fore chains.

With the coming of the ram the old type of heads had to be discarded. In the earliest ships they were placed forward of the main-deck, but the poor ventilation made them objectionable. Later in the 1860s, most ships had heads built in the waist, on both sides of the ship, level with the upper-deck and projecting outboard, with soil pipes down to the waterline.

The provision of proper toilet facilities for the men was often neglected. The old wooden depot hulks were often the worst of all. The *Duke of Wellington* at Portsmouth had a normal complement of 1,000 men, but with ships commissioning and paying off and drafts of men passing through, the *Duke* often had some four thousand men on board. For all these there were twelve latrine holes, six on each side. From 4.00 a.m. until long after pipe-down at night there were queues of men on each side of the ship struggling to reach the heads. In spite of sentries posted to stop them, any number of desperate men could wait no longer and were put in the 'report' for offences against decency. Every morning, the sweepers had to remove the evidence from scores of places on the upper-deck.

The living conditions on a Victorian mess-deck were described by Admiral Ballard, who was a midshipman at the time:

The bare bleakness of the mess-deck with its long range of plank tables and stools had as little suggestion of physical ease as a prison cell. It was damp and chilly in a cold climate, and damp and hot in the tropics. It was swept by searching draughts if the ports were open, and nearly pitch dark if they were closed, glass scuttles not having been invented. It was dimly lit at night by tallow candles inside lamps at long intervals, and as there were no drying rooms it reeked of wet serge and flannel in rainy weather. In short the living quarters of the mid-Victorian bluejacket, stoker, or marine were as widely dissociated from any ideal of a home in the usual sense as could well be imagined.

Moreover, he was always in a crowd by day or night. His work and his leisure, his eating, drinking, washing and sleeping were all in crowded surroundings. He swallowed his bully beef and hard tack, his pea soup, 'copper rattle', and rum, at a mess table so congested that he had absolutely no elbow room and scarce space to sit. He washed himself twice a week on deck at the same time as he washed his clothes, in the two tubfulls of cold water which formed the allowance for the whole twenty-five men in his mess, in the middle of a splashing mob at other tubs all round; and he slung his hammock at night among hundreds of others so tightly packed that they had no swinging room however much the ship rolled. Even in the head he had no individual privacy.

There were no bathrooms on board for officers or men. Henry Capper, who served on the lower-deck at the time of which the Admiral was writing, said that in his experience, each mess drew half a gallon per man of fresh water daily. They all washed in this, stripped to the waist. Before using that water to scrub tables, stools and the deck, they washed feet and legs to the knee, rinsing with salt water. Any man who missed this ritual had a rough time from his messmates.

The sail sizes of the early ironclads were as large as could still be worked by manpower. Thirty men were about as many as could get on a yard, and a fore or main topsail in *Achilles*, for example, with an area of 4,000 square feet and a spread of 95 feet from clew to clew, was just about as much as they could humanly handle in a gale of wind. Once such a giant sail had been started by slacking off sheets or halliards, it took on a brute force of its own, tons of wind pressure behind it making the canvas thunder and boom and try to thrash itself to pieces. While men on deck tried to restrain it with bunt-lines, braces and reef-tackles, aloft the yardarms whipped about like fishing rods and every topman on the footropes hung on for dear life while he tried to do his part in furling or reefing. The men hung like dots in the sky, while the ship swung thirty or forty degrees each way for hours at a time. Very occasionally the force of the wind defeated them, and they had to cut a sail loose.

At sea and in harbour, ships were constantly competing against each other at drill. Every day, except Saturday and Sunday, there were drill evolutions before colours, and every evening gear was sent down from aloft after evening quarters. At sea, besides the ordinary work of making, shortening and trimming sail as wind and weather changed, there would be an evolution on the watch twice a day and a drill for all hands in the evening.

Admiral Ballard has described one ordinary ten-day cruise of the Channel and Reserve Squadron. Twelve ironclads took part: *Minotaur, Agincourt, Northumberland, Achilles, Audacious, Valiant, Warrior, Hercules, Lord Warden, Hector, Defence* and *Penelope*. They weighed from Berehaven in Ireland on a Thursday evening and on getting outside they sent down royal yards and pointed other yards to the wind. On Friday morning

> they exercised general quarters, and in the evening crossed royal yards, made plain sail, shortened and furled all sail. On Saturday, struck topgallant masts. On Sunday there were no drills, but the yards were braced round twice to shifts of wind. On Monday the watch was exercised morning and afternoon in shifting main topsail. In the evening they sent up topgalland masts, crossed upper yards, made all plain sail, reefed topsails, shook out reefs, furled sails, sent down upper yards, struck topgallant masts. On Tuesday, the watch exercise was shifting foresail; in the evening the hands were exercised at fire quarters, which included getting up the tackles for hoisting out boomboats. On Wednesday they exercised each watch in shifting jibboom, and in the evening sent up topgallant masts, crossed upper yards, made plain sail, furled again. Thursday being small-arm Company day, no watch drills took place aloft; but in the evening hands made plain sail, set stunsails one side, shifted topsails and furled sails. On Friday morning they prepared for action aloft, which meant unbending all square sails, sending topgallant masts, upper yards and stunsail booms on deck, and running bowsprits in. They then exercised general quarters, and after general quarters bent all sails again, sent up all spars that were down, and ran out the bowsprits. On Saturday they moored in Vigo Bay, hoisted out boomboats, and in the evening sent down upper yards.

When the admiral signalled a ship: 'Evolution well executed', spirits on board would soar. Conversely, 'Repeat the evolution' would cast a gloom on deck for days. In such an atmosphere of intense competition, the men took risks aloft and a ship might suffer half a dozen deaths from falls in a commission. In *Achilles*, for example, there were twelve fatal accidents in one Mediterranean commission: one petty officer, one leading seaman, six A.B.s and four ordinary seamen. Ballard, then a midshipman in *Achilles*, remembered all his life 'the sickening horror with which as quite a youngster I first saw a blue-clad human figure whirling down with an awful rush from a hundred and fifty feet above the deck and striking violently against the spread of the lower rigging rebound overboard with a plunge to sink from sight instantly and forever'.

One special evolution was 'hauling up the ruddy old twiddler', or hoisting the propeller. It was a major undertaking to draw a propeller, weighing as much as ten tons and measuring over twenty feet across, up into a well in the ship. Sheer legs were rigged over the well and the falls led forward along the main-deck. Lower-deck was cleared of both watches, and about 600 men

HMS *Achilles*, 1865.

manned the falls, one watch each side, ready to 'Stamp and go!' from the order 'Hoist away!' When high enough, the propeller was locked in place by large pawls, and the sheer legs and falls unrigged. If necessary propellers could be hoisted right up on deck for emergency repairs.

The anchors were also hoisted by hand, with up to a hundred men manning the capstan bars, all stamping their feet in time to the quick march played by the ship's band. The band struck up the moment the flagship hauled down the flag hoist to 'Shorten in' and when ships were in company the anchorage would resound to the lively music of the ship's bands, each playing a different tune. When a ship was hoisting her anchor for the last time before going home after a foreign commission, the band would have to play faster and faster and, though they would soon be playing at top speed, they would still get left behind the men's feet.

The anchors were still hoisted by a method which went back to the Middle Ages. The capstan was in two parts, the upper normally on the quarter-deck where it was manned by men at the bars, and the lower on the main-deck where it did the work of hauling in. The massive hemp cables of the days of sail were too large to be brought to the capstan. The capstan actually hauled on a much smaller cable, called a messenger, which was rigged so that it formed an endless chain, leading forward to the hawse-hole and back aft again along the main-deck to the capstan. As the messenger was pulled along the deck, the anchor cable, which lay beside it, was stopped to it every few feet with some turns of small rope, known as 'nippers'; so, as the messenger was hauled aft, it took the cable with it. When the cable reached the navel pipe (often aft of the funnel and the machinery spaces) the nippers were unwound so that the cable could descend through the navel pipes into the cable locker, while the messenger, freed of nippers, went on aft to the capstan and round again. Although the ironclads of the 1860s all had chain cables and not hemp, the old method of messengers was still used (and needed expert and agile seamen to wind and unwind the nippers at the right time while the cable was moving along). *Bellerophon* was the first ship to have her anchor cable led to her capstan. Her 'patent' capstan, as it was called, was worked by hand in her first commission, but a steam engine was fitted later.

Some naval officers, although they never disputed that sail training was essential, still regarded the ironclad's sailing qualities with scepticism. In June 1863, Captain Geoffrey Phipps Hornby, flag captain in the two-decker *Edgar* of the Channel Fleet (incidentally, in March 1865, the last line-of-battle-ship to sail out of Portsmouth Harbour) referred to the five ironclads with which he was going to tour the British Isles as 'dummies'. From Yarmouth to Sunderland was one day's sail for *Edgar* 'but if the dummies were to go under sail I shall think it lucky if we get there in ten'. In fact, it took five, as the squadron had to get up steam to avoid some dangerous shoals off the Norfolk coast.

The five were *Warrior, Black Prince, Resistance, Defence* and *Royal Oak*. Besides *Edgar*, the squadron also had two frigates, *Emerald* and *Liverpool*, and the despatch vessel, *Trinculo*. The object of the cruise was to show the flag; as Hornby said, 'we are doing popularity to a great extent. Ostensibly we are to show the ships, and what happy fellows the British mariners are in a man-of-war—nothing but porter and skittles!'

After Sunderland, they went to Leith, Invergordon, Kirkwall, Lough Foyle, Lough Swilly, the Clyde and Liverpool. Everywhere crowds of people visited the ships, and the townsfolk got up balls, dinners and festivities in the Navy's honour. The welcome was particularly warm at Liverpool where the squadron arrived, under sail, in September 1863. Hornby went shooting with his kinsman Lord Derby at Knowsley, the officers were dined out by the Mersey Yacht Club, and the sailors were banqueted by the Mayor and Corporation.

When Hornby visited *Black Prince* he thought her very fine, though he did have some criticisms about her vulnerable (uncladded) ends and her three masts instead of four, but he found 'the men in the ironclads are so disgustingly proud of their ships that they will allow them *no* faults'. The sailors' opinion was fully shared by the citizens of Liverpool who flocked on board to look and marvel at, for instance, the electric telegraph in *Resistance*; the officer of the watch on the forward bridge moved a dial on a plate which was repeated on another dial in front of the quartermaster below. The same ship had oil which was burnt in a retort in a 'small caboose' and the gas generated by the heat was passed to a gasometer on the upper-deck, between the booms and before the main hatch.The gas was piped below to light the engine room and the screw alley with twelve burners which gave a 'truly brilliant effect, so wonderfully different to the old oil lamp'. Everybody was very impressed with the guns and the engines and the boats and the massive anchors, and *Black Prince*'s two 'telescopic funnels'. The ladies especially admired the drying room in *Warrior*, fitted with a heating apparatus for drying the sailors' laundry in bad weather.

A visitor to *Warrior* was very pleased by the courtesy everybody on board showed to him and the way they all vied to explain the parts of the ship:

Along the broad white deck, which looked like a great broad street, men were seen rope making, carpentering, making hammocks, and hand ropes, &c. Sentries were walking their quiet rounds as silently as if there were no crowd around them. Going down the ladder to the main-deck, the ear was greeted with the bleating of sheep, and the cackle of domestic fowls in spacious coops, and the animals seemed quite at home among plenty of clean fodder and food. Large quantities of butchers' meat hanging up ready for cooking. Cooks busy at work in the galley, preparing all sorts of dishes—the smell set up is savoury, and calculated to give one an appetite. It is not yet meat time, yet here and there are seen some of the fine fellows leisurely (it being their watch below, as it is termed) dispatching their 'levener', from the hour 'eleven' at which it is taken; and which, in one instance, was a goodly snack of fried beefsteaks and onions; and another mutton chops and boiled rice; and in both cases plenty of biscuits. While a great many were eating, many were engaged in reading (Newspapers mostly) or writing letters; some working hearthrugs by a quilting process, or embroidering pictures. Many lay asleep, having to go on deck at twelve o'clock; some sat wrapt in their own meditation, as if unconscious of what was going on around them; one man, a marine, chaunted a song, with a fine cultivated voice; and an artillery-man tried to get up a laugh in his own mess, by pretending to read from a newspaper of a man being drowned by a cart wheel passing over him, but the joke was too stale. It is generally understood on shore that 'Jack', when not on duty, is passing round the grog or smoking, but here you found the seamen better occupied in their leisure moments . . .We are all familiar with the British seaman as a daring man, and a light-hearted cheery man; we read of him as a hero, and we find him on shore with a soul lifted above all mean and common cares; but we have to visit him in his abode, in order to see him as the homely man.

The Channel Fleet's visit to Liverpool in 1863 is one of the very few mid-Victorian encounters between people and bluejacket which is fully documented. The sailors' behaviour, manners, conversation and conduct were all closely observed and recorded. The banquet for the sailors was not on the original programme. Several Liverpool gentlemen wrote to Admiral Dacres that 'a very strong desire exists to extend the hospitality of the town to the seamen and marines of the Channel Squadron.' Forty shipowners and merchants each contributed £10 towards the expenses of a dinner. In fact, 800 bluejackets, 200 marines and 200 gentlemen of Liverpool sat down to dine together on 22 September, at St George's Hall.

The men, all specially selected for their good conduct and for having never broken their leave in their present ship, landed at Prince's stage at twelve noon, in a gale of wind and pelting rain, and were well soaked before they moved off at 12.30. However, neither the men nor the citizens of Liverpool were daunted by the weather. Preceded by a contingent of Liverpool police and by *Edgar*'s band, the men marched off by ship's companies. They were cheered all the way from the pierhead to the city centre, the men of HMS *Liverpool* especially. Crowds packed the route, hats were thrown into the air and trampled underfoot, the bells of St Nicholas pealed out, the cheering was deafening, and the constabulary had to clear a way. The sailors were visibly amazed by the warmth of their reception and one bluejacket was quoted as saying, 'Well, we'll think ourselves somebodies arter all this. Blow me if ever I see'd such a sight as this. Just let 'em attack Liverpool and send for the Channel Fleet, that's all.'

To the music of the bands, the men marched through the streets of Liverpool, where every corner was decorated with flags, and every window packed with cheering, waving spectators. They gave three cheers at Nelson's Monument, and another three for the Queen, before arriving at St George's Hall shortly before two o'clock.

The hall, too, was decorated for the occasion. 'Exotic plants and floral rarities' had been brought from the Philharmonic. Mrs Lynn, of the Waterloo Hotel, supplied several handsome silver candelabra, which were all decked with flowers. The organ gallery above, where there was a choir, was decorated with flags and bannerets, the Royal Arms, and a scroll saying 'The Brave British Tars of Old England'. The men sat down at some sixteen or seventeen tables, each holding over sixty men. Every man had a bottle of three-water grog and a quart bottle of Alsopp's Pale Ale. He also had a place card, with the event inscribed upon it in gold, and a list of 'viands and toasts'. The Bill of Fare was:

DINNER—Beef, roast and boiled, Ham, baked and boiled Potatoes, and other vegetables
REMOVE—Plum pudding and Crimean sauce
DESSERT—Apples, Ale, and Punch

The bugle sounded, and the whole thousand were on their feet as one, for grace, said by the chairman, Mr S. R. Graves, who had been one of the moving spirits behind the dinner. The band of the 11th Liverpool Artillery Volunteers played a selection of popular airs during dinner. 'Ample justice having been done to the feast, and the tables cleared, the bugle again sounded, this time to do honour to the Queen.' After the chairman had given them the toast, 'the Queen', everyone rose and 'the seamen sent forth such a cheer as only such men could vociferate—loud and continuous'. Mr Best played 'God save the Queen' on the organ, and the choir and the whole audience joined in the anthem.

There now followed a programme of songs, speeches, toasts and recitations, the bluejackets and their hosts taking part in turn. Then John Grant, captain of the foretop of *Royal Oak*, rose to speak and propose a toast. Of all the sailors' speeches recorded that day, this was perhaps the best. It was a large hall, and a huge audience, and even encouraged by Allsop's Pale Ale and Virginia tobacco, a speech must have been something of an ordeal. But John Grant rose to the occasion with humour and sincerity:

> Mr Chairman and to all the kind entertainers of this feast I rise, and was going to say something when I did get up, but actually that 'ere gentleman (pointing to Mr Cowper) has taken all the stiff'ning out of my shirt-collar (loud laughter). It is a fact I am not much of a chap to spin a long 'denda. I hope you will excuse me if I lose the steerage of my tongue, and if I break down you'll lend a hand to help a stranded vessel to get off the shore (cheers). They say we live in an iron age. No doubt of it; many of us here present live in ironclad ships, but we are not the only ones, for I believe the fair sex can boast of that as well as us (roars of laughter). But I was going to say when I rose in this place that the Fleet raised a great deal of excitement on shore, and only on one occasion was there a greater one, and that was the arrival of her most gracious Majesty the Queen. Not the slightest doubt of it. . . . Now I hope for a little drop of the royal yard, not forgetting the stunsail booms, and we'll all drink success to every female in Liverpool (convulsive laughter), also to our worthy chairman and our kind entertainers. I know my fellow-shipmates, both seamen and marines, will join me in returning their heartfelt thanks, and let us give three hearty cheers. 'The Lady Mayoress, and all the ladies of Liverpool.'

A seaman of *Edgar* called for three cheers for the ladies, and then on went the celebrations; the chairman responded, saying 'We hope the Channel Fleet will revisit Liverpool (loud and repeated cheering)'; Mr Stoyle, of the Prince of Wales Theatre, sang 'Simon the Cellarer', and 'his mimicry of Dame Margery's voice gained for him round after round of deafening cheers'; A. S. Callaway, a seaman of *Black Prince*, sang 'The White Squall', Petty Officer J. Fraser, of *Defence*, sang 'The Anchor's Weighed' and the choir sang 'Rule Britannia'. By the time they drank to 'Sweethearts and Wives' and sang 'God Save the Queen' again, it was half past five o'clock.

In his *Memories* which he dictated many years later, in September 1919, Jackie Fisher also remembered that day. He was then gunnery lieutenant of *Warrior*, at the age of twenty-two, and already a man marked for promotion.

When the banquet was over, John Kiernan, captain of the maintop in *Warrior*, got up unsolicited in his chair and said that 'on behalf of his topmates he wished to thank the Mayor and Corporation for a jolly good dinner and the best beer he'd ever tasted'. He stopped there and said: 'Bill, hand me up that beer again.' Bill said there was no more! A pledge had been given by the Mayor that they should have only two bottles of beer each. However, in came 'beer by the dozen'. That, at least, was Fisher's recollection.

By this time, some 60,000 people were lining the sailors' route back to the landing stage. Some women stationed across the road caused the bluejackets to break ranks and at once there were high jinks, with sailors commandeering hansom cabs, riding on top and taking over the reins. One sailor, on coming down from the cabby's seat, was quoted as saying that 'He'd be blow'd, if ever he'd had such a jolly cruise in his life'. Fisher's version is that he then appealed to the *Warriors'* 'honour and affection', thinking that they might have had 'a good lot of beer'. When they marched back to the ship in fours, he asked them to 'take each other's arms. They nobly did it! And I got highly complimented for the magnificent way they marched back through the streets!'

Jackie Fisher had a strong streak of native cunning in him, and he was quick to commend what would now be called 'one-upmanship' in his sailors. During Admiral Dacres's inspection of *Warrior*, Fisher's chief gunner's mate Abraham Johnson was down in a magazine when the admiral was just about to descend the ladder. (Johnson had come to Fisher beforehand and said he knew his admiral and would Fisher let him have a free hand?) Johnson called up to the admiral, 'Beg pardon, sir! you can't come down here!' 'Damn the fellow,' said the admiral, 'what does he mean?' Johnson said again, 'You can't come down here, sir.' 'Why not?' asked the admiral' 'Because no iron instrument is allowed in the magazine, sir.' 'Ah!' said the admiral, unbuckling his sword, '*that* fellow knows his duty! This is a *properly* organised ship!'

Jack's table manners had been seen and approved of in Liverpool. 'He could, though used to his basin, politely use his punch-glass without spilling its contents—aye, and in a manner that would have done credit to a professional toast-master.' Again, 'though none had studied the rules laid down for after-dinner etiquette, he could recline on the back of his chair, and peel his apple with all the dignity of an alderman at the civic feast.'

'The British Tar of the Future', from *Punch*, 12 April 1862.

Liverpool was the highlight of the cruise. From figures kept by *Warrior*, more people (57,400) visited the ship in Liverpool than anywhere else. The total number visiting *Warrior* during the cruise was 270,834; extrapolating from these for the whole fleet, a total of well over a million and a half people must have visited the ships. For *Warrior*, the busiest day had 14,273 visitors, at Sunderland, and the greatest number of steamers alongside in one day was 194.

The ironclads were, of course, a godsend to *Punch*, which published cartoons of 'The British Tar of the Future', clanking about in heavily rivetted metal bell-bottoms. In April 1862 they printed a parody of Charles Dibdin:

Iron-clad Jack
A sea-song of the future

Go, patter to soldiers and swabs not at sea
   'Bout danger and fear and the like,
A full head of steam and good iron-ship give me,
   And 'taint to three-deckers I'll strike!
Though such shot on our iron sides smack, smash, and smite,
   As would shiver a frigate of wood,
What of that? sheathed in plate we'll right gallantly fight,
   Till our foes for the fishes be food.
In armour cased for'ard, amidships, abaft,
   In our sides neither crevice nor crack,
All safely we steam in our blacksmith-built craft:
   Naught to fear now has Iron-clad Jack.

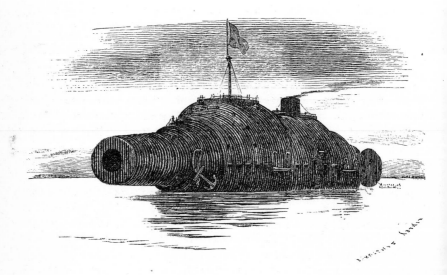

Punch's view in 1870 of what the ironclads of the future would be like.

Captain and *Eurydice*:
two mid-Victorian naval tragedies

Some of *Punch*'s 'ironclad verse' parodies were not all that far from current naval thinking. At a time of such rapid change, when almost every new ship had different guns, different machinery, different armour, to her predecessors, there was always a danger that sooner or later invention would outrun discretion. Over-confidence, compounded by flouting of some basic principles of ship stability, undoubtedly contributed to the greatest disaster of the mid-Victorian Navy, the capsizing of HMS *Captain* with the loss of 472 lives in the Bay of Biscay in September 1870.

Captain's designer, Captain Cowper Coles, was a brave, inventive and persistent officer, who knew how to marshal what would now be called the mass media to his side. He had served with great gallantry in the Crimea; as Admiral Sir Edmund Lyons's flag lieutenant in *Agamemnon* at Sebastopol he was recommended for the Victoria Cross and was unlucky not to get it. He was promoted commander in November 1854 and commanded the paddle-steamer *Stromboli* in the Black Sea. On his own initiative he built primitive forms of monitor for shore bombardment. The first, called *Lady Nancy*, was made of some thirty casks lashed in the form of a raft and carrying a 32-pounder gun. It had a crew of eighteen, carried a hundred rounds of ammunition and drawing only twenty inches, could get close inshore. A later version had a 68-pounder gun mounted on a centrally-pivoted platform, and protected by a metal shield, shaped like a dishcover, which Coles called a 'cupola'. So, in these early experiments in which, as Coles insisted, one trained the *gun* and not the ship, the turret-ship was developed.

Coles strongly pressed the idea of turret-ships on the Admiralty and his arguments were backed up by the success of Ericsson's *Monitor* in the American Civil War. The Admiralty went so far as to commission two ships, *Royal Sovereign*, converted from a first-rate of 130 guns, and *Prince Albert*, designed as a turret-ship. Both were formidably armed, with the new 9-inch 12½-ton rifled muzzle loaders designed at Woolwich, firing a 250-lb shell with a 43-lb charge. But they had very limited endurance, and were not much more than coast defence ships; in Admiral Ballard's phrase, they were 'lionesses on a very short length of chain'.

Although Coles used the *Monitor* as evidence for his argument, he himself did not read the full message of her experience (she capsized in a gale with all hands). Coles advocated a ship with a low freeboard, offering a smaller target to an enemy. The guns should be mounted in turrets, placed on a deck comparatively close to the water.

The Admiralty were sufficiently impressed by Coles's ideas to appoint a committee of officers and members of the Chief Constructor's department who, led by Edward James Lyon, the Chief Constructor, produced the *Monarch*, the world's first ocean-going turret warship. In all the furore over *Captain*, *Monarch*'s excellence has been obscured. She was the first ocean-going warship to fight under steam instead of sail, to be built of metal and not timber, and to have her main armament outside rather than inside her hull—in short, she was the first to embody all of the three great changes in Victorian fighting ship design.

The Admiralty deeply mistrusted Coles's own design and, normally, that would have been that. But Coles and his partisans, aided and abetted by *The Times*, launched and sustained a strong campaign to show that Coles was being hampered in his attempts to improve the country's sea defences by an ignorant, conservative and obstructive Admiralty Board in general, and Lyon in particular. As a result of this intense pressure, the Admiralty took the amazing and unprecedented step of commissioning a ship of Coles's design. She was built at Cammel Laird's, a private yard, at Birkenhead.

Captain had a designed freeboard of $8\frac{1}{2}$ feet but as she neared completion it seemed to experienced onlookers that she was going to draw much more, and so she did. When all coal, ammunition and provisions were on board her freeboard was reduced to $6\frac{1}{2}$ feet. Coles had originally intended *Captain* to be a mastless hull, like a coast defence ship, but with two propellers, as an extra safeguard, if anything went wrong with one. However, the Admiralty stipulated that if *Captain* was to take her place in a deep-water fleet she must carry enough canvas for a moderate rate of progress without using steam. The Admiralty would have been satisfied—or so they said—with a sail plan for a second or third-rate ship. But Coles was so confident that he added the maximum standard spar and sail plan for a first rate, with a sail area of 50,000 square feet. This meant that three masts were now necessary. Normal staying arrangements could not be fitted because they would have interferred with the arcs of fire of the two turrets. So tripod masts had to be used, adding to the top weight and to the wind resistance. Furthermore, Coles had the sail plan erected using the top of *Captain*'s superstructure, and not the top edge of her freeboard, as a base line. The effect was a drop of only a few feet in the sails' courses, and also an added leverage, because the centre of wind resistance had been raised that much higher. Thus everything seemed to conspire to make *Captain* top-heavy and cranky.

She was also awkward and uncomfortable to work and live in. She had no proper upper-deck, but a broad passageway or flying deck, passing over the two turrets running from the forecastle to the poop. This deck was lined on both sides with hammock boxes and also carried much of the gear normally stowed on a ship's upper-deck: booms, boats, ropes for handling the sails, bitts and fife rails for running rigging, and a small conning-tower. The space was very cramped and there was no proper run for sheets and halliards (there was no way men could 'stamp and go' as in *Achilles*). This flying deck was also used for ship's company musters, divisions, and small arms drill at sea because the deck below was awash in all but the calmest weather. A light bridge crossed the flying deck just forward of the funnel, with engine-room telegraphs and voice pipes to the threefold steering wheels on the poop and lower-deck.

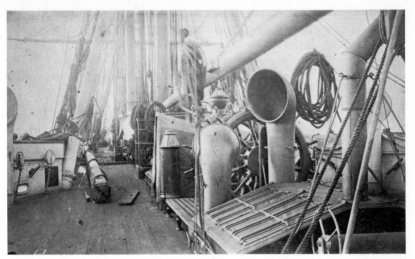

On board HMS *Captain*: awkward and uncomfortable to work
and live in, she had no proper upper-deck.

There was only one internal accommodation deck and everybody lived on
it except the captain, the commander and the navigating officer, whose cabins
were under the poop. Such space as was available was curtailed by bulkheads
and wing compartments and the ship's company would have been seriously
overcrowded had the ship not carried about a hundred men fewer than a
wooden ship of the same tonnage. The main-deck had no port-holes and there
were only two hatchways, one on the poop and the other on the forecastle.
Ventilation was bad, although the main-deck was quite well lit by two large
deadlights. The upper or gun deck was nearly always flooded at sea, and in a
force 6 or 7 wind the turret ports had also to be shut.

Captain was delivered as ready for sea in January 1870. That extra two feet
of draught was too much for the Admiralty, who refused to pay the last
instalment of her cost. She commissioned on 30 April, at Portsmouth, and
lower-deck legend said afterwards that the signalman hoisted the ensign
upside down by mistake that day. She had a maximum safe heeling angle of
21°, less than a third of the normal for her time (*Monarch*'s was over 70°) and to
many people she 'looked all wrong'. But they were mostly being wise after the
event and her first captain, Hugh Burgoyne VC, professed himself quite
satisfied with her.

Captain carried 600 tons of coals but she was less economical in steaming
than *Monarch* and trials showed that she was inferior to *Monarch* in every
other respect: her turning circle was larger, her speed was lower at every point
of sailing, her ability to fire her guns in heavy weather was less. However, she
did ride out one gale off Ushant quite safely and her sea-worthiness seemed
proved. Reed and others still had misgivings, but there was now no doubt in

the popular mind that *Captain* had fully vindicated Cowper Coles in his struggle against the fuddy-duddy Admiralty.

In August 1870 *Captain* joined the Channel Fleet for the passage south to Gibraltar to combine with the Mediterranean Fleet for a cruise in the Atlantic. After coaling, the combined fleet sailed north from Gibraltar, with Admiral Sir Alexander Milne flying his flag in *Lord Warden*. Milne had never seen *Captain* before she joined his flag on the morning of 6 September, when he boarded her to witness sailing trials and target practice.

The weather worsened during the afternoon and Burgoyne asked the admiral to stay and dine on board, returning to his flagship the next morning. Milne decided to get back and his boat was called alongside *Captain* at 5.00 p.m. In the sea already running, *Captain*'s lee rails were awash, and Milne had the greatest difficulty in getting into his boat. He was drenched to the skin, the boat was very nearly swamped, and when he got back to *Lord Warden* he was reported as saying, 'Thank God I'm on board my own ship again.'

By about six o'clock it was dark and the weather was getting worse. The wind steadily freshened as the barometer dropped. Upper sails were furled, topsails double reefed through the squadron, but by eleven o'clock proper station-keeping was no longer possible, and the flagship signalled 'open order'. *Captain* answered this signal. Shortly after midnight, when the watches were changing, there was a particularly fierce squall. Every ship in the fleet lost sails and had rigging damaged; it was almost certainly this squall which was too much for *Captain*. She heeled over, turned turtle, and sank.

There were no legends of heroism about *Captain*'s end: there were so few survivors and so little time. Both watches of seamen were probably on deck, the oncoming watch being mustered by the midshipman on the forecastle, while the offgoing watch were still struggling to clew down the topsail yards; the ship was lying over too much for the yards to come down of their weight, and not an inch could they gain on the weather braces. Burgoyne himself was on deck, in an old pair of trousers, cap and pilot cloth reefer, showing that he had wakened suddenly and had had no time to dress properly. One of the survivors, Gunner's Mate James Ellis, heard Burgoyne ask the officer of the watch for the angle of the ship's heel from the bridge clinometer. The answer was 'eighteen degrees' and Burgoyne at once ordered both fore and main topsail halliards and sheets let go. This, if it had ever been done, might have spilled enough wind pressure out of the sails to save the ship. But there was no time. At about five minutes past midnight, the squall hit the ship and took her over.

Before they could collect themselves, Captain Burgoyne, the officers of the watch and both watches of seamen were either thrown into the sea or were supporting themselves in wreckage or boats. *Captain* herself was bottom up, with her keel showing. She soon sank, taking with her the whole of her engineroom branch, all her marines and the rest of her officers; amongst the young men who died were the sons of Mr Erskine, the Minister of War, Lord Northbrook and Admiral Sir Baldwin Walker. Also drowned was Captain Cowper Coles, who had been on board as an observer. He had been sleeping in a cabin aft, and nobody saw him after the accident. Very probably he never woke.

Several seamen had saved themselves by climbing into the 36-foot pinnace which was floating clear. Near them was an upturned steam-pinnace, with Burgoyne and Gunner James May clinging to its keel. May had made a remarkable escape. He had awoken when he felt the ship rolling violently and he had gone on deck to check the security of the turrets. He was inside the after one when he felt the ship going. He climbed out through the sighting port at the top which, when he left, was level with the water. Burgoyne and May saw *Captain*'s bows rear up before she sank.

Later, May remembered their conversation. Burgoyne said, 'My God, May, I never thought we were coming to this.' When May shouted that *Captain* was going, and that they would soon follow her, Burgoyne replied, 'I'm afraid so, this boat shows no signs of righting.'

But they were not lost. They drifted towards the other pinnace, and May managed to get across to it. Burgoyne was a non-swimmer, but another survivor, Able Seaman John Heard, implored him to come across and held out a boat-hook. According to Heard, Burgoyne told the seaman to save himself and 'I shall not forget you one day'. Burgoyne was not seen again.

The pinnace lost another man, swept overboard by a wave, but the rest, eighteen of them, survived to sight Cape Finisterre just before dawn and eventually to get ashore in Corcubion Bay on the coast of Spain, the next day.

The officers and men of *Captain* had as their memorials two plaques in St Paul's Cathedral, and a sad little card, price 2d, sold on the streets of Portsmouth and Chatham:

> In Memory of the
> 506 Gallant British Sailors
> Who Perished in HMS *Captain*
> Which foundered off Cape Finisterre on
> the morning of September 7th 1870.

> 'There is on the lone, lone sea
>   A spot unmarked, but holy;
> For there the gallant and the free
>   In their ocean bed lie lowly.

> 'Down, down beneath the deep.
>   That oft to triumph bore them;
> They sleep a calm and peaceful sleep
>   The soft waves dashing o'er them.

> 'And though no stone may tell
>   Their name, their worth, their glory.
> They rest in hearts that loved them well.
>   They grace Britannia's story.'

Cowper Coles may have drowned, but his idea of guns in turrets lived on. When the first true mastless capital ship in the Navy's history, HMS

Devastation, completed for sea in 1872, her four 12-inch, 35-ton muzzle-loaders were mounted in two huge turrets, 31 feet in diameter and capable of training and firing through arcs of 280. Her accommodation was not so impressive: the sailors called her, and the seven *Cyclops* class armoured defence ships of about the same period, 'rat-holes with tinned air'. Phipps Hornby, now an admiral, took *Devastation* upon a round-Britain cruise in 1873, where she was as popular and as reassuring to the masses as *Warrior* and the others had been a decade earlier. (The ships were acclaimed everywhere, and in Aberdeen Phipps Hornby had respectfully dedicated to him a 'Devastation Galop', composed by a Mr James Scott Skinner, dancing master of Aberdeen, and played at the Grand Ball given to the Channel Fleet.)

By 1878 there were fewer than a dozen pure sailing ships in the Navy List and they were all employed for training officers and men. One of them was an old so-called 'Jackass' frigate of 900 tons, built in 1842, called HMS *Eurydice*. She was commissioned as a training ship for young seamen in February 1877. Her captain, Marcus Hare, had been specially chosen for the appointment; he had been commander in command of *Boscawen*, the training ship at Portland, and *Eurydice* was his first command as a captain. The first lieutenant was Francis Hope Taybor, another picked man, who had just spent four years as first lieutenant of HMS *Cruiser*, the seamen's training ship in the Mediterranean.

In November 1877, *Eurydice* went on a cruise to the West Indies, leaving Bermuda on 6 March 1878 for Portsmouth. She had over 300 people on board: her fifteen officers, sixty permanent ship's company (including a barber, a lamptrimmer and a 'musician' called Seidenstucker), and over 200 seamen under training. She also had, for the passage home, a Royal Marine detachment of a corporal and fourteen privates, a captain of the Royal Engineers and half a dozen time-expired soldiers, and four or five court-martial prisoners being sent home to serve their sentences.

By noon of 24 March, after a quick passage, *Eurydice* was off the Isle of Wight, and everybody expected to anchor at Spithead that evening. The weather was fine but cold, with a steady northerly (offshore) wind, but the glass was dropping slightly. *Eurydice* was carrying all plain sail, with studding-sails, and making about seven knots against an ebb tide. The Isle of Wight, and its steep cliffs split by deep chines running down to the sea, is particularly dangerous for squalls. Hare was cutting corners somewhat, steering as close to land as he could. That afternoon, merchantmen further out to sea could be seen shortening sail but they had far fewer hands than *Eurydice*. Her crew were numerous, superbly trained and fit, and could be relied upon to have everything off her in double quick time. At about 3.30 p.m. Hare ordered men aloft to shorten sail but evidently decided there was not time before the squall arrived. The men were ordered down again. Sheets and halliards were cut, but it was too late. A snow squall overwhelmed *Eurydice*, pushing her over on to her starboard beam ends. Her main-deck gun ports were open, the main-deck flooded, and *Eurydice* sank, righting herself as she went down, in 7 fathoms of water.

HMS *Devastation*, the first mastless capital ship, in 1873.

Hare was last seen standing high on the port weather gunwale, directing sails to be shortened and then, when it was too late for that, giving orders for boats to be lowered. One survivor said Hare had told him to save himself, saying, 'It is of no avail.'

The snowstorm at first obscured what had happened but when it cleared the schooner *Emma* closed the spot, where *Eurydice*'s royals could still be seen flapping above the water. *Emma*'s boats picked up five men, Taybor, the sapper captain, a petty officer, Able Seaman Cuddiford and Ordinary Seaman Sydney Fletcher, of whom only Cuddiford and Fletcher lived. The other three and everybody else on board died (including Daniel Harley of *Alert*, and one prisoner found still in his cell when the ship was raised five months later).

Ordinary Seaman Sydney Fletcher (on the left) and Able Seaman Cuddiford, the only two survivors of HMS *Eurydice*.

The court-martial of Cuddiford and Fletcher (a technical necessity; they were both of course, acquitted of any blame) decided that *Eurydice* was lost because of 'a sudden squall whose approach was invisible from the ship'. The squall probably was sudden, but it hardly seems likely that it was invisible from the ship. It seems much more probable that Hare simply sailed *Eurydice* under. He was relying on his razor-sharp crew, and the thought of getting home that evening was in his and everybody's minds, but the squall caught him and *Eurydice* with the gun ports open. Two years later, by one of those eerie coincidences that occur at sea, another sail training ship with trainees on board, HMS *Atalanta*, a very similar ship to *Eurydice*, also coming home from a cruise in the West Indies, was lost with all hands somewhere between Bermuda and home.

The loss of *Eurydice* sent a thrill of horror round not just Portsmouth, but the whole nation. Reginald Bacon, then a cadet in *Britannia*, felt that squall on the Dart that afternoon and he remembered later that an old sailor with him said: 'That is the sort of squall to capsize a ship if she is not properly handled.' Agnes Weston, who had started a branch of her Royal Naval Temperance Society on board, was on a trip to York but she had visited *Eurydice* before she sailed: 'I can almost see those hundreds of bright, young faces now.' The pledge book and cards went down with the ship, but months later she got them back when the ship was raised. They crumbled to dust after a little exposure, but she was able to read the names. Marcus Hare was a good friend of Agnes Weston's and she was delighted when Cuddiford told her that Hare had clasped his hands in prayer as he went down with the ship; 'I don't profess to be a Christian man,' said Cuddiford, 'but if there ever was one, it was our captain.'

A memorial to the men who died in *Eurydice* was erected in the Naval Cemetery at Haslar, Gosport. It was a large granite monument, surmounted by one of the anchors recovered from the ship, and inscribed with the ship's name on one side. Names of the dead were inscribed on panels, and many of those whose bodies were recovered from the sea are buried in graves around the memorial.

But the young men of *Eurydice* had another memorial, probably more lasting, and certainly far less predictable. At Mount St Mary's College in Derbyshire, Gerard Manley Hopkins, a young Jesuit priest, read the accounts of the disaster in *The Times*, and in April 1878 he wrote a poem called 'The Loss of the *Eurydice*'. Hopkins felt almost guilty at writing poetry, and thought it 'unprofessional', but three years earlier he had read in *The Times* of a similar disaster and with great diffidence had turned an account of the wreck of the *Deutschland* on Kentish Knock, in December 1875, into one of the greatest religious poems in the language. Now, he took the story of *Eurydice* and wrote a poetic parable, linking this naval disaster, so many men drowned with no chance of absolution, to the greater disaster to the nation, the abandonment of the Roman Catholic religion.

> She had come from a cruise, training seamen—
> Men, boldboys soon to be men:
>   Must it, worst weather,
> Blast bole and bloom together?
>
> No Atlantic squall overwrought her
> Or rearing billow of the Biscay water:
>   Home was hard at hand
> And the blow bore from land.

And you were a liar, O blue March day.
Bright sun lanced fire in the heavenly bay;
    But what black Boreas wrecked her? he
Came equipped, deadly-electric,

A beetling baldbright cloud thorough England
Riding: there did storms not mingle? and
    Hailropes hustle and grind their
Heavengravel? wolfsnow, worlds of it, wind there?

Gerard Manley Hopkins was no seaman but he had no doubt what had gone wrong:

Too proud, too proud, what a press she bore!
Royal, and all her royals wore.
    Sharp with her, shorten sail!
Too late; lost; gone with the gale.

This was that fell capsize.
As half she had righted and hoped to rise
    Death teeming in by her portholes
Raced down decks, round messes of mortals.

Then a lurch forward, frigate and men;
'All hands for themselves' the cry ran then;
    But she who had housed them thither
Was around them, bound them or wound them with her.

Hopkins gives poetic expression to the feeling the country had for its sailors. Sydney Fletcher and Cuddiford would have been astonished to be referred to in such a way, but there is no doubt Hopkins was touching some deep-rooted chord in the national temperament:

They say who saw one sea-corpse cold
He was all of lovely manly mould,
    Every inch a tar,
Of the best we boast our sailors are.

Look, foot to forelock, how all things suit! he
Is strung by duty, is strained to beauty,
    And brown-as-dawning-skinned
With brine and shine and whirling wind.

O his nimble finger, his gnarled grip!
Leagues, leagues of seamanship
    Slumber in these forsaken
Bones, this sinew, and will not waken.

He was but one like thousands more.
Day and night I deplore
    My people and born own nation,
Fast foundering own generation.

Tea, temperance and Aggie Weston:
promotion for the sailor

It was almost impossible for the nineteenth-century sailor to reach wardroom rank. In theory, a man could be promoted for gallantry in the presence of the enemy. In practice, nobody was so promoted after the Crimean War. This very important reform—promotion from the lower-deck to the wardroom—had to wait until the twentieth century.

Some boys joined the Navy from the industrial schools ships, and there were several of them at seaports around the British Isles. A boy was sent to such a ship if, under the Industrial Schools Act, he had been found begging, or wandering with no proper abode or guardianship, or destitute, or frequenting the company of thieves, or if he was under twelve years old and had been charged with an offence punishable by imprisonment. A typical ship was *Formidable*, at Portishead, Somerset, which opened in December 1869.

The boys were housed, clothed and treated very much as if they had joined the Navy. They had school on board and games on playing fields ashore. They learned swimming, gun drill and boat drill, and all the normal business of living on board. By the end of 1878 *Formidable* had received 891 boys. Of them, 594 had left the ship, 415 to the merchant service, thirty to the Royal Navy. Others emigrated, or took other employment, or were claimed back by their families or friends. The boys were asked to write and tell the ship how they were getting on in their new lives, and some of them did. One boy wrote from HMS *Sylvia*:

> Sir, in obedience to your request at leaving your ship, I write to inform you of my progress in your profession. Since leaving the *Formidable* I went to the *Impregnable*, and from there to this ship, which is a surveying ship. We are surveying the south coast of Russia. We are A.B.s; so you see we are not doing so badly. I am sorry I have not written to you before; I hope you will excuse me for my silence. Will you remember me to the instructors, by whom I gained so much; to Mr Rice, the schoolmaster; and I should like this to be read to all the boys. I should not ask you, but knowing it is your pleasure to assist any boys that have been under you; and will you tell them from me that the Service is a fine thing, it has done me a wonderful deal of good, and I recommend them to do the same.

With its good grammar and flawless spelling, it is a curiously cool and dutiful letter. The writer obviously had his own way to make in the world, and that involved fulfilling past obligations; if his old captain asked him to write, he wrote. But there were still romantics joining the Navy. Charles Humphreys joined at Uxbridge, aged thirteen, in October 1870 and was sent to the old hulk

Hebe, off Woolwich Dockyard, tender to the *Fishguard*. He was lost in wonder at all he saw: *Hebe*, 'although she had no guns on board', and the 'dockyard was also a wonderful place to me'. His first impressions of sea life 'were very romantic, but I soon found that it was a very rough life. I was soon sorry that I joined the Navy and wanted to go home.' There was the authentic voice of a homesick, frightened, overawed child, like thousands of others who joined the Navy.

The training ship *St Vincent* at Portsmouth was full, so Humphreys was sent to the *Boscawen* at Portland, joining in November 1870. He did not enjoy his year on board, 'learning discipline' as he put it. The instructors were very cruel, the captain very stern, the boys were short of food, and 'many a rope's end' did Humphreys feel. He learned 'sail drill, knots and splices, boat rowing, school, gun drill, rifle and cutlass drills, and everything that goes to make a sailor'. They were taught how to make and mend clothes, were paid 3d a week, and could go ashore every Sunday afternoon until sunset. There was three weeks' leave at midsummer and at Christmas. As Humphreys was a long way from home and his parents were very poor, he stayed on board during the leave. They had to clean the ship, but they did no drills. However, they did get plum duff at Christmas 'and we thought we were very well off'. Humphreys gives one revealing sidelong glimpse of the sailor's social status at the time: 'life in the Navy was not much thought of.'

'Merrily Round the Capstan': boy seamen of the training-ship
Boscawen shortening in cable.

From *Boscawen* Humphreys went to *Excellent* for gunnery training, as a boy first class. The boys were oppressed by thieving seniors. 'At that time honesty was not the best policy in the Navy, at least, not with the ship's stewards. Boys were robbed of their money; clothes were put down to them, which they never received, and as I suppose I was a "green horn", I was one of those who had to suffer.' He was paid two shillings a week but because he was 'in debt to the Crown for my uniform', he was not paid anything until the sum was wiped off.

Humphreys left *Excellent* in January 1872 and joined *Vulture*, 10-gun steam-corvette for the East African Station. Their commission, from Humphreys's own account, was much more exciting than many others in the tropics. There was boat-work, searching for, and attacking, slavers. The slave-masters were always ready to fight back and once Humphreys was nearly killed by an Arab who rushed at him with a scimitar. He had other escapes, one of them from the common fate of falling from aloft. It was off the east coast of Africa, when the ship was rolling hard. 'My mate, next to me, caught hold of the rope I was going to catch hold of, when it parted and down he went and was killed. He died within 20 minutes and the last words he said were, "Lay me on my left side." Had I caught hold of that rope, it would have been me killed instead of him.'

Humphreys left the Navy in 1881, aged twenty-four, a comparatively young man. He had a fund of stories to take with him, one of them a most revealing account of how popular *Vulture*'s captain must have been: after paying off, they went up to London by train and 'our captain travelled with us, and he was so much liked, that when we arrived at Victoria, some of the men took the horses out of the carriage that was waiting for him, and dragged it through the streets. This of course caused quite a sensation, but it was all taken in good part.'

Henry Capper joined *St Vincent* as a boy in 1869. He was born in 1855 in Portsmouth and, most unusually for the lower-deck, came from a middle-class family. His father had 'a responsible post' in Portsmouth Dockyard and Henry had relatives who were naval officers. How great a social gulf Henry Capper had created by joining the lower-deck was shown him when he took passage in the trooper *Orontes* for the North American and West Indies Station in January 1873. His cousin, a sub-lieutenant, was also taking passage in the same ship. Capper 'kept as far away from him as possible' and did not try to presume upon their relationship. It was just as well he did not, for one night he was look-out on the forecastle when his cousin was the officer forward. 'Taking advantage of our being alone, I made a perfectly respectful remark to this young officer— only two years my senior in age—in regard to our common family affairs. He at once lost his temper and said: "If you ever again have the presumption to address me except on duty I'll have you caned." He had but to report me for impertinence and that would have happened!' It was largely because of this bitter snub that Capper made up his mind that he would, by hook or by crook, become an officer, and in so doing reopen the blocked channels of promotion from lower-deck to quarter-deck.

Capper's memories of his first ship, the *Inconstant* in the Flying Squadron in 1870, show how high passions ran in the Navy and how terrible was the retribution for striking a superior officer, no matter what the provocation. At Cape Town, on passage home, a marine coming on board after forty-eight hours' leave was ordered by a sergeant to give a hand in getting up ashes, a job which would normally be done by one of the watch on board. When the marine protested there was an argument, in which the sergeant taunted the marine, saying that he had slept with the marine's wife and would do so again when the ship got back. Infuriated, the marine made a lunge at the sergeant with the gun lever he had in his hand. He was convicted by court-martial and sentenced to fourteen years' hard labour on Cape Town breakwater.

Ordinary Seaman Henry Capper wearing the collar of his Good
Templar regalia, 1873.

The convicted man was brought up in the presence of the ship's company. The captain read out his sentence, and ordered his badges and regimental buttons to be cut off. Then, according to a common custom of the time, the captain began a homily on the enormity of the crime, but the marine interrupted fiercely and shouted:

Captain Waddalove! If you are a gentleman, don't strike a man when he's down. If the admiral had taunted you that your wife was his whore wouldn't you have downed him as I did this white-livered Sergeant as did that to me? If I live to find him after fourteen years in prison, I'll give him a civilian's dose, and so would you! Now let me go, you have no right to add to the punishment. I'll suffer that like a man!

Needless to say, the sergeant was transferred to another ship within a day or so, for his own safety, or 'he would have been dropped overboard some dark night'.

In Capper's opinion, one of the chief reasons why sailors were kept low on the social scale was the custom of paying them only once in six months. Each man was then given a printed form, called a Slop List, showing the 'wages due' and the 'nulcts' such as 'slops, charges and arrears', and 'soap, tobacco and religious books'. Many men were illiterate (the boys, better-educated, made themselves pocket money by reading and writing letters for them) and often could not understand the items, especially the last, which was really the method of paying the chaplain.

Men could allot half their pay to someone at home. But even this was open to exploitation, by ladies of the seaport towns taking advantage of the long foreign commissions to 'marry' two or even more men at the same time. *Inconstant* had one A.B. who was a very clever needleman. At Bombay another expert needleman joined for the passage home. Both joined forces and by the time they got to England had earned themselves a large sum to hand over to their wives. 'They landed on leave together, and only then learned that their wives lived in the same street, and same house. Each then discovered his wife to be one and the same woman, at that moment in association with a marine from another ship, to whom she was also married.'

Capper's next ship, in the West Indies from 1873–74, was the sloop *Spartan* (Captain J. S. Hudson, the officer who had been attacked by John Dalliger). Capper himself was a teetotaller and he formed a branch of the Good Templars on board. This was a quasi-secret society whose members swore amongst others things to abstain from alcohol. Many of the older and more conservative officers and men scoffed at such an organisation, because of its aims, or looked askance at it, because any assembly on board not attended by either the captain or the chaplain was technically illegal.

Within a year, half of *Spartan*'s complement of 272 were members and from being the 'drunkenest ship in the squadron' *Spartan* had the smallest punishment returns. On board, they held their meetings in a storeroom, or, when not steaming, in the stokehold. Once they joined the Good Templar Lodge, the sailors learned recitations and songs and took part in simple ceremonies. But most important of all, as Capper pointed out, 'coming thus into association with decent folk ashore (upon whom they had previously looked as far above them) many became attached to young women and made excellent marriages.'

Henry Capper was one of the first to realise that temperance and the raising of the bluejacket's self-esteem were closely linked. Nobody did more for both causes than Capper's friend for more than thirty years, Agnes Weston. Aggie Weston had her critics, in and out of the Navy, but in her own way and in her own chosen field she was one of the great reforming figures of the nineteenth-century Navy. She was born in London in March 1840, the eldest daughter of a successful barrister. Her family had naval connections, but her work for the Navy, though it now seems predestined, actually came about in a series of unplanned steps. As an unmarried daughter and a deeply religious young woman, she naturally turned her hand to local affairs and welfare. When the family were living in Bath she held prayer meetings for the Somerset militiamen. She wrote to soldiers on foreign service. One of them knew a bluejacket and asked her to write to him as well.

Miss Agnes E. Weston.

By May 1871, Aggie's letters had grown into a home industry. She began to write a general letter and have it printed, for distribution to ship's companies all over the world. One officer, serving in the West Indies, wrote to Aggie about the scene on board after he had distributed a parcel of her letters on the lower-deck. 'I went round the decks half-an-hour afterwards, just to note what they were doing with them. It would have cheered your heart to have seen that sight—groups of men sitting cross-legged on the deck round one, the best reader probably, who was seated in the middle reading the letter to his messmates. It was a good sight indeed on board a warship on a Sunday afternoon.'

In 1872 Aggie went to stay with friends at Devonport where, every Sunday afternoon, she saw hundreds of sailors strolling aimlessly about with nowhere to go. She held meetings with hymn singing and Bible readings, and tea, in her friend's kitchen. One of her first bluejacket friends, a young seaman called Arthur Phillips, must have been a very brave man. 'He was never ashamed,' wrote Aggie, 'to kneel down under his hammock for prayer, before the hands turned in.'

The temperance cause had already made progress in the Navy. The National Temperance League had taken up work started years before in HMS *Reindeer* by the men themselves. As captain of *Russell* in the 1850s Admiral Sir William King-Hall offered to sign a pledge of abstinence if men punished for offences of drunkenness on board would do the same. He and Agnes Weston were both present at the inaugural meeting of the Royal Naval Temperance Society at Devonport on 28 April 1873. Aggie was a tireless worker for the cause. In May she visited *Impregnable* and addressed the boys; 225 of them signed the pledge. Aggie went on to visit thirty-eight ships that year, took some 1,600 pledges and formed many branches of the Society.

Several bluejackets had told Aggie they wished they had 'a public-house without the drink'. She and her indefatigable friend Miss Wintz found a house which had been a large grocery store, at the bottom of Fore Street, near the dockyard gates in Devonport. With money raised through the temperance movement, the ladies converted the house into a restaurant and kitchen, with a reading room. It was furnished with tables and settles, and Aggie had it decorated with bright colours, mirrors, and a little gilding, for, she cannily said, 'I was competing against public houses.' The doors opened officially on 8 May 1876. The building became internationally known as Aggie Weston's Sailors' Rest.

To the ordinary bluejacket, Aggie Weston's was an eye-opener.

To men accustomed to eat from tables covered with tarpaulin cloths [wrote Henry Capper], their own knives and never even a two-pronged fork in the mess, and only basins and plates when these were purchased by themselves, the change was startling indeed. Many of the waitresses were unpaid volunteer ladies, and the rule enforced was to avoid all familiarity, so that whereas in their own haunts they were called 'Jack', 'Tom', or 'Bill', here each customer was 'Mr——', and 'Yes, sir', and 'No, sir', the method of reply. What wonder that a new atmosphere created new desires, and that in some measure what they had experienced on shore began to be the rule afloat.

Another Sailors' Rest, in Portsmouth, opened in June 1881.

Henry Capper also became involved in the reform of the Sailors' Home at Portsea, which had been open since 1852. Though under distinguished patronage, it was badly managed, uncomfortable, ill-furnished and out-of-date, and 'the attendants acted as though they were ships' police afloat'. As his ship's representative, Capper was one of a committee which brought about changes, including the resignation of the superintendent. The Home eventually was run as a club, by the bluejackets themselves.

Capper's own career was progressing towards his goal. He qualified for gunner in 1879, and in February 1881 he shipped his first thin gold stripe as a warrant gunner. But he still had some way to go, as he soon found out, at his first dinner in the warrant officers' mess in *Excellent*. The president announced him as a new member, and the sixty officers present all clapped. Capper rose to express his thanks and said how much he appreciated their welcome 'but had done my best to reach this mess only as a half-way house to a commission', whereupon there was a great roar of derisive laughter. Mr Cleverley, the chief gunner in the chair, explained: 'My boy, don't you know that there *is* no further promotion open to you until in some thirty years' time you may get this stripe (the chief gunner's) for a few months before retirement. No naval warrant officer has had a commission these last seventy years: if you want one you must get the system altered first.' That was precisely what Henry Capper was determined to do.

Henry Capper was butting his head against the ceiling of his ambitions, but below that there was, by the last three decades of the century, a recognised career structure in the Navy up which an intelligent, ambitious and resourceful man could climb if he wished. Just such a man was Patrick Riley, who was born of an Irish Roman Catholic family in March 1859. His father was a contractor working on the forts on Drake Island, overlooking Plymouth Sound. Riley was another romantic, keen on the sea and eager to see the world, and when his family moved to South Wales he stayed behind, to live with an aunt in Plymouth so that he could join the Navy. At his instigation his aunt got him a letter of recommendation from a magistrate. Although his aunt made a mistake so that he was only thirteen and a half, and although he was a ¾ inch below the minimum of 4 feet 10 inches, he duly entered in October 1872 as a boy second class, signing on for ten years' continuous service, from the age of eighteen. He had the standard year's training in *Impregnable*, getting 3d—or a 'Holy Joe'—a day as pocket money, and then went to the training brig *Squirrel*, cruising to Portland and to Dartmouth. After a year he was rated boy first class, his pay went up to 7d a day, and he did a gunnery course at *Foudroyant*, attached to *Cambridge* which was the gunnery school ship for the western divisions. He then went to sea, aged fifteen. The majority of boys went to big ships, where cruises lasted only a fortnight, they had salt pork only twice a week, and the battle squadron spent their time in hectic drills; but Riley went to the 14-gun corvette *Amethyst*, on the South American station, where they were often at sea for months, ate salt pork almost every day, and very seldom saw another white ensign.

Except for one mishap, when he had a 'reprimand' written in pencil on his service certificate in the *Calypso* in 1890, Riley was the kind of man to do well in and for the Navy. In *Amethyst* he kept his wits about him and was always interested in his surroundings. He sailed the skiff for the officers and had a better chance than most to get ashore and see the sights. He was nearly

Boys of the Tyne training-ship *Wellesley* at South Shields, 1876.

drowned while swimming off Rio, where the ship's company had general leave in September 1874—the first since commissioning in June. There were no recreational facilities or sports of any kind for the sailors there, so Riley and his mates went for long walks, or to a dance hall, or drinking. Very few overstayed their leave and those who did were hunted down by the local Brazilian police vigilantes, who were rewarded for bringing a man back on board. At that time a man lost a day's pay for every twenty-four hours adrift. From 1 January 1875 new regulations were introduced: a day's pay forfeit for every six hours or part adrift, and the much-disliked 10A punishment was revised and tightened up at the same time.

In his memoirs Riley notes the excitements of the commission, which stick out of the routine like currants in duff; Juan Fernandez, Robinson Crusoe's island; an earthquake at Coquimbo in Chile; the fierce *pampero* winds in the Plate estuary; the tour of the islands and towns north of Vancouver with the Governor General Lord Dufferin and his entourage on board; the run ashore at a place called Talcahuaro where fifty tars had a race on horseback. At gun target practice, the prize was won by Bob Sargent, who fired eight rounds from his 64-pounder in four minutes and ten seconds. At San Francisco they saw two men who had deserted from *Amethyst* at Monte Video; they were 'as bold as brass', but they were on American soil and nothing could be done. A seaman called Bill Stapleton was drowned. There were no pensions for the dependants of men killed on active service, so the ship's company subscribed £80 between them for Stapleton's mother, who was a widow. They had four days' leave at Esquimault and the men were allowed to come back on board to sleep and return to shore the next morning, so saving themselves lodging allowance. This was, as Riley said, 'a very valuable concession'.

The captain was a popular man and at Christmas made the traditional round of the mess-decks while 'the Negro Minstrels assembled with their full orchestra, the sweepers in their grotesque get-ups'. Every mess had its savings, money kept by the ship's steward for food not taken up, which could then be spent on extras. On passage to Valparaiso, for instance, each man was allowed to bring on board two sacks of potatoes and $1\frac{1}{2}$ hundredweight of flour. There were also fourteen sheep and live poultry on board.

On 14 September 1875 Riley was officially eighteen (although due to his aunt's error he was actually only sixteen and a half). He was rated ordinary seaman after a practical examination, 'the bosun taking me on the fo'c'sle, where I was questioned about the fittings of the spars and sails that had been carried away and was also examined by questions about other parts of the ship'. He then went before the captain to be rated, and his pay went up to 1s. 1d. a day. Very soon afterwards he also passed for trained gunnery rating, with an extra penny a day. His new seniority meant that he could draw a pound of tobacco a month, but he did not start smoking until he was thirty years old. However, he did take his tot, of half a gill a day. He had graduated to a man's estate: 'Shall I ever forget the feeling of shyness that came over me when I arrived in my mess for dinner as "man"? I had finished with the drudgery of a mess-boy and all that it meant, and in future I would have more time to myself.'

In November 1875 *Amethyst* took part in the action between HMS *Shah* and the rebel Peruvian turret-ship *Huascar*. *Huascar* escaped and then surrendered, to the disappointment of everyone in *Amethyst* (who had already been disappointed by being ordered to break off). But although *Amethyst* fired at *Huascar* for three hours, her 64-pounder had almost no effect, while a few direct hits from *Huascar*'s 10-inch 300-pounder might easily have sunk *Amethyst*. So discretion was the better part, but Riley said that 'wherever we went ashore, and got into conversation about it, the impression was that the British had lost a certain amount of prestige in failing to capture the *Huascar*.'

Their last Christmas was spent at sea. The messes strung up decorations of ship's biscuits, carved and drilled to make pretty patterns and spell out 'Happy Christmas'. At last their relief arrived, but before leaving they embarked prisoners, including an old shipmate, 'whose spirit', Riley noted, 'was completely broken', to serve the rest of their sentences at Portland. After some more excitement, when they went aground and damaged the bows so badly they had to pump all the way home, they were off (while they were aground the captain enquired where the ship was built and, interestingly, seemed reassured to be told that it was Devonport Dockyard). They sighted

Eddystone Light on 18 May 1878, after a commission of very nearly four years.

A week earlier, the men had been asked to declare which depot they wanted to return to when their fourteen days' leave had expired, and whether they wanted to do a gunnery school course or remain on general service. On paying off, the men went to the *Royal Adelaide* at Devonport or the *Duke of Wellington* at Portsmouth—both hulks. Stokers went to the *Indus*, another hulk, at Devonport. To do the gunnery course a man had to have served as A.B. for twelve months, be of Very Good character or have a special commendation from his commanding officer instead, and sign for five years' service (if he had not already signed for continuous service). Riley took the course; the examination was a stiff one (an officer took a day to examine just four men), but he passed and his pay went up by 4d a day. He then volunteered for a two-month torpedo course.

Riley's progress was steadily upward. He was examined for leading seaman on board the *Defence*, the guardship at Rockferry in the Mersey, in December 1880, and rated on 1 February 1881. He became petty officer second class in June 1882, and first class and gunnery inspector in September 1883. In July 1884 he was gunnery instructor in *Belleisle*, the guardship and training ship for coastguards at Kingstown, Co. Dublin. As a combined gunnery-torpedoman rating he not only took charge of drill but supervised the ship's divers, as well as 'Morris tube firing' for the whole ship's company. He also took charge of swimming instruction: in his last ship, the first class cruiser *Edgar* in the Far East, seventy-eight of her ship's company of 555 could not swim, and Riley taught them all.

Edgar commissioned in March 1893, and by that time Riley was one of the lower-deck's senior citizens. He was the chief petty officers' representative on the canteen committee. He was president of the mess when the chiefs and petty officers dined their counterparts of the Italian fleet at Taranto. As chief gunnery inspector, he and the other 'senior statesmen' of the ship—the ship's steward, ship's cook, chief waiter, chief bosun's mate, chief torpedo instructor—had their own special mess, with a messman to themselves. Riley retired in 1895, but returned to serve during the 1914–18 war.

Fortunately, it was generally the best seamen who served long enough in the Navy to make their memoirs of the lower-deck worth reading and who remembered the Navy kindly enough to think their memories worth writing down. One of the ablest, Thomas Holman, published his *Life in the Royal Navy* in 1892 (anonymously, because he was still serving). Holman was one of those truly irrepressible spirits who took the Navy as it was, but saw how it could be improved and also how it should be preserved. He heartily recommended the life. 'I now have to answer the question as to whether we should send our boys to the Navy,' he wrote. 'I say "Yes", emphatically "Yes"—after a period of twenty years on its lower ranks. My school contemporaries may now be a bit ahead of me, but I doubt if many of them have extracted so much fun and enjoyment out of the last twenty years of life as I have done.'

Holman was natural recruiting material. He first ran away to Portsmouth to join the Navy when he was eleven years old but was told that 'Her Majesty was not in want of such giants to man her fleet just then, as the Russian war was concluded'. Later, he was a cabin boy in a local gentleman's yacht, and though the yacht's owner joined with Holman's mother in painting a horrific picture of the dangers and hardships of a naval life, nothing would shake his determination to join the Navy. Eventually, in 1872, Holman joined *St Vincent* with a certificate of character as 'a badge of respectability' from a clergyman, and a quiet recommendation from the owner of the yacht to the captain of *St Vincent*.

His description of *St Vincent* is typical—hard work and drill, basic food, a 'Holy Joe' for pay once a week, severe punishment and a rigorous life—but Holman enjoyed it. His days were 'exceedingly bright and cheerful'. From *St Vincent* Holman went out to the North American and West Indian squadron where, after six ships in six months, he joined the sloop *Spartan* (in which he served with Henry Capper). Like Patrick Riley, Holman discovered the advantages of being boat's crew. He was bowman in the captain's boat which brought him 'many enjoyable little trips in the way of picnics and excursions on water and land and gave me many chances of accompanying officers' shooting parties up the lagoons in central America after alligators, or on shore hunting'.

Together, Capper and Holman volunteered to transfer to *Dryad* when it was time for *Spartan* to go home. The captain of *Dryad* wanted Capper on board so that 'what had been accomplished in regard to temperance in *Spartan* might be similarly carried out in his smaller command'. Capper had passed for leading rate and wanted to qualify at *Excellent*, wanted to get on, in fact, but eventually 'it was at last agreed that my transfer should take place provided I could find another man of the temperance party to accompany me'. This man was Thomas Holman. But both of them watched the *Spartan* leaving harbour 'with somewhat misty eyes'.

Holman was also a Good Templar, but although he did not take his tot at first, he wrote, 'I like my grog now as well as most.' As in *Spartan*, he was bowman of the captain's boat, where on one occasion alcohol got him into trouble and, revealingly, showed how readily flogging still sprang to the minds of some captains. It was Holman's job as bowman to take the captain 'piggy-back' through the surf. One day, when he had taken him ashore to watch a cricket match, Holman accepted the captain's offer of three brandies and sodas. When they got back to the beach, Holman was hardly in a fit state to walk himself, let alone carry anyone, and, inevitably, he dropped his commanding officer in the surf.

At once the captain shouted, 'Bring him here, coxswain, bring him here; he tried to drown his captain. I'll flog him.' Holman was taken on board and placed in irons. Later, of course, when the captain was dry and warm and had had his dinner, Holman was released and put in his hammock with a sentry to see that he did not choke himself. Next day he was given a dressing-down and suspended from the boat for a week 'in lieu of receiving four dozen with the cat'. The captain had exceeded his authority by threatening flogging, which had been suspended in peacetime since 1871. Even if *Dryad* were considered on a war basis, the captain could still not have flogged a man in the first class for conduct, like Holman, except by court-martial. But, obviously, old ways of thinking and old turns of speech died hard. Before Holman could go to *Excellent* he was examined and passed for leading seaman by *Dryad's* first lieutenant, who said he would be glad to have him in any future ship he served in.

Holman came home after nearly seven years abroad with about £40 back pay in his pocket, and went on six weeks' leave to see his friends at home. He was confident that 'no one among them was so happy or more thoroughly in love with his own profession nor had they the same stock of stories about lions, sharks, elephants, and sea serpents'.

At *Excellent* Holman spent among the happiest twelve months of his life, 'the days were only just long enough to squeeze all the good things into. True, we were at instructions all day long, but then it was being instructed among so many young men of my own age and temperament that made it so delightful; always a keen competition among us to be first at our drills and always a keen competition also as to who could play the biggest joke.'

Holman passed as seaman gunner and was rated leading seaman. He went up to Lerwick in the Shetland Islands as gunnery instructor to the Royal Naval Reserve. He enjoyed himself; his health improved, and he liked the cold, the food and the skating. His next ship was *Bacchante*, for the world cruise of the two sons of the Prince of Wales (later Edward VII), Prince Edward and Prince George, leaving Portsmouth in October 1880. During the voyage, Holman passed the selection board for warrant officer. He joined *Excellent* again for a year's course, and passed out top. He was now a warrant gunner, aged twenty-six, and, like Capper, was eventually promoted to lieutenant-commander—once the system had been changed.

When Henry Capper, wearing plain clothes, went into a world-famous firm of naval tailors on Portsmouth Hard to be measured for a new uniform, all went well until he said that 'the marks of distinction and buttons were those of a gunner'. The assistant at once put down his tape and went for the manager, 'who blandly informed' Capper that 'they did not make uniform for warrant officers, as such garments on their "finished rack" would be seen by senior officers and would be very likely to cost them the loss of their customers'. He recommended Capper to go to Messrs Larcom and Veysey in Queen Street. Capper went, and was well served, but he never forgot that insult.

But if such discrimination existed within the Navy, there was an even greater social distance between the public and the bluejacket. In 1877 an anonymous petty officer published a pamphlet called *The Seamen of the Royal Navy, their Advantages and Disadvantages as viewed from the Lower-deck*. By far the greatest disadvantage, in the writer's view, was the way people looked at the 'common sailor'. It was, he said, not possible for a petty officer or a sailor in uniform to walk through any public street in any naval port with his wife or other respectable female on his arm and not be insulted. The writer himself and another petty officer once went ashore in Malta to see a performance at a regimental theatre. With time to kill, they tried to use the N.C.O.'s mess, but were thrown out, and told they could only drink in the canteen, with the private soldiers. What made the incident even more galling was that they could see the schoolmaster and the captain's steward, who were not dressed as bluejackets in 'square rig', calmly playing billiards inside with two sergeants.

The same two, in Portsmouth, bought stall tickets for the Music-Hall in St Mary's Street. They were told that bluejackets were not allowed in that part of the house. What made this more galling was that while they were arguing with the manager a soldier and a half-drunk navvy were allowed to sit where they had just been refused. They were offered seats further back but, understandably, left in a huff.

The final example quoted was the most remarkable of all.

A petty officer, desiring to avail himself of the privilege of travelling double journey for single fare (as granted by several companies during the Christmas holidays) started in uniform, and was speedily reminded of the fact by the uncouth treatment, coarse language, and impertinent familiarity of a fellow passenger, who eventually quitted the carriage, with the offer to send him [the sailor] 'a gal'. Finding matters so unpleasant, the sailor thought it were the better to try plain clothes. The effect was magical: the porters offered to find him a carriage; to place his carpet-bag in safety; enquired kindly after his luggage, as though it had recently been in a delicate state of health; in fact, they were all suavity, and overflowing with the milk of human kindness, where but a short time previously they had been begging a 'chaw of baccy', whilst a gentleman suffering from 'stopped watch' very politely asked, 'Can you tell me the time, sir?'

Although promotions to wardroom rank were very rare, two warrant gunners were promoted to lieutenant at the Queen's Golden Jubilee (and were known henceforward as 'Jubilee Memorials'), but these were the only two, except for Gunner Lyne, who had a most remarkable record of promotion in the Navy. He showed that with luck and ability it was possible to rise in spite of the system. Thomas Spence Lyne joined *Impregnable* as a boy seaman, aged fourteen and a half, in January 1885, although he was two inches under the height limit. He was a 'natural' sailor, and he thoroughly enjoyed the life. He soon became an expert topman; during the 1887 Review, royal eyes were particularly directed to the top of the main royal mast of the 16-gun *Valorous* where, 130 feet above the deck, Boy Seaman Lyne sat on the truck, the lightning conductor tucked between his legs, cheering and waving his cap as the Queen passed by. His first ship was the five-masted *Agincourt* and, although he could see the usefulness of sail drill as training, he soon recognised the futility of sail in an operational warship. 'Why carry it about?' he asked. He was Arthur Moore's coxswain in *Dreadnought* and his boat picked up thirty-two of *Victoria*'s people on that day. As a gunner, he was given command of Torpedo Boat No. 60 during the Boer War and he commanded her in operations off the west coast of Cape Province with such flair and

The old training-ship *Implacable* at Devonport, 1901.

resourcefulness (once, after the propeller shaft broke, he rigged jury masts and got TB 60 home under extemporised sail) that he was promoted lieutenant. He eventually retired as a rear admiral and a knight, the first man from the lower-deck to achieve such rank since Jacky Kingcombe.

Lyne was an exception. Despite the efforts of Henry Capper, who became secretary of the warrant officers' society and, in 1888, founded the monthly *Warrant Officers' Journal* to publicise their case, the normal avenue of promotion stayed blocked. In 1890 the First Lord, Lord George Hamilton, announced that the Navy needed a hundred more lieutenants. The warrant officers issued an 'Earnest Appeal on Behalf of the Rank and File of the Navy'. They were able to show that warrant officers were already doing the duties of lieutenants and sub-lieutenants. They asked to be allowed to take the examination for sub-lieutenant. They had strong support in Parliament, and in the press, from *The Times* to *Punch*, who commented:

If every brave French soldier, with a knapsack on his back,
May find a Marshal's baton at the bottom of that pack,
Why should not a true British Tar, with pluck, and luck, and wit,
Find at last a 'Luff's' commission hidden somewhere in his kit?

Why not indeed, and a motion to that effect was put down in the House. But
the Government opposed it. So, too, did some serving officers, whose families
regarded the Navy as a private preserve. As one otherwise kindly and sensible
lady told Henry Capper, 'I have the greatest sympathy with you personally in
your desire to rise, but you have chosen the wrong service. The Navy belongs
to us, and if you were to win the commissions you ask for it would be at the
expense of our sons and nephews whose birthright it is.' Lieutenancies for
warrant officers were not awarded until 1903, and other promotion schemes,
whereby young petty officers of any branch could reach the wardroom, were
not introduced until 1912.

Sailors were potent advertising symbols throughout
the late nineteenth century, especially for soap and
tobacco.

'A British tar is a soaring soul': *naval songs of the 1870s*

'Can you sing?' asked Sir Joseph.

'I can 'um a little, your honour,' replied Ralph.

'Then 'um—*hum*, this at your leisure. It is a song that I have composed for the use of the Royal Navy. It is designed to encourage independence of thought and action in the lower branches of the service, and to teach the principle that a British sailor is any man's equal . . . excepting mine.'

Thus George Grossmith, as the Right Hon. Sir Joseph Porter KCB, First Lord of the Admiralty, to George Power, Able Seaman Ralph Rackstraw, on the first night of Gilbert and Sullivan's *H.M.S. Pinafore, or The Lass That Loved A Sailor*, 'an entirely original nautical comic opera in two acts', which opened under the direction of Mr R. D'Oyly Carte, at the Opera Comique on 25 May 1878.

Besides poking satirical fun at the then First Lord, William H. Smith, the piece made delicate play of the absurdities in the contemporary view of the sailor. Captain Corcoran, of *Pinafore*, is horrified to discover that his daughter Josephine is in love with a *common sailor*. Josephine herself concedes the enormity of her passion—'I hate myself when I think of the depth to which I have stooped in permitting myself to think tenderly of one so ignobly born.' However, Josephine can marry *upwards* in class, to Sir Joseph, although she confesses that he nauseates her.

W. S. Gilbert made more fun of sailors' education, writing with tongue in cheek a speech for Ralph Rackstraw such as:

I am poor in the essence of happiness, lady—rich only in never-ending unrest. In me there meet a combination of antithetical elements which are at eternal war with one another. Driven hither by objective influences—thither by subjective emotions—wafted one moment into blazing day, by mocking hope—plunged the next into the Cimmerian darkness of tangible despair, I am but a living ganglion of irreconcilable antagonisms. I hope I make myself clear, lady?

Although Sir Joseph is willing to demean his own awesome rank and marry Josephine, as he confirms in one of the opera's great set-pieces, 'Never mind the why and wherefore, Love can level ranks and therefore', he too is horrified to discover Josephine's passion for a common sailor, especially one he has patronised himself (and specifically warned Corcoran against patronising). Sir Joseph's fine sense of social distinction, and his male jealousy of a rival, combine perfectly to dispatch Ralph to the cells.

The play makes it clear that Ralph's lowly rank is a real obstacle, only removed by the bumboat woman Little Buttercup's revelation: in her youth she did some baby-farming, and mixed two babies up. Corcoran is of 'low condition' and Rackstraw is a 'regular patrician'. It is now possible for Rackstraw to have his Josephine. Nobody points out that the dénouement means that Josephine is now a common sailor's *daughter*, and Rackstraw himself must be literally old enough to be her father. Thus the piece mocks both class and age distinctions.

H.M.S. Pinafore, or The Lass That Loved a Sailor: Dick Deadeye
(on the left) and Ralph Rackstraw. Deadeye:

'Forbear, nor carry out the scheme you've planned;
She is a lady – you a foremast hand!
Remember, she's your gallant captain's daughter,
And you the meanest slave that crawls the water.'

The song Sir Joseph composed for the Royal Navy,

> A British tar is a soaring soul
>   As free as a mountain bird,
> His energetic fist should be ready to resist
>   A dictatorial word.
> His nose should pant and his lip should curl,
> His cheeks should flame and his brow should furl,
> His bosom should heave and his heart should glow,
> And his first be every ready for a knock-down blow,

might well have been appreciated on the lower-deck. It has a good tune and a popular sentiment and if there was one thing the bluejacket enjoyed it was a rousing song. There was very little entertainment for the sailors at sea. Singing was something they could all do, with no prior preparation of gear or expense. How much part singing played in the sailors' lives is vividly shown in the autobiography of Sam Noble, perhaps the most romantic view of the lower-deck in the whole of the nineteenth century.

Sam Noble joined in 1875, during a depression in the jute trade in his native Dundee. Several local lads went along to *Unicorn*, the receiving ship, to join the Navy and Sam went with them, for the excitement and not really intending to join. For some reason the recruiting sergeant immediately fixed on Sam, turning the others away. On learning that Sam was past sixteen years old, he whipped out a tape measure. He was an inch under the height but half an inch over the chest measurement and the sergeant said he would make that right. 'He then', said Sam, 'drew such a picture of the sea: how I should have nothing to do but sit and let the wind blow me along; live on plum-pudding and the roast beef of old England; lashings of grog and tobacco; seeing the world the while and meeting and chatting with princesses and all the beautiful ladies of other lands—ah! it was a gay life . . . !'

That did the trick. Sam was fired with enthusiasm to join the Navy and be a Jolly Jack Tar. But there was a hitch. Six months before, in a mill accident, he had had the tips of two of the fingers of his right hand torn off in the wheels of the machine he was tending. The sergeant was most put out, looked at the fingers, tugged his moustache and then had a solution. 'When you are asked to show your hands,' he told Sam, 'you twirl the left in front of him for all you're worth, and keep the right in the background.'

Sam's mother was a much harder problem. She was, frankly, appalled. It took all the sergeant's considerable powers of persuasion to win her over, but in twenty minutes he had done it. The papers were signed, the Queen's shilling was in her hand and the sergeant left the house 'with the strut of a general who has won a battle'.

Sam went down to Portsmouth that September in the train, with another lad from Dundee. They arrived on a cold raw morning, having had nothing to eat since they left home the night before. With every sense sharpened by hunger and anticipation, Sam remembered all his life the jam tarts the kindly ship's

corporal bought for them on the way down to the boat. The harbour, when he
saw it, was the stuff of romance: 'stately ships, with their white and black
hulls; tall tapering masts and snowy sails; the bewildering array of cordage
and rigging; the gilded trucks at the mastheads gleaming like stars; and the
commission pendants streaming away beneath them like long white serpents.'
All the old songs came back to his mind, which his mother used to sing—
'Black-eyed Susan', 'The Red, White and Blue', 'Rule Britannia' and 'Hearts of
Oak'—and Sam was proud to become part of it all.

A popular view of Jolly Jack ashore (from *Army
and Navy Drolleries*, by Captain Seccombe,
c.1870).

This feeling survived the ragging of newcomers in *St Vincent* which had an
added element for Sam because he was a Scotsman. In his first ship, Scotsmen
were very much in the minority and he had to suffer a good deal of chaffing.

Sam says nothing of his education, but he was patently well-read and writes
in vigorous and vivid prose. After fisticuffs with a messmate in *St Vincent* they
both made it up and, the best of friends, sat down to their dinner. Sam's eye
was blacked, his neck was twisted and his tongue was bitten through. But the
day was his and, he wrote, 'I felt like an admiral back from a tough, totally
unexpected engagement "with all his blushing honours thick upon him".' He
had a photographic memory and when he passed out of *St Vincent* very
creditably and went to *Victory* he used to show 'yokels and farmers from up
country' round the ship and earn himself an extra shilling or so by reciting all
forty verses of a poem about Nelson and Trafalgar composed by a tar who had
been at the battle.

Sam was a day-dreamer, and a poet. 'Poetry engrossed me. I read and mused over every scrap I laid hands on; and to turn out a "bit" myself seemed to me the very height of human achievement. When an idea came into my head I would sit for hours pondering over the words "the world forgetting" but not "by the world forgot".'

His day-dreaming got him seven days 10A when the first lieutenant saw him crooning the words of 'All's Well' when he should have been keeping a look-out:

> And while his thoughts doth homeward veer
> Some well-known voice salutes his ear—

and it was the first lieutenant's well-known voice which saluted Sam with a jerk that nearly jumped him off the yard.

As a rule, Sam thought very highly of the officers, especially Mr Routh the second lieutenant, 'a bold, intrepid, daring fellow, ready for anything. Game, romp or race, fun, fight or frolic—there was Routh, always at the front, and always the gentleman.' When he heard Sam's mother was poorly, Mr Routh pressed two sovereigns on him, to send home. The captain, John Borlase Warren, 'was one of the finest men that ever breathed'. He instituted 'a Savings Bank (an uncommon thing in those days) started a (weekly) Penny Readings night, and contributed himself; giving us such pieces as "The Demon Ship" and "The Sailor's Apology for his bow-legs" from Hood who seemed to be his favourite author'. The captain also got the British Consul for the West Coast on board to read Dickens.

Swallow sailed from Queenstown, bound for the South Atlantic, on 20 May 1877. In the first dog-watch, from 4.00 to 6.00 p.m., the hands were looking at the land receding in the mist when an ordinary seaman called Lucks, who was a 'bit of a musician', struck a chord on his concertina and began to play 'Isle of Beauty, fare thee well'. He was joined by Curly Millet, a tall, slim ordinary seaman from Canterbury, and together they sang:

> Shades of evening close not o'er us,
> Leave our lonely barque a while;
> Morn alas! will not restore us
> Yonder dim and distant isle.
> Still my fancy can discover
> Sunny spots where friends may dwell;
> Absence makes the heart grow fonder,
> Isle of Beauty! Fare thee well!

It was a lovely evening. Regular 'ladies weather'. With the passing of the sun the wind had fallen and the sky turned like maple, dappled over with beautiful spots like the eyes of angels looking down upon us, and the sea stretched away, a broad belt of azure slashed here and there with silver. A gentle breeze a little abaft the beam blew us along, and there was nothing to disturb the performers. The only sounds heard were the

lap-lap of the wavelets licking the side of the ship as they flowed by, the
flap of a restless sail, or creak of a mast, and these seemed to form the
ideal orchestra necessary to complete the accompaniment. They went
through the song to the end, and oh, it was sweet—sweet! Not an officer
or man lost a word or note of the music.

Swallow's voyage lasted exactly four years. She returned to Chatham to pay
off on 20 May 1881, having sailed 60,000 miles, in the South Atlantic and along
the coasts of South America and West Africa. Her ship's company had long
enough to get to know each other, and to hear each other sing.

They must have been a typical ship's company of their time, and everybody
had his party piece. Even Billy the first lieutenant 'could sing, but was too
affected; wouldn't let himself go'. One night he did give them 'Nancy Lee' and
the rousing chorus he got should have warmed and reassured him. But it
didn't. The next morning, he heard somebody singing, not the correct 'see,
there she stands an' waves her hands upon the quay' but 'See, there she stands
upon her hands and waves the key!' The man meant no harm but Billy
unluckily heard him, thought the hands were making game of him, and sang
no more.

However, everybody else did. Mr Baynham would rig himself up in a gown
and say with a nasal intonation, like a parson in church, 'Brethren, we will
now sing the one thousand one hundredth and onety onth ps-a-a-lm', which,
to the tune 'Ye Banks and Braes o' bonnie Doon' was 'There were three crows
sat on a tree, And they were black as black could be.' Mr Richmond, the
paymaster, used to sing a song with a tremendous chorus:

> Tis oh! for a gay and gallant bark,
>   A brisk and lively breeze;
> A bully crew, and a captain, too,
>   to carry me over the seas,
> To carry me over the seas, my boys,
>   To my own true love so gay . . .
> For she's taking a trip in a government ship
>   Ten thousand miles away!
>
> Then blow ye winds heigh-ho!
> A-roaming we will go;
> I'll stay no more on England's shore,
> Then let the music play!
> I'm off by the morning train,
> Across the raging main;
> For I'm on the rove to my own true love,
> Ten thousand miles away!

Fred Booth, the bunting-tosser, was a good singer, and 'a proper hero' to
Sam. 'An all-round handy man was Fred. He could make a signal, fire a gun,
write a rhyme, paint a picture, sing a song, clap a sole on a boot, or make or

patch a pair of trousers—anything that came his way. Fred was "Ready, ay Ready". And besides, he was a decent, genial good-hearted buttie.' He used to sing 'When the swallows homeward fly', 'Love, once again', 'Come into the garden, Maud', and 'Odds, Bobs!':

> Our captain stood on the carronade, to his first lieutenant said he,
> Send all my merry men aft here, for they must listen to me.
> I haven't the gift of the gab, my boys, for I was bred to the sea,
> But yonder lies a Frenchman, that wants to fight with me.
>
> Odds, Bobs! hammer and tongs! As long as I've been at sea
> I've fought against many long odds, my boys, but I've gained the
>   victory.

The song was written by Marryat and its descent from a rougher navy shows in the sardonic humour of the captain in the last verse:

> Our captain stood on the quarter-deck, to his first lieutenant said he:
> 'Send all my merry men aft here, for they must listen to me—
> 'You've done your duty manfully, each man stood to his gun,
> 'If you hadn't, you rascals, as sure as fate, I'd have flogged each
>   mother's son.'

The ship's star singer was Marchand, the ship's corporal, who had a great repertoire of English and Irish tunes.

The corporal had a rich baritone voice, and a bland, graciously urbane manner—for singing! On duty—a different man altogether. *Then*, he was the policeman—'Navy' all the time! But get him up in the dog watch for a song and then he took you in his arms. The most popular of his batch in the fo'c'sle was 'Ratcliff Highway', to the tune called 'The Ash Grove'. I think I see him standing on the fore hatch, arms outspread as if embracing everybody, face lifted to the sky, body bent forward, eyes half shut, and a positive sob in his voice:

> I love her dear mother,
> I'm fond of her brother,
> On sister and father I spend half my pay,
> But oh! give me Nancy,
> The girl of my fancy,
> To go for a ramble down Ratcliff Highway!'

The chorus was the last three lines repeated, and didn't we roll them out!

Their pet elocutionist was Leading Stoker Bill Grimshaw, a tall man, 'standing over six feet high and as thin as one of his own cinder-rakes', with a wrinkled left side to his face, where his eye had been injured in a boiler accident. He used to recite 'Jack Oakum', and 'Sunday at Sea', and 'Two Hearty Tars' and 'Jack and the Jew'. He could also recite a piece called 'The Sailor's Apology' but he never did, because the captain had once recited it. 'Whoever sang a song, or did anything else, first, that item belonged to him right through the commission'.

Then there was Harry Watson, the next best singer to Curly Millet, a born musician though he could not read a note of music, who used to sing one much-loved song, a homeward-bounder, called 'We'll soon sight the Isle of Wight, my Boys'. Sam once heard a whole fleet sing it, at Montevideo when *Bacchante*, with the royal princes on board, arrived on her world cruise. Somebody in, say, *Swallow* would start the first four lines, and then every ship joined in the chorus:

> And now we're paid off,
>   And happy are we,
> With a glass in each hand,
>   And a lass on each knee!
>
> We'll soon sight the Isle o'Wight, my boys,
> We'll soon sight the Isle of Wight, my boys,
>   If the breezes don't fail!
>   If the breezes don't fail!

There were twenty men-of-war in harbour that night, including some Americans, and they all joined in. 'One ship started it, another took it up, and away it went right round the lot, covering miles of sea-water, the sound rising, billow upon billow, wave upon wave, like some mighty organ pealing to heaven. That night the very stars seemed to sing!'

Sam had his own party pieces, especially 'Willie brewed a peck o'maut' with the chorus:

> We are nae fou', sae very, very fou',
>   But juist a wee drappie in oor e'e,
> The cock may craw, the day may draw',
>   But aye we'll taste the barley bree!

'You never realise,' Sam wrote, 'how sweet the songs of your own country can be till you hear them far away from home. There they speak to you with a different meaning altogether.' The Admiralty, however, did realise it. They were well aware of the importance of these songs to the sailors' well-being and contentment. In 1841 the Admiralty bought 500 copies of Charles Dibdin's *Songs*, collected by Thomas Dibdin, with sketches by George Cruickshank. The book ran to three editions. In 1867, the Reverend William Guise Tucker, Chaplain of Greenwich Hospital, published a book of 180 songs, 'loyal, patriotic, national, martial, naval, maritime, merry, humorous, entertaining, domestic, and even (in a legitimate sense) amatory'. The Admiralty bought 750 copies and two were issued to each ship.

In 1887, Mr Evans, the chief instructor in singing under the School Board for

One of the most famous of all naval songs, 'A Life on the Ocean Wave'.

London, visited several boys' training ships and recommended a suitable selection of songs. The boys were taught by the tonic sol-fa method, and it was generally thought that singing was good for boys. Chief Bandmaster G. W. Bishop, of HMS *Ganges*, edited the *Royal Naval Song Book*, a collection of fifty national melodies which appeared in 1890. A naval song book of some kind, with words and music, has been in print ever since.

Sam Noble's naval career was ended by an accident. He does not reveal what it was, possibly a fall from aloft: he wrote his memoirs in 1925 from a wheelchair. But he never forgot those songs of nearly half a century before.

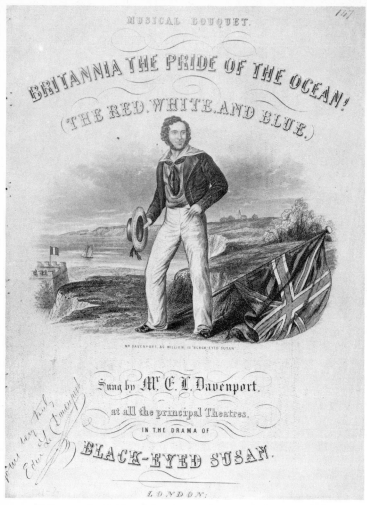

'Brittania the Pride of the Oceans!', a patriotic song of the
1850s, but popular long after the end of the decade.

Lord! what choruses some of these old sea songs have. They mount and
soar in swelling billows of melody, rolling waves of glorious sound that
fill the ship fore and aft, flooding it in harmony; reverberating among
the cordage, echoing and re-echoing from the sails aloft till the soul of
man is absolutely filled with rapture. Their words carry you to the ends
of the earth, and back from there to the scenes of your boyhood, and
home and friends, who are waiting with yearning hearts to grip you by
the hand, just as you yourself are yearning to grip theirs.

And now these dear old anthems are never heard at all, they tell me.
Commissions are so short. Nobody pulls on anything; you just touch a
button and steam does all the work.

The Slave Chase: *the Navy against the African slave trade 1820–80*

Slaves cannot breathe in England; if their lungs
Receive our air, that moment they are free;
They touch our country, and their shackles fall.

So wrote William Cowper in 'The Task' in 1784. But, with an enthusiasm which Lecky called 'among the three or four perfectly virtuous pages in the history of nations', Great Britain pursued the freedom of slaves at sea as well as on land. The carriage of slaves in British vessels was abolished in 1807. In 1811, slave trading was made a felony, punishable by fourteen years' imprisonment. In 1824, slaving was declared piracy punishable by death (a penalty changed to transportation for life in 1837). In 1833 the great Act of Emancipation was passed. From 1 August 1834 all slave children under six years were free at once. Adult slaves served some years longer before they too were free.

Britain not only freed her own slaves but, largely through the agency of the Navy, waged a campaign lasting most of the nineteenth century to free all slaves. Liberia, the state established by freed slaves in 1822, would soon have been overrun by hostile neighbouring native tribes but for the protection of Captain Ashmun RN and the African squadron. By 1815 most civilised countries had declared slavery illegal and the trade should have been extinct. In practice it flourished, and thirty years after slavery was 'abolished' nearly twice as many slaves were being exported from West Africa as before. The Scandinavian countries co-operated with Britain, but for political and legal reasons it was impossible for British ships to stop and search ships of the United States, Spain, Portugal and France. As countries signed Right of Search treaties, so slaving captains sailed under other flags and carried false sets of papers.

The Navy maintained patrolling ships off both coasts of Africa, the Cape of Good Hope, the coasts of Brazil, and the islands of the Caribbean, especially Cuba. The Navy's main instrument against slavers in the first half of the nineteenth century was the West African squadron, which Dr Alexander Bryson, Medical Director General of the Admiralty, called in 1847 'the most disagreeable, arduous, and unhealthy service that falls to the lot of British officers and seamen without, it is to be feared, much prospect of its coming to a speedy termination'. The main slaving territory stretched for some 3,000 miles down the west coast of Africa, from Gambia down to the Congo. Slavers operated from every river mouth and creek. The few white European settlers lived in the scattering of forts and factories along the Gulf of Guinea. Because of the climate, the country, and the incidence of disease, they very rarely penetrated the interior. There were almost no harbours and very few anchorages which could shelter a fair-sized warship. The principal slaving ports were Lagos and Whydah, in the Bight of Benin, where the rivers of the coast, the Bonny, the Calabar, the Cameroons and the Oil River branches of the Niger had been slaving posts since time immemorial.

The task of intercepting slavers was very difficult. The slavers were fast sailors and very manoeuvrable. The slaving captain knew the coast and used darkness and local weather conditions skilfully; even when they had been overhauled, captains produced false papers and documents to prove that all the blacks on board were indentured household servants. In some circumstances, chains and shackles were thrown overboard beforehand; sometimes even the slaves themselves were jettisoned. When a slaver had been captured, the prize crew put on board had to take the greatest care they were not themselves surprised and overtaken. Man-of-war captains were often misled by officials ashore who themselves profited from the slave trade, passing false information to the ship's captain, and accurate intelligence of the Navy's movements to the slavers. Ashore, the Navy had to patrol river estuaries in small boats, destroy the depots or barracoons where the slaves were kept after their journey down from the interior and before they were embarked on board, and, not least important, continue to supervise native chiefs who had agreed to give up slaving.

The officers and men of the Navy were themselves accused of being hypocrites and taunted with greed, because they were given prize money for slaves captured. The rules for arresting slavers were often so complicated that a captain might easily make an error. But any captain who did so found that he had to defend himself at law, at his own expense. Often proceedings were bureaucratically delayed until the captain concerned had left the station, and the case then lapsed for lack of evidence.

Once rescued, the slaves were taken to Freetown (hence the name) where there was an Admiralty Court empowered to condemn prizes, and where there were facilities for watering ships and for obtaining fresh food. However, Freetown had one of the worst climates for Europeans on the whole coast. It was, as somebody said, 'a pestiferous charnel house, a detestable spot, with not one good quality to recommend it'. The sailors had a somewhat macabre joke about Freetown, that the standing orders permanently detailed one party 'employed digging graves as usual', and another 'making coffins until further orders'.

Freetown was one of the few places where ships gave leave. After months on board sailors flocked ashore to drink the fiery native spirits, and to lie about in the gutters to be attacked by mosquitoes until the next morning. The sickness rate on the Station was appalling. The old rhyme,

> Beware and take care of the Bight of Benin
> There's one comes out for forty goes in

was only a slight exaggeration. Malaria, yellow fever, blackwater fever were all endemic on the coast. Whole ship's companies were reduced to skeleton crews by sickness, and some ships were actually forced to leave the station. In

Eden, between May and December 1829, 110 out of 160 men on board died. In *Sybille*, 101 men died in two years, most of them of yellow fever, and by February 1830, when the ship was cruising off Lagos, about 180 miles from land, there had been so many deaths on board and the ship's company's morale had been so depressed that, according to Mr McKechnie, the assistant surgeon, 'at meal hours, when smoking was allowed, the men used to congregate together with despair depicted in their faces to learn from one another who had gone to the doctor, or who was likely to die during the night.' The men had actually caught yellow fever from *Eden* whom they had met at Fernando Po, but the infectious nature of the disease was still unknown (the mosquito's function as a vector in malaria was not discovered until 1880) and there were various theories about 'solar heat, damp mists and miasmas' to account for the infection.

To restore morale on board and to convince the *Sybille*'s officers and men that the disease was not contagious, the surgeon, Dr McKinnel, performed an act of peculiar gallantry, braver in its way than any action for the Victoria Cross. He told McKechnie to

collect some black vomit from the first patient who was attacked by that fatal symptom; accordingly I collected about a pint of it from a man named Riley about two hours before he died. Shortly after, the doctor came to the starboard side of the halfdeck, when I told him what I had done. He then went down to the gunroom, and about half past twelve o'clock (the men being then at dinner) returned with a wineglass. Mr Green, the officer of the watch, was then going below, when he called him over, and filling a glassful of the black vomit, asked him if he would like to have some of it; being answered in the negative, he then said, 'Very well, here is your health, Green,' and drank it off.

Dr McKinnel then went up to the quarter-deck and walked about for two hours, to prove to everybody that he had not done or taken anything to try to counteract the effects of the black vomit. 'It is almost unnecessary to add,' said McKechnie, 'that it did not impair his appetite for dinner, nor did he suffer any inconvenience from it afterwards.'

The disease went in epidemics, sometimes with an interval of years between them. In *Eclair* in 1845 so many men died of yellow fever that she was sent home. Five men actually died in Portsmouth harbour, although they were not allowed ashore because the ship was refused permission to land her men. The case of *Eclair* and the nature of the disease on board her caused a major row in medical and governmental circles.

Out in West Africa there were ways of reducing infection, but the best prophylactic was a visit to Ascension Island or St Helena, where the cooler climate, fresh meat, fruit, fish, turtles, eggs and fresh water worked wonders for the ship's company's health.

The French Revolution of 1830 brought to the throne Louis Philippe, who favoured abolition and signed rights of search conventions. Many slavers turned from the French to the Spanish or Portuguese flags. There was still a demand for slaves in the southern States of America, in Cuba and in Brazil. In theory, the United States was against slavery and sent a few cruisers on anti-slaving duties, but largely through pressure from the southern states, the Unites States did little in practice to discourage slaving until the election of Abraham Lincoln. In the 1840s more rights of search treaties were negotiated, especially with Portugal, and the size of the West African squadron was increased, from about seven cruisers and 700 men in the 1820s to about thirty cruisers and 3,000 men in the 1840s. The increase led to an outcry at home against the expense of keeping so many ships and men on the station, and the efficiency of the squadron was also questioned and debated frequently.

A boat's crew from a man-of-war capturing a slaver off Fish Bay, on the west coast of Africa, 1840.

By 1848 the Navy had twenty-four cruisers off West Africa, nine off the Cape, twelve off Brazil and another ten in the West Indies or off North America. One of those who served in the West African squadron in the 1840s was William Petty Ashcroft, then a signalman in *Actaeon* (24). They arrived at Freetown on 1 June 1845 and embarked native Kroomen 'to do the dirty work and work in the sun such as watering ship'. They all had, as Keppel in *Childers* in 1837 noted, 'incomprehensible names', so they were given 'pusser's names': Doctor Inman, Sea-breeze, No Grog, Prince of Wales in *Childers*, Tom Bottle Beer, Jack Frypan and the captain's 'fancy black coxswain' Jack Peasoup in *Actaeon*. (Kroomen with pusser's names such as Sea-breeze and Jack Nasty Face served in *Express* with Henry Fleet in 1888; they had their own mess on the upper-deck and were not allowed on the main-deck. The Head Krooman maintained discipline with a punishment known as 'Fum Fum' inflicted with a rope's end.)

Actaeon chased several slavers, sending the empty prizes to St Helena for condemnation and the full ones to Freetown. One or two gave themselves up, knowing that the 'fregatta' could catch them. They missed another promising slaver at night by bad seamanship. The helm was put up too sharply at the last moment and *Actaeon* passed under the quarry's stern instead of closing her gently from windward and taking her wind. The captain had the officer of the watch relieved of duty and exchanged him to the next man-of-war they met.

The very next day they sighted a brigantine who innocently thought *Actaeon* was a whaler, due to her unusual sail arrangement at the time. She proved to have 500 slaves on board. Another time, three steamers, *Terrible*, *Penelope* and *Styx*, were sighted from the masthead while *Actaeon*'s cutter was away taking charge of a prize. The rule was that if a ship came in sight while another was in action she was entitled to a share. *Actaeon*'s captain ordered down the royal and topgallant yards, topsails and topgallant masts. The three steamers thus saw nothing, and missed *Actaeon* and their prize money.

The struggle to suppress slavery fluctuated, depending upon political, legal and technological changes. There were particularly energetic officers, such as Captain Denman of *Wanderer* who in 1840 destroyed a large slave barracoon on the Gallinas river and negotiated treaties were several local chiefs to burn down others in the area. The immediate interests of the slaves actually inside the barracoons were not best served by having them burned down. They were deprived of rest and shelter at a time when they were exhausted by their long march, chained, shackled and beaten, down to the coast from the interior. But the burning of barracoons, the harassment of slavers ashore and the intense blockade mounted at sea succeeded for a time in bringing the trade with Cuba almost to a halt. (The Gallinas river operations also took their toll of *Wanderer*'s ship's company: the conditions, when the men waded waist-deep in muddy brackish water and often slept in wet clothes on damp, marshy ground, were ripe for malaria and sixteen men were incapacitated by the disease.)

The greatest technological advance for the anti-slaving ships was the coming of steam. At last the elusive slavers could be run down and captured, whether or not the wind failed at the critical time. The large sailing frigate *Penelope* (16), which had had engines and paddlewheels fitted in 1842, arrived on the station in 1845. The slavers themselves soon used steamships and one of *Penelope*'s most notable *coups* was the pursuit and capture of the large slave steamer *Cacique*, with 1,500 slaves on board, in March 1846. In March 1848 Captain Hotham, then commanding *Penelope*, reported that of fifty-nine

A moonlight chase of the brigantine slaver *Windward* by HM steam-sloop *Alecto*, 1858.

slavers captured in the previous year, twenty-three were taken by steamers.

In 1850 there were high hopes that slavery might be put down entirely in a few years. Brazil passed laws prohibiting slavery, and a Brazilian squadron operated off the African coast. In December 1851 the British squadron arrived off Lagos, under Commodore Jones, flying his broad pennant in *Penelope*. On 26 December a force embarked in the paddle-steamer *Bloodhound*, with Teazle and the boats of the squadron, accompanied by an iron, rocket fitted ship, *Victor*, owned by Mr Beecroft, the British Consul, assaulted and stormed the town. The slave barracks were destroyed and this important slaving port was turned over to legitimate commerce.

As the decade went on, the Royal Navy was not able to give so much attention to its anti-slaving duties, with other preoccupations in Burma, the Crimea, India, China, followed by Franco-Italian tensions and fears of a French invasion. The French, now ruled by Napoleon III, were hostile to the British, the Americans only lukewarm. But once President Lincoln had been inaugurated in 1861, the prospects changed completely. Lincoln was whole-heartedly against the slave trade. In 1862 he hanged a convicted American slave trader, *pour encourager les autres*. Slavers could no longer use the American flag. In 1865, the slave trade had diminished to the point where no ships at all were brought into Freetown for adjudication. By 1866, the trade was almost extinct.

But not quite. In 1866, Phipps Hornby was out there in *Bristol*, with an epidemic of yellow fever on board, of which twenty-two men died. In 1867 he was writing to Sir Alexander Milne to say that if the Admiralty did not intend to maintain the minimum number of cruisers, which he put at fourteen, then the blockade ought to be relaxed. In two sentences he summed up the task of the Navy: 'The work is very hard; there is no excitement, not even hope, nothing but a dogged pressing on to the duty because it is ordered. Very fine to contemplate, doubtless; but it is destroying promising young men, officers principally, but also seamen largely.'

However, there was still some chance of excitement. *Swallow* once chased a slaver off the west coast, when Sam Noble was there to see. She was a Portuguese brig called *Pensamento*, 'a long sinister-looking craft'. *Swallow* got steam up, took in sail, altered the rig by housing topmasts and shortening the jibboom, and hoisting an American flag. *Pensamento*'s deck was 'full of black, woolly heads, which bobbed over the rail from every part of her'.

They waited for two days and then, at sunset on the third day, the look-out man reported that the brig was putting to sea under full sail. The chase began.

A fine spanking breeze from the land sent us along in grand style. At first we couldn't see the brig, but when the moon gained her splendour and turned the sea into a glory of molten silver, *then* we saw her—although not so much her in reality as the black velvety shadow she threw on the glittering surface over which she went like an ominous bird. My word, couldn't she sail! Bending over so that sometimes we could have seen her bilge-boards had we been nearer, she simply flew over the water.

Certainly, *Swallow* was no match for her in that wind. 'She easily went one and a half knots to our one. She bounded over the silver wavelets like a thing of life, clothing herself in glittering sparks from her forefoot, like the girls in the African village with their fireflies, leaving a wake behind her like the steam of a railway train; and seeming to laugh at our efforts to catch up with her.'

Though *Swallow* had full steam up, so that the screw added to the sails, and though two warning shots were fired from the 7-inch gun, the brig's captain merely twiddled his fingers contemptuously ('twisting himself side-on to let us see him do it') and the brig gradually edged away. Her captain set stunsails which

> put more life into the brig than ever, and she began to leave us hand over fist—melt away, in fact, before our eyes—till by and by all we could make out was a glittering pin-point on the horizon.
>
> But then the wind changed, and there was a lull. The way we lifted the brig now showed that she had hardly any wind at all. We overhauled her as an express does a goods train. Soon she began to show up; then to take shape; then we could distinguish her individual sails; then out popped her black hull, and she lay broad to view just as we had seen her at first.
>
> Our fellows went dancing mad about the t'gallant fo'c'sle, shaking hands and telling each other about the prize money that would line our handkerchiefs by and by, crying, 'Good little girlie', 'Pretty little swallow-tail!', 'Catch her pussy; there's the mouse ahead, dear!' and Buntin, whose watch below it was, began to carol: 'When the swallows homeward fly.' Oh, we were the happy crowd!

The cutter was lowered and on its way, when the wind sprang up again, and the brig was off. 'A sharp shower came on, just heavy enough to soak the sails and give them a better draw—as if to help her, you would have thought!—and away she went like a racehorse. It was like snatching a bone from a dog! If you had heard the remarks on the *Swallow*, you would have thought sailors a rum lot—which they are, really.'

But it was only an expiring puff of wind, and it soon dropped. 'In half an hour we were lying within a couple of cable-lengths of her, on a sea like a lady's mirror, just dimmed occasionally by the clouds crossing the moon, as her breathing does when she brings the glass too close.'

Once more the boat was lowered, and the reality of the brig was much less idyllic than the sight of her. 'We smelt the brig as we came nearer. By the time the bowman got hooked on alongside we felt almost suffocated. What a stench! One of the fellows remarked: "It'll take a lot of prize money beer to wash this down, hearties!" I never came across a smell like yon in all *my* life.'

But in the event they got no prize money beer.

It seemed that although there were over 700 negroes—men, women and children—on board that brig, we couldn't touch her skipper because he

had papers certifying every one of them to be labourers going to South
America to be employed in the rice and cotton fields. Not a manacle nor
an iron was aboard of her—I believe they got rid of these things during
the last lap of the chase. She was a slaver all right, only the brutes that
commanded her were too cute to let themselves be caught.

Anyway, they got clear. It was a terrible disappointment to us; and it
took the splicing of the mainbrace and a sing-song under the glorious
moon to cheer the way back to port, and make up for it.

On the east coast of Africa the slave trade thrived and lasted well into the
twentieth century, while on the west coast it had more or less ended as an
organised business by 1870. There were two main slaving routes in the east,
one from the northern part of Central Africa through Zanzibar to Arabia and
southern Asia, and the other from the southern regions of Central Africa across
to Madagascar. The trade was seasonal, depending entirely upon changes in
the prevailing winds and currents of the Indian Ocean. The slaving dhows
made two voyages a year, one on each monsoon, coming southwards with the
stream of legitimate traffic to Zanzibar on the north-east monsoon which lasted
from November to April. Having embarked slaves, they sailed northwards
again on the south-west monsoon, between April and September. The south-
west monsoon tended to be a blusterer, and was especially turbulent during its
middle period. The worst weather of the year in the Arabian Sea occurred just
off Socotra and the African coast from the end of June to the end of August, so
the 'up' trade of slave-carrying dhows generally sailed as soon after the
beginning, or as near the end, of the monsoon as they could.

Galla slaves on board HMS *Daphne*, 1874.

Knowledge of these climatic limitations was very useful to the naval squadron, but it was about their only advantage. Slavery was legal in all Muhammedan countries and HM ships could only be concerned with slaving when it took place on the high seas. Various treaties and right of search agreements were negotiated as time went on with local potentates such as the Sultan of Oman, The Sultan of Zanzibar, and the governments of Persia and Turkey, but in practice the captain of a British man-of-war was very much his own judge, jury and executioner. The only port to which he could take prizes and where he could release slaves was Bombay, and to go there meant that his ship was off her station for a long time.

The largest dhows were about 300 tons, but most of them were very much smaller, and none of them left the sight of land if they could avoid it. With their very shallow draught, high poop and low freeboard forward, they looked like delicate ladies' slippers skimming over the water. Their single large white cotton lateen sails were very conspicuous, but the dhows were very fast sailers, often faster than the naval brigs pursuing them. Most had only a handful of slaves on board, and though boat's crews were briefed to look for signs of slaving, such as spare planks for laying down as a slave deck, or more water or rice than the number of people on board justified, or actual shackles, bolts and handcuffs, it was often difficult to establish whether any extra negroes on board were slaves on their way to be sold. A chase and an interception by a man-of-war's boat sometimes doomed the slaves on board the dhow. The slaving captains carried the minimum food and water on board for their voyage; any lengthy delay meant that the slaves starved, or died of thirst.

The essence of east coast slaver-catching was boatwork. A ship's boats were kept at five minutes' notice, ready equipped with water casks, salt pork, biscuits and a small cask of rum with a lock on it. The bluejacket crews had to wear uniform only while they were in sight of the ship. Once clear, they opened their bundles, to blossom out into 'pirate rigs' of ragged serge jumpers, worn serge or blanket trousers, and a red or blue night cap. The more lawless and piratical they looked, the better the sailors liked it.

With a midshipman or a junior lieutenant in command, a boat was often away from the ship for two or three weeks. They normally anchored every night, the men off watch sleeping along the thwarts; there was no bedding on board, but each man took a blanket from his small painted clothesbag or bundle and used his cork lifejacket as a pillow. The stores and oars were levelled up to make room for the sleepers. The midshipman, the interpreter and the coxswain, normally a leading seaman, slept in the stern-sheets. Under the stern grating was the 'canteen store' of condensed milk, sardines, jam and other small luxuries. There, too, was the rum barricoe in the coxswain's charge, and a ditty box containing the boat's signal book, rockets, slave trade instructions, boarding forms, log book, and a bag of local pice (currency) for purchases. The galley was a small coal-burning cooking stove, standing on copper-covered boards just forward of the mast and secured by wire stays. There was a large compartment in its top, where tea, cocoa or pea soup could be brewed. The lid had an inner compartment with a pot let into it, for boiling porridge or cooking meat. The funnel was lowered when under sail and was then a hazard to all on board; almost everybody on board was scalded or burned by it, in time. To counterbalance the stove's weight forward, the coal, water, harness cask and ammunition were stowed well aft. The rifles were kept in painted canvas sheaths under the seats.

There was normally a crew of nine. The midshipman was armed with a service revolver and a sharpened cutlass instead of his dirk; the crew all had cutlasses. Everybody kept one-hour watches, the cook always having the dawn watch. The midshipman's watch was normally the only timepiece on board and if this were lost, they called their reliefs by marking an eight-hour candle in hours and keeping it burning in a bucket of water.

The ship's biscuit was made at Bombay especially for the Navy, and it was unusually good: the 'intermediate' round white-flour type packed in tin-lined boxes. Empty, the boxes were then used again for stowing peas, oatmeal, cocoa, tea, sugar, in compartments with canvas lids. Or they were used as coal bunkers, magazines, stores for crockery, candles, soap and firewood.

Boatwork was marvellous experience for young officers and sailors, but it had its dangers. Boarding a dhow had always to be done from the weather side: a slaver's crew once lowered their huge sail on top of a steam-boat from *London* and stabbed the bluejackets through the sail. The only man uninjured was the stoker below, who managed to reverse the engines and get the boat clear. Boarding boats sometimes capsized, or were sunk by the slavers hurling heavy stones through their bottom boards. Most slavers offered no resistance but if they were near their destination or if the boarding party looked weak in numbers, the slavers sometimes replied with musket fire, or tried to repel boarders were sabres. Occasionally, a dhow would have an ancient brass gun, captured from some long-forgotten prize, lashed to the gunwale and filled with black powder and bits of old iron, as a sort of makeshift grape shot. Fortunately, these weapons generally misfired.

Sometimes, slavers were caught by accident or because of their own guilty consciences. One evening in 1888, when *Garnet* was anchored off the north-west coast of Zanzibar, the forecastle sentry fired off a blank cartridge at 9.00 p.m. to mark sunset. A dhow just rounding the point hurriedly lowered her sail, obviously thinking she was sailing into a trap. A boat was sent away to board her and she was found to have slaves. In June that year, the same ship was off Zanzibar carrying out prize firing at a target, and a cutter was sent to tow away a dhow which was fouling the range, as it was a flat calm. She was found to have forty-seven slaves on board.

The method the Navy used to patrol the coastline was well described by Thomas Holman who served on the station himself.

Each ship is assigned a few hundred miles of coastline up and down which she constantly cruises, dropping boats at all the principal sheltering places or anchorages. These boats establish depots at these places, and from them patrol a certain amount of coast on either side,

HMS *London*, the headquarters of the British squadron on the
east coast of Africa in the 1880s.

usually meeting the boats stationed at the depot above and below them.
In this way 700 or 800 miles of coastline can be fairly well looked after;
the boats forming a continuous line of inshore patrols, while the ships
steam leisurely to and fro in the offing.

The boats normally operated in pairs so that should a slaver sink or repel one
boat there was always another nearby. But if the dhows were coming in twos
and threes, this plan would break down and the dhows would escape. 'This,'
wrote Thomas Holman, 'the British sailor would not allow.' The boats then
split up, to chase dhows as necessary.

Once recovered, the slaves hardly appeared worth all the trouble that had
been taken over them. Their captors had been indifferent rather than cruel,
treating the slaves as cattle, but the slaves were generally in poor physical
condition, mentally very backward, and always illiterate. Like their brethren
on the west coast they were prone to disease and a man-of-war captain had to
watch his charges carefully for signs of cholera, smallpox or dysentery. The
slaves showed no interest whatsoever in their new surroundings when they
came on board. They were dirty but docile, defecating on the deck because
they had never been acquainted with any sort of hygiene. They were washed
as soon as they came on board by 'seedies' (natives) in the ship's company
behind specially erected canvas screens. Their hair was closely cropped. They
were given white or coloured calico which they wore as sarongs. They were
fed boiled rice and ship's biscuit, laced with treacle or condensed milk.

Sometimes they were reluctant to eat, having been told by the dhow's crew that 'the yellow funnel of the big white ship was for the smoke of the fire of the huge kettle in which the white man would boil and then eat you all'.

The bluejackets always took the greatest care of the freed slaves. Captain Philip Colomb, commanding *Dryad* in 1872, wrote that he

> did not expect to see a prettier sight than I was witness of for several days in succession when watching the conduct of the bluejacket towards the negroes. Some of them who had been captured on shore after landing were sadly cut about the feet—especially the women and children—from running over the rocks. It was an established habit of the men—notably of the older petty officers—to carry them about in their arms, when it was necessary to move them from one part of the ship to another, so as to save them from putting their wounded feet to the deck. Then the doctoring which went on, the care with which cooling poultices were applied, and the careful bandaging, would have done credit to a village hospital; and that it was a spontaneous piece of charity made it all the more engaging to observe. I should say the poor creatures never had before, and certainly will never have again, such gentle treatment as they received at the hands of our English seamen.

Later in the century, slaves were released at Zanzibar and received schooling at the mission stations there and on the mainland. They often took the names of their delivering ships, so that there were dozens of Mr and Mrs and Miss Boadiceas, Garnets, Turquoises, Reindeers, Mariners, Kingfishers, Penguins, Griffons, Algerines, Conquests, Brisks, Cossacks, Satellites, Pigeons, Redbreasts, Londons and Bacchantes.

The naval ships had many seedies in their ship's companies. One of them, Seedie Tindal (bosun's mate) Farabani was serving in *Wild Swan* off Mozambique in August 1880 when a recovered slave boy called Farejallah fell into the water and was attacked by a monster shark. The boy's leg was bitten off at the knee, and three other sharks appeared, attracted by the blood. Farabani dived into the water and rescued the boy, although the unfortunate lad had his other leg bitten off before he could be brought ashore and later that afternoon died of his injuries. Farabani was awarded the Albert Medal First Class for lifesaving at sea (the medal was instituted by Royal Warrants of 1866 and 1867, and was won by several serving members of the Navy, notably Quartermaster William Bridges for gallantry as a member of a shellroom crew after a gun explosion which killed eight men in *Thunderer* in 1879).

Throughout the reports and reminiscences of the battle against slavery on the east and west coasts of Africa, the moral certainty of the officers and sailors taking part is evident. Slaving was not only a legal but a moral crime, a sin against humanity. The deaths, the ruined constitutions, the hardships, the ill-informed criticisms, the boredom were all worth enduring in the long run. The ordinary bluejacket was quite certain in his own mind that what he was doing was absolutely right. The slavers were utterly wrong, offenders against God as well as man.

HMS *London*'s pinnace capturing an Arab slaving dhow off
Zanzibar, 1880.

The case for suppressing the trade was well summed up by John Barton, a
seaman gunner, at that memorable banquet in Liverpool in 1863, a city whose
fortunes had to a great extent been founded on slaving. As an encore, Barton
sang the ballad 'The Slave Ship':

> The first grey dawn of the morning was beaming,
>   The bright rays shone forth the glad spirits of light,
> The rising sun o'er the ocean was streaming,
>   That dispelled with its rays the dark shadows of night.
> The air, oh how pure, and the morning how mild,
>   And the waters lay hushed like a sleeping child.
>
> Then up—up with the anchor let us away,
>   Spread the sails 'tis a favouring wind;
> And long ere the break of the morning we'll leave
>   The coast of old Afric behind.
>
> Gloomily stood the captain
>   With his arms upon his breast,
> His cold brow firmly knitted,
>   And his iron lips compressed.
> Are all well whipped below there?
>   Ay! ay! the seaman said,
> Heave up the worthless lubbers,
>   The dying and the dead.

Help! oh help! thou God of Christians,
  Save a mother from despair.
Cruel white men stole my children,
  Oh God of Christians hear my prayer;
I am young and strong and hardy,
  He's a weak and feeble boy;
Take me, whip me, chain me, starve me,
  Oh God in mercy save my boy.

They've killed my child, they've killed my child,
  The mother shrieked now all is o'er,
Down the savage Captain struck her,
  Lifeless on the vessel's floor.

Old England—old England, the land of the free,
Whose home is the waters, whose flag sweeps the sea;
Still stretch out thy hand o'er the ocean's broad wave,
Protecting the helpless unfortunate slave.
And nations that call themselves free shall repent,
Of the thousands in pain to eternity sent;
Each who forwards the cause on the verge of the grave,
Shall gain strength from the prayer of the poor negro slave.

Sunday morning at sea:
the Navy of the 1880s

As late as the 1880s, the reputation of the 'old Navy' was still dying hardly. In 1882, Admiral Kennedy was appointed to command *Lord Warden*, the coastguard ship at Queensferry, in the Firth of Forth. His duty was to inspect the coastguard stations and drill-ships of the naval reserve on the coast of Scotland from Berwick-on-Tweed round the north coast to Ullapool, and including the Orkneys and Shetlands. Besides the coastguardsmen, he had about 5,000 naval reserve men under his command, mostly fishermen from the Orkneys and Shetlands, Aberdeen, Wick and Inverness, some whalers from Dundee and Peterhead, and some ocean-going seamen from merchant ships. Although the guns they drilled with were exactly the same as those used at Trafalgar, the men were so zealous and such good seamen that, at Kennedy's suggestion, *Lord Warden* paid a recruiting visit to the Shetlands, where there were some 1,800 reservists.

No sooner had *Lord Warden* anchored in Lerwick than every able-bodied young man fled to the hills, for fear of the press gang. Kennedy hired the town hall to hold a meeting and point out the advantages of joining the Navy. Not a single recruit did he get. It was later explained to him by the fishermen that it was more to their advantage to keep their boys to help with the fishing than to hire others in their place. Much disgusted, Kennedy returned to the Firth of Forth and never repeated the experiment.

In some ways, the Navy had not changed at all, just as human nature had not changed. Sympathy, commonsense and a sense of humour always scored with sailors. Admiral Bacon served as a watch-keeping lieutenant in *Cruiser*, the last ship under sail in the Navy, in the Mediterranean. *Cruiser* was employed as a training ship for midshipmen and young seamen, and there were some comedians on board. 'Unusual' punishments were rightly forbidden; the Navy knew what devilish ingenuity men could use against each other in the tedium, close proximity, and possibly the heat, of a long commission on a remote station. But it was still permissible to make the punishment fit the crime. One man in *Cruiser* was found drunk on board and, to raise a laugh on the lower-deck and to go as near to impertinence as he dared, he claimed that somebody had a 'down' on him and had put gin in the water tank on the main-deck. The commander therefore put the man on sentry duty over the tank, fully accoutred with cutlass, webbing and bayonet belt; he had to have his meals on the spot and sleep on the deck nearby, for a fortnight. Another man, an excellent petty officer, was a Plymouth Brother, and insisted on holding bible classes for the ship's company. The first lieutenant objected to sectarian doctrine being preached to young seamen, and told the man to desist. But he went on, and so was taken before the captain as a defaulter, where he explained how the Bible ordered him to preach the Gospel. The man was in

danger of having his career broken for insubordination, continuing to insist
that he must obey his Father's orders. The situation was saved by Captain
Sacheverell Darwin's common sense. 'Look here, my young man,' he said, 'I'm
captain of this ship and you're captain of the quarter-deck of the ship. When I
give you an order you have got to obey it; when we are both cold meat in a
box, then the other man steps in. Do you see?' He did see, and never held
another prayer meeting.

Ridicule was sometimes more effective than anything else. One man in
Portsmouth Barracks could not, or would not, learn to swim. Everybody could
see he was not really trying. The commander then made him wear a lifejacket
at all times, in case he fell into the puddles on the parade ground and drowned.
The man passed his swimming test within a month. Bacon himself, as a
commander of a ship in the Mediterranean, thought that want of exercise and
lethargy of the liver were responsible for at least three-quarters of the cases of
slackness and laziness brought before him. So he instituted an extra drill class
for persistent offenders. It was explained to them that this was not a
punishment, they merely had to keep on the move for an hour without
stopping, with physical drill, followed by a run over the masthead, then
exercises with dumb-bells, then three or four times round the deck, then out
over the lower boom, down into a boat and back again, and so on. Punishments
on board dropped to half.

It was Kennedy's flag captain in the East Indies, Captain Giffard, who was
told by an old lady at one of Kennedy's wife's 'At Homes' in Calcutta that 'she
so loved to see the dear sailors lying drunk about the streets, it reminded her of
home!' Kennedy protested that his ship's companies were very well-behaved,
but the old lady had a point. A midshipman of a boat always had to watch his
crew like a hawk to see they did not get hold of spirits while they were inshore.
A drunken crew reflected on the midshipman, and he was likely to be
punished himself with a spell of 'watch and watch'.

Many educated sailors liked to keep diaries and logs, and to write down
poems or songs which caught their fancy. Richard Cotten was a seaman in
Comus on the China and Pacific Station from 1879 to 1884. At Callao in 1883 he
bought himself a smart notebook with stiff board covers and filled it with
poems, verses and songs, with titles such as 'The Sailor's Christmas Day', with
the chorus:

> Then messmates be merry
> We'll dance and we'll sing
> And scrape the old fiddle
> Till we search every string
> Tho' his ship bears him fast
> To his home that's afar
> Christmas tide cheers the heart
> Of a brave British tar.

One or two are more directly related to life in a man-of-war, such as
'Saturday Morning at Sea':

> Eight Bells being struck poor Jack awoke
> Before the dawn of day had broke,
> The Boatswain's Mate the stillness breaks
> Rousing the Watch to Holystone the decks.
> Then around the Capstan musters he
> Picks up a stone and bends the knee.
> He bends the knee but not in prayer.

Another justifiably complains about the social status of the sailor, who was still thought of, and referred to, as a 'common sailor'. With their lack of punctuation (as written in Cotten's book) and somewhat fractured scansion, the lines could have been composed by Cotten himself,

> I am a man before the mast
> I plough the trackless sea
> And on this simple subject
> Will you please enlighten me
> Common Sailors are we called
> Pray tell the reason why
> This sneering objective unto us
> Which you so often reply
> When speaking of a man ashore
> I never hear you say
> He is a common this or that
> Be his calling what it may
> Be he a travelling tinker
> A scavenger or sweep
> Then why term common unto those
> Who travel on the deep

A third poem may also be Cotten's own work. It concerns a long-standing grievance of the lower-deck, that six days should they labour and the seventh have no rest, having to work even harder to prepare the mess-decks for inspection and themselves for divisions. As a midshipman in the steam-frigate *Forte* on the East African station in 1868, Percy Scott learned how the men hated Sunday. It was

> hurry out, it is Sunday; hurry over dressing, it is Sunday; get out of this, it is Sunday. At 9.00 a.m. he was fallen-in on deck and his clothes were inspected by his lieutenant, whereby he might get into trouble. Then the captain walked round and inspected clothes, and he again ran the risk of some thing being wrong with his uniform. Then the captain went below and inspected every hole and corner of the ship. This occupied about two hours, during which the men were left standing on deck. At 11 o'clock there was church, which generally was not over until after 12, so the men got a cold dinner.

When Scott became a captain himself he always arranged for church to be over by eleven, so that the men had an hour to themselves to write letters, have a hot dinner, and a peaceful Sunday.

Cotten's lines capture the very tone of voice of an inspecting officer, eager to find every fault, in 'Sunday Morning on board ship',

> If you are Cook on Sunday morning
>   My friends look out for squalls
> For No. 1 will go his rounds
>   And give you frequent calls
> I want to see those mess traps shine
>   And look here Sir at once
> Ships Corporal put him in the bouse
>   He has not cleaned his sconce
> Send for the PO of his mess
>   There is White-wash on the shelf
> They will not do a thing unless
>   I find it out myself
> And corporal look at the deck
>   It has not seen a brush
> If they don't choose to do it now
>   At dinner time they must
> Who is the cook of No. 9
>   He has not cleaned the Pot
> Send for the caterer of his mess
>   Put both in the report
> And 16 too look at their tubs
>   Without blacking on the hoops
> And corporal pull them dish cloths down
>   And take care of them boots
> There is 18 Mess they have not cleaned
>   The boxes in the rack
> I told them of it yesterday
>   They have had time for that
> And so he goes from mess to mess
>   Finding fault with all he sees
> Let it be this or that.

Comus paid off at Sheerness in March 1884; after four weeks' leave, Cotten joined the 3,900-ton steam-corvette *Bacchante*, flagship of the East Indies Station, in April 1884. Cotten was a gunnery rating and *Bacchante* had a fine selection of guns: ten 4-ton 7-inch guns, four 6-inch breech loaders, seven 9-pounders, two Gardners, six Nordenfeldts, six saluting guns, 140 rifles and eighty-five pistols. Cotten details their numbers lovingly in his diary, along with pictures of turret drill and loading procedures for 25- and 35-ton guns, notes about Nordenfelts, and drawings of types of shot.

The personal side of *Bacchante* was not as satisfactory for Cotten as the gunnery. Clearly, as time went by, the Captain (Arthur Moore) came to be at odds with the ship's company. 'Our Nice (underlined) Captain sent forward', Cotten notes, 'to ask men to attend evening service but none would go.' However, the captain was equal to behaviour like that. Cotten's diary for the very next day records: 'Piped scrub and wash clothes before the middle watch turned out and had several rubs at sail drill, stations, etc., the same afternoon and both Dog Watches and clued up with down screw, another day of agony towards the end of commission.' It took them all the next day to moor ship at Mauritius, having got a hawser round the screw. A week afterwards they had their 'Annual Firing'. The feud went on: 'Middle watch crossed and set top-gallant sails, a very nice little night's work but nothing unusual as our mutual Friend the Captain could not rest without giving us our usual.' The next morning, there was a 'shortened breakfast, and the morning watch furled sails'. The same day Cotten reported smallpox on board. However, they were not downhearted: 'Had a nice sing song on the Forecastle just to let the Gentry aft see we were alive.' Cotten himself seems to have been personally involved in the unrest: 'Went before the bloak [*sic*] expecting 5 days 10A for flapping too much but I beat him off.' Before the end of the month, Cotten was one of a party of bluejackets sent on a punitive expedition against Burmese dacoits. They marched up to Ava fort and hoisted the Union Jack above it. They spent one night in a bloodstained hut, which Cotten called the 'Chamber of Horrors', but normally they slept in the open. They were eight days on the march, doing twenty-six miles a day, with no tents or blankets to shelter them. Cholera broke out and one man, Marine Jones, died of it on Christmas Day 1885. In February, they were all paid their well-earned 'hard-lying money of sixteen rupees, nine annas each'.

Cotten's verses (if they are his) and all the other sailors' logs, diaries and reminiscences of the time are often critical of the Navy, but the criticism is passive. It is as though the sailors knew that it was beyond them to bring about change, and what could not be changed had to be born. Good and bad ships, good and bad officers, were like good and bad weather, to be enjoyed or en-dured as the case might be, and the sailor had no more effect on either than he had on the weather. As a bluejacket grew older, he even had a strong desire to keep things exactly as they were, if only so that the newcomers might have just as tough a time as he did. However much sailors complained about their life, their food, their paymasters, their police and their 'green rubs', there was absolutely no spirit of revolution, no determination whatsoever that things must be changed.

The Navy of the '70s and '80s was spiritually and materially somewhat in the doldrums. In such a long period of peace, the only 'war' was in drill, and sail drill at that, against other ships in the same fleet or squadron. But, as so often in the Navy's history, changes were brought about by some mysterious process in which external pressures chimed with internal ambitions. At least one officer, Lord Charles Beresford, understood the power of press and Parliament to bring about changes in the Navy, and as a Sea Lord and as a member of Parliament he used both.

Meanwhile, on the lower-deck a man appeared at last—perhaps the very first bluejacket ever—astute enough to understand and employ the press to raise the ordinary sailor's valuation of himself and his social status. His name was James Wood, but he wrote under the pseudonym of Lionel Yexley. He not only published, in forceful and critical language, his own reminiscences of his naval career, but he later edited influential newspapers such as *The Fleet*, which provided a voice for the lower-deck.

His mother 'had planned a different career' for him, but in 1879 he succumbed to the fascinating yarns of the RMLI recruiting sergeant at the old Swan and Horseshoe at Westminster. He joined *Impregnable* at Devonport and his first meal (so many naval reminiscences include details of the first service meal) was five squares of bread and a steaming cup of tea. Yexley also records the first racket he found in the Navy: when the new entries' uniforms arrived, the ship's corporal sold their civilian clothes ashore, at great profit to himself.

The *Impregnable* boys were brought up on the rope's end. Yexley recalled 'an otherwise quite kindly old bosun' standing at the top of a companion-way and cutting at random with his 'stonnachy' at the boys' heads and shoulders as they doubled past him on their way on deck. Every petty officer, everybody in any sort of authority, was armed with his 'stonnachy', a short length of rope with a large Matthew Walker knot like a bunched fist tied in the end.

Nobody thought anything of corporal punishment. According to Yexley, up to six or a dozen boys were flogged every day. Two hammocks were lashed crossways on each other and the culprit spreadeagled across them. Up to twelve strokes of the cane, which was forty inches long and as thick as a man's thumb, were inflicted by the ship's corporal. For serious offences such as smoking, or breaking out of the ship and trying to run away, boys were birched with up to twenty-four strokes on the bare breech.

The boys had a bath once a week, on the upper-deck. None of the boys wore any underclothes so the water turned dark blue after a few of them had been through; but they all had to go in and the petty officers saw that each put his head underwater.

Yexley's first ship was a gunboat in the East Indies, with a ship's company of 126, armed with two 64-pounders and one 7-inch pivot gun. Life on station in the Persian Gulf was hot and deadly dull. No leave was allowed and one of the few excitements was the quarterly gun firing. Even then, Yexley says, some ships simply put the ammunition over the side. The food, fat salt pork and pea soup, was exactly the same as if they had been in colder northern waters. The captain did not favour having a canteen on board, but the men bought bottles of pickles, flour, bread biscuit, basins, plates and salt out of their own money. They also exchanged their clothing for whisky whenever they could.

With nothing to spend their money on, men would leave it openly on a shelf. If a thief were discovered, he suffered a terrible retribution. One man, at the gunner's mate's suggestion, was given a 'cobbing'. A 'thieve's cat' of twenty-two tails was made from hammock clews, and he was given four dozen; he had stolen three shillings, so he had one for each shilling, and one for the money. The strokes were laid on by his messmates, in turn. In the tremendous heat below decks they were all naked, except for a black silk handkerchief round their waists, and perhaps a cloth tied round their foreheads.

In the heat, boredom and loneliness of his position, the captain took to drink and eventually fell out with the ship's company. When he piped 'Hands to dance and skylark' one evening, not a man moved. He waited and took his revenge by rousing all hands at four o'clock in the morning to holystone the decks, weigh, and drop the anchors again, make and then furl all plain sail. He sent the hands to general quarters in the middle of the night, and exercised 'man and arm all boats'. He ordered both cutters to be lowered and hoisted again, a job which required clearing lower-deck. The ship had twenty men down with fever at the time, and the remainder had the very greatest difficulty in hoisting the boats. It was some hours before the exhausted, sweating men had the heavy boats properly up to their davits. In time, in Yexley's account, the captain lost control of himself and the ship's company, and was invalided home.

Yexley's next ship was *Euryalus*, flagship on the station. He wrote of his experiences on board nearly a quarter of a century later, when he had become virtually a professional critic of the Navy but, even allowing some licence for his disgruntlement, it seems clear that *Euryalus* was a typical ship of the time, on a remote station in a long time of peace. There was no heavy gun drill, only sail drill. The only gunnery knowledge demanded of the sailors was 'polishing two iron slides of a 64-pounder'. The only seamanship consisted of 'polishing brass work on the fore bitts'. 'The idea of instructing youngsters on professional subjects', Yexley wrote, 'had never been thought of.' The seamen treated the stokers with contempt. Stokers from the stokehold were not allowed on deck in stokehold dress at any time, on pain of 10A punishment. The officers showed little interest in the sailors. At Bombay, when forty-eight hours' general leave was given, the first time anybody had been on shore for seven weeks, 'the first thing everyone wanted was a feed'. Yexley noted disgustedly that neither the padre nor anybody else on board interested themselves in organising anything for the men, who were left entirely to their own devices ashore.

In that atmosphere of heat and boredom, naval discipline insensitively and inflexibly applied could easily ruin a man. Disaster could come, seemingly inevitably, from a petty little offence. One able seaman was picked up for some flaw in his uniform at divisions and was ordered to muster his bag in his dinner hour. The man was exasperated by the punishment and was rash enough to show it. Because of his attitude he was charged with disrespect to a superior officer, given ten days' 10A punishment and ordered to muster his bag in the dinner hour every day for a week. The man's feelings naturally mounted, and eventually he put a 7-inch projectile in his bag and threw it overboard. But as he had paid for the uniform, and the bag, out of his own pocket, his offence must have been hard to define. The court-martial, however, made no bones about it, and sentenced him to five years' imprisonment for insubordination.

In 1881 Yexley was drafted to *London*, the store, hospital and guard-ship for the southern part of the East Indies Station. She provided base support and boat's crews for the suppression of the slave trade between the African mainland and Pemba Island, north of Zanzibar, but otherwise she was little more than a hulk. Her guns had been removed, her awnings were kept permanently rigged, and her rigging was so rotten it was not safe to climb aloft. Bats flew out of her sides whenever a bugle blew. Her decks were infested by rats and cockroaches. Some of the cockroaches were more than two inches long and the sailors used to hold cockroach races.

London was also a prison ship, where men condemned to imprisonment on the station served their sentences until they could be sent home. In that climate and in that ship, their lives were a living hell. The cells in which they spent most of their day, in solitary confinement, were six foot by four. They lived on a reduced diet, had to pick 2 lbs of oakum daily, and do $2\frac{1}{2}$ hours of shot drill, in two poeriods of $1\frac{1}{4}$ hours each.

For shot drill, large wooden blocks were placed at nine foot intervals around the upper-deck. Each block had a concave depression carved in its upper face. A 32-lb round shot was placed in the concavity. The prisoner stood to attention facing the block, then bent from the waist, picked up the shot, held it in both hands with his forearms stiffly at right angles to his body, turned, marched to the next block, turned, lowered the shot onto the block, paused, lifted the shot, turned, marched to the next block, turned, lowered, paused, lifted, turned, marched, turned, lowered, paused, and so on, for $1\frac{1}{4}$ hours, without rest.

Shot drill was unpleasant in temperate climates. In the tropics it was torture. Sweat soon saturated the men's rough canvas clothing and ran down their legs to stain the deck in a great dark circle, as they steadily shuffled round in their misery. Shot drill had its own rhythm of agony, as the men lifted, and marched, and dropped the shot. The ship's police stood round to call the time and make sure that the prisoners grounded their shot in unison. From the decks below, shot drill had a characteristic sound, of the rumble of shots grounded, the pad of bare feet and the rumble again. In *London*, the captain stood with his watch, to measure the number of times the shot was grounded every five minutes.

London had a 'wet and dry' canteen, for beer and dry stores. But there was no leave throughout the commission, except a couple of hours on Sunday afternoons for privileged men on the 'special leave' list.

On 20 January 1883 *London* was relieved by *Windsor Castle* and sailed for home four days later. Although, as Yexley says, the paymasters on board had nothing whatsoever to do during the passage home, the men's paying-off accounts were not ready when the ship arrived in England and they had had to wait seven days to be paid. Meanwhile they were allowed ashore at Mutton Cove, where all the 'gay women' of the town were waiting for them. Although the ship's company were mostly east-coast men, no decent lodgings were arranged for them nor any means of transport laid on to take them home. It was no wonder that many of them 'bought a white horse'—behaved in a recklessly extravagant manner.

Yexley had volunteered for a course at *Excellent* and was, in the meantime, discharged to the old receiving ship *Duke of Wellington*. Here, he found corruption and bribery reigning on an oriental scale. There were thousands of men temporarily drafted to the *Duke*, passing through with nobody much interested in them. The ship was run by the naval police under a system of graft and bribes. Nothing could be done without first bribing the police. Yexley himself 'broke' his leave because, he said, he simply did not understand that a bribe was expected of him. Although Yexley and every other proper seaman had a fierce contempt for the police ('failed able seamen', Yexley called them) he conceded that they made the system work and, to a certain extent, mitigated its worst effects. Had the police applied all the Admiralty rules and regulations rigorously there would have been an instant mutiny. As it was, corruption held hands with theft and misappropriation. The butchers of Gosport ran their businesses on sailors' beef. Many married men wanted shore billets and were willing to pay to get them. When the C-in-C held a muster by open list at the end of 1885 it was found that hundreds of 'extra' supernumary billets had been created, quite illegally, both in the *Duke* and in *Asia*, the receiving ship for stokers and artificers.

When Yexley went to *Excellent*, the men were still living in the old hulks, although the gunner's house, the 'Excellent house that Jack Built', had been put up ashore by that time. Whale Island was still Mud Island, with a resident population of several thousand rabbits and about one thousand convicts, levelling the island off with earth from the new dockyard extensions. The atmosphere at *Excellent* could hardly have been more different than in the old *Duke*. 'You', the men on the course were told by the staff, 'know nothing. You must start again from scratch.' *Excellent*'s slogan was: 'Attitude is the art of gunnery and whiskers make the man', and Yexley enjoyed every moment of it. Jackie Fisher was then captain, Percy Scott and John Jellicoe were on the staff. Yexley was in Jellicoe's class and a member of one of the earliest 'field gun's crews', who exercised dismantling, transporting and reassembling a field piece against the clock. They worked hard and they played hard. Instruction began at 9.30 a.m. and went on until 3.45 p.m. with, as Yexley said, 'no red tape' and no distractions. But leave was given until 7.00 a.m. five nights a week.

After *Excellent* Yexley went to *Vernon* to do the ninety-days course on torpedoes and passed out with a first class certificate, adding 2d a day to the extra 4d he got from *Excellent*. When he left the Navy he joined the Coastguard, but he resigned prematurely from that service too (thus forfeiting the pension for which he had so nearly qualified) so as to be free to edit a paper called *Hope, The Bluejacket and Coastguard Gazette*. It was published by Masters Ltd. in Ryde, Isle of Wight, with a readership in the naval ports and the coastguard stations round the country.

Yexley was an intelligent and able man whose chief service to the Navy was rendered after he left it. From the moment he became editor in January 1897, he set himself to the task of improving the bluejacket's lot, ashore and afloat, inside the Navy and out. Having been 'inside the whale' himself gave his writing an added conviction, and sometimes an added venom. His campaigns on behalf of the working class in the Navy belonged in spirit as well as in time to the next century. In a sense, Lionel Yexley was the first man on or from the lower-deck to make the mental transition from the nineteenth to the twentieth century.

In 1902 he resigned from *Hope* after a disagreement with J. N. Masters, the proprietor. Three years later he started his own paper, *The Fleet*, which was perhaps the first true bluejacket's newspaper. He commented upon uniform, pay and fleet manoeuvres. He campaigned for improved victualling scales. He attacked brutal punishments for boys, and absurd restrictions upon leave. He ran a lively correspondence column and kept a close watch on other newspapers such as *The Times*, often quoting or commenting or apostrophising them for the benefit of his own readers. He published obituaries of senior offices who had behaved with particular consideration to the lower-deck. He printed satirical contributions on the Navy written by serving bluejackets, which would have seemed incredible only a few years earlier. He published a pamphlet attacking the financial structure of Aggie Weston's Sailors' Rests, and he kept up the attack for some time; he believed that her brand of well-meaning philanthropy was insulting to the sailors and misleading to the public. He was quick to note social tensions in the Navy itself, such as those between artificers and 'mechanicians' promoted from the stoker branch. Whenever the sailor was abused afloat or slighted ashore, *The Fleet* retaliated with a full account of the offence.

In the broader publishing field, Yexley also edited a series of Ship's Logs. These were accounts of a ship's commission, written by members of the ship's company and published with photographs, details of cruises, names of football teams etc. In all there were some forty of them published in the first decade of the twentieth century and they now give valuable insight into the lives and living conditions in the Fleet at the time. Yexley's work made the way easier for many of the reforms introduced by Fisher.

In the late 1870s and 1880s, as for most of the century, the Mediterranean was the most important station for the Navy; it was almost constantly in a state of political tension. In February 1878 war between Russia and Turkey seemed imminent and a British fleet under Phipps Hornby steamed through the Dardanelles and calmed the situation. Some warships remained in Besika Bay, at the entrance to the Dardanelles, for more than a year, their ship's companies fighting off boredom by riding horses ashore and hunting hares.

The next Mediterranean crisis came in the summer of 1882. Though Egypt was nominally a vassal state to Turkey, Khedive Ismail was in fact an autonomous ruler, with a taste for high living in the European style for which he borrowed enormous sums of money from London and Paris. When, inevitably, he defaulted on his debts, the British and French governments held an audit of Egyptian affairs and ordered certain restraints. Ismail objected, was deposed, and replaced by his son Tewfiz. However, the economies aggravated an anti-European feeling which already existed in Egypt. Taking advantage of this, Arabi Pasha, a brigadier in the Egyptian army, seized effective power and forced Tewfiz to do as the army ordered.

This was a state of affairs which could not be tolerated for long, but although British ships were anchored in the roadsteads off Alexandria, Arabi was defiant. He built extra shore fortifications, drilled troops and gun crews within easy sight of the ships, and generally strengthened the defences of the seafront. The French ships withdrew from the scene. The situation deteriorated during June 1882, until Admiral Sir Beauchamp Seymour, who had relieved Phipps Hornby as C-in-C, sent Arabi an ultimatum to withdraw his troops from the strongest fortifications and hand them over.

There were violent anti-foreigner riots ashore, one naval officer was killed, and Europeans left by every available ship. Arabi had gone so far, and his control over a highly excited population rested so much upon his own personal prestige, that it was impossible for him to back down, even had he wished.

By 10 July 1882, the last European ship had left. Seymour's ultimatum expired at 5.00 a.m. on 11 July. By that time his eight bombarding ships were in position: *Monarch, Invincible* and *Penelope* were close inshore, opposite a strong-point known as Fort Mex; *Temeraire* and *Inflexible* were further out, lying off the breakwater; and *Superb, Sultan* and *Alexandra* lay to the northward, opposite a line of guns on the Ras-el-Tin peninsula. The corvettes *Helicon* and *Condor* were stationed as repeating ships. To be closer to events, Seymour shifted flag to *Invincible*, the middle ship of those opposing Fort Mex.

Sailors of the Mediterranean Fleet practising with the
Nordenfeldt gun on board HMS *Monarch*, 1881.

Seymour's ships provided a perfect example of the miscellaneous nature of the mid-Victorian fleet. Not one of them was alike any of the others, and only one of them had a sister-ship in the Navy. The other seven were individual designs. Among them they mounted guns of 6-inch, 7-inch, 8-inch, 9-inch, 10-

inch, 11-inch, 12-inch and 16-inch calibres. Six of them had central batteries, and the other two a pair of turrets each. Between them they steamed on single screws, twin screws, simple engines, compound engines, horizontal engines, vertical engines, high pressure cylindrical and low pressure rectangular boilers.

The fleet and forts were actually well matched. The forts mounted some 250 guns, 200 of them smooth-bores, but forty-five of them modern rifled guns capable of piercing armour plate. The ships mounted many more modern guns, but because five could only bring half their armament to bear on one side, they only had forty-three guns able to train on the shore at one time.

One of *Sultan*'s seamen kept a diary of the bombardment. His name was Arthur Bowes, and he had joined *Ganges* in May 1874. He qualified as a Trained Man and joined *Sultan* in 1882. *Sultan* coaled ship all night on 4 July, went to sea on the night of the 5th, and prepared for action. She came in again on 8 July and replaced gear. On Sunday the 9th, shell parties of both watches filled shell. The next day, the anchor gear was rove and the cable shortened in, the men prepared aloft for action and rigged barricades on deck with hammocks. Bowes and his mates slept on deck that night and were called at 4.30 a.m.

The sun rose on a flat calm sea. Seymour's ultimatum expired at five, but he was in no hurry. The low sun was hanging right in his gunners' eyes and he had the whole day still in front of him. Still hoping that there might come a white flag from the forts, Seymour kept his ships steaming up and down for nearly two hours before signalling to the leading ship *Alexandra* to open fire, which she did at 6.59 a.m. One of the largest forts, Fort Ada, replied at once, and the battle was on.

Bowes's diary is maddeningly laconic about the bombardment. '7.10 a.m. engagement commenced,' he wrote, '6 p.m. ended', and nothing else. The slight wind was north by west and carried the guns' smoke in front of the ships so that at first the gun crews could not see their fall of shot. However, the forts should have been reduced in a couple of hours. But most of the ships' outfits of shells were for use against other armoured ships, not against earthworks, and of the hundreds of shells fired that day almost half failed to explode properly because of faulty fuses. Thus the bombardment lasted for nearly nine hours. The intensity of fire fluctuated considerably as the day went on, as one or other of the forts was silenced. *Superb* gained an important success by blowing up Fort Ava's magazine shortly after 4.30 p.m. and the firing was only desultory after that. At last, the forts were all quiet. Many of their big guns had been dismounted or wrecked, and their crews had joined the rest of Arabi's army in a general retreat through the town into the open countryside beyond.

However, the Egyptian gunnery was good enough, while it lasted, to inflict damage and casualties on every ship except *Monarch* and *Temeraire*. Six men were killed in the fleet and another twenty-seven wounded. *Sultan* had two killed and seven wounded, one seriously, besides suffering damage to her fo'c'sle and anchor gear, and having her funnel shot away. *Invincible*, the flagship, was hit some twenty times and her armour plate was dented, though not pierced. *Inflexible* was hit by one shell in the after superstructure which killed two officers.

Condor, with the other gunboats, had been stationed to pass on signals and was not expected to take part in the main engagement. However, her captain Lord Charles Beresford took her inshore to engage singlehandedly, with her one large gun, the rows of 10-inch Armstrongs bristling from the sides of the formidable Fort Marabout, the most southerly of the Egyptian fortresses. Beresford handled his ship so skilfully and aggressively that for some time *Condor* attracted upon herself the fire of the fort, so assisting the larger ships further out. At one point, she was so close to the shore that the Egyptian gunners could not depress their guns far enough to fire at her. Eventually *Condor*, and the other gunboats who came to assist her, reduced Fort Marabout to silence. *Condor's* action was greeted by general cheering through the British squadron and Seymour had one of the most famous signals of the Victorian Navy hoisted in *Invincible*, 'Well done, *Condor*!'

'Well done, *Condor*!': Lord Charles Beresford's sloop in action off Alexandria, 1882.

As leading ship, *Alexandra* took the brunt of the Egyptian fire. She was hit more than sixty times. One man was killed and three more wounded, and there was considerable damage to her upper-deck, officers' cabins, the ship's boats and the standing and running rigging. The hull was penetrated twenty-four times above the armoured plate. One of these penetrations was caused by a 10-inch shell which landed on the main-deck but did not explode. Hearing the shout of 'There's a live shell just above the hatchway!' Mr Israel Harding, the gunner, dashed up from below, saw that the shell fuse was still burning, took

A popular music-hall song written in honour of the bluejackets
of England, and those of HMS *Condor* in particular, 1883.

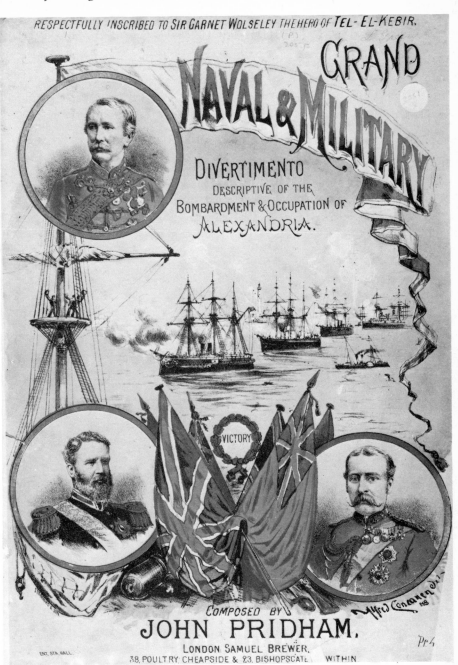

Pianoforte piece composed to celebrate the bombardment of
Alexandria, 1882.

some water from a tub nearby and threw it over the shell and fuse. He then seized the shell and threw it into the tub. This quick thinking and brave action saved many lives. Israel Harding was awarded the Victoria Cross, which was presented to him by Admiral Seymour (who was then Lord Alcester) at Malta in November 1882.

Harding died in May 1917 and the C-in-C at Portsmouth gave him a full naval funeral with all the honours on 26 May 1917. In his will he left to his daughter Sophia a portrait of his father and mother; to his son Joseph, his Brazilian Order, his Baltic Medal, his sword and a photograph of Lord Alcester presenting him with his VC in Malta; to his daughter Louisa Clara, his Ashanti Medal and a work table; to his daughter Annetta, his Egyptian Medal, his Khedive Star and a picture of Queen Victoria on satin; to his daughter Victoria Maud, a photograph of her father and mother; to his son-in-law Norman, his silver watch; and to his grand-daughter Ivy, her grandmother's gold watch. His Victoria Cross was to be drawn for by all these beneficiaries.

Gunner Israel Harding, VC.

A few days after the funeral, Joseph Harding received a most graceful letter of condolence from a man who had known his father:

Will you allow me to write and express my great sympathy with you and your family in the death of your gallant father, he was a grand old gentleman and a brave seaman, the heroic act he performed at Alexandria justly earned him the Victoria Cross. He was a very old friend of mine and I always regarded him with respect and esteem.

Yours sincerely,

Charles Beresford, Admiral.

Bluejackets clearing the streets of Alexandria with a
Gatling gun, 1882.

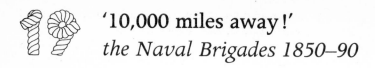

'10,000 miles away!'
the Naval Brigades 1850–90

'Arm, man and send away boats!' was a regular evolution in warships of the nineteenth century. It was understood that most ships, at some time during a foreign commission, would have to send bluejackets ashore, to quell an insurrection, or to restore order after a natural disaster, or simply to put out a fire. Every few years, a Naval Brigade was needed somewhere in the world, to operate ashore in defence of some part of the British Empire. At a time when there was no wireless telegraphy and reinforcements of any kind took months to arrive, a man-of-war was often the quickest and best way of bringing some force to the required spot.

The Naval Brigades often landed with wildly unsuitable food and clothing for the locality, with very little knowledge of the local political situation, with almost all their intelligence supplied by officials of the Crown or by the army, and with no facilities for transport, or hospitals, or gun carriages, except what they could improvise for themselves. Yet, as he showed in the Crimea and in India, the bluejacket was a superb campaigner.

Whilst the Naval Brigades of *Shannon* and *Pearl* were winning Victoria Crosses and immortality in India, the Naval Brigade of *Pelorus*, in a now quite forgotten campaign, operated ashore for some months in Burma, where they quite possibly prevented a Burmese mutiny. After the end of the second Burmese War in December 1852, the province of Pegu was annexed by Britain and was administered by the Honourable East India Company. In 1857 the King of Ava took advantage of the turmoil of the Indian Mutiny and gathered together a force of 15,000 men, which was far more than he needed for self-defence or for normal policing of the countryside. The British Commissioner in Pegu became alarmed at the possibility of a large scale insurrection in Pegu and asked for assistance. The troops in Burma had been depleted (because of the demands of India) and the Navy had to step in. The senior naval officer, Commodore Randle Burges Watson, ordered *Pelorus* (Captain Beauchamp Seymour, the same Seymour who commanded at Alexandria) to Rangoon where she arrived on 27 January 1858. On 4 February, Seymour took a force of fourteen officers and 162 men, with *Pelorus*'s launch, barge and other boats and field guns, up the Irrawaddy in the flat *Bhagarittie* which was towed (like those in India) by a river steamer, the 200-ton 90 h.p. Bengal Marine ship *Damoodah*. They arrived at the fort of Meaday ten days later.

Because of the incompetence and laziness of the East India Company's military officials, Meaday was filthy, insanitary and almost impossible to defend. There was no well or any other supply of water inside; all water had to be carried four hundred feet up the hill from the Irrawaddy. The magazine was 200 yards away from the fort, and unconnected to it by any passage or defence works. However the sailors made the best of it. They cleaned and whitewashed the barracks and living spaces, and put the cookhouse into working order. There were six bricklayers amongst *Pelorus*'s sailors, but when Seymour asked for tools and mortar he was told that it was 'customary to send into the jungle and get some Chinamen who, in the course of two or three days, would come in and see what was to be done'. So the sailors made their own mortar and, in Seymour's words, proceeded to show 'the authorities here that the British Navy can do without having to "send into the jungle for Chinese bricklayers" to execute repairs in the Hon. East India Company's forts'. With the help of local bhisties (water carriers) and sweepers, the sailors 'worked with a will', made their barracks 'thoroughly clean and sweet' and also fitted out a roomy cargo boat, the *Luchia*, as a hospital ship. Five men died of dysentery while they were up river, and twelve more were sent down to Rangoon.

On 6 April, the Naval Brigade was relieved by a detachment from the 1st Battalion, The Worcestershire Regiment, and came downriver again without seeing action. But because of the presence of the Naval Brigade the commodore at Calcutta was able to keep on reporting, as the months went by, that all continued to be quiet in Burma.

The Admiralty were relieved to hear this but 'still disapproved of the efficiency of H.M. ships being impaired by detaching their crews for land service'. The Admiralty hoped that everybody would return to their proper duties as soon as possible. There was a case for using seamen-gunners as artillerymen, but the Admiralty were quite right in principle in opposing the use of expensively-trained, scarce, long-service sailors as infantrymen on foreign stations. But the truth was that the country was hard-pressed to provide any sort of troops in Burma at that time.

The Burmese expedition of 1858 was a classical example of the Navy bringing force to the required spot, and remaining until relieved, or the situation returned to normal. Another such situation, in which the Navy were involved in actual fighting, occurred two years later in New Zealand.

This time the opponents were the valiant Maori race who were, as Commodore Loring, senior officer on the Australian station, said, 'by no means contemptible foes: man to man they are equal to ourselves'. The cause of the trouble was the ownership of land—which had been at the root of the previous Maori War from 1845 to 1847 and, although the Maoris were nominally subdued, disputes had rumbled on ever since. In November 1859 the Governor of New Zealand, Colonel the Hon. Gore-Browne, arrived at Taraniki, a province on the west coast of the North Island, and offered to buy any land that the Maoris were willing to sell. One offered 600 acres. The offer was genuine, the man's title was good and he was the proper owner of the land, but when surveyors came to mark boundaries a local chieftain, Wiremu Kingi Te Rangitake (William King), declared that he would not allow the land to be sold. Gore-Browne then sent a force to compel King to accept the sale. There was a general uprising amongst the natives, who made good use of their local knowledge to wage guerrilla warfare: here and there they built forts, or *pahs*, which they occupied as long as need be, knowing just when to evacuate and slip away to safety. While the settlers of Taranaki retired to New Plymouth on the coast, the Maoris burned their houses and ravaged their settlements for a distance of twenty miles along the coast and eight to ten miles inland.

The uprising seemed to be spreading and, as one naval officer wrote later, Auckland was 'nearly in a panic'. The citizens of New Plymouth were therefore overjoyed and relieved when the steamer *Adelaide*, with troops of the 65th Regiment, and the 13-gun steam screw sloop *Niger* (Captain Peter Cracroft) arrived off their town on 1 March, 1860. The ship's company of *Niger* assisted the small garrison of New Plymouth to guard the town while the 65th Regiment, with militia and mounted volunteers, went inland.

After nearly a month of operations, a party of volunteers and some settlers were besieged and under attack by the Maoris at a fortified place called Omata, a few miles south of New Plymouth. On 28 March, there were reports that the Maoris had massacred two men and three children at a farmhouse near Omata. A relieving force of about 300 officers and men of the 65th, with militia and volunteers, and including *Niger*'s first lieutenant, Lieutenant William Blake, two officers and twenty-five seamen, advanced towards Omata stockade.

At about 1.00 p.m. the men still on board *Niger* heard two guns, the signal of alarm, from the barracks on the hill in New Plymouth. Two surf boats came out and Cracroft and six officers, thirty-two bluejackets and ten marines, with a 24-lb rocket tube, went ashore, leaving about fifty stokers and boys to look after the ship (thus justifying one of the Admiralty's complaints about Naval Brigades; there was, however, no seaborne danger to *Niger*). The party formed up on the jetty, put their ammunition and rocket tube in a bullock cart, and with a further force of 250 men of the 65th and some volunteers set off for Omata. They reached the place at about 5.00 p.m. and found Lieutenant Blake and two volunteers badly wounded, and one volunteer dead.

About a mile further up the road from Omata, the sailors could see a large fortified *pah*, with three Maori battle flags flying from it, on a hill called Waireka. Although an order had been given to retire, Cracroft led his men down the road towards the *pah*. According to one officer's account, Cracroft said, 'My lads, there are three flags flying in defiance of the Queen and our men. Ten pounds to the man that hauls the big flag down.' One sailor said, 'We'll do it, sir'. So they went another half a mile further on the Omata road. They could hear the Maoris in the *pah* firing at the 65th in a nearby gulley. They fired four or five rockets at 700 yards range 'and then stepped on easy like as it was getting quite dark. When we got about sixty yards from the *pah*, the rascals saw us and began cheering so we gave our cheers and in we went amongst them, cutting and popping away quite lively, killed as many as we could see, tore down the flags, and then as we could not see friends from foes, we fell in and marched off in the best order we could.' Their dusk attack was so sudden that they suffered only four casualties, all wounded.

The three flags had patriotic Maori emblems on them: Mount Egmont rising above the blue, Ngamotu (the Sugarloaf Island), and a bleeding heart. The first into the *pah* and the man who captured the largest flag was the captain's coxswain, Leading Seaman William Odgers who, with Roger Glanville the captain of the foretop, A.B. William Older and William Clarke, a supernumary marine from *Iris*, was recommended for the Victoria Cross. Cracroft actually recommended them all, but if they could not all get it, then he especially recommended Odgers, 'being the most daring'. He was duly gazetted on 3 August 1860 and received his Cross at a ceremony at Devonport from the C-in-C Plymouth, Admiral Houston Stewart, on 23 July 1862.

Lieutenant Blake was promoted commander for his bravery, and Odgers was offered warrant rank. But he is supposed to have refused it, and preferred to remain a petty officer (as he then was). The offer caused some controversy in the Navy. There was a feeling that Odgers should have been offered a commission instead of a warrant, especially as Colour Sergeant McKenna V.C. of the 65th (Yorks and Lancs Regiment) was given a commission for a gallant action in September 1863—also in New Zealand, so the two cases were directly comparable.

The Maori rebellion died down and flared up again several times in the next three years and Naval Brigades took part in several of the actions. The Navy's last serious battle with the Maoris began in April 1864 at Tauranga in North Island, further north than the scene of Odger's exploit, on the Bay of Plenty on the west coast. On 26 April, a force of nearly 1,300 men under General Sir Duncan Cameron and a Naval Brigade of 429 officers and men of the Waikato flotilla under Commodore Sir William Wiseman of *Curaçao* (21) landed at the Mission Station at Tauranga to attack a strongly fortified Maori position at Pukehinahina, some three miles from a village called Te Papa. The fortification was called the Gate *pah*.

During the night of 27th/28th, the seamen set up three Armstrong guns from *Esk* about 700 yards from the *pah*.. When it was light enough to see next morning, the naval guns and the 24-pounders of the Royal Artillery began to batter away at the corner of the *pah*. The naval guns each fired over a hundred rounds that day, without any misfire or mishap. At about 10.00 a.m. Captain Jenkins of *Miranda* was ordered to bring out two of his ship's 32-pounders, with a hundred rounds for each gun. He had the guns in position and ready for mounting by 3.00 p.m.—a notable feat of seamanship and gun-handling—but by that time the Gate *pah* was very nearly breached.

The assault began at 4.00 p.m. when a storming party of eighty sailors and seventy marines under Commander Edward Hay, of the steam sloop *Harrier* (17), and 150 soldiers of the 43rd Light Infantry (Oxfordshire and Buckinghamshire Regiment) ran to within 100 yards of the *pah*, where they paused to regain their breath under cover of a small hill. When ordered to advance the storming party ran with tremendous dash up the slope and over the walls of the *pah* and actually succeeded in establishing themselves inside. But then they had a severe setback. The Maoris were well entrenched in camouflaged positions, and the interior of the *pah* was complicated, with many passages and hiding places. The Maori fire was heavy and accurate and all the officers were either killed or badly wounded, including Commander Hay. Some of the Maoris had rushed out of the back of the *pah* but then came back face to face with their attackers. Leaderless and subjected to very heavy fire, with several casualties, the storming party wavered and began to fall back. At that moment the supporting party, consisting of the rest of the Naval Brigade (except for thirty-four men under Lieutenant Hotham of *Curaçao* who were with the 68th Regiment) under Captain Jenkins and some troops from the camp arrived at the wall of the *pah* to find the storming party retreating in confusion. The reinforcements also turned about and the whole force retired in a disorder which was very near to a rout. Sailors and soldiers retreated together, and there is no way of knowing who first began what was perilously close to a panic.

A breastwork was made on the ridge where the storming party had rested before they began their assault, and guns were brought up to it for a bombardment the next day. But at 5.30 a.m. the next morning A.B. John Colenutt from *Harrier* entered the *pah* alone and came back to report that the Maoris had left it during the night.

Later, garbled accounts of the somewhat disorderly retreat appeared in newspapers in Australia and New Zealand, implying cowardice on the part of the Naval Brigade. The sailors resented this accusation so bitterly that when *Esk* next visited Auckland a party of her sailors, who had been accused of deserting their captain, Hamilton, who was killed inside the *pah*, gathered outside the office of the local newspaper, shouting that they were 'downing house'. The office was a wooden building and the sailors, who were in a highly excited and riotous state, were quite clearly going to carry out their threat, when the editor himself came out and promised to publish an immediate retraction of his libellous statements.

That the statements *were* libellous is shown by the despatches, in which several officers, petty officers and men were mentioned for gallantry. Commander Hay was accompanied into the *pah* by his coxswain, *Harrier*'s captain of the foretop, Samuel Mitchell. When Hay was wounded he ordered Mitchell to leave him and go to safety. Mitchell refused and carried Hay out of the *pah* on his back. Hay died of his wounds the next day. Mitchell was recommended by Commodore Wiseman for the Victoria Cross and received it from the Governor of New South Wales, at a ceremony attended by a crowd of more than 10,000 people in Sydney on 24 September 1864. Afterwards he was born shoulder-high through the streets of Sydney.

The 43rd Light Infantry had their revenge for the reverse at the Gate *pah* when they defeated the Maoris at Te Ranga in June, but no Naval Brigade took part. The Tauranga chiefs made peace in August, although the war dragged on for another two years. A third Maori war did not end until 1870. At home, *Harrier*'s Naval Brigade were commemorated by a handsome white Carrara marble monument erected in Kingston churchyard in Portsmouth. A sculptured anchor and chain cable, with *Harrier*'s name engraved on the anchor, were mounted on a slab of black Belgian marble; the names of Commander Hay and sixteen others were engraved on the side.

While the war in New Zealand had been going on, the Navy had also been in action off Japan, where its opponents were as martial and proud a race as the

Maoris, and where the impact of Europeans was as great a cultural and racial shock as in New Zealand. In August 1863 the screw frigate *Euryalus* (35), flagship of Vice Admiral Sir Augustus Kuper, had bombarded the batteries at Kagoshima, stronghold of Prince Satsuma (incidentally showing up serious design faults in the Armstrong breech-loading guns and causing the Navy to revert to muzzle-loaders).

Captain of the foretop Samuel Mitchell, VC.
However, Mitchell lost his medal, and the VC in
this picture was made of cardboard.

In the next twelve months there were several incidents of racial tension in Japan. Two officers of the Lancashire Fusiliers visiting a Buddhist shrine were attacked by a band of samurai and hacked to death. The British Ambassador and his entourage were also attacked by would-be assassins who raided the legation late at night. The samurai were feudal retainers of the powerful Japanese chieftains, or Daimios. Amongst the most hostile of these were Satsuma and Choshiu, whose territory bordered the entrance to the Inland Sea at Shimonoseki. Kuper sent the screw corvette *Barrosa* (Captain Dowell) and the despatch vessel *Cormorant* to negotiate with Choshiu, but the ships were fired on as they entered the Straits of Shimonoseki and had to turn back.

The Government of the Mikado said that they were unable to coerce the Daimios and could take no action. An international squadron of British, French, Dutch and one American ship anchored off Hima Shima, a small island twelve miles east of Shimonoseki in the Inland Sea on 3 September 1864. Kuper flew his flag in *Euryalus*, with the screw battleship *Conqueror* (78) which had a battalion of marines under Colonel Suther, the corvettes *Tartar* and *Barrosa*,

A Japanese battery captured by the Naval Brigade at
Simonoseki, in September 1864.

the paddle-frigate *Leopard*, the gunboats or sloops *Perseus*, *Coquette*, *Bouncer*
and *Argus*, and the collier *Pembrokeshire*. The French had a screw frigate, a
screw corvette and a despatch vessel, the Dutch three screw steamships and a
paddler, and there was a chartered steamer with one gun, manned by
American naval personnel and volunteers.

The squadron got under way at 9.00 a.m. on the 4th, the British ships in the
centre, one half towing the other to economise on coal, and the whole force
anchored in the Straits. Choshiu, to the north and west, was the only hostile
Daimio; fortunately, Buzen on the southern side was strictly neutral.

Kuper was allowed to reconnoitre the Straits strangely unmolested. There
was a wooded valley, six or seven miles wide, between two lofty bluffs. Along
the foreshore, above the highwater mark, batteries of guns were ranged,
protected by parapets of palisades. One small battery was hidden among the
trees on the northern bluff.

The following day the ships ranged themselves in front of their targets, the
smaller warships about 1000 yards off the shore, with *Conqueror*, *Euryalus* and
the French flagship *Semiramis* further out. The bombardment began at
3.00 p.m. and within an hour most of the Japanese guns were silent. By
6.00 p.m. they had stopped firing altogether. It was considered too late for an
assault landing but a party from *Perseus* under Commander Kingston and from
the Dutch corvette *Medusa* landed and spiked the guns in No. 5 Battery—
the only Japanese guns which did not resume the action the next day.

At daylight Commander John Moresby of *Argus* collected a party of marines and bluejackets and successfully landed and captured the batteries, despite some damage and casualties from the Japanese guns while the boats were alongside *Tartar*. Their only real difficulty was the fierce tide which swept through the narrow straits. The Japanese retreated up the valley. 'It was a marvel to me,' Moresby wrote, 'that they had held out so long, for excepting the traverses between the guns there was not the slightest protection from our shellfire, which struck them full in the face.'

The guns were spiked and dismounted, the platforms and magazines were blown up, the French and Dutch landing parties were re-embarking, and Moresby himself was actually back in *Argus*, 'thinking all was over', when the first real action occurred. The Naval Brigade at No. 5 Battery, which consisted of one 8-ton and six 24-pounder guns, were suddenly attacked by a strong force of Japanese who had gathered in a shallow valley immediately behind the battery. Just then, *Perseus* grounded in a vulnerable position under the captured batteries, and it was necessary to secure No. 5 Battery and drive the Japanese out before dark.

Colonel Suther led the marine battalion up one side of the valley, while Captain Alexander, flag captain in *Euryalus*, led the Naval Brigade up the other. They were met by hot fire from the parapet of a ditch in front of the battery and from the top of an 8-foot wall protecting the palisade. Seven seamen were killed and there were twenty-six wounded, including Captain Alexander who was hit by a musket ball in the ankle. But, in Moresby's account, 'our men never checked, and rushing on, swarmed over the wall and won the stockade, the enemy disappearing in the bush.'

The Queen's colour was carried into action with the leading company that day by Midshipman Duncan Gordon Boyes, of *Euryalus*, who kept the flag flying to the fore in spite of fierce fire which killed one of his colour sergeants at his feet, and wounded the other, Thomas Pride, captain of *Euryalus*'s after guard. Boyes was only prevented from going forward further by Captain Alexander's express orders. The standard he carried was afterwards found to have six musket ball holes in it.

Boyes, Pride, and William Seeley, another sailor from *Euryalus*, who had distinguished himself by carrying out a daring reconnaissance and then, though wounded, taking part in the rush for the Battery, were all awarded the Victoria Cross.

The total Allied casualties were twelve killed and sixty wounded. Sixty guns were captured and taken off to the ships. On 10 September, a plenipotentiary from Prince Nagato, the ruler of Kyushu, came off to negotiate a settlement under which it was agreed that the Straits were to be open to vessels of all nations, the shore batteries would not be rearmed or repaired, and the Allied Powers would receive an indemnity to be fixed by their representative in Tokyo. Once again, the right force had been applied to the right place.

When *Euryalus* returned to England in September 1865, Queen Victoria issued a special command that the Victoria Crosses for Boyes, Pride and Seeley should be presented 'in such a public and formal manner as might be

Ordinary Seaman William Seeley, VC,   Captain of *Euryalus*'s after-guard,
the first American citizen to win a   Thomas Pride, VC.
Victoria Cross.

considered best adapted to evince Her Majesty's sense of the noble daring displayed by the officer and seamen concerned before the enemy'. Their Lordships added that 'nothing was to be omitted which might tend to redound to the honour of this officer and of these seamen'.

At the presentation ceremony on Southsea Common, on Friday 22 September 1865, the C-in-C Admiral Sir Michael Seymour took this to heart. Officers, petty officers, seamen and marines who had already won the VC were assembled to right and left of the C-in-C to witness the presentation. Captains, commanders and officers of the fleet attended, all in full dress uniform with white trousers. Seamen and marines of Her Majesty's ships in port and at Spithead, and marines from headquarters at Fort Cumberland, were all in full dress.

The Naval Brigade, under Captain Astley Cooper Key of *Excellent*, had two battalions with companies from *Excellent, Terrible, Recruit, Scorpion*, and *Royal Sovereign*, a battery of field pieces with their crews from *Excellent*, and the officers and ship's company of *Euryalus*. So many thousands of people congregated that the Marines, doing duty as policemen, had the greatest difficulty in clearing a space for the Naval Brigade to form up when it marched onto the Common. The admiral arrived in his carriage, to the general salute. After the Crosses had been presented, *Victory* fired a gun salute, and the sailors doffed caps and gave three cheers.

Two years after the bombardment of Shimonoseki, the same pattern of insult to British interests followed by swift retribution and redress recurred, this time in Abyssinia, where King Theodore, fancying himself slighted by the British government, imprisoned in his great fortress of Magdala the British Consul in Massowah, the British Resident in Aden (who had gone in good faith to negotiate) and every other British citizen he could lay his hands on. In the winter of 1867 the Navy transported an expeditionary force under Sir Robert Napier from Bombay across the Arabian Sea. The force consisted of 4,000 British and 8,000 Indian troops, 14,000 'camp followers', and over 36,000 beasts of burden including baggage elephants and over 6,000 camels. It was one of the most massive logistical exercises of the Victorian era, in which 235 sailing ships and ninety-five steamers were engaged. A Naval Brigade of eighty-three men, with twelve 12-pounder rocket tubes in two batteries, landed under Commander Fellows of *Dryad* and marched to Magdala with the army. They played a large part in defeating King Theodore's troops, who were demoralised by the rockets and forced to abandon their own guns. The town and fortress were destroyed and within a week the troops had re-embarked and were on their way back. King Theodore committed suicide.

When the fierce Ashantee troops of King Coffee crossed the river Prah early in 1873 and swept the Fanti country with fire and spear, the only force to oppose them was a Naval Brigade of 110 marines and a party of seamen from *Barracouta*, who were reinforced by Commodore Commerell VC and another 400 seamen from Cape Town in July. With a handful of loyal Hausa troops and one West Indian Regiment, Commerell successfully defended the coast and kept the Ashantee in check until Sir Garnet Wolseley and an expeditionary force arrived at the end of the year.

To the tune of their favourite song 'Ten Thousand Miles Away', which never failed 'to lift them along', a Naval Brigade of 250 officers and men under Commodore Hewitt VC marched out with the army in January 1874. They helped the sappers bridge the river Prah, took part in the most arduous fighting at Amoaful and shared in the capture and destruction of King Coffee's capital Coomassie. Ninety-five per cent of the Naval Brigade were on the sick list at one time or another and thirty-nine per cent of them had to be invalided to England, but Sir Garnet Wolseley wrote in his despatches, 'All fought throughout the campaign with the dashing courage for which seamen and marines are so celebrated.'

The next despatches to commend the Naval Brigades were for the expedition to Perak in the Malay peninsula in 1875 where the success of the operation was attributed 'mainly to the special and professional aid given by the Naval Brigade as rocket and gun parties, and in fitting and managing the country boats, which alone could be used'. The Sultan Ismail of Perak had attacked the British Residency, murdered Mr Birch the resident, and torn down the Union Jack. A corvette and three gunboats from the China station arrived and landed a Naval Brigade to co-operate with the troops which had been sent up from Singapore.

Campaigning conditions were as hard as anywhere in the world. There was virtually no fresh food. In the muddy rivers, oars were almost useless and the heavy boats had to be poled upstream for days, under a hot sun and against currents of up to four knots an hour. Men sank waist deep in the marshes, and in those malarial jungles many men went sick. However, Sultan Ismail was attacked and defeated, and then hunted through the jungle until he surrendered in March 1876. He was taken down to Singapore as a prisoner.

The Naval Brigades had their share of the fighting in the Zulu War in 1879.

The Zulu Medal, 1877–79.

The Ashantee Medal, 1873–74.

At Isandhlwana, when a British column advancing into Zululand from Rorke's Drift was attacked by the main Zulu army—15,000 to 20,000 strong—and virtually slaughtered to the last man, the Navy was represented by a signalman from *Active*, who was personal servant to Lieutenant Berkeley Milne, on Lord Chelmsford's staff. He was last seen with his back to a wagon wheel, defending himself with his sword-bayonet until a Zulu brave came behind him and assegaied him through the spokes of the wheel. When the news of the disaster at Isandhlwana reached St Helena, where *Shah* was on her way home, her commanding officer Captain Bradshaw on his own initiative embarked most of the island's garrison and took them to Durban where he landed them, with seamen and marines and guns from the ship. *Shah*'s unexpected appearance did a great deal to restore civilian morale in Natal at the time.

As the Zulu war went on, the ships provided some forty officers and over 800 men in all, from *Active, Shah, Boadicea* and *Tenedos*. Sailors manned defences at Inyezane. The only survivor of one Zulu assault was a boy, only ten or twelve years old. He was sitting, stunned and bewildered, in the ditch when a large sailor from *Boadicea* reached over the parapet, grabbed him, cuffed his ears until he stopped squeaking, and then sat on him until the attack was over. The lad was adopted by *Boadicea*'s sailors as a mascot and later joined the Navy.

The sailors were at the great Zulu defeat at Gingilhovo and took part in the relief and occupation at Eshowe. Lord Chelmsford wrote that 'it is impossible for me to speak too highly of the conduct and behaviour of the bluejackets and marines whether in camp or under fire.' Certainly the sailors' discipline in camp was excellent. According to Captain Fletcher Campbell, of *Active*, only one man suffered corporal punishment in his brigade, in more than eight months' campaigning: a stoker who stole a bottle of brandy from a stores wagon.

But valuable though the sailors were in action, their most important contribution was probably the skill and ingenuity they showed in bringing up the army's men and supplies. To cross the great river Tugela, which was two hundred yards wide and running strongly, the sailors constructed and manned a haul-over punt which ferried across 5,000 men, a large wagon train and hundreds of tons of stores. The coast of Zululand was harbourless, so the ships lay off a place called Port Durnford, and the crews warped boats through the surf to the shore. By August 1879, 2,000 tons of stores had been landed at Durnford and 500 tons had been shipped off by this method.

As always, the Admiralty were anxious about their ships. As early as April they were ordering that all officers and men were to be re-embarked as soon as the 'exigencies of war should permit' because they did not like the prospect of valuable ships in an exposed anchorage half-manned during the approaching winter season. In July 1879 the Naval Brigade embarked at Port Durnford, after seven months' service on shore. King Cetewayo of the Zulus was deposed.

Not all the Navy's opponents were as powerful as Cetewayo or as numerous as the mighty Zulu tribe, but their fate was generally the same. In March 1880, the bluejackets of *Boadicea* were in action again ashore, at Batanga on the West Coast of Africa. *Boadicea* was then flagship of Commodore Frederick Richards, C-in-C of the Cape Station. Six months earlier, two local chieftains, King Jack and King Long Long, had attacked an English trader's boat and taken the mate prisoner. The commodore summoned them both on board to explain their conduct. Both refused, and were given forty-eight hours to remove their women and children. The punitive action which followed was like a hundred other incidents up and down both coasts of Africa in the nineteenth century. It was succintly described in the diary kept by C. H. Macklen, as able seaman in *Boadicea* at the time.

> 22nd March. *Boadicea* accompanied by *Firebrand* and *Forester* at 6.30 a.m. proceeded off the villages. Gunboats on nearing the shore opened fire, hundreds of natives being assembled on shore, wildly brandishing their weapons; but after the second shell burst in their proximity they decamped, not one being visible a few minutes afterwards. A party of 200 seamen and 50 marines put off from the *Boadicea* and pulled for the shore, the Commodore leading in the galley.

Altho' the surf was exceedingly high the boats pushed through it, crews
jumping into the surf as the boats touched bottom; the pinnace partially
came to grief owing to a tremendous breaker lifting her stern high in the
air and pitching a few of her crew into the surf, thereby giving them a
nice cooler, which was enjoyable owing to the intense heat of the sun.
All having reached the shore, a line of skirmishers was thrown out,
consisting of marines, and ordered to occupy a slight eminence in front,
the bush being so dense that enemies could lay concealed ten yards away
without the slightest danger of being seen. Brigade under Commander
Romilly ordered to advance with gatlings, rockets, etc. The Commodore
with his boat's crew led on, marines skirmishing on either side. In this
formation a village was reached; no sign of human being was visible.
Houses were searched, animals and fowls driven out and the houses then
burnt to the ground. Later the column arrived at a stream of beautifully
cool water, which was a great boon. Water supplies replenished and the
stream waded waist deep. The force surrounded a village of large
proportions which the guide said was King Jack's Town, pointing out a
very respectable-looking two-storey house as His Sable Majesty's
dwelling. Skirmishers being thrown out and guards posted the work of
destruction began. The houses were razed to the ground and burnt.
Later a few more villages were destroyed, the Kroomen being employed
to catch all the animals and drive them to the beach. Long Long's villages
were destroyed in the same way.

So much for Their Sable Majesties. But by the end of that year the *Boadicea*'s
sailors were on their way to fight a far more formidable enemy, in a war which
ironically was partly caused by their success against the Zulus. Fear of a Zulu
invasion had united the people of the Transvaal, so that most of them were
quite content when the British annexed the Republic, for its own protection,
in 1877. But a minority of Boers, led by Paul Kruger, bitterly resented the
British. Once the Zulu threat was removed, they began to defy British civil
power and finally, in December 1880, attacked British troops and occupied
garrison buildings.

Like Bradshaw in *Shah*, Richards acted swiftly and without waiting for
Admiralty sanction. He left Simonstown in *Boadicea*, having coaled and stored
for war, on 1 January and anchored in Durban roads on the 5th. When General
Sir George Colley, the Governor, asked for assistance, Richards sent ashore a
Naval Brigade of five officers, 124 petty officers and men, two Gatlings and
three rocket tubes. They travelled to Pietermaritzburg by train on the 7th.
Commander Francis Romilly was in command of the brigade, but Richards
himself also went with them.

On 9 January the Naval Brigade set out to march from Pietermaritzburg,
with the Gatling guns and the rockets to Newcastle, where the army was
mobilising. They marched 225 miles in very rugged country in ten days, one of
the fastest long-distance marches of any force in South Africa, arriving in
Newcastle on the 29th.

The short campaign of 1881 was one long disaster for the British. It began on

28 January with an attack by inadequate forces on a pass in the Drakensburg Mountains (between Transvaal and Natal) called Laing's Nek which was driven off with heavy losses. The Naval Brigade occupied Laing's farmhouse and garden, and at one critical point their well-laid rockets drove off the Boers and allowed remnants of a party of the 58th Regiment who had been cut off to rejoin the main body. Then, on 8 February, the day Richards was ordered by the Admiralty to return to Durban, there was another action on the Ingogo river, with more heavy losses. Finally, on 28 February, there was the disaster at Majuba.

At about 9.00 p.m. on the 26th, some of the Naval Brigade under Romilly and single companies from the 3rd, 60th and 58th Regiments, in all about 450 men led by Colley himself, left the main encampment and climbed Majuba mountain. Half their number stayed on a plateau, while the rest went to the top, only about half a mile from the Boers' camp. Early next morning the Boers saw Colley's force and prepared to retreat, but when they realised that there were only a handful of British on the mountain top they surrounded them and attacked.

> Now commenced the firing on both sides, [wrote Macklen] sometimes hot, sometimes desultory. Other reinforcements arrived for the Boers. Fire again became rapid, but few casualties occurred until midday, when an ill-fated ball struck Captain [sic] Romilly in the left extremity of the bowels exploding as it passed out behind. The enemy now charged the hill, retreated, but charged again, pouring a dreadful volley which killed and wounded many . . .

Hundreds of Boers stormed the mountain top and began to kill everybody there. Colley ordered a retreat. It was every man for himself, but Lieutenant Trower, now commanding the Naval Brigade, stayed with a few of his sailors. They were all killed to the last man. In the retreat all semblance of discipline collapsed. There was utter confusion, with order and counter-order leading to disorder. The Naval Brigade, now under their third commanding officer of the day, were told to get their guns into a small fort, provision and water it for two days, and block up the entrance. They had barely done so when they were told that everything had been changed.

To complete the rout of the British, a violent thunderstorm broke and turned the camp into a morass. Burial and relief parties had to feel their way about the mountain side in blinding rain and darkness. Romilly was found lying on the hillside next day and brought in. 'Every man of the Brigade, to whom he was endeared,' wrote Macklen, 'endeavoured to do something for him.' But Romilly died on 2 March. Colley himself had been killed and in all thirteen officers and 210 men were killed or wounded, seven officers and 50 men taken prisoner. Of the sixty-four members of the Naval Brigade at Majuba, thirty-three were killed or wounded.

Captain Compton Domvile of *Dido* took over command of the Naval Brigade and brought them back to Durban where they embarked on 19 April. They marched to *Boadicea*'s band, cheered by the citizens of Durban who turned out *en masse*. Well-wishers asked if they could send grog on board but when told this was against regulations they bought up all the fruit in Durban and pressed it on the sailors. Paul Kruger, on this occasion at least, did not suffer any of the fates of Kings Theodore, Cetewayo, Jack or Long Long. A preliminary peace treaty was signed, followed by the Convention of London in 1884, confirming Transvaal's suzerainty.

Once again, the Admiralty were unhappy about the landing of a Naval Brigade, especially without their prior knowledge or approval. But Richards was the calibre of man to reassure them and eventually they telegraphed their complete approval of his actions. Richards was a very able officer, who eventually rose to be an admiral of the fleet. The sailors respected him, but he drove them as hard as he drove himself. Years later, when Richards was an admiral, he hired a one-legged cabman, a well-known character, to take him from Portsmouth railway station to the dockyard. The fare was a shilling, but Richards, although he did not recognise the man as one of his old *Boadiceas*, offered five. The cabby refused the money. 'You drove me for nothing on the coast of Africa,' he said, 'I will drive you for nothing now!' Delighted to get his long-awaited revenge, the cabby shook up his horse and rattled off, leaving Richards speechless with rage.

Naval Brigades had a knack of making news. Their part in the 'small wars' of the nineteenth century was generally well reported in the daily and illustrated newspapers of the time. They made excellent subjects for the war artists who sent home a stream of vivid action-packed pictures of bluejackets doubling up to the front, trundling guns into action, charging down native village streets, chasing slavers, boarding pirates, storming Maori *pahs* and Boer *laagers*, or wrestling hand to hand with Zulu and Sudanese spearmen.

After the bombardment of Alexandria the ships sent armed parties ashore which for two days were the only force for law and order until the arrival of the army. In the campaign against Arabi, the press were especially intrigued by the naval armoured train mounting Gatlings and a 40-pounder gun, devised by Captains Jackie Fisher and Arthur Knyvet Wilson. War artists followed the sailors to the battles in the Sudan where, at El-Teb, Captain Wilson, who had really only walked up to the front to see what was happening, won a Victoria Cross in a singlehanded combat. Bluejackets were ashore in Burma (again) in 1885, in the Sudan (again) in 1894, and in scores of other minor affrays. Naval guns took part in many of the most famous Victorian battles, at Colenso and at Ladysmith, and in suppressing the Boxer Rebellion in China. As always, the sailors were ready to campaign anywhere.

The best description of service in a Naval Brigade of the 1880s is by Thomas Holman, who hits off exactly the heat, the exhaustion, the labour of fighting on after a wound, the high morale in spite of the sensation of being isolated and surrounded by a fierce, athletic and seemingly irrepressible enemy who keeps on attacking. His account is of an engagement in which sailors from *Dolphin* took part at a place called Tofrik in the Sudan in 1884. The Arabs attacked while the defenders were still putting up a brushwood defence barricade and

The bluejackets' armoured train at Alexandria, 1882.

before the Gardner guns were properly in position. Holman, in the crew of one of the Gardners, had a spear thrust through his thigh. One officer and four sailors were killed, and only the stoutest resistance prevented a massacre.

There we lay, an isolated and small party of Britons, infuriated and as callous to danger as the Mohammedan fanatics around us, who were calling on Allah to preserve them and deliver us into their hands, keeping them at bay from the shelter of the gun wheels, determined to sell our lives dearly, and encouraging each other to use such limbs as

'Bluejackets to the Front': the war in the Sudan, 1884.

were not yet wounded for the preservation of those that were. Now our hearts would cease to beat as we curled up our bodies to evade, or stretched out our arms to ward off an impending blow; and the next moment it would go on at double speed and pump up into our heads that throbbed and thrilled and maddened us, as with frenzied haste we hacked at our opponents with our swords or shot them with our pistols.

A mass of white, black and brown wounded humanity, mad with pain and excitement, slashing, hacking and heaving at everything around us; each cursing the other in a different tongue, and all determined to die hard, and endeavouring with their last breath and strength to hasten the end of their dying opponents. Panting, howling, bleeding, cursing, raving, praying, kicking, gnashing their teeth, biting the dust; it was sad, grand, bewildering, awful to view, to contemplate. Yet these things were as naught to us, our own life was all.

And, when it was all over, the sailors embarked again, taking their guns with them, and went back to the ship's routine, to salt beef, salt pork and biscuit, but ready for the next expedition, or for whatever might turn up. As Holman said, 'You surely get your money's worth out of these tarry souls, do you not?'

20 'They all love Jack': the Navy in the 1890s

'The people love their Navy and believe in it,' said the *Daily Telegraph* in July 1887, during Queen Victoria's Golden Jubilee review at Spithead. Certainly there seemed good reason for popular confidence: 128 warships were on view, with some foreign visitors from France, Germany and the Netherlands, drawn up in three review squadrons and five flotillas. Every ship was from home waters, from the Reserve Training or Channel Squadrons. Not one had come from a foreign station.

But to experienced eyes (including those of the French naval attaché) the review showed the Navy's weakness as well as its strength. To make the numbers more impressive, the Navy had commissioned all manner of warships, some of which had not seen service for years. Sydney Eardley-Wilmot called them 'a motley collection of ancient constructions', and to get them to sea at all the Navy had to man them with inexperienced crews. There was a gun accident in the gunboat *Kite*, with one man killed and several injured, and there were several collisions: the Royal Yacht with the troopship *Orontes*, the *Black Prince* with *Agincourt*, and the notoriously unhandy *Ajax* with *Devastation*, so that the *Daily News* advised the Navy to keep foreign visitors out of the way 'until our bumping races of ironclads have come to an end'.

Nevertheless, the 1887 review contributed to a growing national awareness of the Navy and its problems (just as Lord Charles Beresford, one of its chief instigators, had hoped it would). In the 1880s there were a number of naval 'panics'. In 1884 Mr W. T. Stead caused one on his own with the publication in the *Pall Mall Gazette* (of which he was editor) of 'The truth about the Navy by one who knows the facts'. In 1885 the Poet Laureate Lord Tennyson published his celebrated accusatory poem 'The Fleet', addressed to the Sea Lords. In 1888, with rumours of a possible Franco-Russian alliance, there was another 'panic', which led to the Naval Defence Act of 1889, with authorised expenditure of £21,000,000 on the Navy and the building of seventy new warships. The Navy, henceforth, was to be on a scale 'at least equal to the naval strength of any other two countries'.

So, in the 1890s, after many years of internal administrative slumber and outward public indifference, the Navy suddenly became fashionable again, a proper subject of interest and debate. The Navy Records Society was founded in 1893, for the printing of papers and documents of naval biography, history and archaeology, and, a year later, the Navy League to secure, 'as the primary policy of national policy, the command of the sea'. Mahan and Colomb published influential works of naval history. Naval history was studied at Oxford and Cambridge. Board games of naval tactics were on sale, played with counters and squares. The ordinary bluejacket, though he remained a 'common sailor' became a national darling, known as 'The Handyman', from Harold Begbie's verse, 'Handy afloat, handy ashore Handier still in a hole'. The name caught on, and the sailor was a potent selling symbol, on advertisements, posters and cigarette cards, especially for tobacco and soap. The 'Handyman's' portrait, by R. Caton Woodville, was exhibited in a London gallery. A Nautical Ballet, featuring Miss Beatrice Ford as a 'Handyman', with a chorus of handy girl 'tars', opened at the Alhambra. Nautical drama had a revival. *Black-Eyed Susan* played to full houses at the Theatre Royal Edinburgh, in 1891, and came to London again in 1896, where the same year, another naval play called *True Blue* opened in March. *H.M.S. Pinafore* was revived at the Savoy Theatre in November 1887, and again in June 1889. Rudyard Kipling went to sea with the Channel Squadron and published *A Fleet in Being* in 1898. Henry Newbolt had a great success with his patriotic poems, *Admirals All*, the same year. W. Clark Russell achieved a considerable reputation with books such as *The Wreck of the Grosvenor*, *The Good Ships Mohock*, and *The romance of a Midshipman*, all published in the '90s.

Anything to do with the Armed Forces, and especially the Navy, seemed sure of a popular success, to an extent which now seems almost incredible. In 1895, a new weekly magazine appeared, called *Navy and Army Illustrated*. Number 1, of 20 December 1895, led with a photograph of Captain HRH The Duke of York (later George V) in full naval dress. Most issues thereafter carried full length, full dress photographs of senior naval or army officers (though more often naval: the magazine's military content was decidedly secondary, both in position and in emphasis). With its large folio format, glossy paper, superlative production, full and complimentary captions, the magazine gave otherwise quite obscure serving naval officers publicity undreamed-of, and unrepeated, far beyond the limits of the service. There were also articles on naval and military life, group pictures of ship's wardrooms on commissioning, reports of naval manoeuvres, short stories, memoirs of famous naval battles, book reviews, a 'gossip column' about officers' appointments and promotions, and 'notes and queries' on naval matters in general. *The Navy and Army Illustrated* also published, week after week, pages of large and lively pictures of life on the lower-deck which remain, even today, unsurpassed for technical accomplishment and human interest.

The Victorian reader was exposed to the virtues of the Navy from a very early age. The *Boy's Own Paper* was one of the most enthusiastic and consistent, not to say relentless, recruiting agencies the Navy ever had. Almost every copy had a story of sea adventure for boys, a picture of naval life commissioned from some well-known artist, an account of a naval battle, or an article on naval customs, naval uniforms, or life on board a man-of-war. Some of these articles, such as 'The Naval Code of Punishment', by 'George Andrew Patterson RN' in December 1890, now seem to be of very doubtful recruiting appeal, but possibly they were intended to reassure parents that flogging had been abolished. The editor himself often used some naval motif, such as a bluejacket reading his mail from home, to head his own correspondence

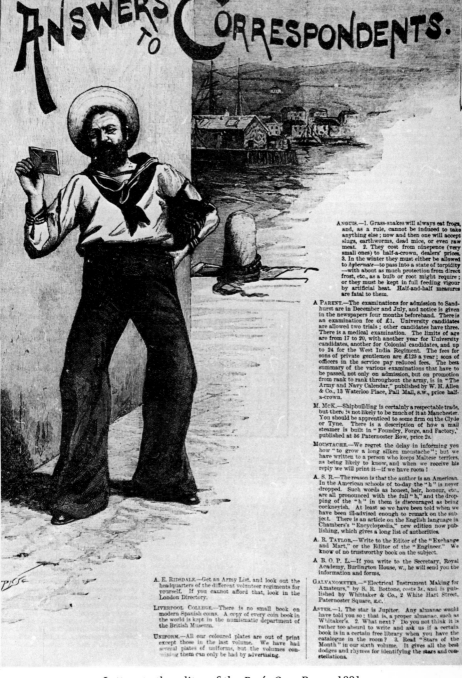

ANSWERS TO CORRESPONDENTS.

ANGUS.—1. Grass-snakes will always eat frogs, and, as a rule, cannot be induced to take anything else; now and then one will accept slugs, earthworms, dead mice, or even raw meat. 2. They cost from ninepence (very small ones) to half-a-crown, dealers' prices. 3. In the winter they must either be allowed to *hybernate*—to pass into a state of torpidity —with about as much protection from direct frost, etc., as a bulb or root might require; or they must be kept in full feeding vigour by artificial heat. Half-and-half measures are fatal to them.

A PARENT.—The examinations for admission to Sandhurst are in December and July, and notice is given in the newspapers four months beforehand. There is an examination fee of £1. University candidates are allowed two trials; other candidates have three. There is a medical examination. The limits of age are from 17 to 20, with another year for University candidates, another for Colonial candidates, and up to 24 for the West India Regiment. The fees for sons of private gentlemen are £125 a year; sons of officers in the service pay reduced fees. The best summary of the various examinations that have to be passed, not only on admission, but on promotion from rank to rank throughout the army, is in "The Army and Navy Calendar," published by W. H. Allen & Co., 13 Waterloo Place, Pall Mall, S.W., price half-a-crown.

M. McK.—Shipbuilding is certainly a respectable trade, but there is not likely to be much of it at Manchester. You should be apprenticed to some firm on the Clyde or Tyne. There is a description of how a mail steamer is built in "Foundry, Forge, and Factory," published at 56 Paternoster Row, price 2s.

MOUSTACHE.—We regret the delay in informing you how "to grow a long silken moustache"; but we have written to a person who keeps Maltese terriers, as being likely to know, and when we receive his reply we will print it—if we have room!

A. S. R.—The reason is that the author is an American. In the American schools of to-day the "h" is never dropped. Such words as honest, heir, honour, etc., are all pronounced with the full "h," and the dropping of the "h" in them is discouraged as being cockneyish. At least so we have been told when we have been ill-advised enough to remark on the subject. There is an article on the English language in Chambers's "Encyclopædia," new edition now publishing, which gives a long list of authorities.

A. R. TAYLOR.—Write to the Editor of the "Exchange and Mart," or the Editor of the "Engineer." We know of no trustworthy book on the subject.

A. B. O. P. L.—If you write to the Secretary, Royal Academy, Burlington House, w., he will send you the information and forms.

GALVANOMETER.—"Electrical Instrument Making for Amateurs," by S. R. Bottone, costs 3s., and is published by Whittaker & Co., 2 White Hart Street, Paternoster Square, E.C.

ASTER.—1. The star is Jupiter. Any almanac would have told you so; that is, a proper almanac, such as Whittaker's. 2. What next? Do you not think it is rather too absurd to write and ask us if a certain book is in a certain free library when you have the catalogue in the room? 3. Read "Stars of the Month" in our sixth volume. It gives all the best dodges and rhymes for identifying the stars and constellations.

A. E. RIDSDALE.—Get an Army List, and look out the headquarters of the different volunteer regiments for yourself. If you cannot afford that, look in the London Directory.

LIVERPOOL COLLEGE.—There is no small book on modern Spanish coins. A copy of every coin book in the world is kept in the numismatic department of the British Museum.

UNIFORM.—All our coloured plates are out of print except those in the last volume. We have had several plates of uniforms, but the volumes containing them can only be had by advertising.

Letters to the editor of the *Boy's Own Paper*, 1891.

column where, amongst letters about pimples and cold baths and nervousness and mange in terriers, he would reply to boys who had enquired about joining the Navy. In May 1890:

> It costs you nothing to be a boy in the navy; your uniform and outfit are found for you. But you must be quite healthy and have the consent of your parents or guardians. A pamphlet, obtainable free from the nearest post office, will tell you how to proceed. In London the naval recruiting office is at Spring Gardens at Charing Cross, a door or two from Drummond's Bank. If you are in the country, and anywhere within walk of the sea, your best plan is to apply at your nearest coastguard station. Of course at a naval port you should apply on board the training ship. You would do well to write for information to the Commanding Officer, HMS *St Vincent*, Portsmouth.

But where there was no hope, the editor was quick to destroy it. To 'H.D.', in November 1892, he replied tersely, 'Bad Teeth will throw you.'

The BOP's advertisements reflected the same interest in the Navy. In the Christmas Number of 1888, Redfern's of Cowes, Isle of Wight, offered 'Man-o'-War Suits & Pea Coats, for Boys and Girls, Made In True Naval Style, Real Government Serge Only Being Employed'. Much more elaborate, from Hinde's London Sample Room, was 'A Sailor Boy Doll'. His name was 'Romping Rollicking Roderick' and he was sold 'with his Sea Chest, 8 in. by 3 in. Containing 3 Suits of Clothes, 5 Hats, all to take on and off. A SLOOP, "The Pinafore", 8 in. long, with sails, rudder, crew, cargo, small boat, oars &c., and a well written booklet, called *He Would be a Sailor*, by Mrs Hayes. The whole Toy comprising upwards of SIXTY ARTICLES, the like of which has never been seen for ONE SHILLING. 4d extra for packing and carriage.'

The launch of one of Her Majesty's ships was always a great social occasion, which often had royal or at least aristocratic patronage. The day was normally commemorated by printed ephemera, such as leaflets giving the ship's particulars, details about her building and the history of past ships of the name. Flags were sold with the ship's name, or balloons, or posters and badges. Tissue handkerchiefs were given away for the launch of HMS *Orion* at Portsmouth by the Marchioness of Winchester. Some dockyards had their own resident bards. At Chatham, there was Philip Thompson, the 'Dockyard Poet', to write appropriate verses for the 'Floating Out' of HMS *Illustrious*, in September 1896, and of the third class cruiser *Pioneer* on Coronation Day, 1899. Composers continued to find the Navy inspiring. Theo Bonheur composed a 'Dreadnought Descriptive Fantasia' for pianoforte, to give a musical impression of life in a man-of-war.

In 1891 Bonheur published 'The Royal Naval Exhibition Polka', in honour of an event which did more to publicise the Navy than anything else (except, perhaps, the loss of HMS *Victoria* two years later). The exhibition, which covered a site of about fifteen acres in the grounds of the Chelsea Hospital on

DEDICATED BY SPECIAL PERMISSION TO
ADMIRAL SIR Wᴹ DOWELL, K.C.B.
AND PERFORMED WITH GREAT SUCCESS AT
THE ROYAL NAVAL EXHIBITION.

THE ROYAL NAVAL EXHIBITION

POLKA

COMPOSED BY

THEO BONHEUR

PRICE 4/
FULL ORCHESTRA 1/6 NET.
SEPTETS 1/

London.
ALPHONSE CARY, 87 OXFORD STREET, Wᶜ
& VOGEL HOUSE, CLAPHAM JUNCTION S.Wᶜ
(ALSO AT NEWBURY)

Polka for piano, specially composed for the Royal Naval
Exhibition on the Thames Embankment in the summer of 1891.

the Thames Embankment, was designed to show off every aspect of the Navy's life and history.

It opened in May 1891 and more than two and a half million people had visited it by the time it closed, 151 days later. One of the most popular exhibits was a model of *Victory*'s lower-deck at Trafalgar, life-size, showing the death of Nelson. The man from *Punch*, who visited the 'Naveries' as he called it, was so moved by this that he wrote: 'who would not, after this, have his back drawing-room converted into the quarter-deck of the *Shannon*, and his spare bedroom into a tiny reproduction of the Battle of Copenhagen!'

There was something for everybody. The 40-ton trawler *Hermione* of Grimsby, sent by the Deep Sea Fishermen's Mission; a National Panorama of the Battle of Trafalgar; an arena, for field gun drill and manoeuvres; a lake, some 250 feet by 150 feet, on which two miniature battleships representing *Majestic* and *Edinburgh*, each twenty-five feet long by six feet in the beam, fought out naval engagements; an ample supply of dining rooms and refreshment rooms and, last but not least, a 'temperance bar'.

Visitors could go by lift to the top of an exact model of the new Eddystone Lighthouse, which was 167 feet high and topped with a five million candle-power light. There were displays of relics and implements from Arctic expeditions, pictures and prints, gold medals, Nelson's blue coat and white waistcoat, a fleet of fifty silver model ships lent by HRH the Duke of Edinburgh, old surveys and charts, guns and ordnance stores, and, in Armstrong's Gallery, a full-sized model of a 110-ton gun mounted in a turret, as fitted to *Victory* and *Benbow*.

The drills with 'field pieces' were always extremely popular with the public at tournaments, exhibitions and carnivals all over the country in the latter part of the nineteenth century (and their lineal descendants, the Field Guns Crew Competitions, are still a major attraction at the Royal Tournaments of today). They were, principally, demonstrations of precise drill, combined with agile smartness. Patrick Riley took part in one at Balls Bridge tournament, Dublin, in 1886. After the men had performed a few preliminary movements with the gun, and fired a few rounds, Riley gave the order 'Cease fire'. 'The men then stood to attention,' he wrote, 'waiting for the next order; facing the captain, I gave the order "Dismount". In a few seconds, the gun was on the ground, wheels off both carriage and limber and the men sitting on the separated parts perfectly still, looking like figures carved in wood.' The crowd loved it.

They all loved Jack, and there was even a song with that very title. It was written by Fred E. Weatherly (who also wrote 'Nancy Lee', 'The Old Brigade', 'Roses of Picardy' and 'Danny Boy') with music by Stephen Adams (who also wrote the tune of 'Nancy Lee'):

> When the ship is trim and ready,
> And the jolly days are done,
> When the last goodbyes are whisper'd,
> And Jack aboard is gone,
> The lasses fall a-weeping,
> As they watch his vessel's track,
> For all the landsmen lovers are nothing after Jack,
> For all the landsmen lovers are nothing after Jack.
>
> For his heart is like the sea,
> Ever open, brave and free,
> And the girls must lonely be
> Till his ship comes back.
> But if love's the best of all
> That can a man befall,
> Why, Jack's the King of all
> For they all love Jack!

ARTHUR LLOYD'S GREAT COMIC SONG
GOOD-BYE JOHN,
OR THE LASS THAT LOVED A SAILOR.

ENT. STA. HALL

Pr 3/-

WRITTEN & COMPOSED BY

G . W . H U N T .

LONDON: J. W. TRAYHEARNE, 419, OXFORD ST. W.

A popular comic song from the music-halls of the 1890s.

Recitations about storms, shipwrecks and disasters at sea were always popular. The worst naval disaster of the 1890s was the sinking of the battleship *Victoria*, flagship of the Mediterranean Fleet, off Tripoli on the Lebanese coast, on the afternoon of 22 June 1893, with the loss of 365 officers and men, including the C-in-C himself, Vice Admiral Sir George Tryon.

Tryon was one of the ablest and best-known flag officers of his day, and he was possibly one of the most autocratic and powerful personalities ever to serve in the Navy. It was, in fact, the sheer force of his personality which allowed the disaster to happen. Tryon gloried in intricate fleet manoeuvrings, which at times became so intricate and involved that his second-in-command, the much staider Rear Admiral Markham (of Arctic note), sometimes confessed that he could not understand them and had to have them explained. (Markham was not alone; Henry Fleet, who served under Tryon some years earlier, said of some manoeuvres in the Channel Fleet that 'we were not taken into the confidence of the Admiral, but simply lived in a nightmare of motion, being whirled about from one position to another apparently without cause, and certainly without effect as the results proved'.)

That afternoon, eight battleships, three armoured cruisers, and two third class cruisers of the fleet were steaming in two columns led by *Victoria* (Tryon) and *Camperdown* (Markham), six cables (or twelve hundred yards) apart, when, to get his fleet into the proper position for anchoring that evening, Tryon ordered the two columns to turn inwards. When that signal was passed to him, Captain Arthur Moore, in *Dreadnought*, two ships behind *Victoria*, remarked, 'Now we shall see something interesting.' For the minimum turning circle of the ships was eight cables (or sixteen hundred yards). Thus the manoeuvre, as ordered, was inherently dangerous. Markham realised there must be something wrong, and delayed acknowledging the signal; he repeated the flag hoist, but kept it 'at the dip', meaning that he did not understand it. But such was the sledge-hammer force of Tyron's personality (and so unusual was it even to breathe the slightest question about an admiral's orders in the Victorian navy) that when *Victoria* semaphored to *Camperdown*, 'What are you waiting for?' Markham ordered the hoist to be hauled 'close up', meaning that he understood, and the evolution was carried out at once. *Victoria* and *Camperdown* put their helms hard over and headed inwards towards each other.

What happened next has often been told but never more succinctly than in the first lines of a thirty-two verse epic 'The Loss of H.M.S. Victoria', by W. A. Eaton, which was sold, price one penny, soon after the accident:

> The sun shone bright, the gentle breeze
>   Rippled the sunny waves;
> Who would have thought four hundred men
>   Would soon find watery graves?
>
> There was no storm cloud in the sky,
>   No breakers on the shore;
> No deadly cannon lifted high
>   Its fierce and sullen roar.
>
> A double line of battleships
>   Steamed onward, side by side,
> Like well-trained warriors marching on,
>   In stern and stately pride.

But now the order flashed across
   To change to single file;
There were but six short cable lengths
   Between them all the while.

The brave ship Camperdown steamed round
   (I cannot tell you how);
Her ram struck the Victoria,
   And crashed into her bow.

The Admiral upon the bridge,
   Had her head turned for shore;
But now the water rushing in,
   Told him that all was o'er.

Collision mats were of no use
   To keep the water out;
The crew with perfect discipline
   Moved rapidly about.

Except for the reference to 'single file' (reconstructing Tryon's probable intentions, it seems that when the fatal move was over the columns were supposed to be two cables apart, not in single file) Eaton's account is fair. Rapidly though her crew moved about, *Victoria*'s watertight doors were open at the time of collision, and she filled forward and sank in about ten minutes. The discipline of the ship's company was magnificent. They fell in on the upper-deck as ordered, and only broke ranks when the ship began to turn over. Many of the engine-room staff below went down with the ship, still at their posts. Many men got clear of the ship but were dragged down by suction, or killed by *Victoria*'s screws which were still revolving or by wreckage which came shooting to the surface amongst the swimmers. Tryon first flew a signal to tell boats to keep clear, obviously for fear they would be drawn down with *Victoria*, but some coxswains disobeyed, and 294 officers and men were picked up. Tryon was not among them.

The survivors were courtmartialled, according to Service custom, but no blame attached to any of them. The accident was, as Arthur Knyvet Wilson (commanding *Sans Pareil* second in *Camperdown*'s column) later wrote, 'apparently an act of madness' by Tryon who simply mistook the fleet's turning circle's diameter for its radius, in a moment of mental aberration. Being the man he was, he did not change his mind, and his captains did not dare challenge him—in fact, most of them thought that he had some clever solution up his sleeve. The disaster did permanent damage to Markham's reputation, and to *Camperdown*'s; Markham went on half pay and rose no further in the Service, and nobody liked *Camperdown* to steam astern of them after that. The sailors called her *Crampherdown*.

In that year of 1893 there was yet another 'naval panic' due to the appearance of a strong Russian fleet in the Mediterranean, and the following year another massive warship building programme was begun. The navies of

Europe were, in fact, already engaged on the 'arms race' leading up to the First World War. The Royal Navy, as always, was in a mixed state of reform and reaction. Fisher, one of the greatest reformers in the Navy's history, became C-in-C in the Mediterranean in 1899 and at once set about changing things at Malta. He took the traditional service view about leave and stood it on its head, making the previous maximum allowance the new minimum, and granting short leave as often as possible to each watch in turn, so that everybody got a few hours ashore. *Mirabile dictu*, the incidence of leavebreaking and drunkenness actually decreased. Fisher's major reforms, such as changes in officers' training, shortening of ships' foreign commissions, and the establishment of the 'stone frigates' ashore for training and housing seamen— and at last abolishing the Victorian hulks—had to wait until the next century when he became a Sea Lord. But in Malta, Fisher let his critical eye rove over every aspect of fleet life, from providing playing fields and recreational facilities ashore, to fresh bread every day on board.

Thomas Spence Lyne, who rose from the lower-deck to the rank of Rear Admiral, had several distinguished naval forbears; his father served in the Crimea but was discharged from the Navy because of ill-health. In this, Lyne was one of the few. As the nineteenth century went on, the number of boy seamen who had fathers in the Navy actually seemed to decrease. By the 1890s, naval fathers were still the largest single category, but overall they were in a minority. Most parents had no connections with the Navy and very few encouraged their sons to join; in almost every case the boy joined of his own accord, with his parents either indifferent or actively hostile (and if the boy decided after a few weeks that he did not like the Navy, the parents' attitude was 'Now you've made your bed, now you must lie on it'). Some boys had been in a naval atmosphere from an earlier age, having been to the Royal Hospital School, Greenwich, for the sons of men who had served on the lower-deck. These boys literally 'knew the ropes', but they were only about one in ten of new recruits. The great majority of the new entries, the 'nozzers' or the 'noojacks' as they were called in the training ships, were wide-eyed and wondering.

Entry was very much as the editor of BOP described it. The boys had to be between $15\frac{1}{2}$ and 16 years old, physically fit, especially their teeth. They signed for twelve years' service, from the age of eighteen. In the training ships they received a general education in reading, writing and arithmetic, geography, religious instruction and some naval history. Their professional training was traditional; knots and splices, sail and arms drill, boat handling and swimming, with boxing, gymnastics and physical training. Their days were still ruled by bugle and bosun's call, they lived under the threat of the rope's end and the cane, and although they were never given quite enough to eat, they had leave at Christmas and Easter and seemed generally content with their lots.

Sail training died hard. After the training ships, the boys went to the training squadron of four corvettes which cruised along the south coast of England and down as far as Spain. Life in the brigs was traditional, too. Fred

Parsons, the son of a Bridport gardener, joined in 1893, aged just under 15½. One day in the brig *Active*, he and his mates were issued with pork from a cask stamped '1805', the year of Nelson's death. Another day, a marine trod on Parsons's bare toe while they were hoisting a boat. When Parsons cried out, the first lieutenant said he could not possibly be hoisting while he was talking, and he was awarded six cuts of the cane. The ship's corporal told Parsons that he had been hoping for the chance to give him six, and bet a pound to a penny he would make him squeal.

> I was laid over the arm of the mainmast bitts, with two other boys holding my arms and legs so that I was helpless. The corporal struck. They never struck straight down, but made a half-circle and struck upwards so as to get more power. I shall never forget the pain of that first cut—it was quite unbelievable. I tried not to squeal; but at the third stroke I let out a scream which brought everybody on the upper-deck to a standstill.

Parsons later became one of the Navy's earliest submariners and he went with Scott in *Terra Nova* to the South Pole.

In 1894 it was thought that public education had improved to the point where boys could enter the Navy later, at the same age as marines. The cruiser *Northampton* was commissioned, a steam vessel but with the inevitable masts and sails, to cruise round British ports, recruiting boys between sixteen and eighteen years as she went. The boys, known as '*Northampton* riggers', volunteered in satisfactory numbers and two more cruisers, *Calypso* and *Calliope*, were commissioned. The Sail Training Squadron lasted until 1899 when it was disbanded because of the manning needs of the Boer War. There were those who deplored its departure for many years.

Photographs of ship's companies in the last quarter of the nineteenth century showed many more men with beards (although, by the 1890s, more officers and senior ratings had beards than seamen). The famous image of the bearded sailor on the cigarette packet actually took many years to evolve. In general, for most of the century, officers and men were clean shaven. Beards and moustaches were deplored. In 1838 the C-in-C Plymouth Admiral Beauclerk issued an order commenting on 'the unofficerlike and dirty appearance of Hair being allowed to grow all round the Visage, making the man to resemble more the Brute than a Christian, and following a foreign practice to the National Character of Englishmen' and requesting that the custom be discontinued. As with other matters, much depended upon the captain's whim: when the frigate *Vernon* was off the coast of Syria for a year in the early 1840s, Captain Walpole (the same man who put all his crew into red frocks) ordered his ship's company to grow beards. *Vernon* returned to Malta on a fresh wind rather more quickly than Walpole expected and though the officers had had time to shave, many of the sailors still had beards when the C-in-C came on board. Walpole explained that *Vernon* had been serving with Orientals who judged a man's virility by his hair and he had thought that the honour of Great Britain must be maintained.

THE NAVY & ARMY ILLUSTRATED.

Vol. VIII.—No. 127.]   *SATURDAY, JULY 8th, 1899.*

'A Sailor and his Lass': a tribute from *The Navy & Army Illustrated* to the domestic phase of bluejacket life, 1899.

Normally, a seaman wore bushy sidewhiskers with no moustache, and showed clean at least three fingers' breadth of chin in front of the jawbone. This left ample scope for individual taste in 'Dundreary whiskers' or 'Piccadilly weepers' as they were sometimes called. By the 1850s, the sidewhiskers joined up beneath the jaw, so that the face was framed in a complete fringe of hair. Many sailors grew beards in the Crimean winter. In 1869 the First Lord, Hugh Childers, proposed to allow beards, after some discussion with the Queen for and against moustaches. He was supported by the captain of the Royal Yacht, Prince Leiningen, who wrote: 'There is more bad language made use of during the quarter of an hour devoted to shaving than during any other part of the day, and no wonder. Jack has had three hours on deck from 4 a.m. aloft, or on the lookout steaming head to wind. He goes below his face as hard as iron. A bad razor, a bit of broken glass, a wet deck, the ship rolling or pitching. Such are the difficulties under which the British seaman shaves.' On 24 July, 1869 a Circular was issued to the fleet permitting the wearing of beards. But there must be no moustaches. It was all or nothing, although beard and moustache had to be kept tidily trimmed. In the 1870s there was a vogue for beards, but by the 1890s most seamen were clean shaven again.

Like the naval beard, the naval salute had also been defined by the end of the nineteenth century. It had always been customary in the Navy for centuries to show respect to a senior by touching or raising one's hat. Although a Circular of August 1873 laid down marks of respect to be paid to superior officers in uniform by parties of seamen armed and unarmed, the actual form of the hand salute was still undefined. In 1882, boys in the training ships were taught to salute 'by touching the hat or cap, or by taking it off always looking the person saluted in the face. By touching the hat is meant holding the edge with forefinger and thumb.' A year later, this method was used generally in the Navy. In January 1890, the taking off of hats was discontinued as a salute, and the salute was ordered to be made by 'bringing up the right hand, with the thumb and fingers straight and close together, to the cap or hat naturally or smartly, but not hurriedly . . .' Either hand could be used. On passing an officer the salute was to be made with the *further* hand from him. When piping the ship's side bosun's mates often held the call in their right hand whilst saluting with their left. Finally, in 1918, the Royal Marines abolished the use of the left hand; all salutes were to be given by the right hand. In 1923, the Navy followed suit.

The sailor of the 1890s was healthier than his predecessors and better educated (to such an extent that a female visitor to the cruiser *Phaeton* in 1893 was told, only half jokingly, that men did not go aloft in the old way because the 'School Board has spoilt them all for that'.) He was better fed, and though he was not much better paid, he could keep his pay in a Savings Bank paying him 2–3 per cent interest per annum. There was a growing interest in his home and family welfare, although a writer in the *United Service Magazine* in 1893 warned that 'to get at a bluejacket's wife is sometimes a matter of difficulty, and when reached she does not always receive the advances of the captain's or commander's wife with effusion or even civility'. The same writer complained that 'no interest was taken in them (the wives). There were no married quarters. A sailor family used the nearest and cheapest doctor. His children's education was left to the School Board.'

But in so many ways Jack was still Jack. He still had his loves and hates, and especially he hated coaling ship. 'Coal ship' was a frequent evolution, which involved almost every man on board in hours of grinding hard labour. The men fell in, wearing their motley 'coaling clothes and hats'; coal-bags and barrows were brought up; the deck was sanded; small boats and other movable items on the upper-deck moved out of the dust. When the collier arrived alongside, some hands went down into her holds to fill bags and fasten them on to the whips. The bags, each weighing some 200 lbs, were hoisted on board, five to ten at a time. On deck, they were wheeled away in the barrows which were generally manned by the marines and tipped down coal-shutes. Down below, in the bunkers, more men were ready to shovel the coal into place. Meanwhile the band played or, if there was no band, the men sang. Flags at the yardarm showed how many tons of coal had been embarked. In company, coaling was done as an evolution and ships competed against each other. After coaling all day, and often into the night, the whole ship and everybody in it was black with dust. On completion of the task, the ship was washed down with water, and the men went below to clean themselves. Coaling ship did have one consolation: the sailors could smoke as much as they liked while they were doing it.

Coaling ship, probably the most unpleasant of all Jack's tasks.

One day's coaling ship, in *Dreadnought* while Lyne was serving in her, showed how the sailor reacted to considerate treatment by his officers. They were ready to begin coaling at 8.00 a.m., but the collier was delayed. As she was expected at any time, the commander piped the hands to make and mend clothes, which meant they could do as they pleased until the collier arrived and they were required for duty. But for some reason the collier did not arrive until the following day at 10.00 a.m. So the hands had a free day off. But that night the petty officers held a conference and the word spread round the ship, on the lower-deck grapevine: 'Tomorrow's coaling will be a record, come what may.'

In the morning, everything went wrong. There were defects in the collier's winches and derricks, with faulty gear, delays of all kinds. But the ship's company allowed nothing to hinder them. In spite of all the difficulties, 'the coaling was accomplished with a smashing record, far outstanding any previous performance, and was not again beaten by any other ship during the commission.' The next day, the commander congratulated the ship's company on their showing. According to Lyne, the sailors 'tittered a bit as sailors do when the commander tendered his lavish mead of praise, apparently quite oblivious of the fact that it was not they but the commander himself who had achieved this result, since it was only in some sort of recognition of his patient toiling to promote their comfort and welfare. It was to him that praise alone was due. I do not suppose Commander Cummings ever knew the secret of that coaling.'

On 26 June 1897, another review was held at Spithead, to honour the Queen's Diamond Jubilee. But this review was a show of real strength. There were 165 warships of all kinds, spread out over thirty miles, in five lines, and each line over five miles long. Once again, as in 1887, not one ship had been drawn from abroad, all were from the home station. It was the greatest show of naval force the world had ever seen.

The men, too, were the envy of the world. The British tar was a remarkable fellow. Properly led, he would go anywhere and do anything and do it with a will. He was 'always in good humour', as 'Martello Tower' described him in the Crimea:

> and if you understood how to manage him, he would do anything he was asked to do—whether he could or not! He would make brooms, milk the cow, play at cricket, march, fight, run, dance, sing, play the fiddle, smoke a pipe, drink a glass of grog (or more!) and mind the baby. That he had his weaknesses and shortcomings cannot be denied, but take him all in all he was a splendid fellow!—and I expect we shall never see his like again.

BIBLIOGRAPHY

MM: *Mariner's Mirror*. NMM: National Maritime Museum. NR: *Naval Review*. JRUSI: *Journal of Royal United Services Institition*. USM: *United Service Magazine*

ACLAND, Sir Reginald, KC 'Crime and Punishments in the Royal Navy during the last fifty years' NR vol. XI (1923)

ASHCROFT, William Petty 'Reminiscences' NR vol. LII (1964)—vol. LIII (1965)

ASHTON, John *Real Sailor Songs* London, Leadenhall Press, 1891

BACON, Admiral Sir Reginald, KCB, KCVO, DSO
The Life of Lord Fisher of Kilverstone 2 vols, London, Hodder & Stoughton, 1929
A Naval Scrapbook, Part 1: 1877–1900; London, Hutchinson, 1932
The Life of John Rushworth, Earl Jellicoe London, Cassell, 1936

BAGGETT, John, Signalman 'Journal of the Cruises of HMS *Alexandra*, flagship of Admiral Lord John Hay' May 1883–Nov. 1885; NMM: JOD 71

BALLARD, Admiral George, CB 'The Navy in Early Victorian England' ed. G. M. Young, 'The Black Battlefleet', 'Ironclads of the 1870s', 'The Unarmoured Branches of the Navy' and many other articles on Victorian warships; MM vol. XV (1929)–vol. XXXII (1946)
'Round Shot': Burma 1885; NR vol. XXV (1937) No. 4
'HMS *Alexandra*'; NR vol. XXVI (1938) No. 3
'Naval Machine Guns and Sudanese Spearmen in 1884' NR vol. XXVI (1938) No. 4
'Recollections of the Passage of the Dardanelles by a British Battle Squadron in the European Crisis of 1878' NR vol. XXVIII (1940) No. 1
'Memoirs', Part One: Burney's and HMS Britannia. MM vol. LXI (1975)
'Memoirs', Part Two: Midshipman, MM vol. LXII (1976)

BATH, Paymaster Cdr. A. G., OBE 'The Victualling of the Navy' JRUSI Feb 1939

BAYNHAM, Henry 'A Seaman in HMS *Leander*, 1863–66' MM vol. LI (1965)
From the Lower Deck: The Royal Navy 1780–1840 London, Hutchinson, 1969
Before The Mast: Naval Ratings of the 19th Century London, Hutchinson, 1971
Men from the Dreadnoughts London, Hutchinson, 1976

BECHERVAISE, John *Thirty-Six Years of a Seafaring Life, by 'An Old Quartermaster'* Portsea, Woodward, 1839
A Farewell to His Old Shipmates Portsea, Woodward, 1847

BENNETT, Captain Geoffrey, DSC, RN *Charlie B* London, Peter Dawnay, 1968

BERESFORD, Admiral Lord Charles *Memoirs* 2 vols, London, Methuen, 1914

BLAKE, Clagette *Charles Elliott RN 1801–1875* London, Cleaver-Hulme Press, 1960

BLAKE, John *How Sailors Fight* London, Grant Richards, 1901

BOLDERO, Mrs *A Young Heart of Oak: Memories of Harry Stuart Boldero, Lieut. RN* London, Hodder & Stoughton, 1892

BONNER-SMITH, David (ed.) 'The Russian War, 1855' Baltic Official Correspondence; Navy Records Society, vol. LXXXIV (1944)

BONNER-SMITH, David and DEWAR, Captain A. C., RN (eds.) 'The Russian War 1854, Baltic and Black Sea' Official Correspondence; Navy Records Society, vol. LXXXIII (1943)

BOTELER, Captain John Harvey, RN 'Recollections of My Sea Life: From 1808 to 1830' ed. by David Bonner-Smith; Navy Records Society, vol. LXXVII (1942)

BOWES, Arthur 'Diary in HMS *Sultan*, 1882–1885' NMM: JOD 104

BOWLES, G. Stewart *A Gun-Room Ditty Box* London, Methuen, 1898

BOWMAN, Rev, E. L., Chaplain RN 'Journal in the *Tribune*, Black Sea 1855, *Shannon*, East Indies including Naval Brigade, Indian Mutiny 1856–9, and *Nile*, North American Station, 1861–3' NMM: JOD 93

BRADFORD, Admiral Sir Edward E., KCB, CVO *Life of Admiral of the Fleet Sir Arthur Knyvet Wilson, Bart., VC, GCB, OM, GCVO* London, John Murray, 1923

BRENTON, Rear Admiral Sir James, Bart., KCB *An Appeal to the British Nation on Behalf of her Sailors* London, James Nisbet, 1838

BRIDGE, Captain Cyprian, RN 'Experiences of a New System of Lighting Her Majesty's Ships' USM April 1878
Admiral Sir Cyprian, GCB: Some Recollections London, John Murray, 1918

'British Log Book, Or Tales Of The Ocean, The': pub. in weekly parts, by Wakelin of Fleet Street, *c*. 1850

British Navy In The Present Year Of Grace, The By an Undistinguished Naval Officer (H. J. B. Montgomery) London, Hamilton Adams, and Devonport, A. H. Swiss, n.d. (1884)

CAMPBELL, Lt. Charles, RN 'The Interior Economy of a Modern Man of War' JRUSI vol. XXVII (1883)

CAMPBELL, Captain H. J. Fletcher, CB, RN 'Naval Brigades' JRUSI vol. XXVI (1882)

CAPPER, Lt. Cdr. Henry D., OBE, RN *Aft—From the Hawsehole: Sixty-Two Years of Sailors' Evolution* London, Faber & Gwyer, 1927

CECIL HAMPSHIRE, A. *Royal Sailors* London, Kimber, 1971

Chads, Memoir of Admiral Sir Henry Ducie, GCB by an Old Follower. Portsea, Griffin, 1869

Chambers Journal vol. LI No. 545, 6 June 1874, 'The Naval Prison at Lewes'

CHARLEWOOD, Cdr. Henry, RN *Passages from the Life of a Naval Officer* Manchester, Cave and Sever, 1869

CHIMMO, Captain William, RN *Midshipman's Diary: A Few Notes* London, J. D. Potter, 1862

CODRINGTON, Admiral Sir Edward *Memoirs of his Life* ed. Lady Bourchier; 2 vols. London, Longmans, Green, 1873

COLBORNE, Hon. John, and BRINE, Frederic *Memorials of the Brave, or Resting Places of Our Fallen Heroes in the Crimea and Scutari* London, Ackermann & Co, 1858

COLOMB, Captain P. H., RN *Slave-Catching in the Indian Ocean* London, Longmans, Green, 1873

COLOMB, Vice Admiral P. H. *Memoirs of Admiral the Rt. Hon. Sir Astley Cooper Key, GCB, DCL, FRS etc* London, Methuen, 1898

"Commander RN". *Crime and Punishment in the Navy, AD 1862–63* Portsea, Griffin, 1866

CORK AND ORRERY, Admiral of the Fleet the Earl of, GCB, GCVO *My Naval Life: 1886–1941* London, Hutchinson, 1942

Cornhill Magazine 'Reform in the Navy' vol. III Jan. 1861
'The Inner Life of a Man of War' vol. VII 1863

COTTEN, Richard 'Diary and book of verse, kept on HMS *Comus*, China & Pacific 1879–84, and HMS *Bacchante*, East Indies, 1885–86' NMM: JOD 119

COX, John George, RN *Cox and the Juju Coast: A journal kept aboard HMS Fly, 1868–9* St Helier, Jersey, C.I.; Ellison, 1968. Also pub. as 'West Coast Gunboat Diary' NR 1968

CRESSWELL, Admiral Sir William, KCMG, KBE, ed. Paul Thompson *Close to the Wind: Early Memoirs, 1866–79* London, Heinemann, 1965

CUMBERLAND, John 'Cumberland's British Theatre', with remarks, biographical and critical by D-G (G. Daniel) printed from the acting copies, as performed at the Theatre Royal, London, 1829–1837
'Cumberland's Minor Theatre', with remarks, biographical and critical by D-G (G. Daniel) printed from the acting copies, as performed at the Metropolitan minor theatres, 1830–1840

CUNNINGHAM, John, Surgeon, RN 'Remarks during a voyage in the Pacific in HMS *Cambridge*, *Fly*, *Spartiate*, and the Ship *Arab*, 1823–1825' NMM: JOD 21

CYRIAX, R. J., and JONES, A. G. E. 'The Papers in the Possession of Harry Peglar, Captain of the Foretop, HMS *Terror*, 1845' MM vol. XL (1954)

DEWAR, Captain A. C., RN (ed.) 'The Russian War, 1855, Black Sea': Official Correspondence; Navy Records Society, vol. LXXXV (1945)

DICKENS, Charles *The Uncommercial Traveller*

DOMVILLE, W. T., Surgeon 'Journal and Observations made in HMS *Resolute*, 1852–53' NMM: JOD 67

DON, William Gerard, MD, Deputy Surgeon General *Reminiscences of the Baltic Fleet of 1855* Brechin, D. H. Edwards, 1894 (repr. London, Cornmarket Press, 1971)

DUNDAS, Admiral Sir Charles, KCMG *An Admiral's Yarns* London, Jenkins, 1922

EAGLESTONE, Constance 'Forty-Eight Hours in a Man-of-War (HMS *Phaeton*)' USM 1892

EARDLEY-WILMOT, Cdr. Arthur Parry, RN *Manning the Navy* London, Cleaver, 1849

EARDLEY-WILMOT, Rear Admiral Sir Sydney M. *An Admiral's Memories: Sixty-Five Years Afloat and Ashore* London, Sampson Low, Marston, 1927
—— *Life of Vice Admiral Lord Lyons* London, Sampson Low, Marston, 1898

EARP, G. Butler *The History of the Baltic Campaign of 1854, from documents furnished by Vice Admiral Sir Charles Napier, KCB* London, Richard Bentley, 1857

EATON, W. A. *The Loss of HMS* Victoria, Eaton's Popular Songs for Recital No. 37; London and Maidstone, Simpkin, Marshall, Hamilton & Kent, 1893

EGERTON, Mrs Fred *Admiral of the Fleet Sir Geoffrey Phipps Hornby, GCB: A Biography* Edinburgh and London, Blackwood & Sons, 1896

ELLIOTT, Admiral Sir George, KCB 'The Naval Exhibition, 1891' USM, New Series vol. III, 1891

HMS Excellent *1820–1930*, third edition, ed. Captain R. D. Oliver CBE, DSC, RN: Portsmouth, Charpentier, 1930

FABB, John, and MCGOWAN, A. P. *The Victorian and Edwardian Navy from Old Photographs* London, Batsford, 1976

FINLAYSON, Robert, MD, Surgeon, RN 'An Essay addressed to Captains of the Royal Navy, and those of the Merchants' Service, on the means of preserving the Health of their Crews, with directions for the prevention of Dry Rot in Ships' Review in the *Navy and Military Journal*, vol. I, 1827

FIRTH, Professor C. H. 'Naval Songs and Ballads' Navy Record Society, vol. XXXIII (1907)

FISHER OF KILVERSTONE, Lord, Admiral of the Fleet *Memories* London, Hodder & Stoughton, 1919
—— *Records* London, Hodder & Stoughton, 1919

FITZGERALD, Captain C. C. P., RN 'Mastless Ships of War' USM, 1887
—— Admiral C. C. Penrose *The Life of Admiral Sir George Tryon, KCB* Edinburgh and London, Blackwood & Sons, 1897
From Sail to Steam: Naval Recollections 1878–1905 London, Edward Arnold, 1916

FLEET, Vice Admiral Henry Lewis, CBE *My Life and a Few Yarns* London, George Allen, 1922

Formidable: *The Story of the Bristol Training Ship for Homeless and Destitute Boys* Bristol, Chilcott, 1879

FORTESCUE, Captain Sir Seymour, KCVO, CMG, RN *Looking Back* London, Longmans, Green, 1920

FOX, Grace *British Admirals and Chinese Pirates, 1832–1869* London, Kegan Paul, Trench, Trubner, 1940

FRASER, Edward 'The *Pearl*'s Brigade in the Indian Mutiny' MM vol. XII 1926

FREER-SMITH, Cdr. Sir Hamilton, CSI, RN *Recollections Ancient and Modern* London, Hutchinson, 1925

FREMANTLE, Admiral The Hon. Sir Edmund, KCVO *The Navy as I have Known It: 1849–99* London, Cassell, 1904

FREMANTLE, Admiral Sir Sydney Robert *My Naval Career: 1880–1928* London, Hutchinson, 1949

Gallant British Tar, The, Or, The Visit of the Channel Fleet to the Port of Liverpool 1863 Portsea, J. & J. Gardner, 1864

GARDINER, Leslie *The British Admiralty* Edinburgh and London, Blackwood & Sons, 1968

GIFFARD, Admiral Sir George, KCB *Reminiscences of a Naval Officer* Exeter, William Pollard, 1892

GILBERT, William Schwenck *HMS* Pinafore, *Or, The Lass that Loved A Sailor* London, Chappell, 1878

GILLESPIE, Captain T. P., MBE, RN 'Plymouth Port Orders of 1858' MM vol. XL (1960)

GLASCOCK, Captain W. N., RN *Naval Sketch Book* London, Whittaker, 1834
Naval Officer's Manual London, Whittaker, 1848

GOODENOUGH, Rev. G., Chaplain RN *The Handyman Afloat and Ashore* London, T. Fisher Unwin, 1901

GOODRICH, Lt. Cdr. Caspar F., United States Navy *Report of the British Naval and Military Operations in Egypt, 1882* Washington, Government Printing Office, 1885

GOULD, Lt. Cdr. Rupert T., RN *Enigmas: Another Book of Unexplained Facts. The* Victoria *Tragedy* 2nd edn; London, Geoffrey Bles, 1946

GRAEME, Captain Alexander John, RN *Memoirs of an Early Naval Life* Teignmouth, G. H. Croydon, 1881

GRAHAM, Gerald *Empire of the North Atlantic: The Maritime Struggle for North America* 2nd edn; London, University of Toronto Press and OUP, 1958

GRENFELL, Captain Russell, RN *Service Pay* London, Eyre & Spottiswoode, 1944

HALL, Captain Basil, RN, FRS *The Lieutenant and the Commander* London, Bell & Daldy, 1866

HALL, John *Staffordshire Portrait Figures* London, Charles Letts, 1972

HALLIWELL, J. O. *Early Naval Ballads of England* Percy Society, 1851

HANNAY, James *Singleton Fontenoy RN* 3 vols, London, 1851

HARLEY, Daniel W. 'Diary in HMS *Alert* (Arctic Exploration) 1875–76' NMM: JOD 116

HARRIS, Admiral Sir Robert Hastings, KCB, KCMG *From Naval Cadet to Admiral* London, Cassell, 1913

HAWKEY, Arthur *HMS* Captain, London, G. Bell & Sons, 1963

HENDERSON, Admiral Sir William H. 'Crime and Punishment in the Royal Navy' NR vol. XI (1923)

HICKLEY, Lieut. J. D., DSO, RN 'An Account of the Operations on the Benin River in August and September 1894' USM 1895

HICKMAN, William *Reports of crime and punishment in the Navy in the year 1862* (London, 1864) *and in the year 1863* (London, 1865)

—— *Reports and Opinions of Officers on the Acts of Parliament and Admiralty Regulations for maintaining good order in the fleet, passed since 1860* London, Harrison, 1867

HINDS, Rev. Robert 'Diary in HMS *Rodney*, Black Sea and Crimea, 1853–1856' NMM: JOD 65

'Historic Tinned Foods' International Tin Research & Development Council, Publication No. 85. Fraser Road, Greenford, Middx.

HOLMAN, Thomas, RN *Life in the Royal Navy* London, Sampson Low, Marston, 1892

HOPKINS, Gerard Manley *Poems of Gerard Manley Hopkins*, 3rd edn, 5th imp. London, OUP, 1960

HOUGH, Richard *Admirals in Collision* London, Hamish Hamilton, 1959 (Repr. London, White Lion, 1973)

HUME, Major General John R. *Reminiscences of the Crimean Campaign* London, Unwin Brothers, 1894

HUNTER, Captain James Edward, RN *Ups and Downs of a Sailor* London, Selwyn & Blount, 1923

HUTCHINSON, Edward, FRGS, FSA *The Slave Trade of East Africa* London, Sampson Low, Marston, 1874 (repr. Allerthorpe, York, K Books, 1970)

IRWIN, D. Hastings *War Medals and Decorations, from 1588 to 1889* London, L. Upcott Gill, 1890

JARRETT, Dudley *British Naval Dress* London, J. M. Dent & Sons, 1960

JERNINGHAM, Cdr. Arthur Wm., RN *Remarks on the means of Directing the Fire of Ships Broadsides* Whitehall, Parker Furnival and Parker for the Military Library, 1851

JERROLD, Douglas *Black Ey'd Susan, Or, All in the Downs*. First performed at the Royal Surrey Theatre, London, 8 June 1829. Nineteenth Century Plays, ed. George Rowell, 2nd edn, Oxford, OUP, 1972

JONES, Captain Oliver, J., RN *Recollections of a Winter Campaign in India 1857–58* London, Saunders, Otley, 1859

KEBLE CHATTERTON, E. *Old Ship Prints* London, John Lane The Bodley Head, 1927 (repr. London, Spring Books, 1965)

KELLY, Mrs Tom *From the Fleet in the Fifties: A History of the Crimean War, with letters written in 1854–5–6 by the Rev. S. Kelson Stothert MA, Chaplain to the Naval Brigade* London, Hurst & Blackett, 1902

KEMP, Peter *The British Sailor: A Social History of the Lower Deck* London, Dent, 1970

KENNEDY, Admiral Sir William, KCB *Hurrah for the Life of a Sailor: Fifty Years in the Royal Navy* Edinburgh and London, Blackwood & Sons, 1901

KEPPEL, Admiral of the Fleet The Hon. Sir Henry, GCB, DCL *A Sailor's Life Under Four Sovereigns* 3 vols, London, Macmillan, 1899

KERR, Lieut. (later Admiral) Lord Frederic 'Acre 1840' MM vol. XIX (1933)

KING-HALL, Admiral Sir Herbert, KCB, CVO, DSO, LLD *Naval Memories and Traditions* London, Hutchinson, 1920

KINGLAKE, Alexander W. *The Invasion of the Crimea, its origin and an account of its progress down to the death of Lord Raglan* 8 vols, Edinburgh and London, Blackwood & Sons, 1863

KINGSTON, W. H. G. *Blue Jackets, or Chips of the Old Block* London, Grant & Griffith, 1854 (rev. and updated as *Our Sailors* by G. A. Henty, London, Griffith, Farran Browne, *c.* 1890)

KIPLING, Rudyard *A Fleet In Being: Notes of Two Trips with the Channel Squadron* London, MacMillan, 1898

KNOCK, Sydney *Clear Lower Deck* London, Philip Alan, 1932

'CLINKER KNOCKER' *Aye Aye Sir: The Autobiography of a Stoker* London, Rich & Cowan, 1938

LAFFEN, John *Jack Tar* London, Cassell, 1969

LAIRD CLOWES, Sir William *The Royal Navy, a History from the Earliest Times to the Present* 7 vols. London, Sampson Low, Marston, vol. VI (1901) and vol. VII (1903)

LANGMAID, J. Chief Engineer, RN 'A Proposed Method of Training Naval Stokers, and Otherwise Increasing the Efficiency of the Steam Branch Personnel' JRUSI vol. XXXV February 1891

LANT, Jeffrey L. 'The Spithead Naval Review of 1887' MM vol. LXI (1975)

LAYARD, General W. T. 'A Midshipman with Marryatt in the First Burma War' NR vol. XLIX (1961)

LEWIS, Michael 'An Eyewitness at Petropaulovski 1854' MM vol. XL (1963) *The Navy in Transition: A Social History 1814–1864* London, Hodder & Stoughton, 1965

LINKLATER, Eric *The Voyage of the* Challenger, London, John Murray, 1972

LLOYD, Christopher *The Navy and the Slave Trade* London, Longmans, Green, 1949

'The Origins of HMS *Excellent*' MM vol. XLI (1955)

The British Seaman 1200–1860: A Social Survey London, Collins, 1968

—— and COULTER, Jack L. S. *Medicine and the Navy: 1200–1900* vol. IV 1815–1900. Edinburgh and London, E & S Livingstone, 1963

LORNE, Marquis of, Kt. *V.R.I. Her Life and Empire* London, Eyre & Spottiswoode, 1901

LYNE, Rear Admiral Sir Thomas J. Spence, KCVO, CB, DSO *Something About A Sailor: From Sailor Boy to Admiral* London, Jarrolds, 1940

MACDONALD, John Denis, MD, FRS, Staff Surgeon RN 'On the Ventilation of Ships, especially of Low Freeboard, and Hospital Ships' USM Feb. 1874

—— Inspector General of Hospitals 'On Ship Ventilation as a Department of Naval Hygiene' USM May 1895

MACKLEN, C. H. 'From a Young Seaman's Diary 1872–1882' NR vol. XXIII (1935)

McPHERSON, Charles *Life on Board a Man O'War, by a British Seaman* Glasgow, 1829

MAIN, Robert 'Our Sailor Boys' USM Jan. 1872

MANSFIELD, J. S. *Remarks on the African Squadron* London, Ridgway, 1851 (repr. Allerthorpe, York, K Books 1973)

MARDER, Arthur J. 'The Origin of Popular Interest in the Royal Navy' JRUSI Nov. 1937

British Naval Policy 1880–1905 London, Putnam, 1941

Mariners' Mirror, vol. I (1911) to vol. LXII (1976). Signed, or pseudonymous, or anonymous or initialled contributions, notes, answers to correspondents on: Crimean Gunboats; Seamen's Uniform in 1861; Captain's Orders in the Indian Navy of 1855; Saluting; British Battleships of 1870; the loss of HMS *Vanguard*; Fanny Adams; Sailors' Songs; Handling Sail; Naval Volunteer Drillships; the RNVR; Ships in Mourning; War Rockets in the Mid-Victorian British Fleet; Rating and Distribution of British Warships in the 19th Century; Simoneseki, Japan, September 1864; 'Dance and Skylark'; Introduction of Canned Food into the Royal Navy 1811–1852; A midshipman in the Royal Navy, 1870–73; Naval Novels; Naval Verse; Ship's Libraries; Royal Naval Bands

MARSHALL, Lieut. John *Royal Naval Biography* 4 vols. London, Longmans, Green, 1823–35

'MARTELLO TOWER' (F. C. Norman) *At School and At Sea* London, John Murray, 1899

MASEFIELD, John *A Sailor's Garland* London, Methuen, 1906

MATHEW, David *The Naval Heritage* London, Collins, 1945

MAXWELL, Sir Herbert, Bart., MP *Sixty Years A Queen* London, Harmsworth, 1897

MAY, Gunner James, RN *The Narrative of the Loss of H.M.S.* Captain, Brompton, Kent, G. James Gale, 1872

MAY. Cdr. W. E., RN 'Face Fungus' NR vol. LII (1964)

MENDS, Bowen S. *Life of Admiral Sir William Mends, GCB* London, John Murray, 1899

MONTAGU, Rear Admiral The Hon. Victor A. *A Middy's Recollections* London, Adam & Charles Black, 1898
Reminiscences of Admiral Montagu London, Edward Arnold, 1910

MONTRESOR, Admiral Sir Frederick *Leaves From Memory's Log Book (by an Ancient Mariner)* London, W. H. Allen, 1887

MOORE, E. Marjorie *Adventures in the Royal Navy: Admiral Sir Arthur Moore* Liverpool, Liverpool University Press, 1966

MORESBY, Admiral John *Two Admirals: Admiral of the Fleet Sir Fairfax Moresby, and his son John, A record of life and service in the Navy for a hundred years* London, John Murray, 1909

MORRIS, Donald R. *The Washing of the Spears* London, Jonathan Cape, 1966

MOSELEY, H. N. *Notes by a Naturalist on HMS* Challenger, London, MacMillan, 1879

Nautical Standard And Steam Navigation Gazette for 1848, published weekly

Naval Review, vol. I (1912) to vol. LXIV (1976). Signed, or pseudonymous, or anonymous, or initialled contributions and letters on: Service conditions in 1816; the bombardment of Algiers, 1816; 1st China War, 1842; actions against slavers on the west coast of Africa; Burma, 1850; Lagos, 1851; the New Zealand War, 1845; Napier in the Baltic; the Crimean War; HMS *Pelorus's* Brigade in Burma, 1858; New Zealand War, 1860; Japan, 1864; the Zulu War, 1879; the Transvaal, 1881; Egypt, 1882; *Alert* in the Arctic, 1875–76; the loss of HMS *Eurydice*, 1878; the loss of HMS *Captain*, 1870; the 1888 Naval Manoeuvres; the Benin Expedition of 1897; Training in Sail; Tinned Food; Scurvy; Saluting

Naval Song Book No date or publisher. *c.* 1904

NOBLE, Sam, AB *'Tween Decks in the Seventies* London, Sampson Low, Marston, 1925

O'BYRNE, Robert *O'Byrne's Naval Annual for 1855* London, Piper, Stephenson & Spence, 1855 (repr. London, Cornmarket Press, 1969)

O'BYRNE, William R. *A Naval Biographical Dictionary* London, John Murray, 1849

OLIVER, Anthony *The Victorian Staffordshire Figure* London, MacMillan, 1971

OXENHAM, Rev. H. N., MA *Memoir of Lieut. Rudolph De L'Isle RN* London, Chapman & Hall, 1886

PADFIELD, Peter *Guns At Sea* London, Hugh Evelyn, 1973

PAGET, Admiral Lord Clarence, GCB *Autobiography and Journals* ed. Rt. Hon. Sir Arthur Otway. London, Chapman & Hall, 1896

PALMER, Charles Stuart *Life and Letters of Sir James Graham 1792–1861* 2 vols. London, John Murray, 1907

PARKES, Oscar, OBE, AINA *British Battleships:* Warrior *1860 to* Vanguard *1950* London, Seeley Services, 1957

PARSONS, Fred 'Terra Nova' NR vol. LIX (1971)–vol. LX (1972)

PAYNTER, Lt. Cdr. H. H., RN 'Battleship Life in the Early Eighties' JRUSI 1929 'A Midshipman in the Egyptian War' JRUSI 1930

PEGG, William 'Glimpses of the Past: Diary in HMS *Basilisk*, 1852–58' NMM: JOD 138

PENN, Cdr. Geoffrey, RN *'Up Funnel, Down Screw!': The Story of the Naval Engineer* London, Hollis & Carter, 1955

PLEMMING, Captain J. W., RN 'Reminiscences of an Early Engineer' NR vol. LIV (1966), LV (1967)

PURSEY, Cdr. H., RN. 'From Petitions to Reviews' *Brassey's Annual* 1937 'Lower Deck to Quarterdeck' *Brassey's Annual* 1938 'The Making of a Seaman' *Brassey's Annual* 1939

RASOR, Eugene Latimer 'The Problem of Discipline in the Mid 19th Century Royal Navy' University of Virginia. Unpub. thesis. NMM: THS/5

REID, J. S., AB, and PEARCE, T. M., Gunner *The Log of HMS* Victorious *1899–1903* London, Westminster Press, 1903

RICHARDS, Admiral of the Fleet Sir Frank, GCB 'Private Papers: Extracts' NR vol. XIX (1931)–vol. XXI (1933)

RICHARDSON, William *A Mariner of England* ed. Colonel Spencer Childers CB, RE. London, John Murray, 1908 (new imp. Greenwich, Conway Maritime Press, 1970)

RILEY, Patrick *Memories of a Bluejacket* London, Sampson Low, Marston, 1931

ROBSON, J. O. 'The First Presentation of the Victoria Cross' JRUSI vol. LXXXVII (1942)

ROBINSON, Cdr. C. N., RN 'Sailors on Shore' MM vol. II (1912) 'Notes on the Dress of the British Seaman' MM vol. III (1913) *The British Fleet* London, George Bell, 1895 *The British Tar in Fact and Fiction* London and New York, Harpers, 1911 *Britannia's Bulwarks* London, Harmsworth, 1904 *The Navy and Army Illustrated* weekly. Editor 1896–1901

RODGERS, N. A. M. 'The Dark Ages of the Admiralty 1869–1885' Part 1: Business Methods. MM vol. LXI (1975). Part 2: Change and Decay, 1874–1880. MM vol. LXII (1976)

ROGERS, Colonel H. C. B., OBE *Troopships and Their History* London, Seeley Services, 1963

ROSE, J. Holland 'The Royal Navy and the Suppression of the Slave Trade (1815–1865)' MM vol. XXII (1936)

ROWBOTHAM, Cdr. W. B., RN 'Naval Brigades in the. Indian Mutiny 1857–58' Navy Records Society vol. LXXXVII (1947)

ROWE, Richard *Jack Afloat and Ashore* London, Smith Elder, 1875

RUSSELL, Sir William Howard *Russell's Despatches from the Crimea 1854–1856* ed. Nicolas Bentley. London, Andre Deutsch, 1966

SABBENS, John C., Surgeon 'Diary in HMS *Sphinx* in the Crimea 1854–57' NMM: JOD 108

SCOTT, Admiral Sir Percy, Bart., KCB, KCVO *Fifty Years in the Royal Navy* London, John Murray, 1919

Sea Songs And Ballads By Dibden And Others London, Bell & Daldy, 1863

SECCOMBE, Captain *Army and Navy Drolleries* London, Warne, n.d. (*c.* 1870)

SECCOMBE, W. E. 'On the Preservation of Biscuit and Other Farinaceous Articles of Diet from Weevil, Maggots, and other insects in H.M. Navy' USM 1875

SENIOR, W. 'The Navy as Penitentiary' MM vol. XVI (1930)

SHARLOCK, William, Painter 'Journal in HMS *Scout* in the Mediterranean, 16 June 1841 to 20 June 1845' NMM: JOD 100

SHORE, Henry N. *Smuggling Days and Smuggling Ways* London, 1892 (repr. London, Philip Allan, 1929)

SIMPSON, William, Sergeant, Royal Marines 'Journal kept in HM Discovery Ship *Plover* 1848–1850, on an Arctic voyage in search of Sir John Franklin' NMM: JOD 76

'C.S.S.' (Captain Cecil Sloane-Stanley RN) *Reminiscences of a Midshipman's Life 1850–56* 2 vols. London and Sydney, Eden, Remington, 1893

SMITH, Vice Admiral Humphrey Hugh, DSO *A Yellow Admiral Remembers* London, Arnold, 1932

SMYTH, Brigadier The Rt. Hon. Sir John, Bart, VC, MC *The Story of the Victoria Cross 1856–1963* London, Muller, 1963

STONE, Christopher *Sea Songs and Ballads* Oxford, Clarendon Press, 1906

Strand Magazine vol. XII July to December 1896. 'Lord Charles Beresford CB, RN' by William G. Fitzgerald and 'Sailor VCs'

STUART, H. *The Novice or Young Seaman's Catechism* Southsea, T. Whitehorn n.d. (1850?)

SULIVAN, Admiral Sir Bartholomew James, KCB *Journals 1810–1890* ed. H. N. Sulivan. London, John Murray, 1896

SUMMERS, Inst. Lieut. D. L., RN *HMS* Ganges: *One Hundred Years of Training Boys for the Royal Navy* Ipswich, W. S. Cowell, 1966

SYMONDS, Rear Admiral Sir William, Kt. *Memoirs of the Life and Services of Rear Admiral Sir William Symonds, KT.* ed. James A Sharp. London, Longman Brown, 1858

TAPRELL DORLING, Captain H., DSO, RN ('Taffrail') 'Adventures of an Officer's Steward' (ed.) NR vol. XXIII (1935) 'The Hanging of John Dalliger' NR vol. XXXIV (1946)

—— with GUILLE L. F. *Ribbons and Medals* London, George Philip, 1963

TAYLOR, R. 'Manning the Royal Navy: The Reform of the Recruiting System, 1852–1862' MM vol. XLIV (1958) and vol. XLV (1959)

'THESEUS' (Late RN). Articles in USM on: Naval Discipline, July 1859; The Recent Mutinies in the Royal Navy, January 1860; Flogging in the Navy, April, 1860; Discontent in the Royal Navy, March 1861; Training Ships for Boys, December 1861; and Naval Discipline and Recent Naval Appointments, March 1862

TROTTER, Wilfred Pym *The Royal Navy in Old Photographs* London, Dent, 1975

TUPPER, Admiral Sir Reginald, GBE, KCB, CVO *Reminiscences* London, Jarrolds, 1929

TURNER, Michael *The Parlour Song Book* London, Michael Joseph, 1972

United Service Magazine. Anonymous articles on: A Proposal for Manning the Fleet, 1830; Jack at Oporto, 1834; Saturday Night At Sea, 1837; Paying Off, 1838; Naval Gunnery Establishment, 1839; Manning the Navy, 1859; The Navy in 1859; The Police of the Navy, 1862; Training for the Royal Navy, 1862; The Church in the Navy AD 1864; Sailors' Homes, 1865; The Health of the Navy, 1866; and Sailors in Embryo, 1867

VERNEY, Lieut. Edmund Hope, RN, Shannon's *Brigade in India, being some account of Sir William Peel's Naval Brigade in the Indian Campaign of 1857–58* London, Saunders, Otley, 1862

—— Captain, RN *The Last Four Days of* Eurydice Portsmouth, Griffin, 1878

HMS Vernon. *A History* Wardroom Mess Committee, HMS *Vernon.* Portsmouth, 1930

VINCENT, Henry. *A Stoker's Log.* London, Jarrolds, 1929

WATTS, Anthony J. *A Pictorial History of the Royal Navy* vol. I 1816–1880, vol. 2 1880–1914. London, Ian Allan, 1970

WESTON, Agnes *My Life Among The Bluejackets* London, Nisbet, 1911

WHITE, Walter 'China Station 1859–1864: The Reminiscences of Walter White' Greenwich, NMM Monographs and Reports No. 3, 1972

WHITE, Walter (ed.) *A Sailor Boy's Log Book: From Portsmouth to the Peiho* London, Chapman and Hall, 1862

WHYMPER, F. *The Sea: Its Stirring Story of Adventure, Peril and Heroism* 4 vols. London, Cassell, Petter and Galpin, n.d. (*c.* 1880)

WILKINS, Philip A. *The History of the Victoria Cross* London, Archibald Constable, 1904

WILLIAMS, Rev. E. A., MA, Chaplain RN *The Cruise of the* Pearl *round the World, with an account of the operations of the Naval Brigade in India* London, Richard Bentley, 1859

WILLIAMS, N. Noel *Admiral Sir Charles Napier, KCB: Life and Letters* London 1867

WILSON, Rev. J. Leighton *The British Squadron on the Coast of Africa* London, Ridgway, 1851 (repr. Allerthorpe, York, K Books, 1973)

WINNINGTON-INGRAM, Rear Admiral H. F. *Hearts of Oak* London, W. H. Allen, 1889

WINTZ, Sophia G. *Our Bluejackets: Miss Weston's Life and Work among our Sailors* London, Hodder & Stoughton, 1900

WOOD, Field Marshal Sir Evelyn, VC, GCB, GCMG *From Midshipman to Field Marshal* 2 vols. London, Methuen, 1906

WORCESTER, G. R. G. 'The First Naval Expedition up the Yangtze River, 1842' MM vol. XXXVI (1950)

YATES, R. W. 'From Wooden Walls to Dreadnoughts In A Lifetime' MM XLVIII (1962)

YEXLEY, Lionel *The Inner Life of the Navy* London, Pitman, 1908
Our Fighting Seamen London, Stanley Paul, 1911
Hope or the Bluejacket ed. 1898–1902
The Fleet Newspaper ed.

YOUNG, G. M. *Victorian England: Portrait of an Age* London, OUP, 1936

YOUNG, Cdr. Robert Travers, OBE, RN *The House That Jack Built* Aldershot, Gale & Polden, 1955

Also miscellaneous articles, picture captions, notes, contributions in
The Illustrated London News
The Illustrated Times
The Graphic
The Sphere
Punch

INDEX

ST A